Microsoft® Office® 2003 Killer Tips

MICROSOFT OFFICE 2003® KILLER TIPS

Microsoft Office 2003 Killer Tips Team

TECHNICAL EDITOR
Polly Reincheld

EDITOR
Barbara Thompson

PRODUCTION EDITOR
Kim Gabriel

PRODUCTION
Dave Damstra
Dave Korman
Mary Maibauer

COVER DESIGN AND CREATIVE CONCEPTS
Felix Nelson

SITE DESIGN
Stacy Behan

PUBLISHED BY
New Riders Publishing / Peachpit Press

FIRST EDITION: July 2004

Composed in Myriad and Helvetica by NAPP Publishing

Trademarks

All terms mentioned in this book that are known to be trademarks or service marks have been appropriately capitalized. New Riders Publishing / Peachpit Press cannot attest to the accuracy of this information. Use of a term in the book should not be regarded as affecting the validity of any trademark or service mark.

Microsoft and Windows are either registered trademarks or trademarks of Microsoft Corporation in the United States and/or other countries.

Warning and Disclaimer

This book is designed to provide information about Microsoft Office 2003 tips. Every effort has been made to make this book as complete and as accurate as possible, but no warranty of fitness is implied.

The information is provided on an as-is basis. The author and New Riders Publishing / Peachpit Press shall have neither liability nor responsibility to any person or entity with respect to any loss or damages arising from the information contained in this book or from the use of the discs or programs that may accompany it.

ISBN 0-7357-1437-1

9 8 7 6 5 4 3 2 1

Printed and bound in the United States of America

www.peachpit.com
www.scottkelbybooks.com

For my Lord,

Jesus Christ.

As with all things

in my life, I give

you the Honor,

the Praise, and

the Glory.

ACKNOWLEDGMENTS

Debbie Stephenson—You've made my life wonderful. You're the best part of every day. Your wonderful sweetness and kindness just makes people want to be around you. Thank you for being my best friend, a loving wife, and an extraordinary mother. You'll always take my breath away. I love you!

Jarod Stephenson—I know that anyone can be a father but Jarod, you make me want to be a spectacular father. One of my favorite things in the world is just going outside and throwing a baseball with you. You've got a heck of an arm for a six-year-old. I'm amazed at who you are and who you're becoming. I'm very, very proud of you!

Jenna Stephenson—If boys make men fathers, then girls make men daddies. Jenna, I absolutely couldn't get through a day without you—you're my little princess. I honestly didn't think that God was capable of making anything so unique, beautiful, sweet, and wonderful as you.

Kleber and Barbara Stephenson—Mom and Dad, as always, I can never thank you enough for everything you do. You're the most extraordinary people anyone could ever know. You're truly a blessing and I only hope that I do as good a job raising my children as you did with me.

My sisters—I'm getting a little tired of always singing your praises. It's exhausting because there are so many to be sung. Cheryl, Kalebra, Julie, Heidi, you're simply the coolest sisters a guy could have. You're all so special to me. Thanks for your love, encouragement, and support. I deserve it. ;-)

Scott Kelby—Bro! You're one of the most creative and talented people I know, as well as being an inspiration and good friend. Thanks for your support, vision, and for creating the most creative environment on the planet.

Dave Moser—The way you do anything is the way you do everything. You have a great talent for doing it right. Thanks for your endless encouragement and constant flow of great ideas.

KW Media Group—A special thanks to Polly Reincheld, Barbara Thompson, Felix Nelson, Kim Gabriel, Dave Damstra, Dave Korman, Margie Rosenstein, Christine Edwards, and Mary Maibauer. All of you are insanely talented. It amazes me how you accomplish what you do. Thanks for your dedication and very hard work.

The Lord, Jesus Christ—God has always blessed me more than I deserve. I can't make it through a day without speaking to Him. Thanks for always listening, allowing me to do what I love, and for blessing me with such a wonderful life.

ABOUT THE AUTHOR

Kleber Stephenson

Kleber Stephenson is Director of Seminars and Director of Windows Technologies for KW Media Group, Inc., a Florida-based software education and publishing firm. He's also the author of the best-selling *Windows XP Killer Tips* and co-author of *The iTunes for Windows Book*, both from New Riders Publishing/Peachpit Press.

A contributing technology reviewer for *Mac Design Magazine* and *Photoshop User,* Kleber has more than a decade of experience analyzing and implementing business computing infrastructures based on the Windows platform. In addition, he has designed and developed real-world network and administrative solutions based on Microsoft technologies and the Windows OS architecture.

Kleber lives in the Tampa Bay area of Florida with his wife, Debbie, his son, Jarod, and his daughter, Jenna.

FOREWORD by Scott Kelby

As Editor for the Killer Tips series, I'm excited not only to bring you another Killer Tips book, but I'm particularly excited to introduce you to an author who is going to take you to a whole new level of speed, efficiency, productivity, and sheer unadulterated out-and-out fun using Microsoft Office 2003. (I just realized that when you put the words "sheer" and "unadulterated" together, it sounds kind of dirty, but it's not meant to be. That comes later.) But first, a little background on this book.

The idea for this type of book came to me one day when I was at the bookstore, browsing in the computer section, when I thought to myself, "Man, these authors must be making a ton of money!" No wait, that wasn't what I was thinking (it's close, mind you, but not exactly). Actually, I was standing there flipping through the different books on Adobe Photoshop (I'm a Photoshop guy at heart). Basically what I would do is look for pages that had a tip on them. They're usually pretty easy to find, because these "rich book authors" usually separate their tips from the regular text of the book. Most of the time, they'll put a box around the tips, or add a tint behind them, or maybe have a tips icon—something to make them stand out and get the readers' attention.

Anyway, that's what I would do—find a tip, read it, and then start flipping until I found another tip. The good news—the tips were usually pretty cool. You have to figure that if an author has some really slick trick, maybe a hidden keyboard shortcut or a cool workaround, he probably wouldn't bury it in blocks of boring copy. No way! He'd find some way to get your attention (with those boxes, tints, a little icon, or simply the word "Tip!"). So, that's the cool news—if it said tip, it was usually worth checking out. The bad news—there are never enough tips. Sometimes there were five or six tips in a chapter, but other times, just one or two. But no matter how many there were, I always got to the last chapter and still wanted more tips.

Standing right there in the bookstore, I thought to myself, "I wish there was a book with nothing but tips: hundreds of tips, cover to cover, and nothing else." Now, that's a book I'd go crazy for. I kept looking and looking, but the book I wanted just wasn't available. That's when I got the idea to write one myself. The next day I called my editor to pitch him with the idea. I told him it would be a book that would be wall-to-wall with nothing but cool tips, hidden shortcuts, and inside tricks designed to make Photoshop users faster, more productive, and best of all, make using Photoshop even more fun. Well, he loved the idea. Okay, that's stretching it a bit. He liked the idea, but most importantly, he "green-lighted it" (that's Hollywood talk—I'm not quite sure what it means), and soon I had created my first all-tips book, *Photoshop 6 Killer Tips* (along with my co-author and good friend, *Photoshop User* magazine Creative Director Felix Nelson).

As it turned out, *Photoshop 6 Killer Tips* was an instant hit (fortunately for me and my chance-taking editor), and we followed it up with (are you ready for this?) *Photoshop 7 Killer Tips*, and then *Photoshop CS Killer Tips*, which were even bigger hits. These books really struck a chord with readers, and I like to think it was because Felix and I were so deeply committed to creating something special—a book where every page included yet another tip that would make you nod your head, smile, and think, "Ahhh, so that's how they do it." However, it pretty much came down to this: People just love cool tips. That's why now there's an entire series of Killer Tips books covering cool applications such as DreamWeaver, QuarkXPress, InDesign, Illustrator, and many more.

So how did we wind up here, with a Killer Tips book for Microsoft Office 2003? Well, there was an intermediate step: I wrote *Mac OS X Killer Tips* for Macintosh users switching over to Apple's UNIX-based operating system. It turned out to be such a big hit, it actually became "biggety-big" (a purely technical term, only used during secret book-publishing rituals).

That naturally led to a *Windows XP Killer Tips* book. The only problem was that I'm really a Photoshop guy and I wanted the Windows XP book to surpass the Mac book's "biggety-bigness," so it needed a pretty special author. That person was Kleber Stephenson. I chose him for one simple reason: The similarity of his first name to my last name. Heck, it's almost the same name (Kleber Kelby. See what I mean?). That was enough for me. Okay, that's actually not the reason at all (just a lucky coincidence). I chose Kleber because he fit every criterion I had set for the ideal Killer Tips author. First, he totally "gets" the Killer Tips concept because, just like me, he's a tip hound—a tip junkie (if you will). Second, I've always enjoyed his writing style, humor, and the completeness of his research and attention to detail, and how he really immerses himself in a project. Third, like me, he's a die-hard Tampa Bay Bucs fan. Fourth (and perhaps most important), he knows more Windows tips and has a better understanding of the Windows operating system than anyone I know. Period.

That's why, when we decided to do this book on Microsoft Office 2003, I called Kleber first. Honestly, if he had decided to pass on the project, you wouldn't be reading this book now, because he was *so* the right person to do this book that I didn't have another person in mind as a backup plan. I wanted Kleber, and if I couldn't get him, I'd shelve the idea and move on to another project. That's how strongly I felt that he was the right person for the job, and I'm absolutely delighted that you're holding his book right now. Kleber has really captured the spirit and flavor of what a "Killer Tips" book is all about, and he proved that with his *Windows XP Killer Tips* book. And I can tell you this—you're gonna love this book, as well!

Kleber has a great sense of humor and a casual, conversational writing style. He has a keen sense for uncovering those inside tips that the pros use to get twice the work done in half the time. He's one of those people who doesn't do anything the "hard way," and he knows every timesaving shortcut, every workaround, and every speed tip to make something different, something special, and to make this the only book of its kind in a very crowded Microsoft Office 2003 book market.

I can't wait for you to "get into it," so I'll step aside and let him take the wheel, because you're about to get faster, more efficient, and have more fun using Microsoft Office 2003 than you ever thought possible.

All my best,

Scott Kelby
Series Editor

TABLE OF CONTENTS

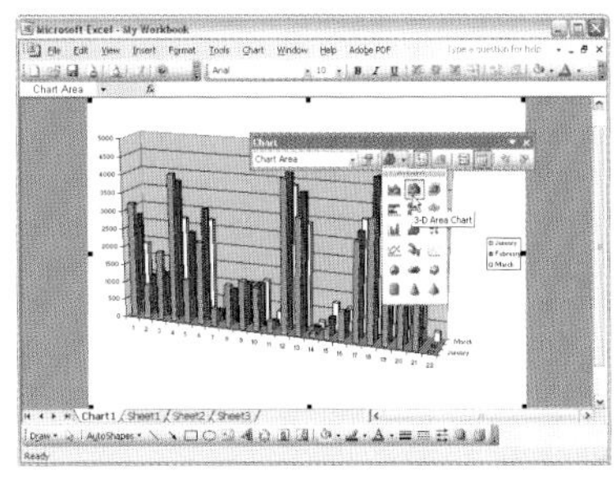

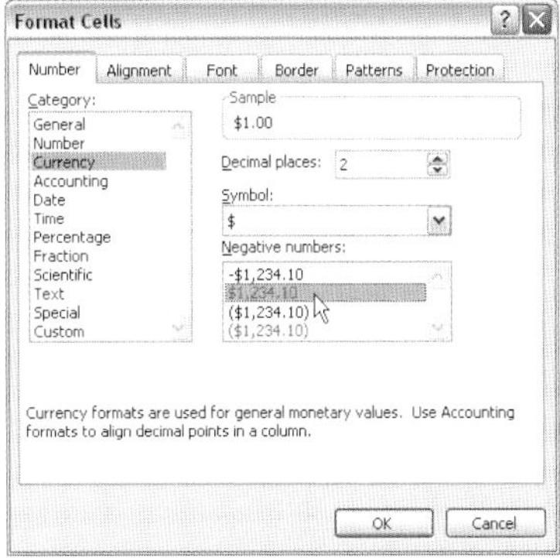

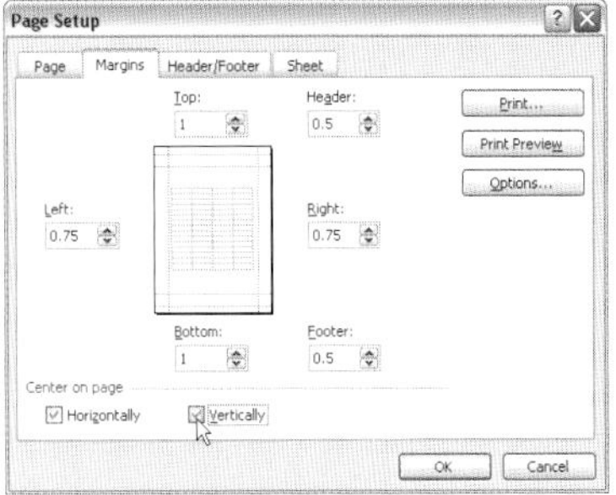

TABLE OF CONTENTS

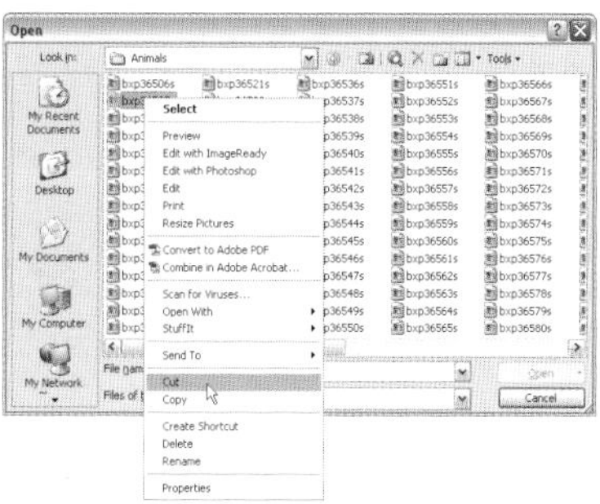

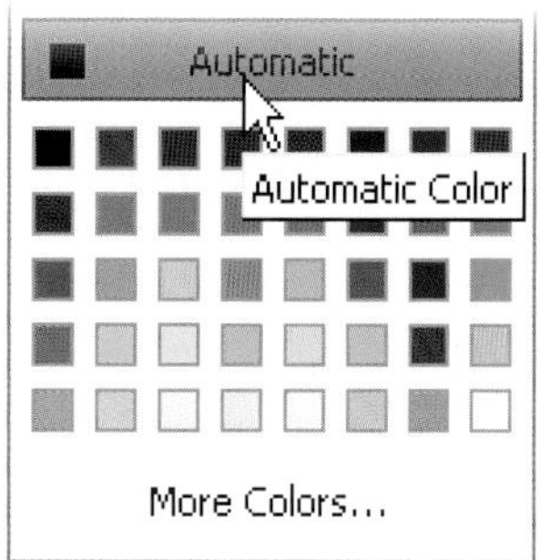

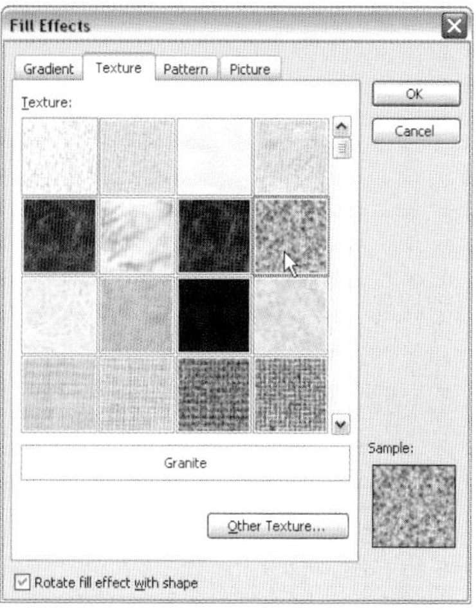

Document2 - Microsoft Word
Clip Art
Search for:
computer
Go
Search in:
Selected collections
Results should be:
All media file types

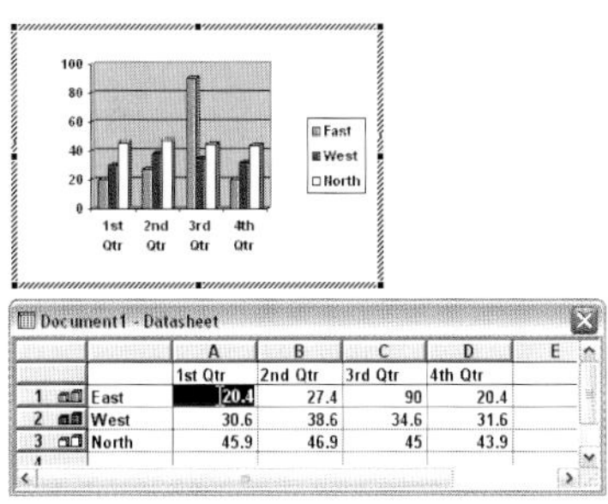
100
80
60
40
20
0
1st Qtr
2nd Qtr
3rd Qtr
4th Qtr
East
West
North
Document1 - Datasheet
A B C D E
1st Qtr 2nd Qtr 3rd Qtr 4th Qtr
1 East 20.4 27.4 90 20.4
2 West 30.6 38.6 34.6 31.6
3 North 45.9 46.9 45 43.9

Create Shortcut
This wizard helps you to create shortcuts to local or network programs, files, folders, computers, or Internet addresses.
Type the location of the item:
mailto:friend@theirdomain.com
Browse...
Click Next to continue.
< Back
Next >
Cancel

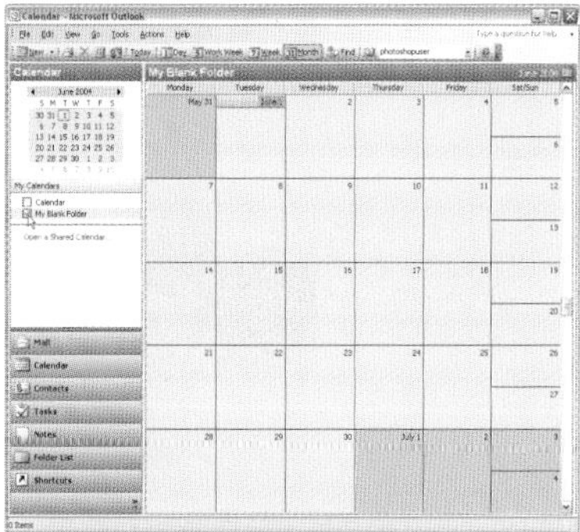

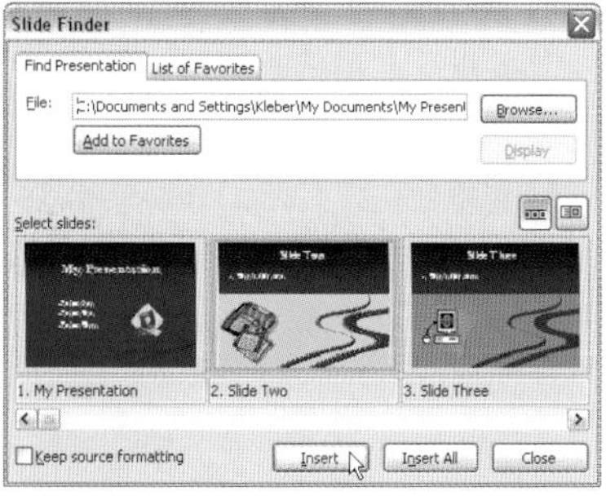
Slide Finder
Find Presentation
List of Favorites
File:
Browse...
Add to Favorites
Display
Select slides:
1. My Presentation
2. Slide Two
3. Slide Three
Keep source formatting
Insert
Insert All
Close

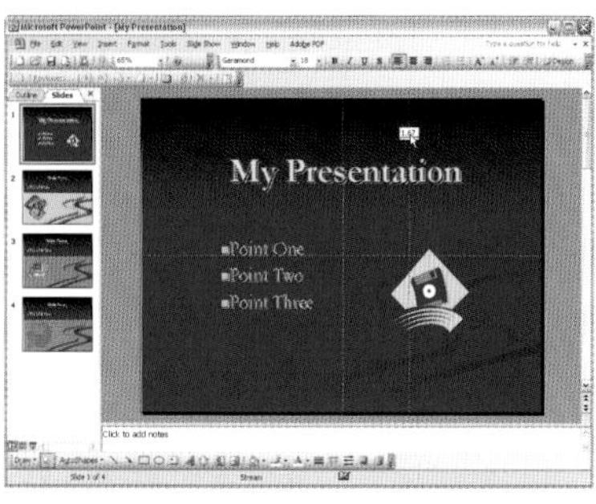
My Presentation
Point One
Point Two
Point Three

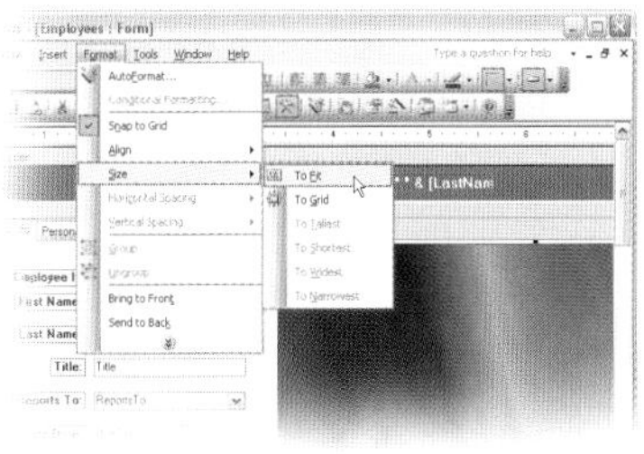

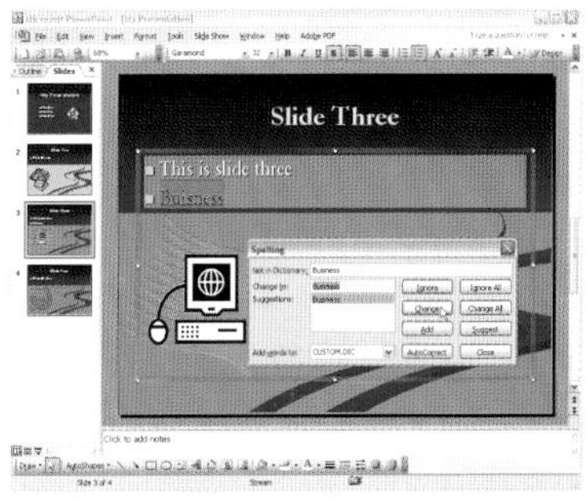
Slide Three
This is slide three

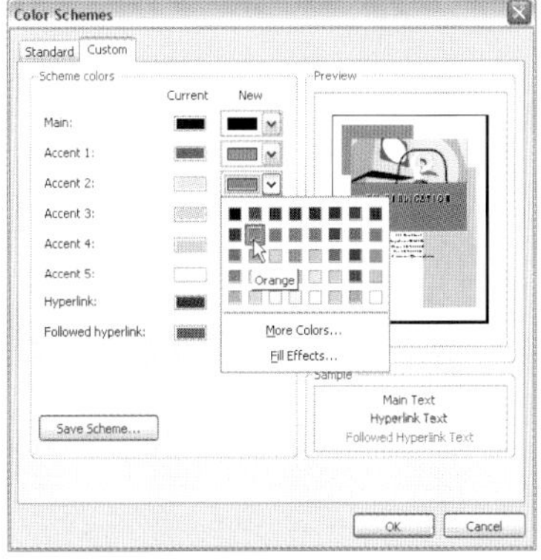
Color Schemes
Standard
Custom
Scheme colors
Current
New
Preview
Main:
Accent 1:
Accent 2:
Accent 3:
Accent 4:
Accent 5:
Hyperlink:
Followed hyperlink:
Orange
More Colors...
Fill Effects...
Main Text
Hyperlink Text
Followed Hyperlink Text
Save Scheme...
OK
Cancel

TABLE OF CONTENTS

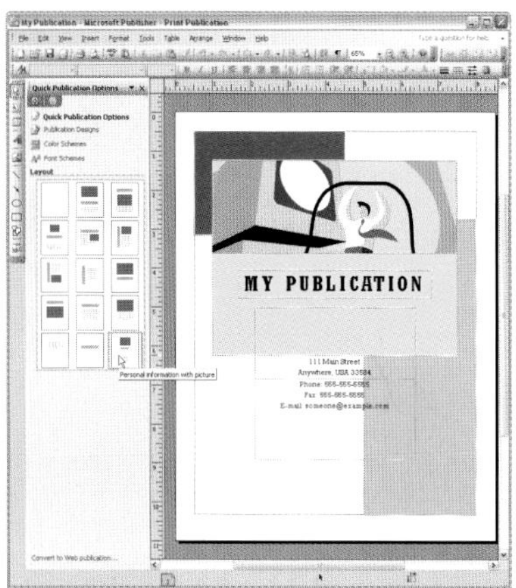

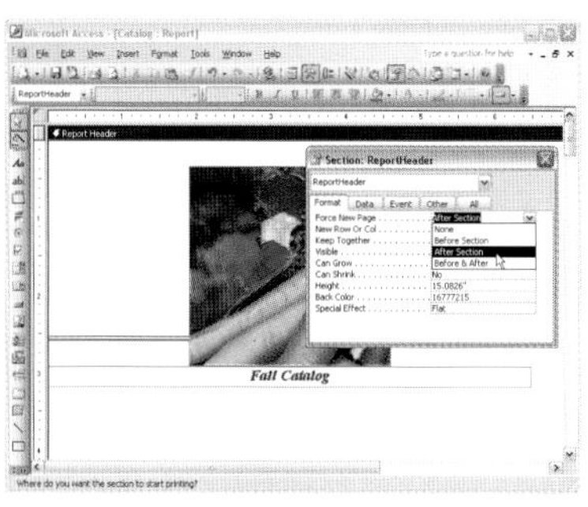

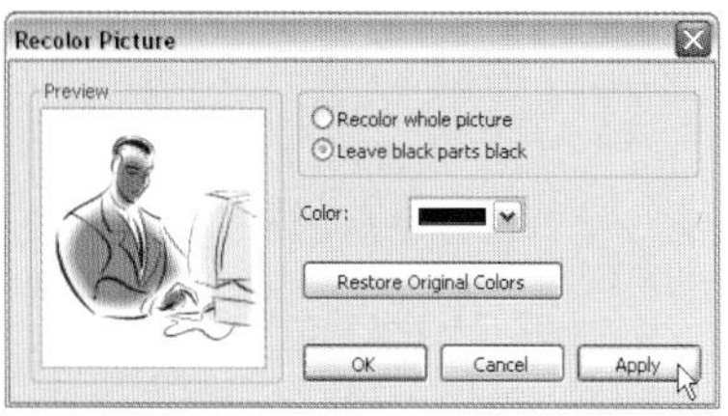

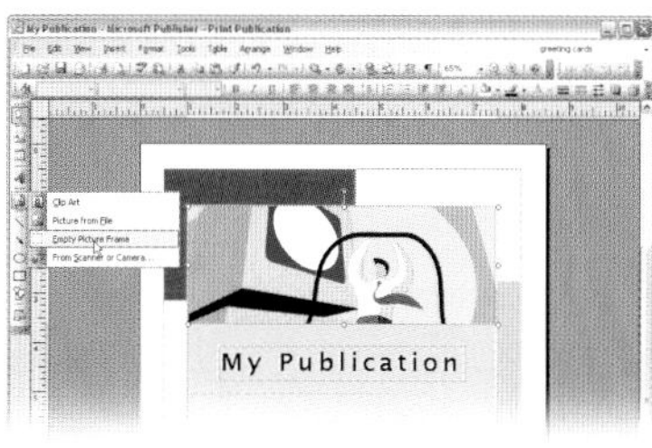
My Publication

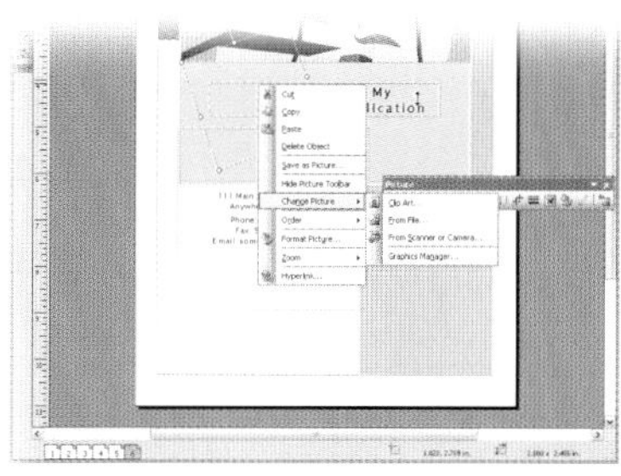

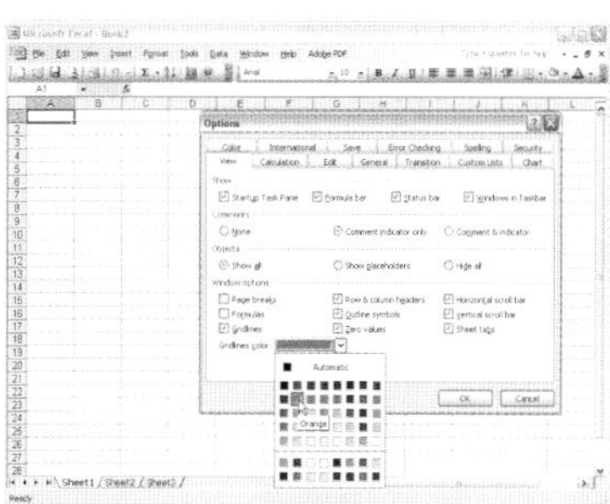

TABLE OF CONTENTS

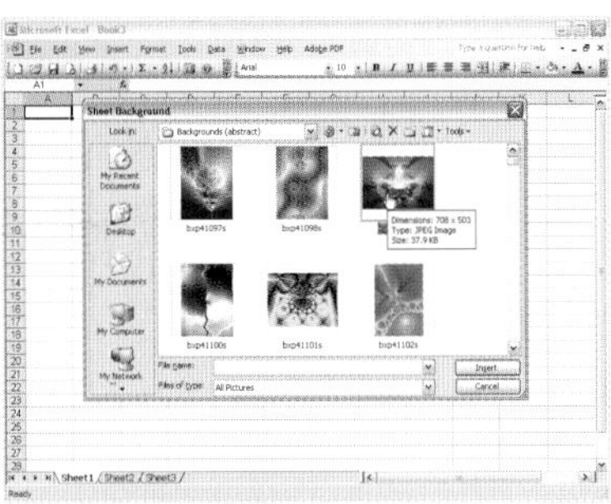

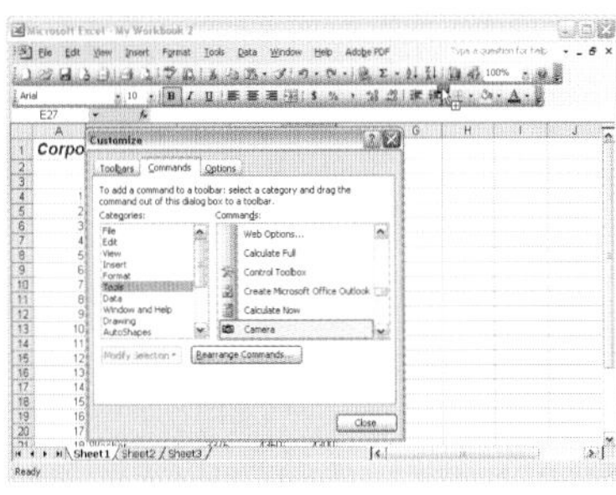

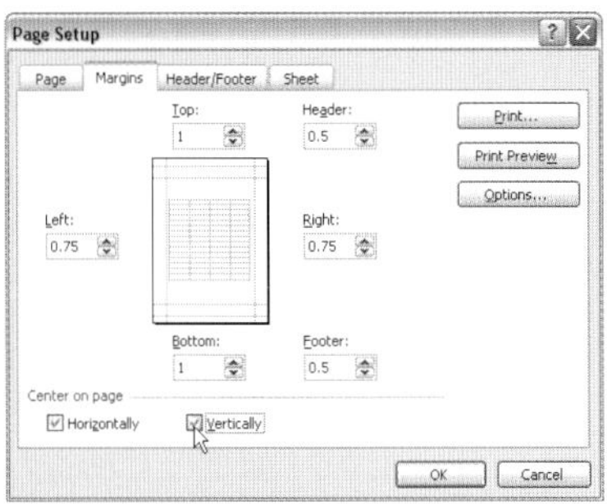

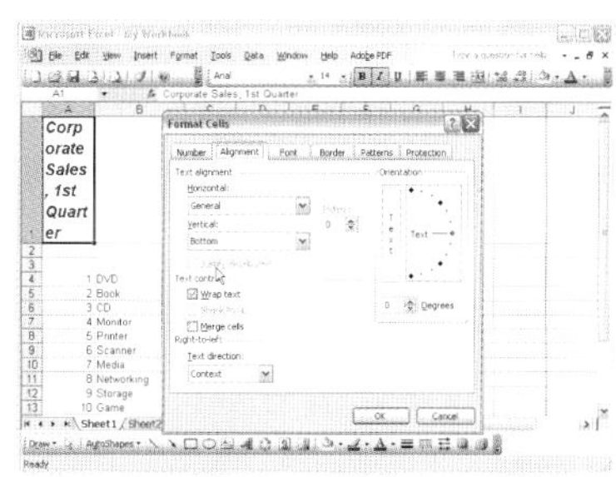

A Day at the Office

GET THE MOST OUT

OF OFFICE 2003

I almost failed kindergarten when I was a child (not as an adult, of course). I couldn't color. I mean, I could color; I just couldn't do it very well. My parents would only

A Day at the Office

get the most out of office 2003

buy me the fat crayons—you know the ones I'm talking about—so I wasn't able to stay within the lines. Who could with those fat crayons? Everybody else had the skinny crayons. They breezed through coloring, but not me. I didn't have the best tools. I had crayons, but not the crayons to get the job done. I still can't color to this day. Every time my children break out the crayons, I get preschool flashbacks, and that's kind of how it must be for anyone anywhere using any other office suite. Microsoft Office is simply the best tool for the job, much like skinny crayons. So I can only assume, since you're reading this book, that you use Microsoft Office. Count yourself blessed and fortunate, because bad tools can really mess you up.

 TURN OFF THE TASK PANES

The first thing I do in just about every Office application once it's launched is click the Close button on the Startup task pane. The task panes are helpful if you've never used an Office application, but for everyone else, they can be annoying (and they take up an enormous amount of workspace). I don't know about you, but I try to keep from being annoyed as much as possible, so I turn off the Startup task pane, and it never appears when an Office application is launched. You too can do this by clicking Tools>Options in the menu bar of most applications. Next, click the View tab in the Options dialog and deselect the Startup Task Pane checkbox located under the Show category, then click OK. Now the Startup task panes will never annoy you again.

THEY'RE EXPANDABLE

Here's a tip to keep in mind when working with task panes: They're expandable. So, when you're forced to scroll through a task pane, don't. Instead, simply place your cursor over the left border until your mouse pointer turns into a two-sided arrow, then click-and-drag the border of the task pane to the left to expand the pane to fit the content. Task panes are already taking up way too much space, so what's a little more space to make them readable?

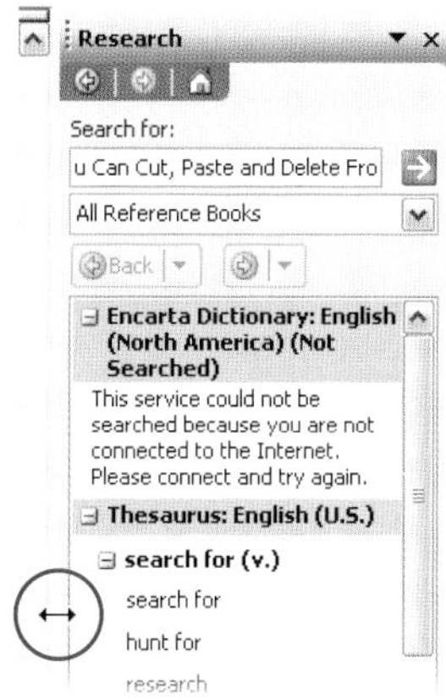

TASK PANES ON THE MOVE

By default, task panes open on the right side of an Office program window. Well, maybe you don't like the task pane on the right. Maybe you'd like the task pane on top of the document window, at the bottom, or on the left side of the window. Well, you're in luck; you can move it to any side you'd like. To do this, move your mouse pointer over the upper-left corner of the task pane until your pointer turns into a four-sided arrow. Next, drag-and-drop the task pane to any side of the program window to dock it, or drag-and-drop it anywhere else on the program window to float the task pane. To move the task pane back, simply drag-and-drop it onto the far right side of the program window.

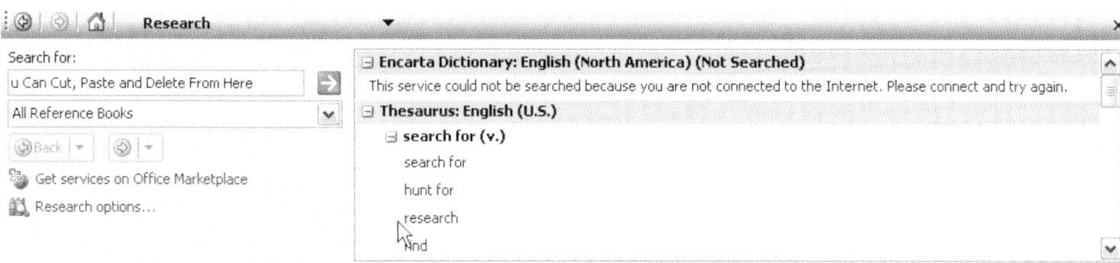

QUICK MENU EXPAND

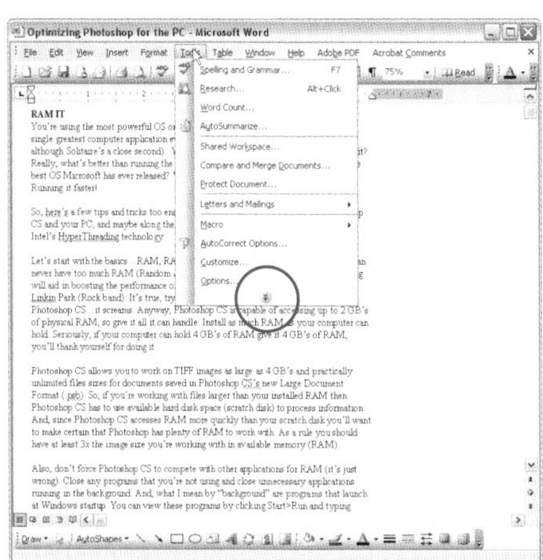

It never fails: The task that you're looking for is always somewhere at the bottom of the menu that you open, which means that you can't see it because Office applications don't fully expand menus automatically. Well, you could click the arrow button at the bottom of the menu to expand it (shown circled), but that's just crazy… there's a better way. To expand menus quickly, simply double-click the menu title. Now you can actually see the tasks you're looking for. However, if you really detest this personalized menu feature, you can get really smart and permanently turn it off. Click Tools>Customize, then click the Options tab in the Customize dialog. Next, select the Always Show Full Menus checkbox under the Personalized Menus and Toolbars category, then click Close.

CUSTOMIZE YOUR MENUS

One of the most useful features of Office 2003 is the ability to create your own custom menus—very handy for grouping tasks that you use most frequently. To create a new menu, click Tools>Customize in the menu bar. Next, click the Commands tab in the Customize dialog, scroll to the bottom of the Categories list, and click New Menu. Drag-and-drop the words "New Menu" from the Commands window onto the menu bar at the top of your screen. Now, give your menu a new name by right-clicking the words "New Menu" and typing a new name in the Name field. To add commands to your menu, drag-and-drop them onto the open menu (not on the menu title). You'll notice a black line indicating where the command will be positioned when you release your mouse button. When you're finished, click OK in the Customize dialog, and all of your favorite commands are now located in one convenient menu. (*Note:* You can only rename and add commands to your new menu when the Customize dialog is open.)

KEEP THE FUN ROLLIN'—CUSTOMIZE YOUR TOOLBARS

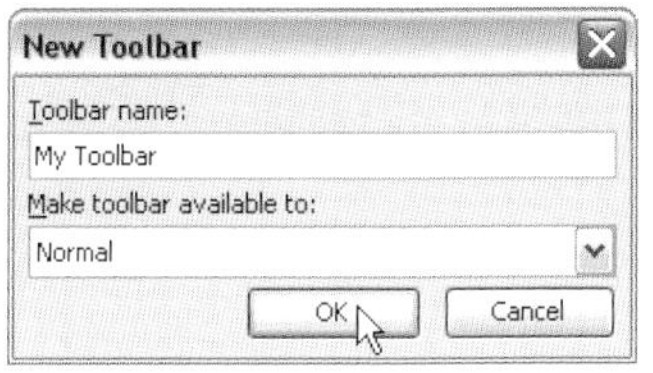

I showed you how to create a customized menu above; well, let's keep the fun rollin' along and create a customized toolbar. It's another great way to increase your productivity in Office. To create a customized toolbar, click Tools>Customize in the menu bar. Next, click the Toolbars tab in the Customize dialog, then click the New button. Type a name in the Toolbar Name field, then, with the Customize dialog still open, drag-and-drop buttons from other open toolbars onto your new toolbar. When finished, click OK in the Customize dialog, and you've just created your very own custom toolbar.

SPLIT THE TOOLBARS

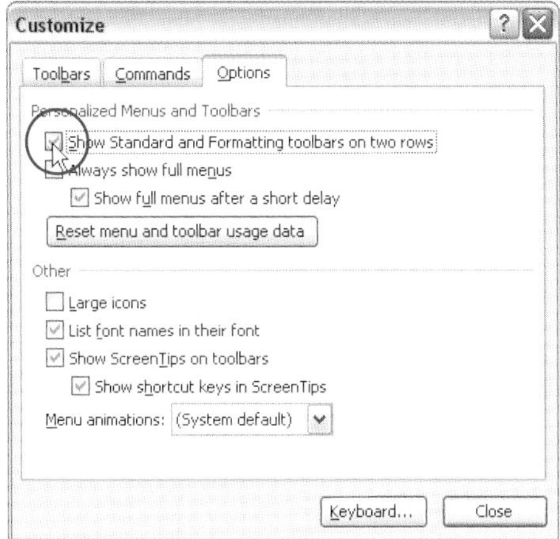

By default, Word, Excel, PowerPoint, and Publisher display the Standard and Formatting toolbars on the same row. This can make things a bit cluttered and, depending on the size of the application's window, makes tasks difficult to access. To show the Standard and Formatting toolbars stacked as two rows instead, right-click anywhere on any toolbar, and click Customize in the shortcut menu. Next, click the Options tab and check Show Standard and Formatting Toolbars on Two Rows, then click Close. You now have the toolbars on two separate rows.

OPEN AND CLOSE TOOLBARS THE EASY WAY

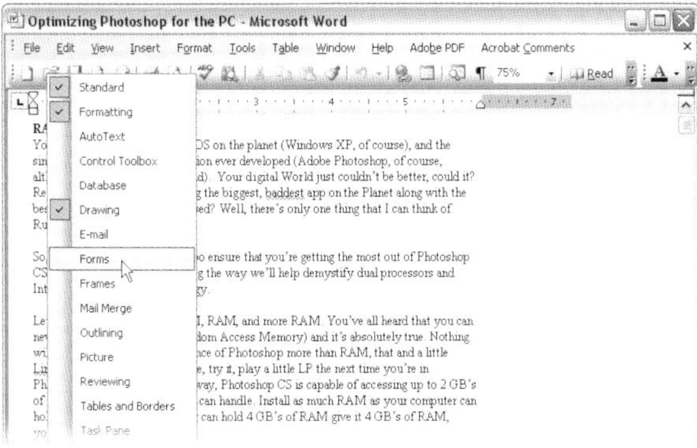

If you need to add new toolbars to your Office applications, you don't have to use the Customize dialog. I mean, you can if you like wasting time and doing things the hard way, but if you don't, try right-clicking any toolbar to view other available toolbars. Next, click a toolbar in the shortcut menu that you'd like to display. If the toolbar is floating when you open it, you can dock the toolbar by dragging-and-dropping it next to other docked toolbars. To close a toolbar, simply right-click any menu or toolbar and deselect that toolbar in the shortcut menu.

 TOOLBARS GETTING CRAZY...RESET 'EM

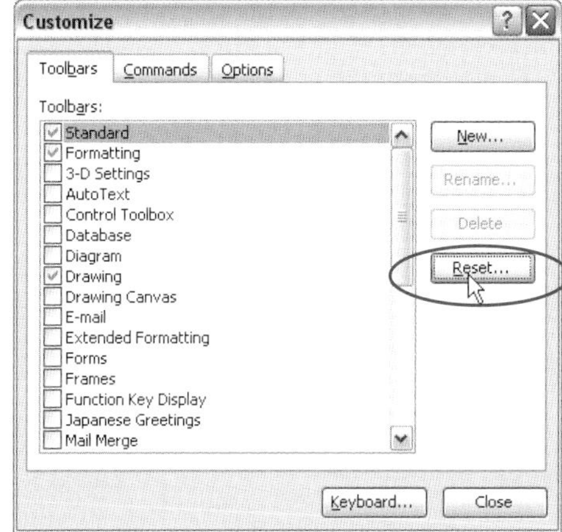

I'm the kind of person who likes to mix things up and, because I'm a rebel, I may not always think that the button layout in the default toolbars works best for me. I find myself changing the position of buttons on my toolbars pretty frequently depending on the project that I'm working on. It just makes sense to have the most frequently used buttons grouped for easier access. This can get confusing at times, however, and will probably make it just about impossible for anyone else to find tasks on these customized toolbars. So...to reset your toolbars to their default state, click Tools>Customize in the menu bar, then click the Toolbars tab in the Customize dialog. Select the toolbar that you want to reset by clicking on its name in the Toolbars window, click the Reset button (to the right), then click Close. Your scrambled buttons are now back to normal.

 LINKING YOUR BUTTONS

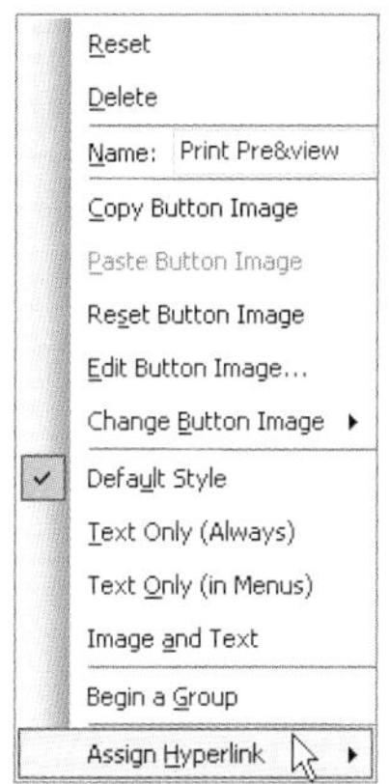

Did you know that you could assign hyperlinks to any button or menu command? Okay, I haven't found a good use for this feature, but it has to be there for a reason, and you may just have one. So, if you want to attach a hyperlink to one of your buttons or commands, here's how. Click Tools>Customize in the menu bar. Then, with the dialog open, right-click a button or open a menu and right-click a command. Next, go to Assign Hyperlink at the bottom of the shortcut menu and click Open. In the dialog, browse to link to a file from your hard drive or type a URL in the Address field to link to a document located on the Internet or office Intranet, then click OK. Click the Close button in the Customize dialog. Now, when you select the button or command, the linked file will open or your Web browser will launch to display the webpage.

GETTIN' GEEKY WITH TOOLBAR BUTTONS

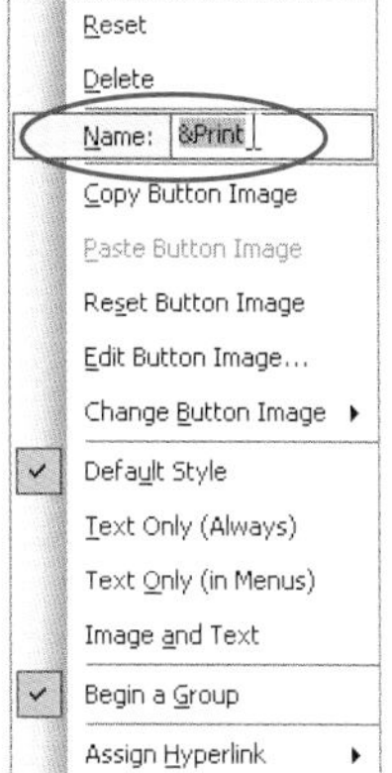

If you really want to get geeky with your toolbar buttons, try this: Click Tools>Customize to open the Customize dialog, then right-click any toolbar button to view its shortcut menu. Using the shortcut menu, you can perform any number of changes to it; you can rename the button (as I did here) or change or edit its image. When finished, click Close in the Customize dialog.

THE MOVE BUTTON TRICK

This trick is for those of you who know how tedious it is to move a toolbar button within Windows (as you know, there's no simple way). Try this to move a toolbar button quickly within any Office application: Press the Alt key on your keyboard, then click any button, and drag-and-drop it to any location on any toolbar. Isn't that great? If you want to delete a button from a toolbar, just press the Alt key and click-and-drag the button off the toolbar. When an "x" appears under the mouse pointer, release the mouse button, and the toolbar button is gone. I really think the Office developers should get together with the Windows developers and share the wealth. This kind of stuff just kills me.

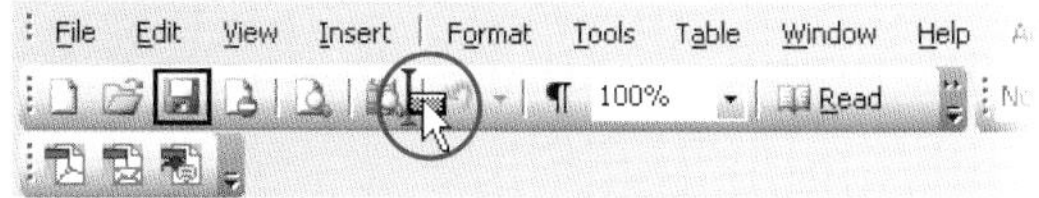

 SIDE BY SIDE...SO COOL

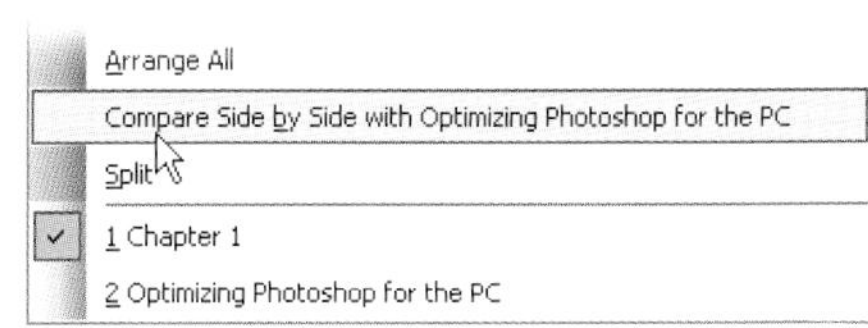

New in Office 2003 for Word and Excel is the Compare Side by Side With option that allows you to, well, compare two open documents side by side. I use this feature all the time, and you probably will too once you know where it is. To compare documents side by side, open at least two documents, then select Window>Compare Side by Side With. If you have more than two documents open, this command will open the Compare Side by Side dialog. Select the document that you want to compare with the document that you're currently working on, then click OK. Your documents will automatically tile vertically.

 ADD PLACES

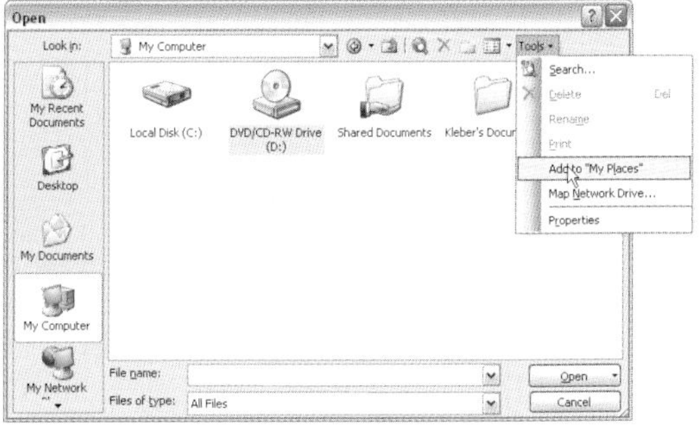

The My Places bar, which appears along the left-hand side of the Open or Save As dialogs, gives you quick access to frequently used locations on your hard drive, but what makes the bar really useful is when you add locations. To add your favorite locations to the My Places bar, go to the File menu and choose Open or Save As to open one of those dialogs, navigate to the folder or drive that you want to add, then click the Tools drop-down menu (at top right of the dialog), and select Add to "My Places." The new location now appears on the My Places bar along the left side of the dialog. To remove a location from the My Places bar, right-click a location icon and click Remove in the shortcut menu.

SHOW SMALL ICONS IN THE MY PLACES BAR

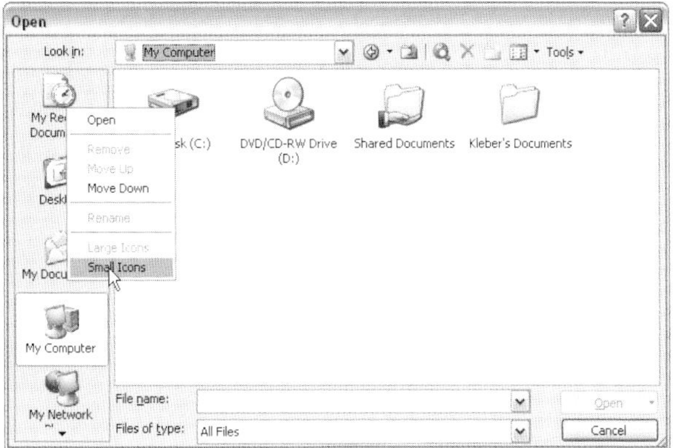

Now that you've added 20 new locations to the My Places bar, you have a new problem: You have to spend more time scrolling to locate your locations than it would take to navigate your hard drive. That's not good. Well, to make the My Places bar a bit more user-friendly, shrink the My Places bar icons. To do this, right-click on any icon in the bar and select Small Icons in the shortcut menu. That's better!

SAVE IT HERE INSTEAD

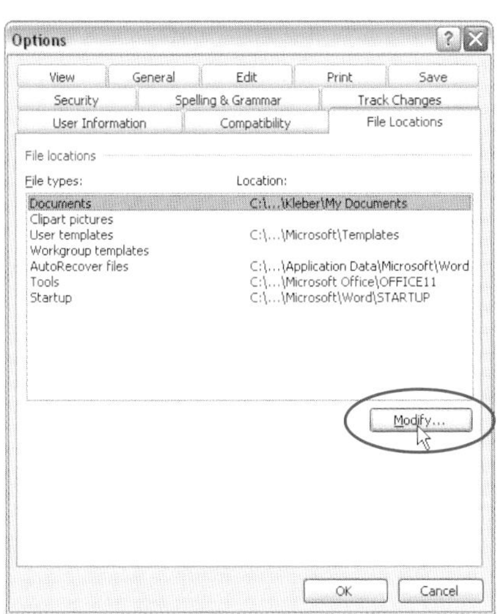

When saving new documents, Office will attempt to save them in your My Documents folder. I guess there should be a default location in which to save all of your documents; however, the My Documents folder may not be the most convenient for you. If this is the case, you can change the default location for saved documents. Click Tools>Options in the menu bar, then click the File Locations tab in the Options dialog. Next, under File Types, click Documents, then click the Modify button. Use the Modify Location dialog to browse your hard drive to select a new location to store your saved documents. When finished, click OK. Now when you click File>Save As, your new location will appear in the Save As dialog.

 NO ACCESS...I'M PROTECTED

Here's one for all of you secret-service agents or seriously paranoid people out there. I'm seriously paranoid, so I password protect just about all of my documents. Actually, there are all kinds of great reasons that any perfectly sane person would want to password protect his or her documents. For instance, I travel a lot, and it's possible that my laptop could be stolen or left behind at any of America's airports, so I always password protect sensitive documents. To password protect your Word, Excel, or PowerPoint documents, click Tools>Options in the menu bar, then click the Security tab in the Options dialog. Type a password in the Password to Open field and click OK, then you'll be prompted to type your password again to verify it. Enter your password again and click OK. Now when you attempt to open the document, you'll be prompted for your password before you can open it. To turn off the password protection, simply delete the password from the Password to Open field in the Options dialog and click OK.

 COPY AND PASTE ON STEROIDS

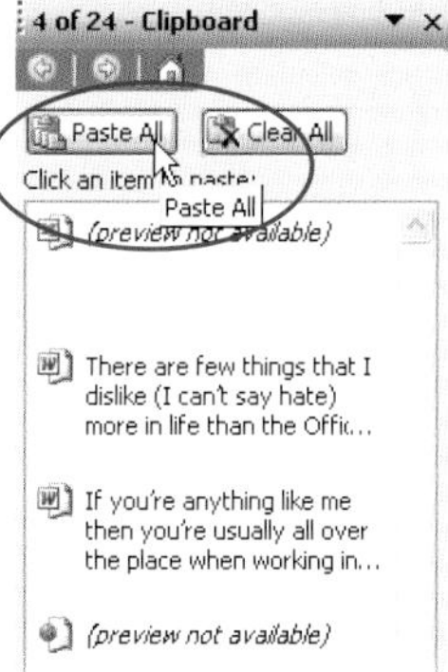

If you're like me, you're usually all over the place when working in Office; I'll be working on related documents in just about all Office applications at the same time. Well, the Office Clipboard can make your life (if not your productivity) much better. For example, you can quickly assemble a presentation in PowerPoint by copying multiple blocks of text in Word (or Excel) and then using the Office Clipboard task pane to paste the contents into PowerPoint. To view the Office Clipboard, click Edit>Office Clipboard in the menu bar. This opens the Office Clipboard, where you can view all of your copied items. Now simply click to insert the item that you want to paste into your document, or click the Paste All button in the top left of the task pane to paste everything from the Clipboard at once.

 THE ASSISTANT'S GOT TO GO

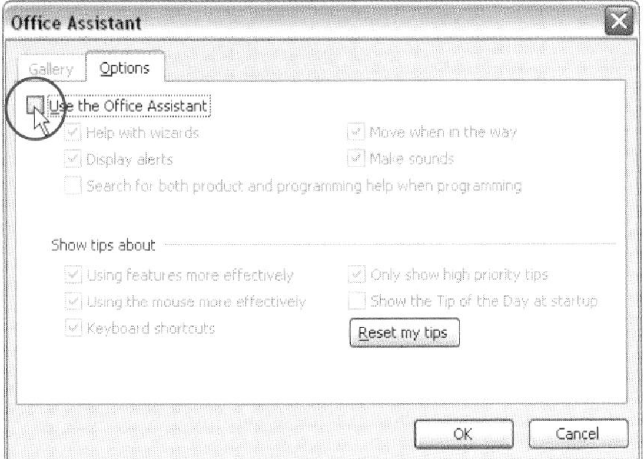

There are few things that I dislike (I can't say hate) more in life than the Office Assistant. I don't know why I hate, I mean dislike, the Office Assistant, I just do. There's no logic behind it. I guess application animations just freak me out. Well, if you're like me, or if you have your own reason for disliking the Office Assistant, you can easily get rid of it: Just right-click the Assistant when it appears, select Options in the shortcut menu; then in the Office Assistant dialog, click the Options tab, uncheck Use the Office Assistant, and click OK. The Office Assistant will never bother you again—sweet!

 HELP ME MADE EASY

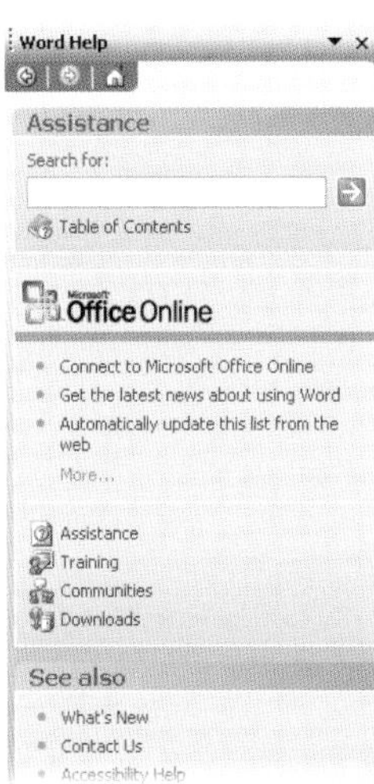

There are probably hundreds of keyboard shortcuts available to Office applications (I haven't actually counted all of the keyboard shortcuts, but hundreds sound about right to me—well, at least tens and tens anyway), but the most important keyboard shortcut to remember in Office is for the Help task pane. Press F1 on your keyboard while working in any Office application to open the Help task pane. Now help is just a keystroke away.

I'M HUNG UP, BUT I'LL RECOVER

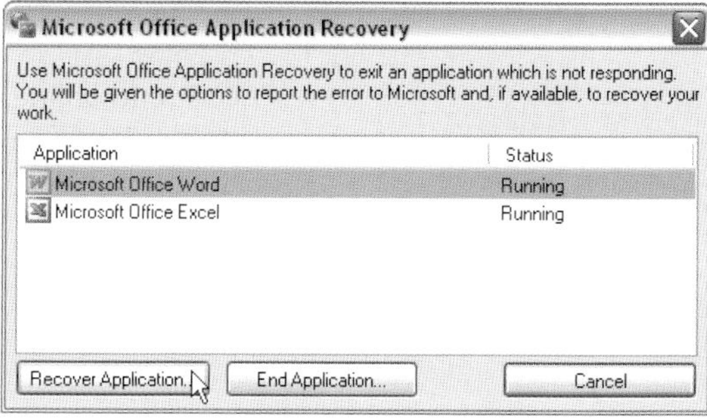

I'm sure that your programs never crash or hang up on you. Mine never do either, but I've heard of it happening. If it ever happens to you, click Start>All Programs>Microsoft Office>Microsoft Office Tools>Microsoft Office Application Recovery, which launches the Office Application Recovery dialog, where you can recover or end an Office application. If your Office program is hung up, then select the program in the dialog window and click the Recover Application button. Office will attempt to recover your documents and help prevent you from losing any of your work.

GET FASTER WITH SHORTCUT KEYS

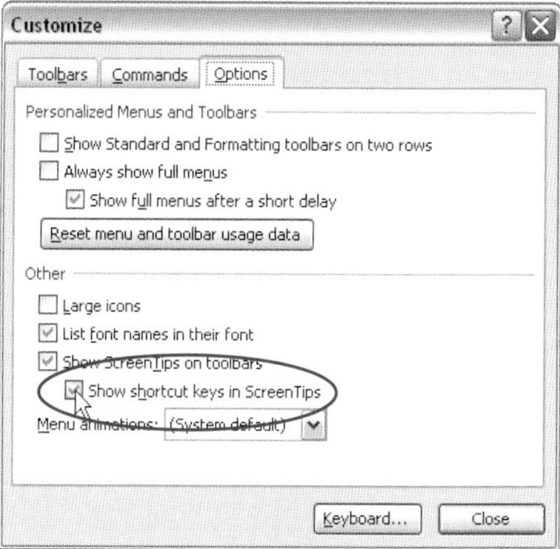

I live by shortcut keys; they make everything faster. Shortcut keys are the quickest way to increase your speed and productivity in just about any program, and Office provides a great way to help you learn shortcut keys. Click Tools>Customize, then click the Options tab. Next, check the Show Shortcut Keys in ScreenTips, then click Close. Now, move your mouse pointer over a button or icon, and you'll see a pop-up screen tip showing that command's shortcut key.

 RESEARCH THIS!

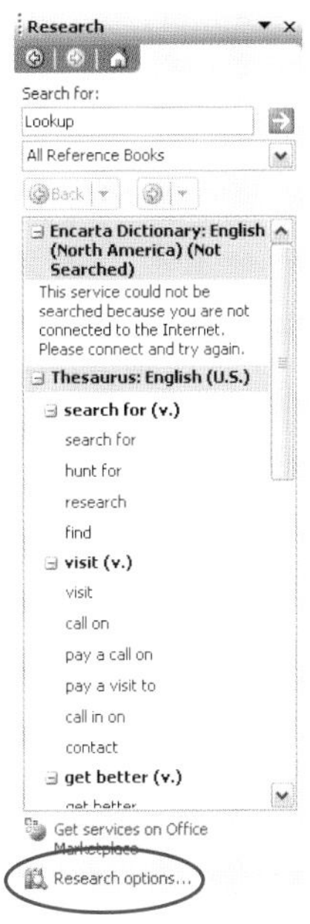

The Research task pane is one of the best enhancements to Office 2003. The Research task pane provides an extensive collection of reference books and online services to help you. For example, you can find the definition of a word, look up a word in the *Encarta Encyclopedia* online, view a word's synonym, or translate words and phrases into different languages. And that's just for starters. To open the Research task pane, right-click any word in your document and click Look Up in the shortcut menu. To set your research options, click the Research Options link at the bottom of the task pane or click the Get Services on Office Marketplace link to add additional services to the Research task pane.

 DO-IT-YOURSELF REPAIRS

If Office starts acting up or you believe an Office document may be corrupt, you can perform a quick diagnostic to try to repair any problems. Select the Help menu and click Detect and Repair to open the Detect and Repair dialog. Next, choose your options and click Start. Detect and Repair automatically finds and fixes errors in your Office files.

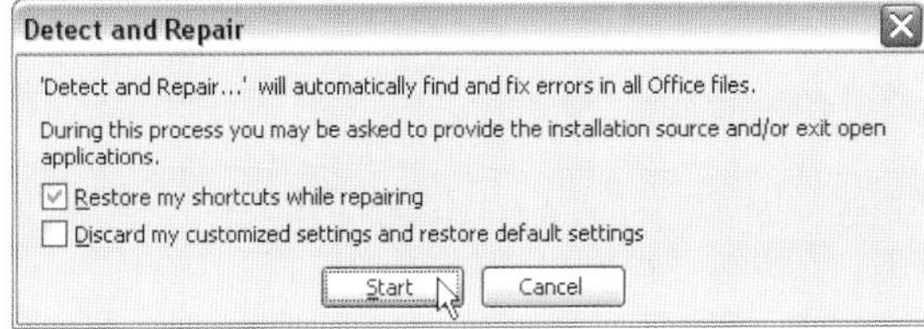

LINK YOUR DOCS

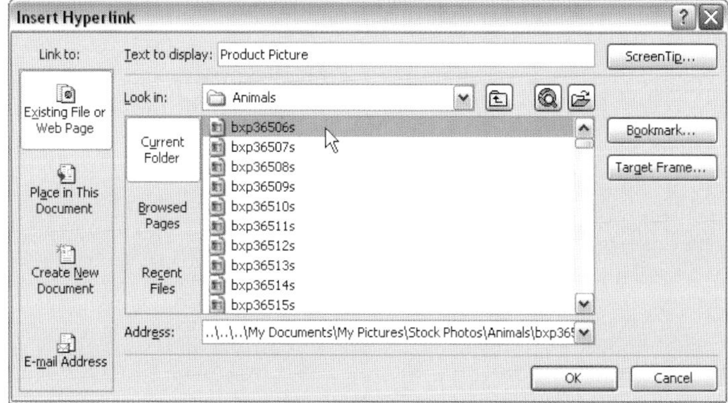

Using hyperlinks in your documents is a great way to include information from other programs or even webpages. For instance, include hyperlinks in a Word document to link to an Excel spreadsheet or to webpages that provide additional information about the subject matter, or even include a link to launch PowerPoint to begin a presentation. To include a hyperlink in your Office documents, press Control-K on your keyboard to open the Insert Hyperlink dialog. Next, click the Existing File or Web Page button in the Link To bar on the left, browse your hard drive to select a document or type a URL in the Address field, then click OK. A new link will appear where your pointer was positioned in your document. Control-click the URL to view the document. If you linked to a webpage or a document in another application, Control-clicking the URL will automatically launch your Web browser or the program that the link refers to.

YOU CAN CUT, PASTE, AND DELETE FROM HERE

You don't have to open Windows Explorer to move or delete files. You can actually use either the Open or Save As dialog for this task. To do this, go to the File menu, choose Open or Save As to open a dialog, then right-click the file you want to move, and click Cut in the shortcut menu (or click Delete to send the file to the Recycle Bin). Now, navigate to where you want to move the file on your hard drive, right-click any blank space in that folder, click Paste in the shortcut menu, then click the Cancel button to close the dialog. You just moved your file!

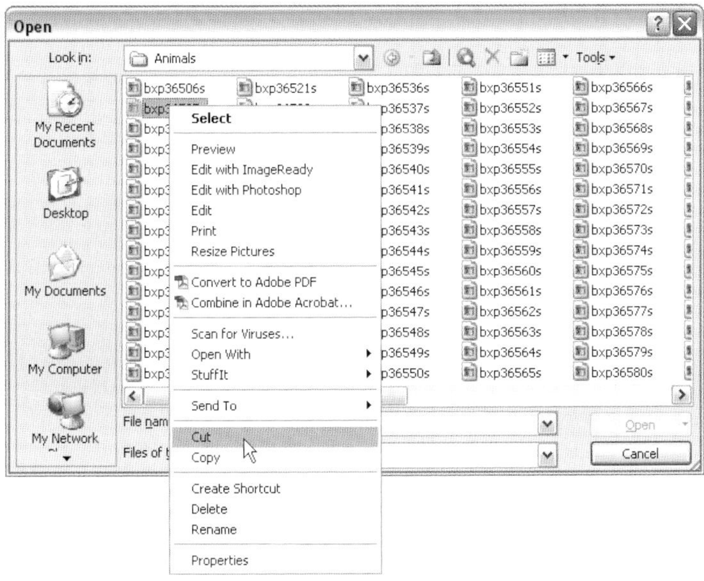

Spread the Word

WORKING WITH WORD

What would the world be like without Microsoft Word? You've probably never given it much thought. Well, I have (I have way too much free time), and it would be

Spread the Word

working with word

awful! It would be an awful, awful world full of typewriters and Wite Out™. People would have to actually learn how to spell and check their own grammar! I don't know about you, but this isn't a world that I'd want to live in. I'm the kind of person who gives credit where credit's due, and I pretty much give credit to Microsoft Word for our civilization as we know it today. Oh, computers played their part, but Microsoft Word gave us something to do with 'em. Grammar! Can you just imagine it? Wait, don't! It's just too painful. Imagine the look on the faces of the typewriter manufacturer executives the first time they saw Word. I bet it was awful!

 PRINT WORD'S SHORTCUTS

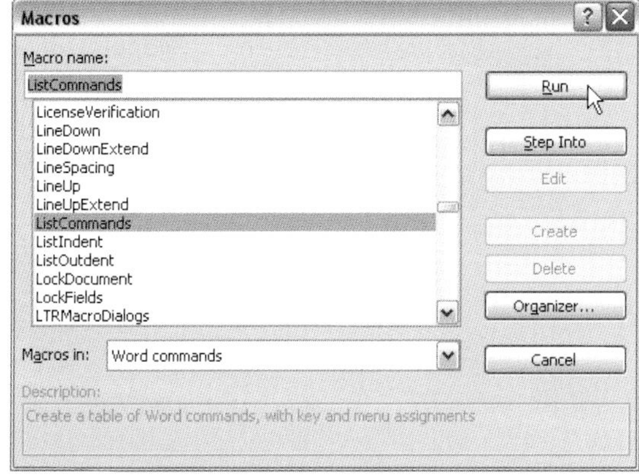

This is probably the best tip in this chapter. I'm sure you've noticed by now that I'm a keyboard-shortcut junkie. I use them as much as possible. They just make everything faster, and when I'm working, faster is always better. Problem is, there's no single place to go within Word to view all of the available shortcuts...or so you might think if you went looking. Actually, there is, and here's how to get to it: Click Tools>Macro>Macros, then choose Word Commands from the Macros In drop-down menu. Next, select ListCommands under the Macro Name field and click the Run button. Check All Word Commands in the resulting dialog, then click OK. Word opens a new document displaying every imaginable keyboard shortcut. Now print the list for future reference, and you'll be flying through Word in no time.

 REPEAT THAT SEARCH

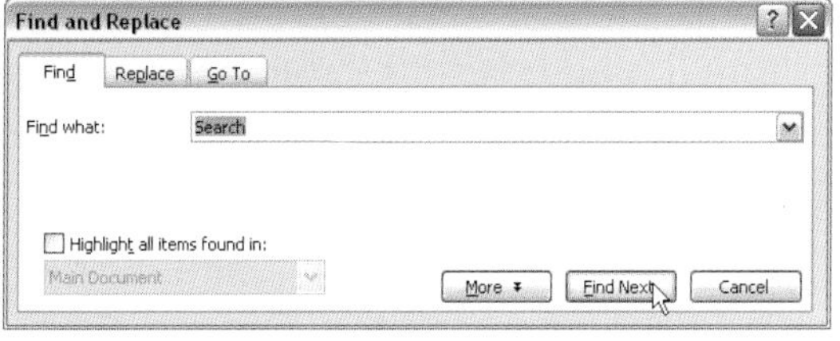

There aren't many occasions where you're going to need this, but when you do, you'll be thankful that you know how to do it because it's really quick—I personally live for tips just like this (sad, isn't it?). Say you've just finished searching for a word or phrase using the Edit>Find command and need to search for the word again; don't open the Find and Replace dialog in the Edit menu and retype the word, just press Shift-F4 on your keyboard. This keyboard shortcut will automatically search your document for the last-searched word or phrase. Faster, better. I bet you'll be using this tip even when you don't need to...just 'cause you can.

INSTANTLY OPEN YOUR LAST-USED DOCUMENT

Oh yeah—shortcuts to shortcuts, can it get any better? Nope! How often do you launch Word by opening the last document you were working on? A lot? Me too! I promise this tip will make your life better (at least your Office life). Locate Word (WINWORD.exe) by doing a search on your hard drive (Start>Search). Then right-click the icon and click Send To>Desktop (create shortcut) in the shortcut menu. Next, right-click the shortcut on your desktop and click Properties in the shortcut menu. Click the Shortcut tab in the Properties dialog and in the Target field type a space, then type "/mfile1" (without the quotes) at the end of the existing target (e.g., "C:\Program Files\Microsoft Office\OFFICE11\WINWORD.EXE" /mfile1). (*Note:* Be sure to enter a space before the forward slash.) Click OK. Now when you click the shortcut icon, Word will automatically launch the last document used in Word.

CUSTOMIZE YOUR DICTIONARY

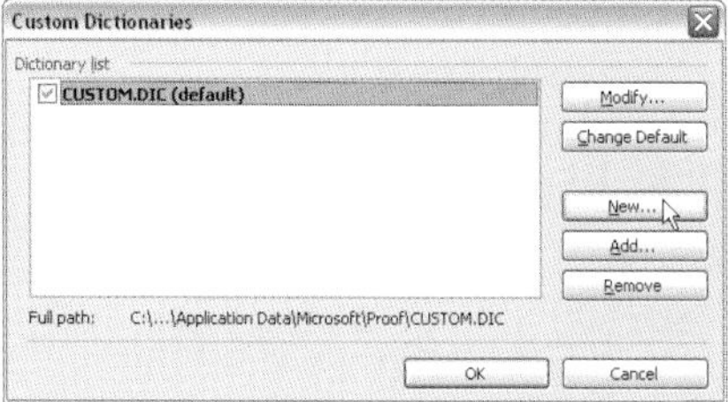

In almost every document that you write, there will be words that Word thinks are misspelled but aren't—especially in documents that include names of people and companies—and adding each word one at a time to the Word dictionary can be almost painful. Well, there's a faster way. Click Tools>Options in the menu bar, then click the Spelling & Grammar tab in the Options dialog. Next, click the Custom Dictionaries button, select the New button, then right-click the CUSTOM file, and click Open With in the shortcut menu. Choose Notepad from the Programs list in the dialog and click OK. Word's dictionary will open in Notepad. Now add as many new words as you'd like to the CUSTOM file, placing each word on its own line. When you're finished, choose File>Save in Notepad to save your changes, and then close Notepad. Click Cancel in the Create Custom Dictionary dialog, then click OK in both the Custom Dictionaries and Options dialogs. Your new words will be added, and Word will no longer ask if those words are spelled correctly.

 SHORTCUT TO YOUR TEXT

Create Scrap Here
Move Scrap Here
Create Document Shortcut Here
Cancel

Here's a really slick way to open a document at the exact text passage you want. Select a block of text, a paragraph, sentence, phrase, or whatever, then right-click the highlighted text and drag-and-drop it to your desktop. Once you drop the text, select Create Document Shortcut Here in the shortcut menu that appears. Now when you double-click the shortcut's icon on your desktop, Word will launch, opening your document at that text passage, word, or whatever. This is a great way to quickly begin a document where you left off, or to jump to the section of your document that you were editing. This shortcut can also be shared with users to provide quick access to important text within a document.

 WORD'S RISING IN THE CHARTS

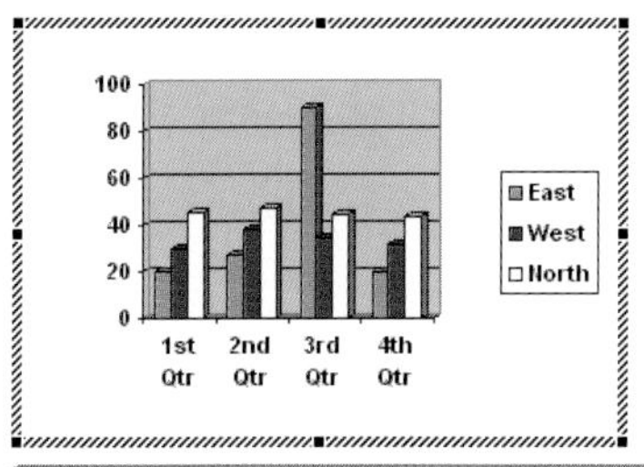

Document1 - Datasheet

		A	B	C	D	E
		1st Qtr	2nd Qtr	3rd Qtr	4th Qtr	
1	East	20.4	27.4	90	20.4	
2	West	30.6	38.6	34.6	31.6	
3	North	45.9	46.9	45	43.9	
4						

Charts are one of Word's coolest tools. I use them all the time for no reason at all, and it amazes me how few users even know about them. Word allows you to add many types of customizable charts to your documents. Here's how: Place your cursor where you want to create a chart in your document, then select Insert>Picture>Chart from Word's menu bar. A chart will appear with an open datasheet. Take note of the menu bar—it's changed. You're now using Microsoft Graph, which has its own menus and tools. Now, update the chart's datasheet with your own numerical values, headings, etc., and your chart is instantly updated. When finished, simply close the datasheet. You can get really geeky by using Microsoft Graph's menu bar to change the type, style, colors, and more in your chart. In addition, you can import existing data into your chart from Excel by choosing Edit>Import File. Go nuts!

 FLIRTING WITH DISASTER

When you're creating a new document, how long does it take before you realize that you haven't saved it? With a distinct feeling of impending doom, you very carefully aim for the Save button in the Standard toolbar and click. Whew, that was close. We've all known the agony of losing documents because our computer decided to crash, freeze, or freak out just prior to saving our work. Good news...you don't have to live in fear any longer because Word 2003 uses AutoRecovery. By default, this feature is enabled and set to save your work automatically every 10 minutes, but I can do a lot of work in 10 minutes. Instead, I like to have Word automatically save my work every minute. I don't mind redoing 1 minute of work, but 10 is just crazy. To access AutoRecovery, click Tools>Options in the menu bar, then click the Save tab in the Options dialog. Next, under Save Options, change the Save AutoRecover Info Every field from 10 minutes to 1 minute, then click OK.

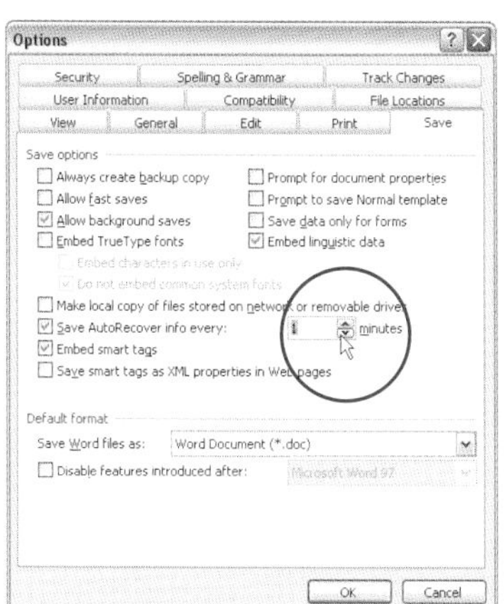

 I'VE ONLY GOT ONE SHEET OF PAPER

Have you ever had several pages to print but only one sheet of paper? It's absolutely pathetic, but this happens to me all the time. I'm always running out of paper. Well, you can use Word's Print dialog to print several pages on one piece of paper. You may have to break out the magnifying glass to read it, but you can at least get it on paper (which is usually good enough for me). Here's how: Press Control-P on your keyboard to open the Print dialog. Next, open the Pages Per Sheet drop-down menu in the Zoom category, select how many pages of your document should be printed to a single piece of paper, then click OK. There you go...a book printed on one sheet of paper.

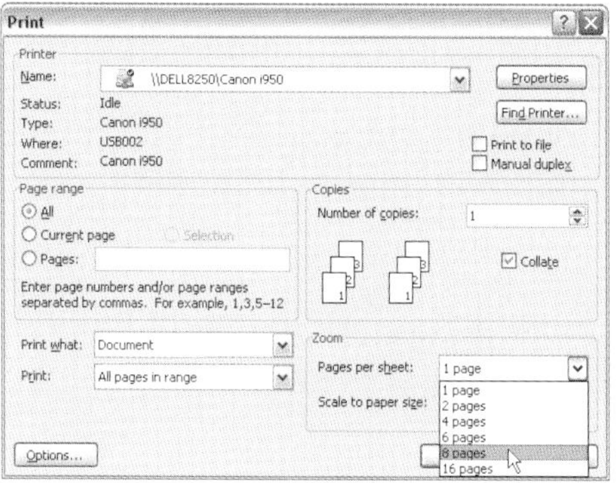

KEEPING UP TO DATE WITH FIELDS

If you use the same document frequently and are continuously changing its date, then make the date a "field" instead. This is very handy for fax cover sheets and form letters. Select Insert>Field from the menu bar, then select Date in the Field Names list on the left. Choose your format in the Date Formats list on the right and click OK. You'll now see the current date appear...this is a field. The cool thing about this field is that from now on, whenever you open the document, the date will automatically update. While you're in the Field dialog, be sure to look around at the different fields that are available—there are a ton.

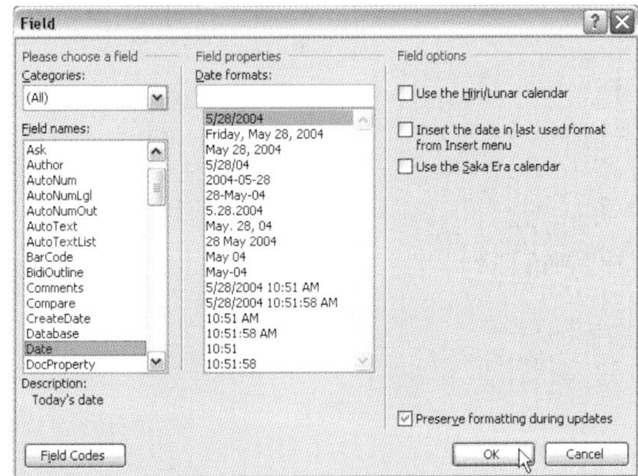

SUPER-FAST TIME AND DATE

Because the current date and current time are the two most frequently used fields, wouldn't it be great if there were a quick way to insert them? Well, there is (otherwise this wouldn't be a tip). Place your cursor where you want to insert a date or time field and press Alt-Shift-D to insert the current date or press Alt-Shift-T to add the current time.

 TURN FIELDS INTO TEXT

In a previous tip, I showed you how to insert a field into your documents, which as you now know is very cool, but if you're going to email the document or share it over a network, then you'll probably want to turn the field into regular text, otherwise the field will continue to update anytime anyone opens the document. To quickly convert your field to text, click within the field and press Control-Shift-F9.

 STOP CONTROL-CLICKING (IT'S BAD FOR YOU)

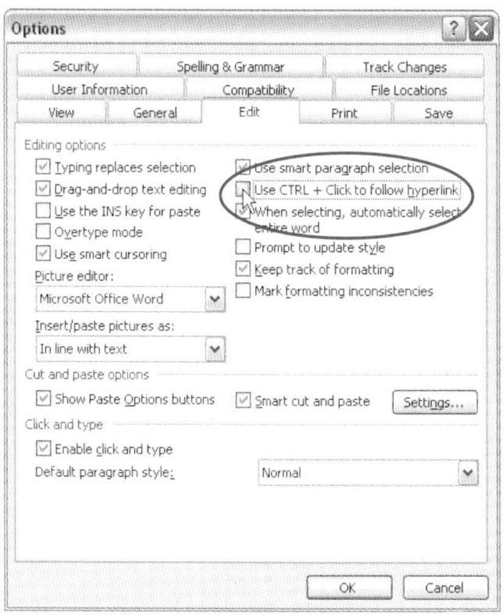

By default, anytime you type a hyperlink into your document, you can only open it by pressing-and-holding the Control key and clicking the link with your mouse pointer. (It's crazy, I know.) This can be somewhat ineffective at times, especially when you want readers to be able to follow your links. You can turn the Control-click feature off by selecting Tools>Options, then clicking the Edit tab in the Options dialog. Uncheck Use CTRL + Click to Follow Hyperlink, and click OK. Now all you have to do is click any hyperlink in your document to immediately open the linked file or URL.

FIND AND REPLACE USING THE CLIPBOARD

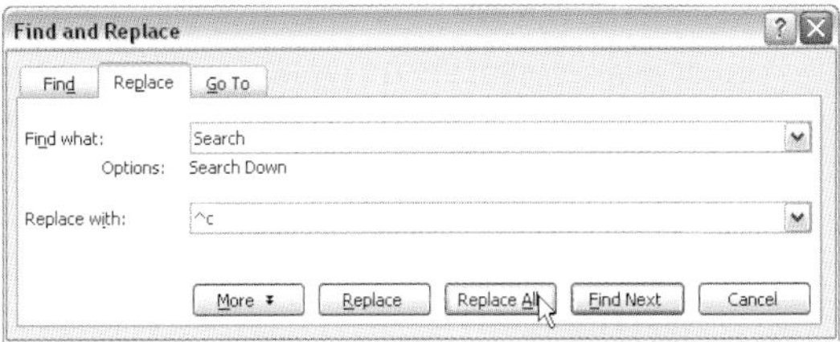

Find and Replace works great for finding and replacing words in your documents, but you can get really geeky with it and replace words with the contents on the Office Clipboard (told ya...geeky). For example, you may want to replace all instances of a word (such as the word "Search") in your document with a picture (of binoculars, for instance). To do this, press Control-F to open the Find and Replace dialog. Next, click the Replace tab and in the Find What field, type the word to be replaced (in our example, "Search"). Then in the Replace With field, type "^c" (press Shift-6 then type a lowercase c), and click Replace All. All of the words are quickly replaced with the Office Clipboard contents. *Note:* Before doing the Find and Replace, make sure to copy a picture of binoculars to the Office Clipboard (by choosing Insert>Picture>Clip Art, choosing your image, and clicking Edit>Copy to copy the image to the Clipboard) or this tip won't work at all.

WORD'S SUPER-SECRET WORK MENU

I love secret stuff! So, I love the fact that Word's most useful menu is completely hidden and undocumented (just kidding!). Word's Work menu is ridiculously useful and allows you to group your most frequently used documents for quick access. Here's how to add the Work menu: Right-click any menu or toolbar and click Customize in the shortcut menu. Next, click the Commands tab and select Built-in Menus in the Categories list. Now drag-and-drop the Work menu from the Commands pane onto the menu bar or onto any toolbar. To add the document that you're working on to the menu, click Work>Add to Work Menu. Your document now appears on the Work menu, ready to be opened at any time with a click of your mouse. To remove items from the Work menu, press Control-Alt-- (hyphen), then click any item in the menu.

 I CAN ACTUALLY SELECT THAT TABLE

I'm all about speed, and anytime I find a quicker way to do something, I'll do it. So, in my quest to do everything faster, I discovered this little shortcut for selecting a table. Click anywhere inside a table and press Alt-5 on the numeric keypad (making certain that the Number Lock key isn't active), and just like magic (it's not really magic), your table is selected. To deselect the table, simply click anywhere inside or outside your table.

 *OUI, OUI*—I CAN TRANSLATE

Have you ever wondered how to spell "bottled water" in Spanish? If you've been to Central America, then you probably have, and fortunately, as long as you have Word and an Internet connection, you can quickly get the help you need to translate just about any word or phrase for numerous languages. To do this in Word, select a word or phrase, right-click the selected text, and click Translate in the shortcut menu. This opens the Research task pane. Now, select the language that you'd like to translate your text into from the To drop-down menu, and the translation will appear at the bottom of the Translation window. Depending on how you've set up Word on your computer, you may have to be online to translate into various languages.

 DON'T JUST PASTE IT, SPIKE IT

Anything called Spike in a computer program just has to be good—and Word's Spike is. The Spike allows you to move multiple objects (text, graphics, etc.) and paste them all at the same time into a document. To "spike" your documents, first select the text and graphics that you want to move, then press Control-F3 on your keyboard. Do this as many times as necessary for as many objects as you want to move (there's no limit to how much you can save to the Spike—actually I'm sure there is, but I've never been able to max it out). When you're ready to paste the objects into your document, place your cursor where you want to insert the content, then press Control-Shift-F3. If you don't want to empty your Spike, click Insert>AutoText>AutoText in the menu bar, then select Spike from the Enter AutoText Entries Here field, and click the Insert button. *Note:* If you don't see Spike listed in the AutoText entries, add it by typing "Spike" (without the quotes) in the Enter AutoText Entries Here text field, then click Add. Spike will now appear as a selection.

 SMART TAGS REALLY ARE SMART

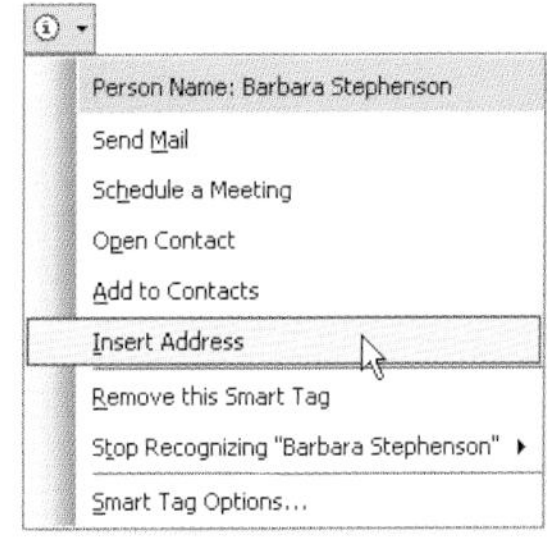

To quickly add an email address for someone in your Outlook Contacts list, simply type his or her name, and the name will appear underlined with a purple dotted line. The dotted line indicates that there are Smart Tags available for the text. Move your cursor over the name and click the down-facing arrow on the Smart Tag's information button. Next, click Insert Address in the Smart Tag menu and Word will automatically add the contact's address to your document. *Note:* If Smart Tags don't appear, go to Tools>AutoCorrect and click the Smart Tags tab in the dialog. Turn on the Show Smart Tag Actions Button checkbox and be sure to select the Person Name (Outlook E-mail Recipients) checkbox in the Recognizers category.

 PRINT LIKE THE POST OFFICE

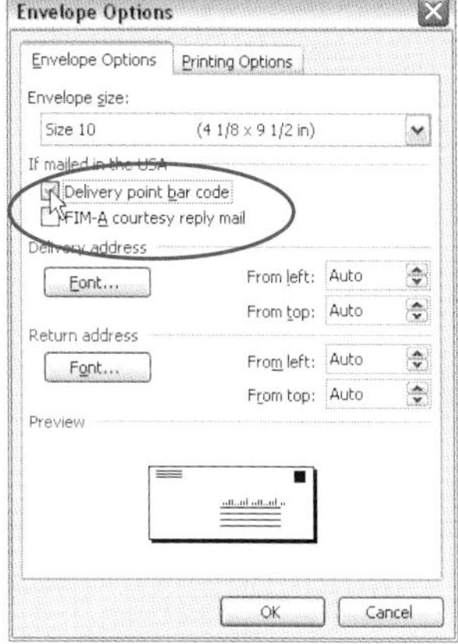

Want to make certain that your mail gets to where it's supposed to? Of course you do, that's kind of the entire point of mailing a letter. Well, you can actually print U.S. delivery point bar codes (postal ZIP codes) on your envelopes (we all know the post office needs the help). To do this, click Tools>Letters and Mailings>Envelopes and Labels. Click the Envelopes tab in the Envelopes and Labels dialog. Now, click the Options button, then check the Delivery Point Bar Code checkbox in the Envelope Options tab, and click OK. Now anytime you print an envelope and include the recipient's ZIP code, Word will automatically print the destination's bar code. The U.S. Postal Service appreciates the help.

 I DON'T USE AVERY LABELS

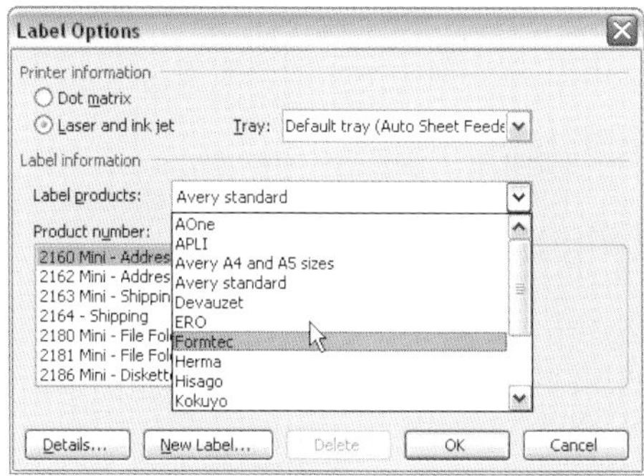

If you print labels, you probably use Avery labels (it's nice to be Avery). Avery labels are so popular that Word uses its label styles by default. Believe it or not, there are other label manufacturers out there, and you just might be using them. Well, Word can actually help you print to labels made by other companies. To select your labels in Word, click Tools>Letters and Mailings>Envelopes and Labels. Click the Labels tab in the Envelopes and Labels dialog, then click the Options button. Click the Label Products drop-down menu in the Label Information category and select your label manufacturer. Now you can locate and print your labels by selecting them from the Product Number list. Click OK when finished.

PRINT A PORTION

Printing a portion of a document is shockingly difficult, so follow along carefully. First, select the text block or blocks that you want to print, then press Control-P on your keyboard to open the Print dialog. Now, check Selection under the Page Range category and click OK. Only the selected text will be printed (unless you're trying to print text that appears within a text box, as part of a table, etc.). I know this is a tough one, so read it a few times if you're not quite getting it. ;-)

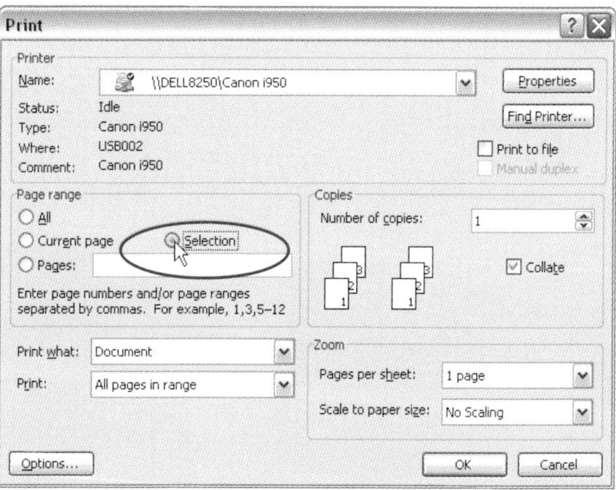

BACKWARD IS BETTER

If you own a printer that prints your documents face up, it just makes sense to change your default print setup. To prevent yourself from having to reorder your printed documents every time you print, change the print order so that the last page prints first, and your pages fall into order (page 1 through whatever). To do this, click Tools>Options in the menu bar, click the Print tab, check Reverse Print Order under the Printing Options category, and click OK. Now when you print your documents, they'll print in reverse order, which is actually the right order.

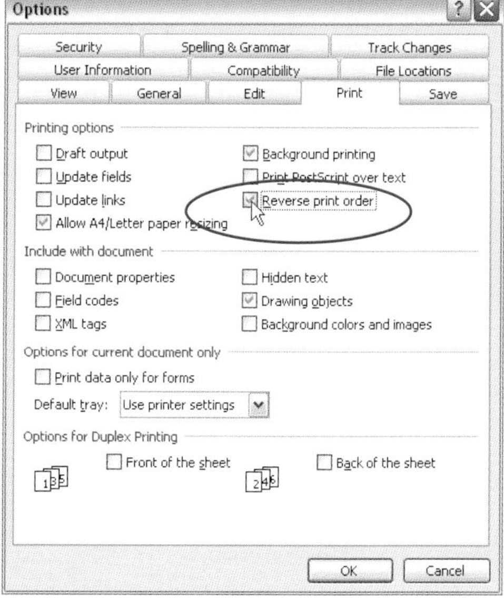

GIVE ME A HUNDREDTH OF AN INCH

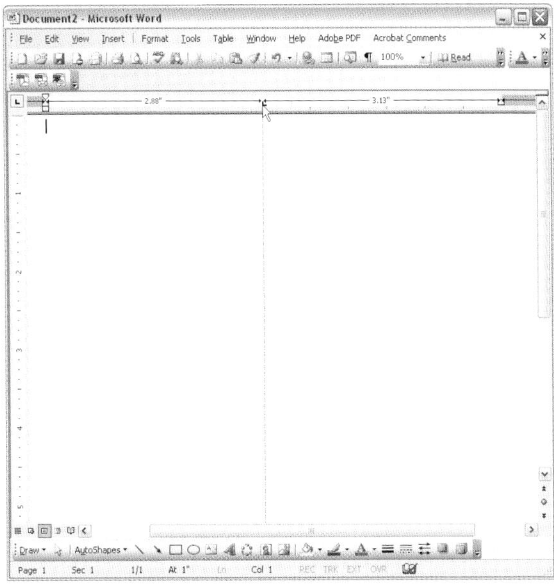

I've never had a reason to use this, but I still think it's pretty cool. If you ever need to use the rulers to measure hundredths of an inch instead of the default tenths of an inch, press the Alt key while clicking on the rulers. You can now move tab stops to measure within a hundredth of an inch.

GROOVY MENUS

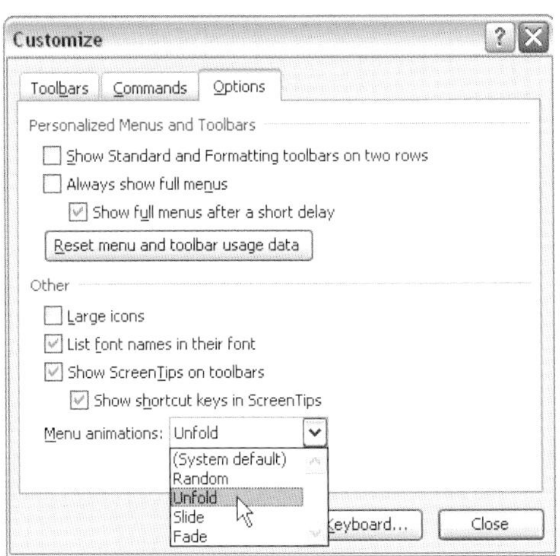

Want to spice up Word's menus? Try animating them. Click Tools>Customize in the menu bar, then click the Options tab in the Customize dialog. Next, click the Menu Animations drop-down menu in the Other category. Here you can select from four different animations for Word's menus (there really should be at least five, but I'll take what I can get). Once you've selected an animation, click Close and then click any menu to see your animations in action. Exciting, isn't it?

SEND, SHARE, COMPARE

You can easily share your documents with friends and colleagues so they can review and edit them. Not me, of course; I hate sharing. But if you want to do this, click File>Send To>Mail Recipient (for Review) in the menu bar. Outlook 2003 will open, and you can add a recipient's email address. When finished, click the Send button to send your document. When you receive the document back, Word will prompt you to merge the two documents to show the changes that were made.

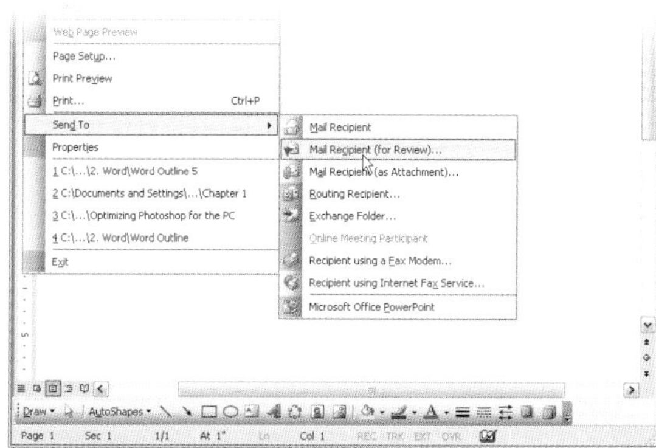

YOU'RE RESTRICTED

If you want to share a document, but you don't want anyone to actually make changes to it, then you should protect your document before sending (this is more my style). Here's how: Click Tools>Protect Document in the menu bar. Now, check Allow Only This Type of Editing in the Document under the Editing Restrictions category in the Protect Document task pane. Next, click the Editing Restrictions drop-down menu and select an option. For this purpose, I'd recommend selecting Comments, which allows recipients to place comments throughout your document but doesn't allow them to edit it. To finish, click the Yes, Start Enforcing Protection button, and Word will prompt you for a password for the document. Type a password and then click OK. Now when you share your document, users can only post comments.

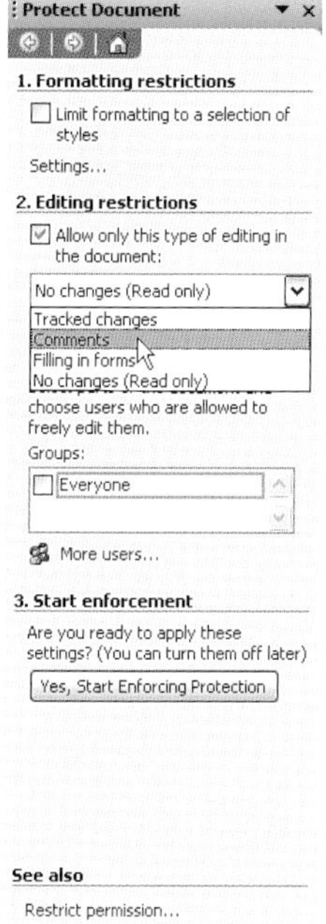

SPLIT AND EDIT

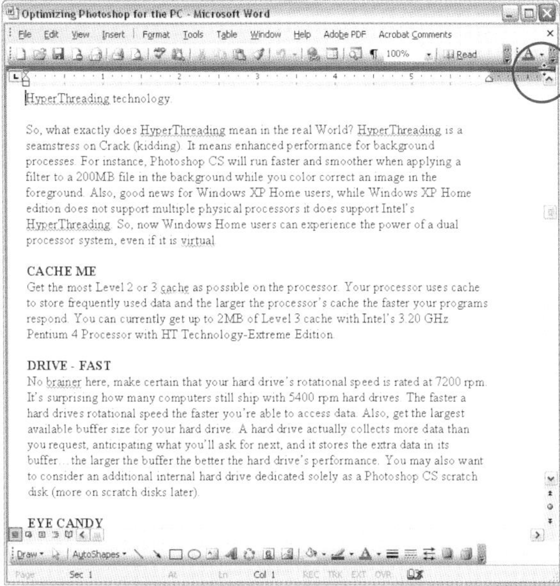

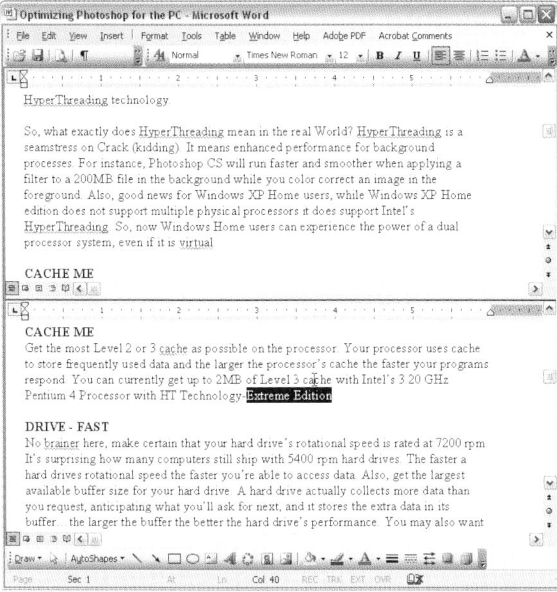

Microsoft is master of the obvious—here's a perfect example: Have you ever noticed the little handle above the right scroll bar? No? Hmm, how did you miss it? Well, even if you had noticed it, you probably never thought to grab and slide it down to split your page. If you had, you'd have found that this little bar does a pretty slick trick: It splits your current document so you can edit two parts of it at the same time, in the same window. Go ahead, grab it, and slide it downward to any position in your document to split the page. Now you can scroll and edit two sections of the same document at the same time. To get back to normal, simply drag-and-drop the divider bar back to the top of the window.

 YOU CAN USE YOUR TOOLBARS IN FULL SCREEN MODE

I have to admit it: I really like working in Full Screen mode in Word and I'm man enough to admit it. I just have more room for everything. Not everyone likes it as much as I do, however, and I found out why: People think you lose your toolbars. Well you do, but you can get them back and dock or float them anywhere on your screen. Here's how: Click View>Full Screen in the menu bar. Now, click the down-facing arrow on the floating Full Screen menu and point to Add or Remove Buttons>Customize. Next, check the Toolbars tab in the Customize dialog, check the toolbars that you'd like to view in Full Screen mode, and then click Close…there's your toolbars! You can now dock or float them anywhere on your screen.

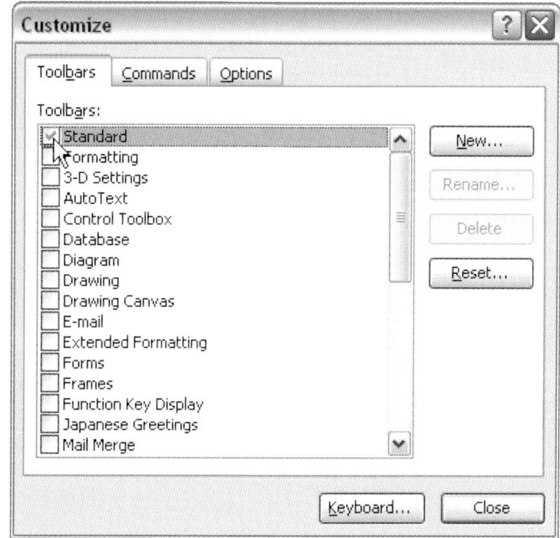

 WORD HOPPING

To quickly jump from word to word in a sentence, press the Control-Left Arrow keys to jump to the start of the previous word; press the Control-Right Arrow keys to jump to the start of the next word. These keyboard shortcuts are a great way to navigate sentences quickly to make changes to individual words.

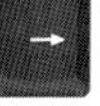

EDIT MULTIPLE PAGES

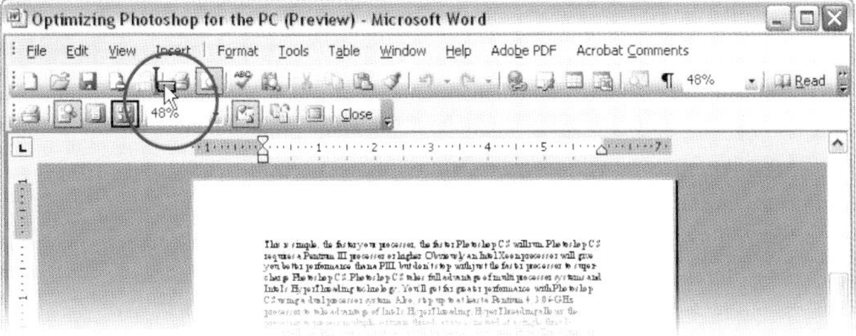

To edit multiple pages in Word, click the Print Preview button on the Standard toolbar, then right-click anywhere within the Print Preview toolbar, and click Standard to open the Standard toolbar. Next, put your mouse pointer on the Multiple Pages button in the Print Preview toolbar and when it highlights, press the Alt key and start to drag. Now, hold the Control key while dragging-and-dropping the Multiple Pages button onto the Standard toolbar. When you click the Close Print Preview window, the Multiple Pages button will still appear on your Standard toolbar. Now you can view and edit multiple pages. Isn't that great?

SAVE 'EM ALL, CLOSE 'EM ALL

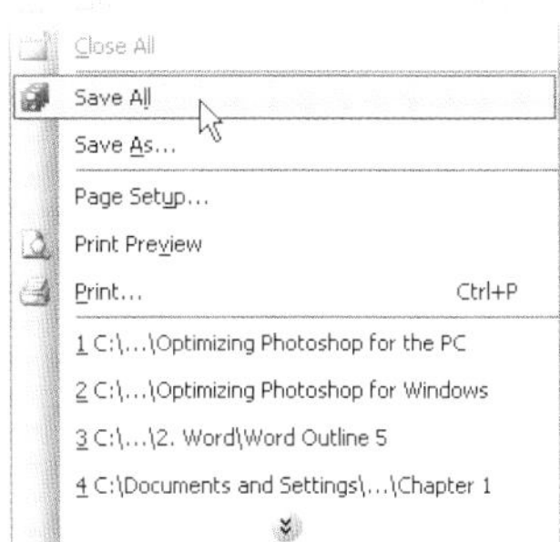

Wouldn't it be nice if we could save all of our open documents at once? But when we click File in the menu bar, we only have the option to save the current document. Well, there's a way around this: Press-and-hold the Shift key on your keyboard, then click File in the menu bar. You now have options to Save All and Close All.

NAVIGATING THE EASY WAY

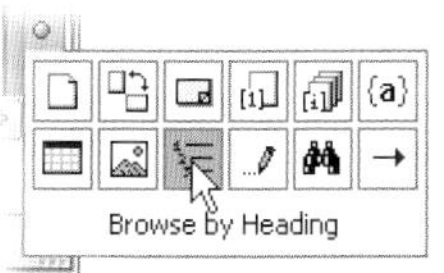

Navigating your documents doesn't have to be difficult, unless you like to do things the hard way. If that's the case, then don't read this tip—it's only helpful and you'll resent it. If you like doing things the easy way, however, try clicking the Select Browse Object button located near the bottom of the right scroll bar. You can quickly browse by field, comment, heading, graphic, and many other objects. Click an object and Word will automatically begin to browse your document for that object. Also, notice the arrows above and below the Select Browse Object button—they turn blue when any option other than Browse by Page is selected, allowing you to search above or below your insertion point.

 YAY, PREVIEWS!

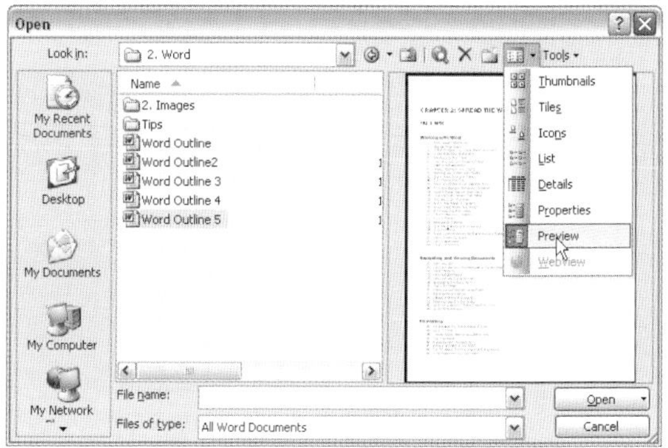

Do you have trouble trying to locate the correct file to open? I always do. I guess I'm just not very good at giving my files very descriptive names. I can't even find a document that I was working on literally five minutes ago…it's bad. Well, I found a way to end my distress. I open my documents with preview images. Now I can see a thumbnail of my document before I open it. To do this, click File>Open in the menu bar. Next, click the down-facing arrow next to the Views button near the top right of the dialog and select Preview. Now, select a document in the Name window, and you'll see a preview of your file in the Open dialog (File>Open) before you open it. If you want to see a thumbnail image of your entire document in the Open dialog, click File>Properties while working in a document that you want to preview later as a thumbnail, and click the Summary tab in the Properties dialog. Click the Save Preview Picture checkbox, then click OK.

THERE'S A COMPARISON TO BE MADE

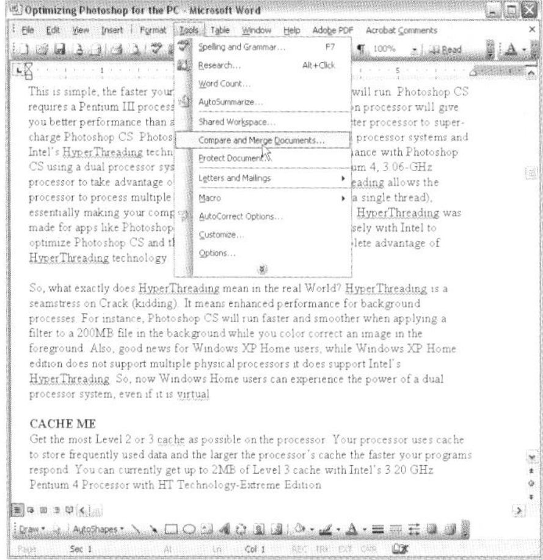

To compare two versions of the same document, click Tools>Compare and Merge Documents in the menu bar. Choose which document to compare with the original or current document, click the Legal Blackline checkbox, and click Compare in the dialog. Word will show you all of the changes made to your document. You can also merge the document into the current document or merge both documents into a new document by clicking Tools>Compare and Merge Documents, selecting the document to merge into your current document, and then clicking the down-facing arrow within the Merge button. Select either Merge into Current Document or Merge into New Document. This is a great way to track changes you've made and be selective about which changes to keep for your final draft.

BOOKMARKS ARE BETTER

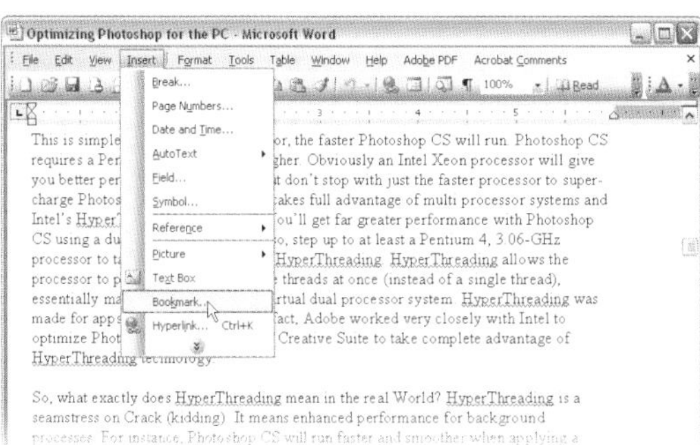

To find your place in a document quickly, just create a bookmark. Highlight text or place your cursor in the document where you'd like to create the bookmark, then click Insert>Bookmark from the menu bar. Type an appropriate name in the Bookmark Name field, click the Add button, and you've created a bookmark. To jump to a bookmark in your document, click Insert>Bookmark in the menu bar, then select the bookmark name in the list and click the Go To button to jump instantly to that location in your document.

 NEED A TABLE OF CONTENTS?

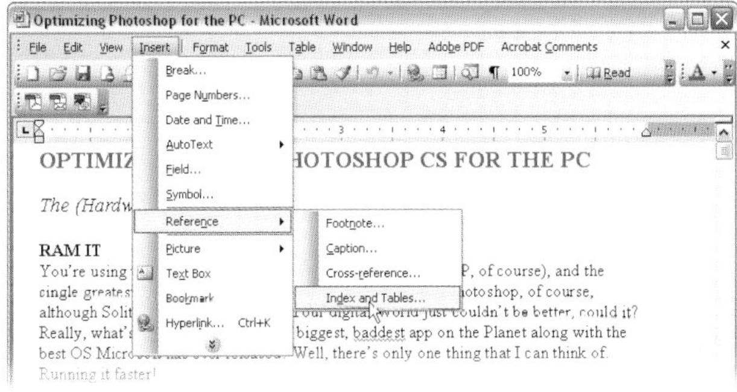

If you've created a long document that includes several headings, you can create a table of contents (it only makes sense). To do this, place your cursor where you want to insert your table of contents, choose Insert>Reference>Index and Tables from the menu bar, then click the Table of Contents tab in the Index and Tables dialog, make any changes you'd like, and click OK. Word will create a table of contents from the headings in your document. Now you can quickly navigate your document using its very own table of contents.

 READING LAYOUT'S GOT TO GO

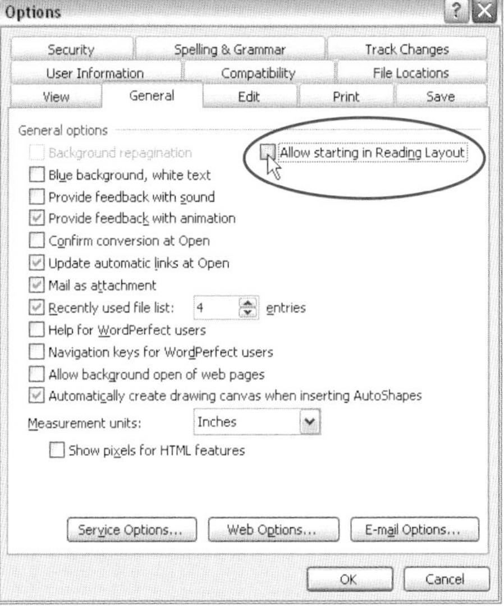

I find it just a little annoying that DOC files open in Reading Layout mode anytime I open an attached Word (.doc) file from an email. I typically receive Word files to edit or comment on; very seldom do I get them just to read. Anyway, I find this annoying enough to do something about it, and you can too. To turn off Reading Layout mode for email attachments, select Tools>Options from the menu bar, click the General tab in the Options dialog, uncheck Allow Starting in Reading Layout (near the top-right corner of the tab), then click OK. Now your attached Word files will launch in an editing mode instead of Reading Layout mode.

 LACKING CREATIVITY? MAKE IT WORK FOR YOU

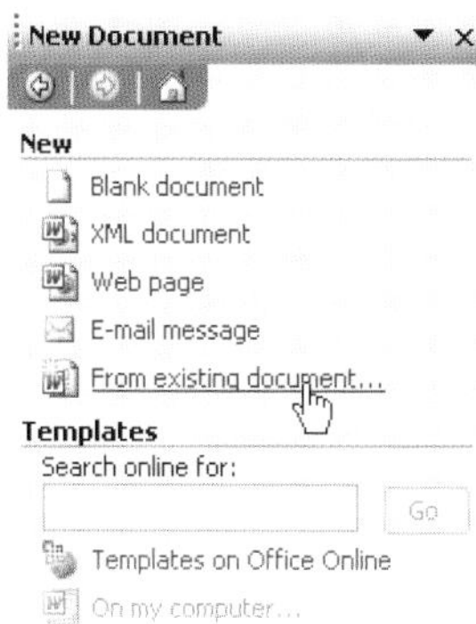

I'm not very creative—most of my documents tend to follow a similar look and feel. I'm working on the problem (without much luck) but I've found a way to make this work for me. I can quickly create a new document that has the look and feel of an existing document (I'm an enabler) by simply clicking File>New in the menu bar and clicking the From Existing Document link in the New Document task pane. This opens the New From Existing Document dialog, where you can select your file, which Word will open as a new document. When you're finished making changes, simply save it with a new file name by choosing File>Save As.

 QUICK PRINT PREVIEW

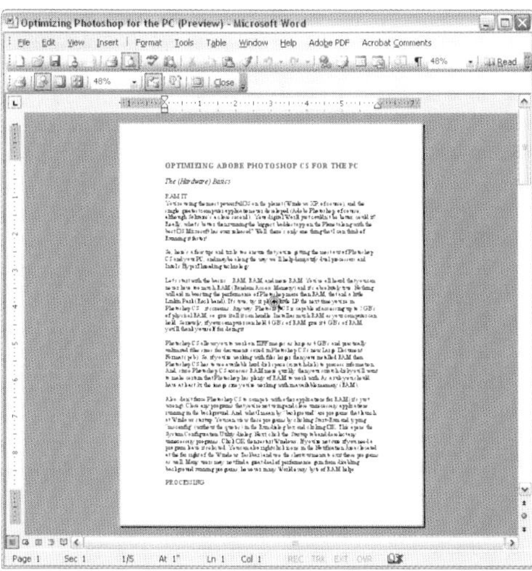

Try this undocumented keyboard shortcut the next time you need to quickly view a document in Print Preview mode. Press Control-Alt-I to switch to Print Preview. Press the shortcut again to switch back to Normal viewing mode.

 AUTOCORRECT MY ABBREVIATIONS? COOL!

AutoCorrect is more powerful than you might think; for example, it has the ability to interpret custom abbreviations of text passages, which is perfect for repetitive text such as your name, address, or for the closing of a letter (name, address, phone, email, etc.). Try this: Type your name and address, select the text, and click Tools>AutoCorrect Options in the menu bar. The AutoCorrect dialog will open, displaying the AutoCorrect tab, which shows your name and address in the With field. Now, type an abbreviation in the Replace field, such as "mna" (without the quotes), short for "My Name and Address," then click OK. Now, type "mna" and hit Enter or the Spacebar, and Word will instantly replace "mna" with your name and address. Very cool!

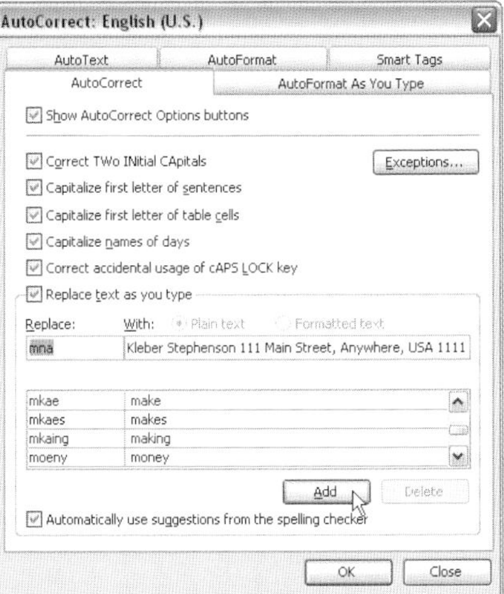

 LOTS O' LINES

You're probably familiar with the trick to create a solid line in Word: Type three hyphens (---) then press Enter on your keyboard. But did you know that you could use similar tricks to create all kinds of lines? For example:

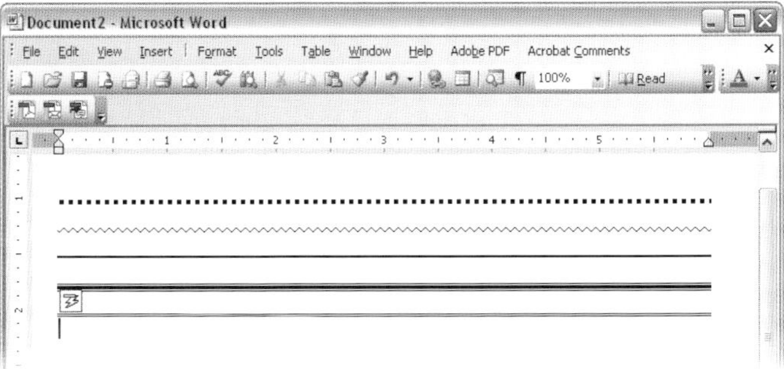

- Type three asterisks (***) then press Enter to create a dotted line.
- Type three tilde symbols (~~~) then press Enter to create a wavy line.
- Type three underscores (___) then press Enter to create a bold line.
- Type three pound symbols (###) then press Enter to create a triple line.
- Type three equal signs (===) then press Enter to create a double line.

 I KNEW THERE HAD TO BE A BETTER WAY

How many of you go to the menu bar to add a row at the end of a table? Yep, we all do, but there's a faster way. Click the last cell in the bottom row of your table, then press the Tab key on your keyboard. This automatically adds a new row to the bottom of the table—now that's faster!

TAB YOUR CELLS

If you've ever had to add a Tab character to a table cell, you probably found yourself scratching your head because you can't add a Tab character to a cell! Pressing the Tab key only jumps you from cell to cell. There's a way around this, though. Press Control-Tab, which will place a Tab character in your cell. Now you can stop scratching your head…problem solved.

 PRESERVE YOUR FORMATTING

If you want to maintain your text's formatting when copying-and-pasting it to a new document, be sure to include the text's last paragraph mark. To view paragraph marks, click the Show/Hide button in the Standard toolbar, then copy (Edit>Copy) your text, including all the formatting marks and paste it (Edit>Paste) to its new location. Click the Show/Hide button again to hide the document's formatting marks. *Note:* This will only work if the Use Smart Paragraph Selection checkbox is selected in the Edit tab of the Options dialog (Tools>Options).

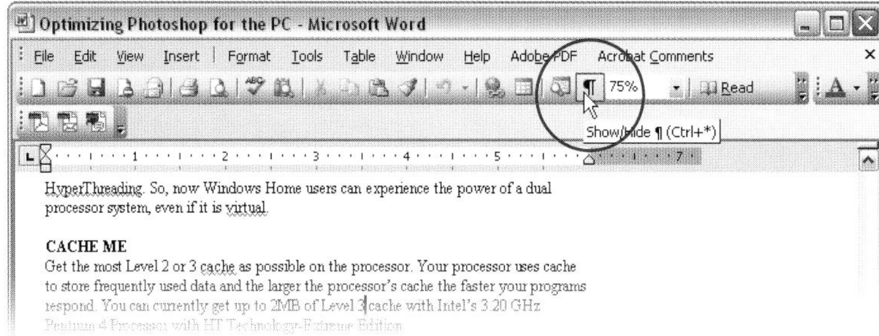

 EXCEL'S GOT NOTHIN' ON WORD

Excel isn't the only Office program capable of calculating numbers. Word can perform calculations in tables, too. To calculate numbers in a table's row, place your numbers in the row's cells, leaving the last cell empty. Next, click the last cell in the row and click Table>Formula in the menu bar. Use the default formula of "=SUM(LEFT)" and click OK. Word will calculate the previous cells and place the added results in the last cell. Repeat the same procedure for calculating columns, using the default formula "=SUM(ABOVE)."

IT'S ALL ABOUT THE PLUS (AND MINUS) SIGNS

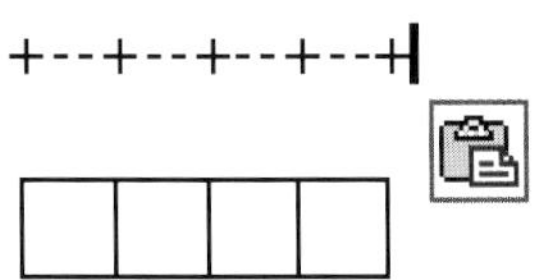

Did you know that tables are made up of plus and minus signs? It's true, try this: Using the number keypad, type a plus sign (+) followed by two minus signs (––) followed by a plus sign (+), then press Enter. You just created a single-cell table. Repeat this pattern (e.g., +––+––+––+––+) for each cell that you'd like to create.

A TEMPLATE OF YOUR VERY OWN

If you've designed your letterhead or other frequently used documents in Word, you may want to save them as templates. To save a document as a template, first apply your formatting and any graphics, then click File>Save As in the menu bar. In the Save As dialog, type a descriptive name for your document in the File Name field, then select Document Template in the Save As Type field, and click Save. To open your new template, click File>New, which opens the New Document task pane. Click the On My Computer link under the Templates category, then click the General tab in the Templates dialog. Now, select your template and click OK.

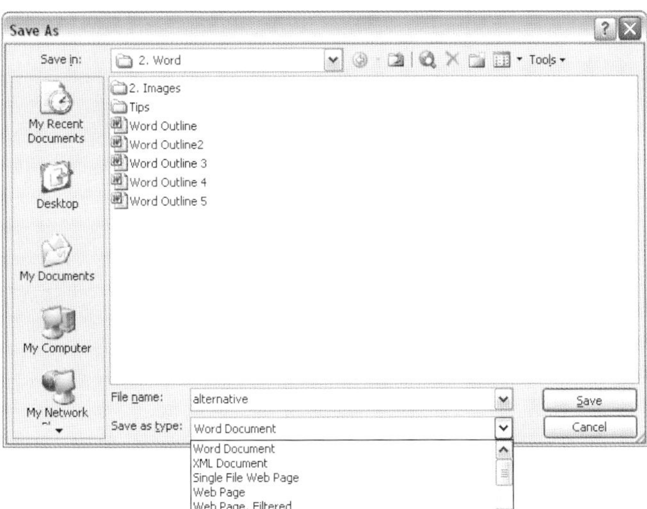

 SPLITTING UP ISN'T HARD TO DO

You've just finished typing a ten-page article and suddenly realize that the editor wanted your story in two columns. Well, too bad; it's too late. You're a loser, and they're gonna fire you (kidding). We can fix it, here's how: First, place your cursor where you want the columns to begin, then click Format>Columns in the menu bar. Next, click the Two icon under the Presets category and click OK. All the text following your cursor is instantly formatted into two columns.

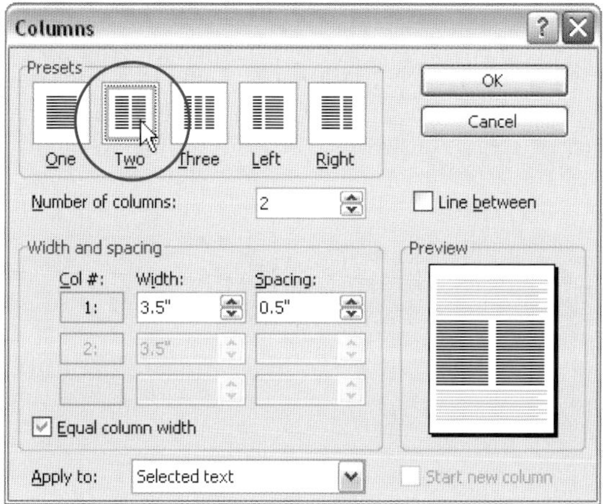

SHRINK YOUR DOCUMENT

It can be a pain trying to get the last couple of sentences to fit onto a page. Most documents fit on a single page (they just do, I'm not making this stuff up), and if they don't, we'll stop at practically nothing to get the last couple of sentences to fit so that we don't have to print a second page. We'll try experimenting with font sizes, deleting every other word—you name it—but there's an easier way. Press Control-Alt-I to view your document in Print Preview and then click the Shrink to Fit button in the Print Preview toolbar. This will shrink your document by adjusting the font size to include the extra text. Now you can print your document on only one sheet of paper.

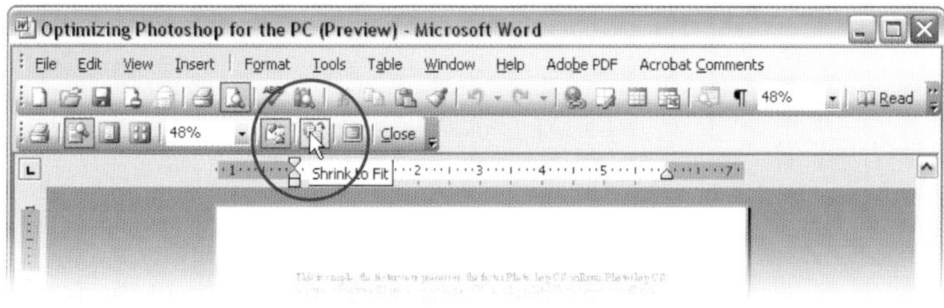

 I'VE MADE A MISTAKE

We can do some pretty awful things to text—too many words underlined, bolded, italicized—it can get crazy. When your formatting gets out of hand, you can get things back to normal by selecting the offending text and pressing Control-Spacebar. This will reset your text style in the Formatting toolbar to Normal. You can do the same to a paragraph's style by selecting it and pressing Control-Q to return it to normal paragraph style.

This *text* is ***awful***

This text is awful

 UNDO IT ALL

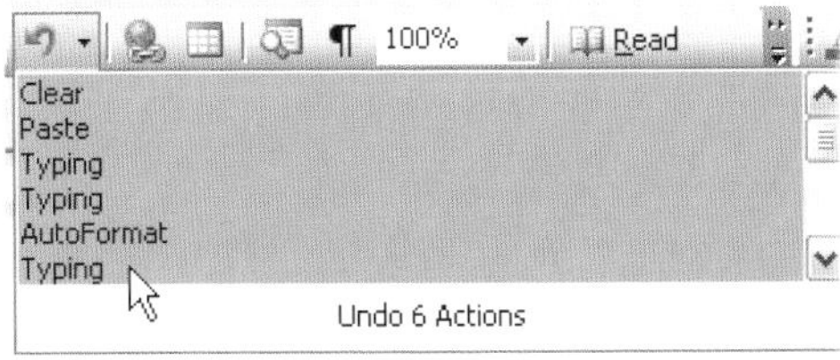

You probably already know that you can perform multiple undos in Word by pressing Control-Z repeatedly, but what if you want to undo tens or even hundreds of changes? That's a lot of Control-Zs. Try this instead: Click the down-facing arrow next to the Undo button in the Standard toolbar, and you'll see a list of literally hundreds of changes that you've made to your document (that is, if you've made hundreds of changes). Now, you can simply scroll through the list until you find the point where you'd like to undo all previous changes. Simply click the item on the list and Word will instantly perform all of the undos that you've selected.

PICK THE PILCROW

When pasting together a document from several different sources, you're going to get several differently formatted paragraphs, but you can quickly give your paragraphs the same formatting. To do this, click the Show/Hide button (it looks like a backward "P") in the Standard toolbar to show your formatting markers. Next, double-click to select the paragraph marker (called a "pilcrow") that you'd like to copy, then right-click the marker, and click Copy in the shortcut menu. Now, double-click the marker at the end of the paragraph to which you'd like to apply the copied paragraph formatting, right-click the marker, and select Paste in the shortcut menu. Your paragraph's formatting will change to reflect the look of the copied pilcrow. Repeat this as many times as you'd like to apply consistent formatting to your paragraphs.

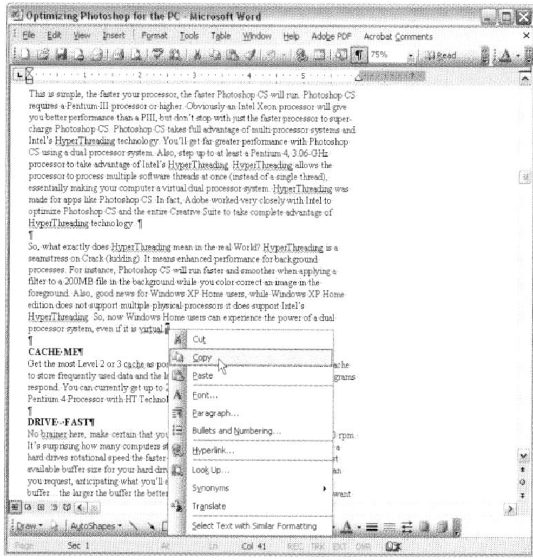

CUSTOMIZE YOUR BULLETS

Do you use bullets? Sure you do, we all do. You don't have to be like everyone else, though. You can customize your bullets for a personal touch. Click Format>Bullets and Numbering in the menu bar, then click the Bulleted tab, click on any style icon, and click the Customize button. Next, click the Character button in the Customized Bulleted List dialog to use one of the Windows character symbols or click Cancel to go back to the Customize Bulleted List dialog and click the Picture button to use a picture or to import your own graphics. When finished, click OK. Now go back to Format>Bullets and Numbering, select your customized bullet, and begin inserting your new bullets.

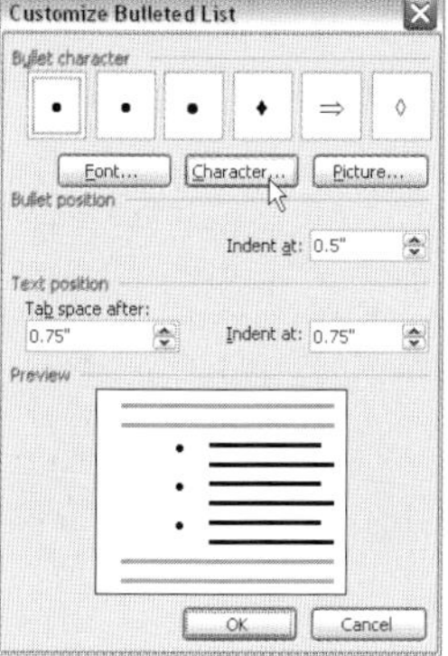

 I NEED A LITTLE ROOM

1. Line 1
2. Line 2
3. Line 3
4. Line 4
5. Line 5
6. Line 6
7. Line 7
8. Line 8
9. Line 9
10. Line 10

Have you noticed how tight the line spacing can appear when using automatic numbering? Personally, I need some room. So, if you need a little more spacing between your numbered lines, try this: Select your numbered text and press Control-Zero on your keyboard. That's better! Press Control-Zero again to return your numbering to its regular line spacing.

TYPE IT AGAIN

Word has a secret key that will repeat the last several words you've typed. I've used this to type repeating words and for adding filler text, and I'm sure you'll find your own uses for it. Try this: Type your name, then press the F4 key on your keyboard. Word inserts your name again. Press the F4 key as many times as you'd like to continue adding the text. Personally, I love seeing my name typed over and over again. It's very soothing.

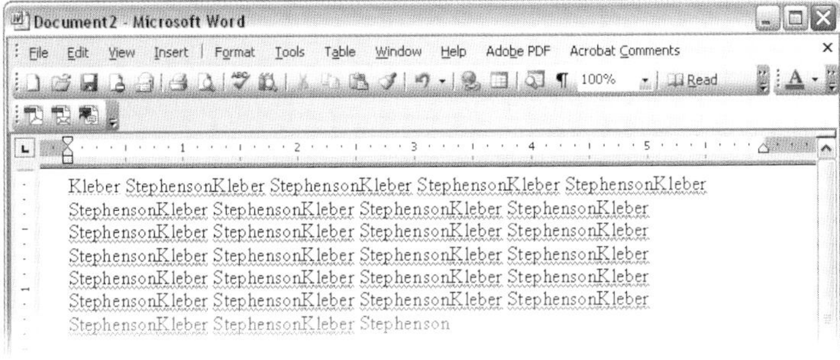

THAT'S NOT PAGE ONE

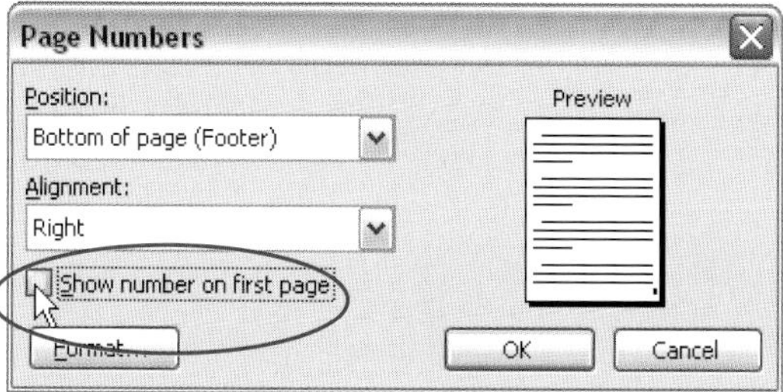

Even Word needs a little help once in a while. Here's an example: You've written a multipage document and numbered the pages (Insert>Page Numbers), but your first page is your title page. Word doesn't know this and will number your title page as page 1, even though the second page is actually page 1. See, Word needs help. To fix this, go to Insert>Page Numbers in the menu bar, select your page number positioning (i.e., the bottom of the page, top, etc.), and uncheck Show Number on First Page. Wait, you're not finished. Next, click the Format button and check Start At in the Page Numbering category and type "0" (zero without the quotes), click OK, and then click OK to close the Page Numbers dialog. Now, check out your page numbering. Page 1 begins on the second page.

SAVE THAT TABLE SIZE

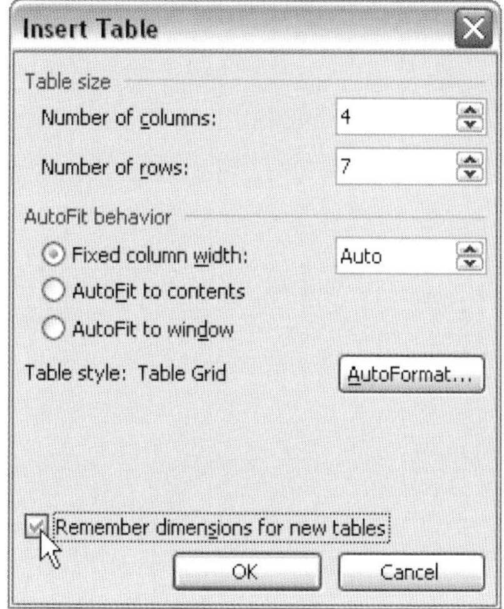

If you find yourself using the same table size over and over again, and it's not Word's default table dimensions, then you should save your custom table size. You can easily do this the next time that you insert a table by clicking Table>Insert>Table. This opens the Insert Table dialog. Now, change the number of columns and rows to whatever you'd like, but before you close the dialog, check Remember Dimensions for New Tables, then click OK. Now, your preferences are saved, so every time you open the Insert Table dialog, your custom table dimensions are displayed by default.

CONTROL YOUR COLUMN WIDTHS

If you want to change only the size of the left or right column in a table, while keeping your other columns evenly spaced, hold the Control key while dragging the column border to the left or right (your mouse pointer will turn into a double-sided arrow). When you release your mouse, the column will be resized, while keeping all of your other columns evenly spaced.

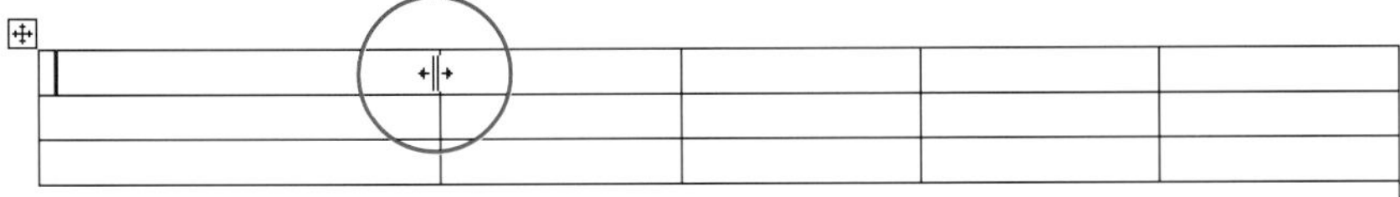

AUTOFIT JUST ONE COLUMN

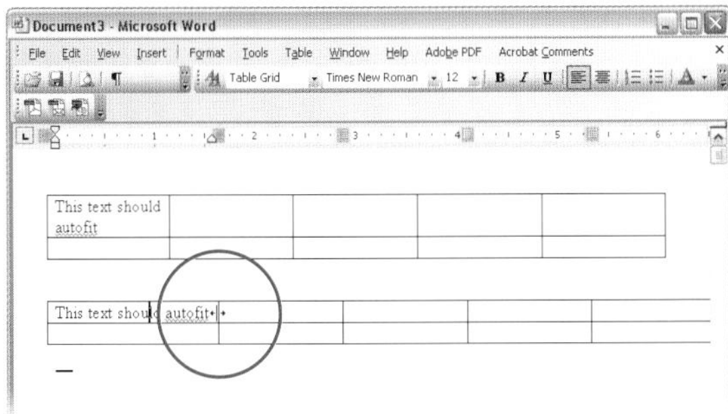

To automatically fit a single column, first select the column by clicking above it, then right-click anywhere in the column, and click AutoFit> AutoFit to Contents. But doing it this way affects every cell in the table. Try this instead: Select the cell that you want to autofit, then double-click the right border of the column (your mouse pointer will turn into a double-sided arrow, as shown) until your text fits...instant autofit. Unlike the AutoFit to Contents command, this technique only affects the cell you're double-clicking; it doesn't affect other cells.

FIND ALL THE SAME

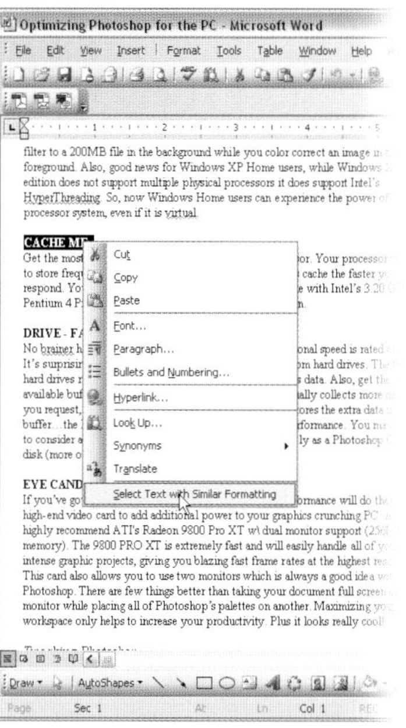

Here's a great shortcut for finding similarly formatted text, whether it's headings, bold or italic text, or any other type of text formatting. Simply select the formatted text, then right-click the text and click Select Text with Similar Formatting in the shortcut menu. Word will automatically select all text in your document that's formatted in the same way. Once your text is selected throughout your document, add any new formatting you'd like and it's applied to all of the selected text. This tip is perfect for quickly changing the format of headings throughout your document.

QUICK SYNONYMS

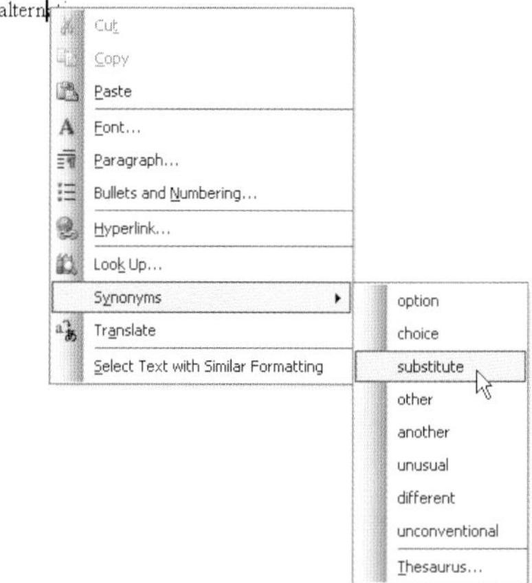

Most of us (especially me) need all the help we can get, and fortunately Word can be very helpful. Here's a good example: If you need a quick list of alternative words (synonyms) for terms in your document, simply right-click the word and point to Synonyms in the shortcut menu for a quick list of alternatives.

IT'S ALL IN THE LINE NUMBER

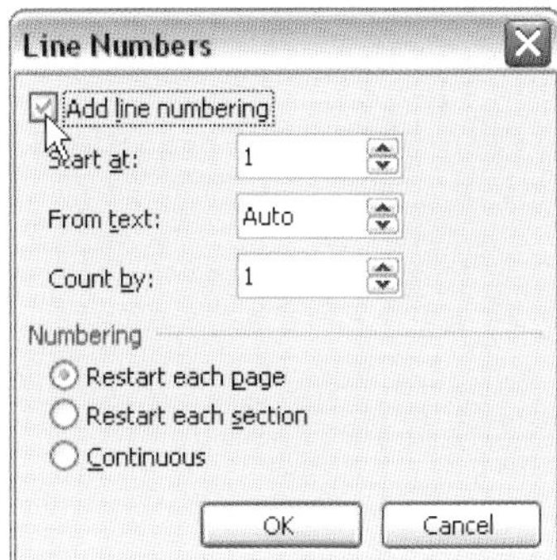

I use line numbers all the time—for referencing important text, debugging code, or as a reminder of edits that need to be made. To turn on line numbers for your document, click File>Page Setup, then click the Layout tab in the Page Setup dialog. Next, click the Line Numbers button and check Add Line Numbering in the Line Numbers dialog. Now, tell Word how to number your pages and click OK. Your new line numbers will appear in the left margin of your pages.

IN SUMMARY…

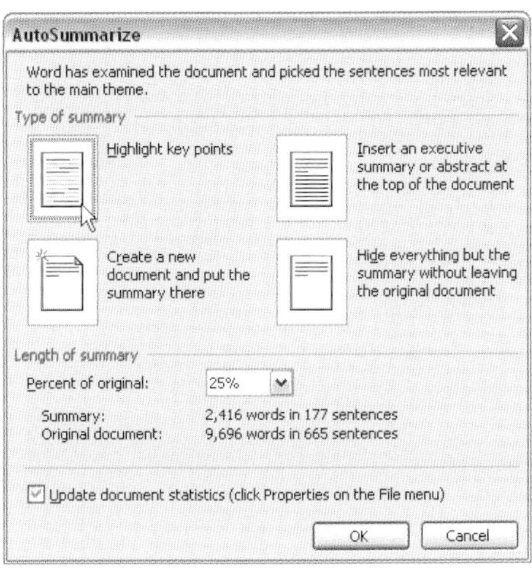

An extremely useful (or useless, I'm not sure which) feature of Word is AutoSummarize. Using AutoSummarize, you can quickly get important info about your document that would otherwise take a considerable amount of time to figure out. You can ask Word to create a quick summary of your document by clicking Tools>AutoSummarize. You'll have several options for creating your document's summary. When finished, click OK in the AutoSummarize dialog.

 GIVE THE SCRAPS TO YOUR DESKTOP

Document Scraps are extremely cool, useful, and one of my favorite features in Word. I use them all the time, especially when writing. Try this next time you're writing: Select a block of text in Word, right-click on it, and then drag-and-drop it onto your desktop. In the shortcut menu that appears, select Create Scrap Here. You just created a Document Scrap. This is a great way to save your ideas and then drag-and-drop them from Scrap into your documents whenever you'd like.

Create Scrap Here
Move Scrap Here
Create Document Shortcut Here
Cancel

 RESUME OR RÉSUMÉ

What's more fun than accented characters? I can't think of a thing (just kidding, accented characters really aren't fun). Follow the keyboard shortcuts below, and you'll actually be able to finally type résumé and other un-American words in no time. Actually, accented characters are a little fun, but be careful: You may find yourself underlining text and creating new documents if you don't type these commands correctly.

(é) Press Control-'-E (apostrophe)
(Ü) Press Control-Shift-;-U (semicolon)
(ç) Press Control-,-C (comma)
(Ñ) Press Control-Shift-`-N (tilde)

Resume or Résumé

REMEMBERING SHORTCUTS

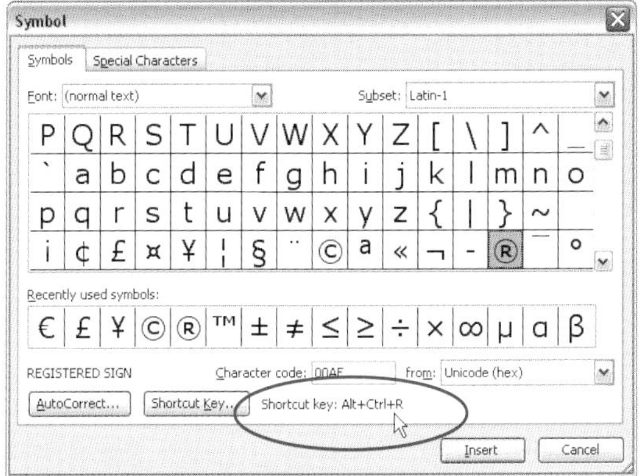

In the previous tip, I showed you how to insert accented characters using keyboard shortcuts. Where can you find these keyboard shortcuts? In Word's Symbol dialog. Using the Symbol dialog is a super-fast way to learn keyboard shortcuts for all of your favorite symbols (such as ©, ®, ™, etc.). Click Insert>Symbol to open Word's Symbol dialog and click a symbol that you'd like to insert into your document. Notice the text just to the right of the Shortcut Key button at the bottom of the dialog; it shows the symbol's keyboard shortcut. Use the shortcut to quickly insert your most frequently used symbols in the future—saves a ton of time.

WANT CONTROL OVER YOUR TEXT? THEN SHIFT

To increase the size of selected text, press Control-Shift-> (period key) or quickly decrease the size of selected text by pressing Control-Shift-< (comma key). You can also select blocks of text above or below the cursor by repeatedly pressing Control-Shift-Up Arrow or Control-Shift-Down Arrow.

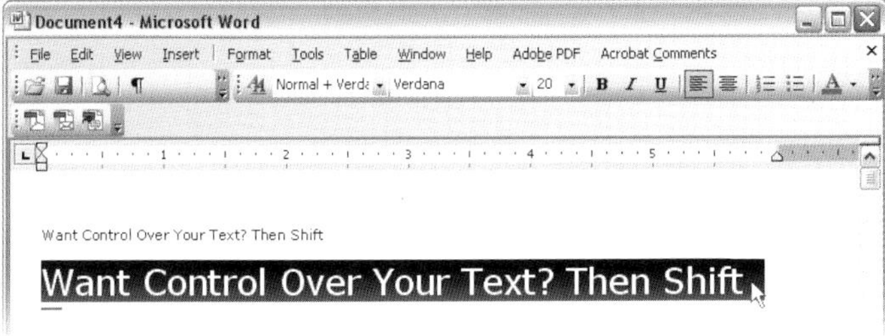

EDITABLE PRINT PREVIEWS

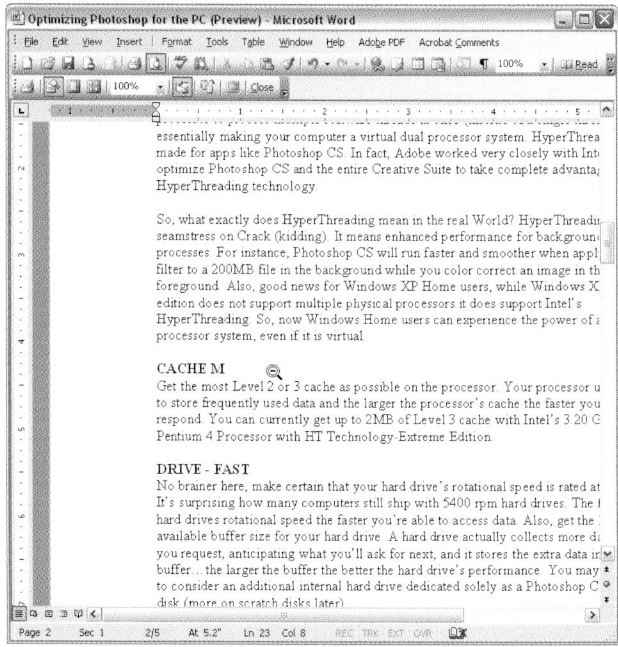

Print Preview is often the perfect view—it allows you to see exactly what your document will look like when printed, but wouldn't it be great if we could edit our documents in Print Preview? Nobody wants to go back and forth between editing documents and previewing them. Well, you don't have to—you can edit in Print Preview. Here's how: First, press Control-Alt-I to show Print Preview. Next, click the Magnifier button in the Print Preview toolbar and zoom in on your text. You won't see your cursor, but all of the other keyboard commands will work. Type and your text will appear, press Enter to create line breaks, or use the Up and Down Arrow keys to navigate in your document. When you're finished making your changes, click the Magnifier button to zoom back out to preview your document again.

QUICK CASE

You can quickly change the case of any word or words by first selecting your text, then pressing Shift-F3 on the keyboard. Continue pressing the F3 key while holding the Shift key to change the case of your text from title case to uppercase to lowercase (as shown).

The Quick Brown Fox Jumps
THE QUICK BROWN FOX JUMPS
the quick brown fox jumps

PICKY SELECTIONS

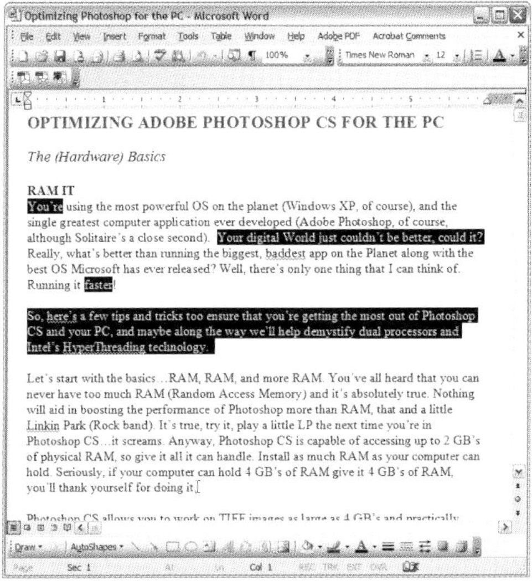

If you ever need to select different text blocks, sentences, or individual words throughout a document to change formatting or text, color, or whatever, press-and-hold the Control key, then make your selections. As long as you're holding the Control key, you'll be able to make multiple selections throughout your document. When finished, make any changes and then deselect your text.

FAKE IT, DUMMY

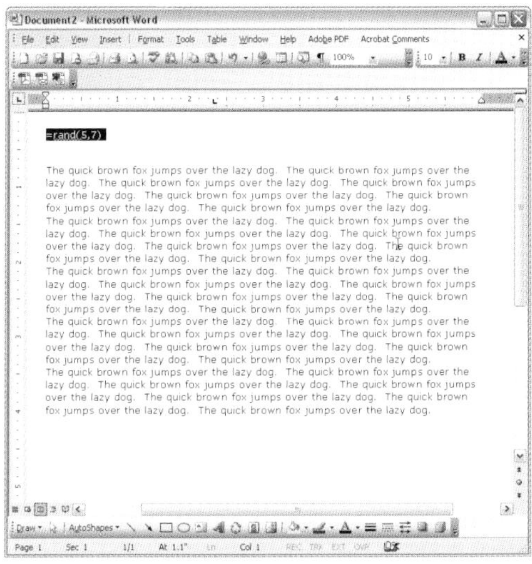

There comes a time in everyone's writing career when we just have to fake it—with our text, that is. You can easily place fake text (dummy text) in your document: Just place the cursor where you want to insert the dummy text, type "=rand(5,7)" (without the quotes), then press Enter on your keyboard. This command will place five paragraphs of fake text, each containing seven sentences. Of course, you can change the (5,7) to any number you'd like—the first number represents the number of paragraphs (5); and the second represents the number of sentences per paragraph (7).

THE EASY WAY TO GET TEXT ABOVE YOUR TABLE

This has happened to everyone—don't deny it. You need to place text above a table at the top of your document and there's only one workaround. You have to cut the table, insert your text, then paste the table back into your document, right? Well, that works, but there's a better way. Click inside the first cell in the top row of the table, then press Control-Shift-Enter on your keyboard to insert a paragraph above the table. I bet you knew there had to be a better way.

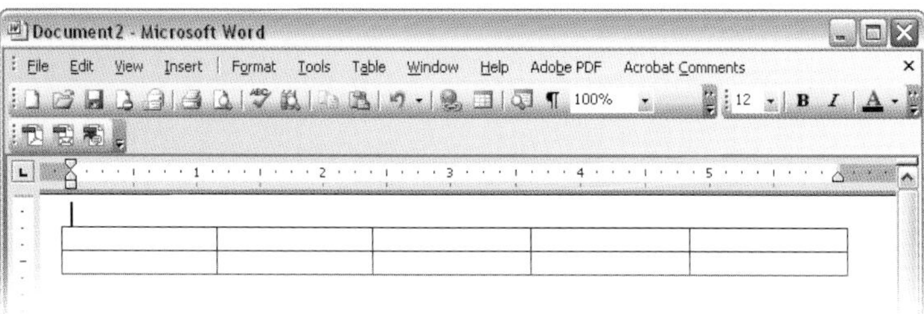

VOICE YOUR COMMENTS

From time to time you're going to want to place text comments into your document—to remind you of edits, check word definitions, or suggest ideas—but did you know that you could also record voice comments? Here's how: Right-click any toolbar and select Reviewing in the shortcut menu. The Insert Voice button isn't on the Reviewing toolbar by default, so if you don't see the Insert Voice button, click the down-facing arrow at the end of the toolbar and go to Add or Remove Buttons>Reviewing and click Insert Voice. The button now appears on the Reviewing toolbar. To insert a voice comment, select the text that you want to comment on, click the Insert Voice button, and then click the Record button.

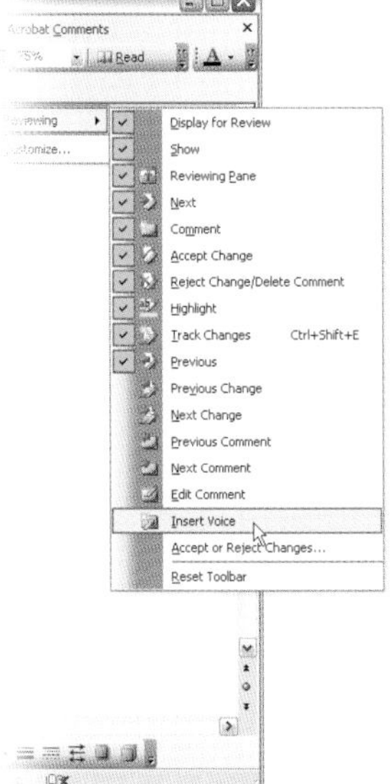

DRAG, HOVER, DROP

To move selected text objects quickly between Word documents (or any open Office applications), click-and-hold the object with your mouse, then drag it to the Windows Taskbar and hover over the document's button where you want to place the object. After hovering for a moment, the document becomes active and appears in the foreground, where you just drop the object into place.

NOW YOU SEE ME, NOW YOU DON'T

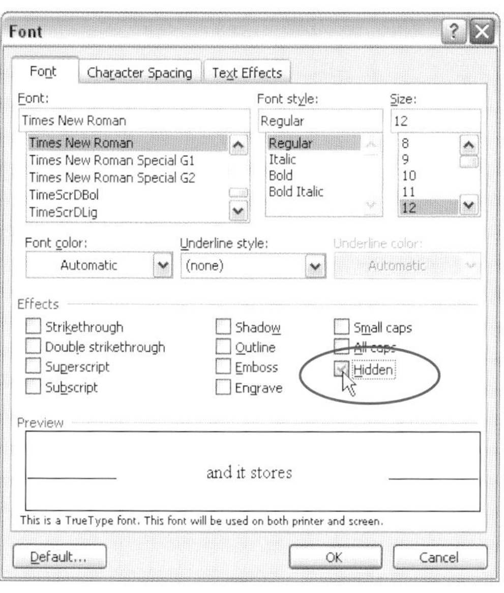

If you have sensitive information in a document that you don't want others to see (or if you're just really paranoid —I'm sure you have your reasons), you can hide your text. Just select the text that you want to hide, click Format>Font in the menu bar, then click Hidden under the Effects category, and click OK. Your text is gone. Actually, it's still there, but you can't see it anymore. To once again display your text, click Tools>Options in the menu bar, click the View tab in the Options dialog, then check Hidden Text under the Formatting Marks category, and click OK. You can once again see your hidden text. It now has a dotted line underneath it, indicating that it's hidden text.

THE KEY TO TESTS

There's actually a great use for hiding your text; for example, educators hide their text all the time (they're very sneaky). Hiding text was made for exams. Teachers (or just about anybody who has to test people) can create one master document with both the questions and the answers, then hide the answers and print the test, and also print an answer key showing only the answers. Brilliant, isn't it? To do this, follow the same steps as mentioned in the previous tip to create hidden text. Once you've hidden the answers, simply print a copy to use for testing by clicking File>Print. To print a copy to use for grading (to create an answer key), go to File>Print, click the Options button in the dialog, and select Hidden Text under the Include With Document category. Click OK to print a test with the answers.

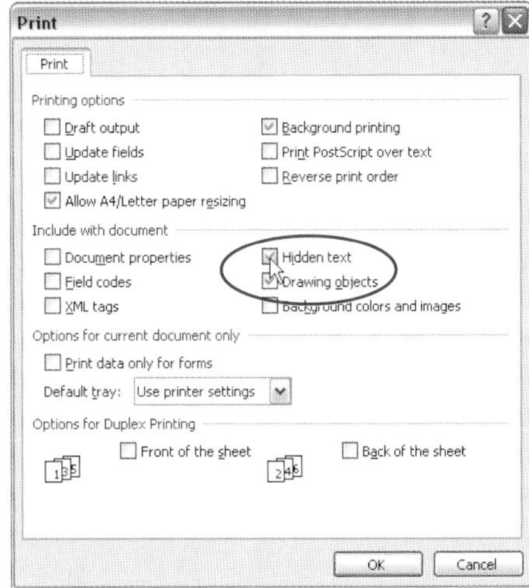

AUTOCOLOR

If you plan to use a background color rather than white, or want to use multiple background colors in your document, be sure to select Automatic Color. This feature automatically chooses a text color that contrasts with the background color, ensuring that you can read your text regardless of the document's background color (which you can change by choosing Format>Background). To use Automatic Color, click the down-facing arrow next to the Font Color button in the Formatting toolbar and click the Automatic Color icon. Now you'll automatically type black text on a white background, white text on a black background, and so on.

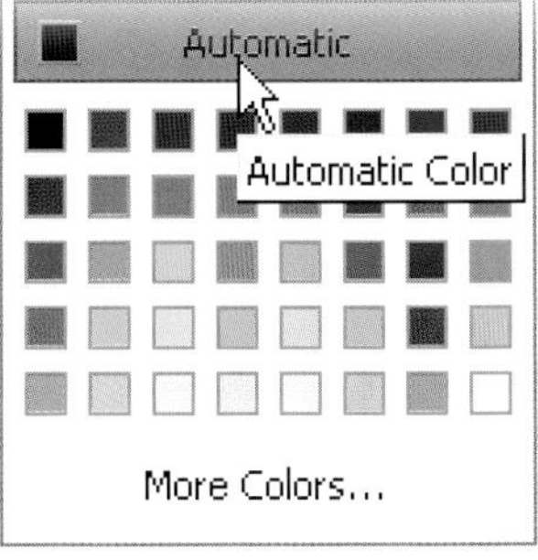

 EDIT CYCLING IN WORD

A super-fast way to find your last three edits is to press Shift-F5. This keyboard shortcut will cycle your cursor through your last three edits, but the really cool thing about the Shift-F5 shortcut is that it's persistent, meaning that even when you close a document, Word will remember the last three edits. When opening a document, this provides a pretty slick way to find where you last left off.

 F8 TO EXTEND

You may know that the F8 key is extremely useful for selecting text in Word. Press the F8 key once and Word goes into extend mode; press it twice to select the current word; a third time will select the current sentence; four times selects the current paragraph; and five or six times selects the current section and entire document, respectively. But you can also make the F8 key select text from the insertion point to a specific letter. Try it: Press F8 and then press any letter. All of the text between the insertion point to that letter is instantly selected (as shown). To escape Word's extend mode, press Escape (Esc) on your keyboard, then click anywhere on the document.

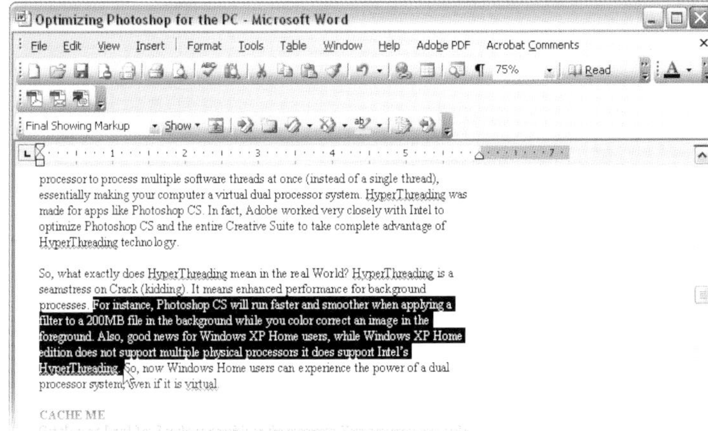

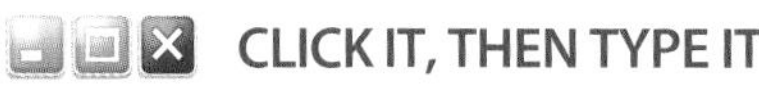

CLICK IT, THEN TYPE IT

A newer feature in Word—Click and Type—allows you to double-click in any blank space in your document to instantly create an insertion point, which gives you a lot more formatting flexibility. There's a catch to using it, however. If you're not able to click and type, then you're using Word's Normal view. For whatever reason, you can only click and type in Print Layout view or Web Layout view. So, to use the Click and Type feature, select View>Print Layout or View>Web Layout in the menu bar. If you still can't use Click and Type, select Tools>Options in the menu bar, then click the Edit tab in the Options dialog. Next, check Enable Click and Type (it's near the bottom of the dialog), then click OK.

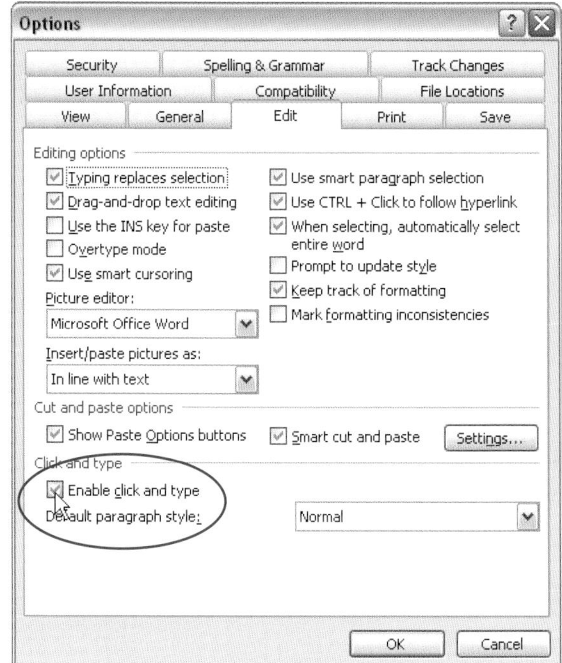

 PERSONALIZE YOUR ENVELOPES

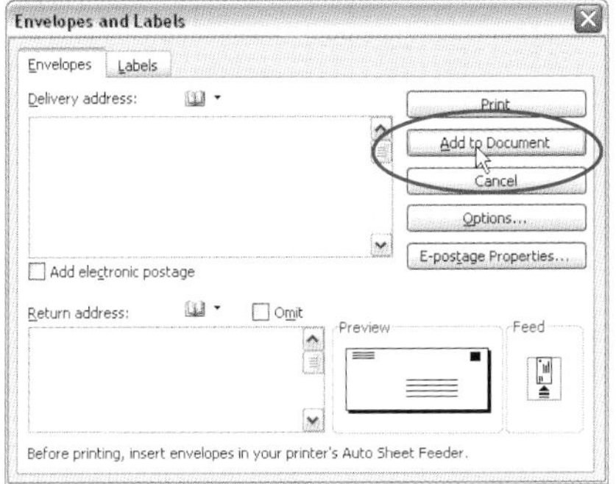

I'm about to share a tip with you that will forever change the way you print envelopes. Keep reading and you'll see what I mean. People love to personalize things—heck, I'd trim my hedges into a big "S" (for Stephenson) if my wife would let me, but if you're not as gung-ho about personalizing your stuff, then start small...start with your envelopes. When you're ready to print an envelope, click Tools>Letters and Mailings>Envelopes and Labels in the menu bar, then click the Envelopes tab in the Envelopes and Labels dialog. Next, add your delivery and return addresses in the appropriate fields, then click the Add to Document button. Your envelope will now appear at the top of your document (as the first page in a multipage document). Now you can edit the envelope as you would any document in Word. Add clip art, text boxes, company logos, and so on.

 SUPER-CHARGE WORD'S PERFORMANCE WITH PLACEHOLDERS

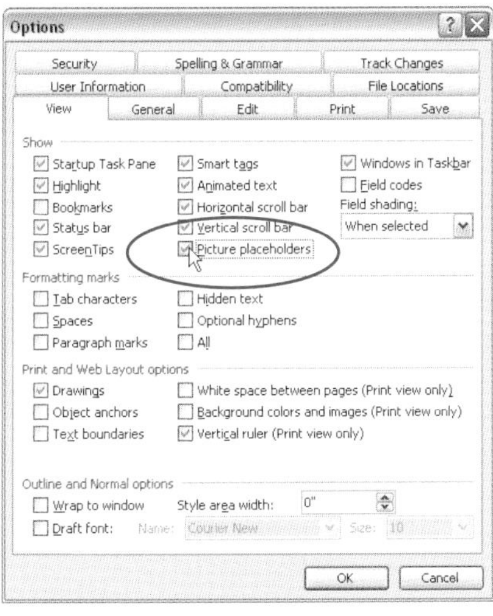

Okay, you've placed about 30 or 40 pictures into your document, which looks great, but now it takes you half an hour to scroll your document (rendering graphics is a tedious business). Well, you could just throw your underpowered PC into the trash, but if this seems a little harsh, you might want to consider replacing your pictures with picture placeholders to improve performance. To do this, click Tools>Options, then click the View tab in the Options dialog. Check Picture Placeholders under the Show category, then click OK. Your pictures are now displayed as empty frames (aka picture placeholders). To show your pictures again, simply uncheck Picture Placeholders in the Options dialog, then click OK.

QUICK GRAPHIC RESIZE TRICK

Okay, you've imported a graphic and resized it so many times that you have no idea what its original size was. You're probably feeling like a loser right about now, and you should be (kidding), but I can help. That's what I'm here for. Simply press-and-hold the Control key on your keyboard, then double-click inside your graphic to get it back to its original size (as I did here for the second image). You're feelin' better already, aren't you?

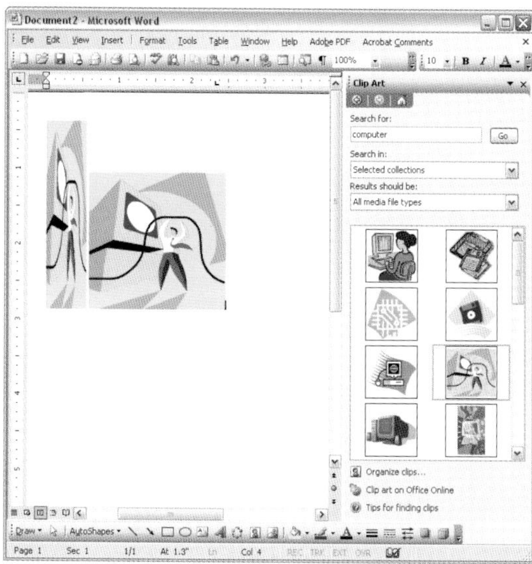

RESIZING THE RIGHT WAY

You probably know that you can simply drag any image's corner handles to resize it as large or as small as you like, while maintaining the image's proportions. However, if you notice, your graphic resizes itself by increments of about a tenth of an inch. I don't pretend to understand Microsoft math, but limiting me to resizing my images by increments of a tenth of an inch is just bad math no matter who's writing it. Try this: Hold the Alt key on your keyboard, then click-and-drag corner handles to resize your image. You can now resize it within a hundredth of an inch. Hmm, shouldn't resizing work this way by default?

 BE EXACT

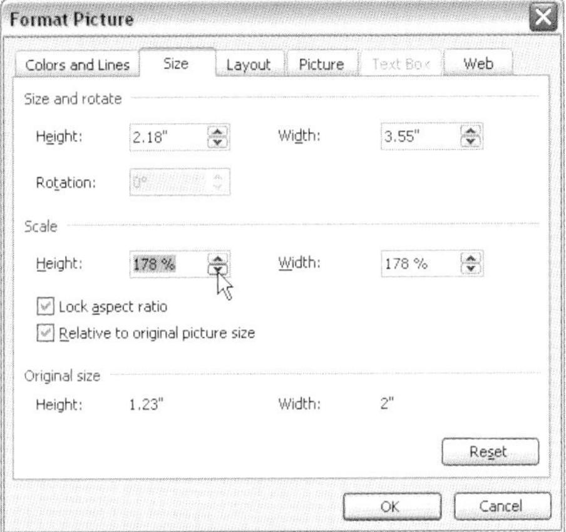

Let's say you have a mildly psychotic client who insists that you resize all of his images to an exact dimension. (Hey, they're out there.) Well, there's a way to be exact: Select an image, click Format>Picture in the menu bar, then click the Size tab in the Format Picture dialog. Look at the Height and Width fields in the Scale category. These numbers tell you what percentage your image has been scaled from its original size. Now, you can use the Height and Width fields to input exact dimensions for your other graphics. When finished, click OK.

GETTING PRECISE WITH WORD'S GRID

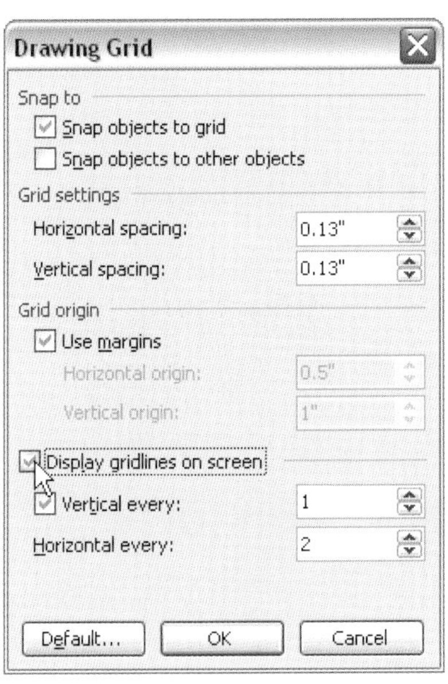

When you need to bring a little order to your layouts and precisely arrange graphic elements, turn on Word's grid. First, display the Drawing toolbar by right-clicking any toolbar or menu and click Drawing in the shortcut menu. Next, click Draw>Grid in the Drawing toolbar. Adjust your grid's dimensions in the Grid Settings category, check Display Gridlines on Screen in the Grid Origin category, then click OK. Now you can lay out your page's graphic elements with precision.

NOT YOUR ORDINARY TEXT BOX

You may think that text boxes are pretty boring, but you can get really geeky with text boxes and add a ton of very cool effects. Try this: Create a new text box by clicking Insert>Text Box in the menu bar, then click-and-drag inside the drawing canvas to create your text box. Next, click Format>Text Box in the menu bar, then click the Colors and Lines tab in the Format Text Box dialog. Click the Color down-facing arrow under the Fill category and choose Fill Effects. From the Fill Effects dialog, you can choose to fill your text box using a Gradient, Texture, Pattern, or Picture. When finished, click OK.

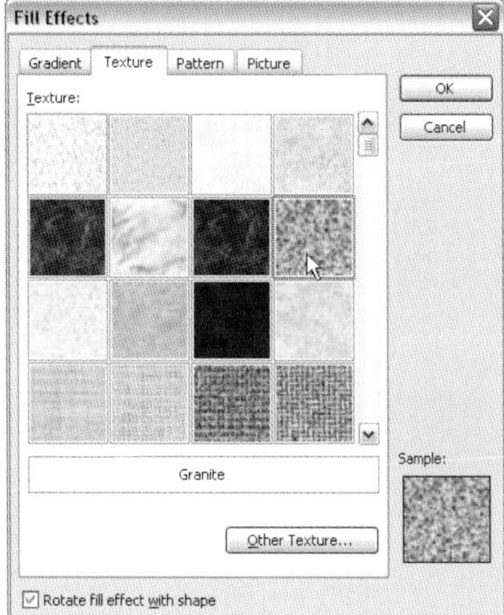

ADDING CAPTIONS

Graphics are great visualizations, but they become even more effective when you add captions to 'em. Here's how: Select your graphic, then click Insert>Reference>Caption in the menu bar. Next, type any additional description in the Caption field in the dialog, then click OK.

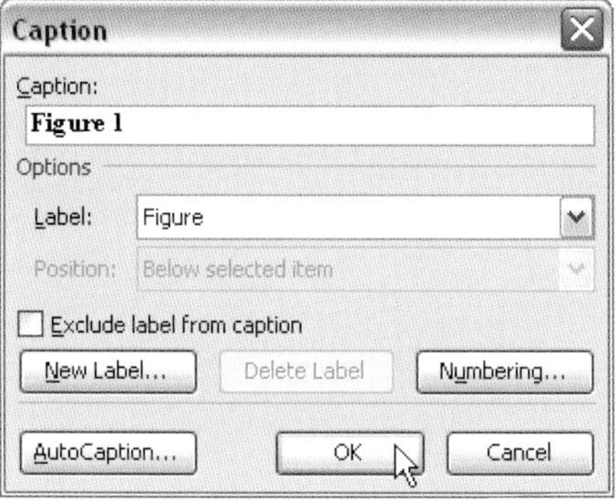

I NEED MORE AUTOSHAPES

There are many things that you can never have too much of, and you can add AutoShapes to that list. I could play around with them for hours. Actually, I have—I honestly have nothing better to do. Anyway, when you do finally get sucked into AutoShapes (if you're not already), be sure not to overlook More AutoShapes (just when you thought it couldn't get any better…). Click the AutoShapes button in the Drawing toolbar, then click More AutoShapes. This opens the Clip Art task pane, with even more AutoShapes to keep the fun going.

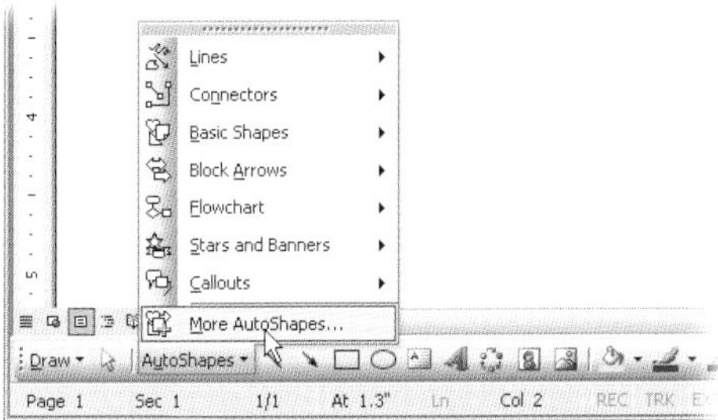

GETTING PRECISE WITH AUTOSHAPES

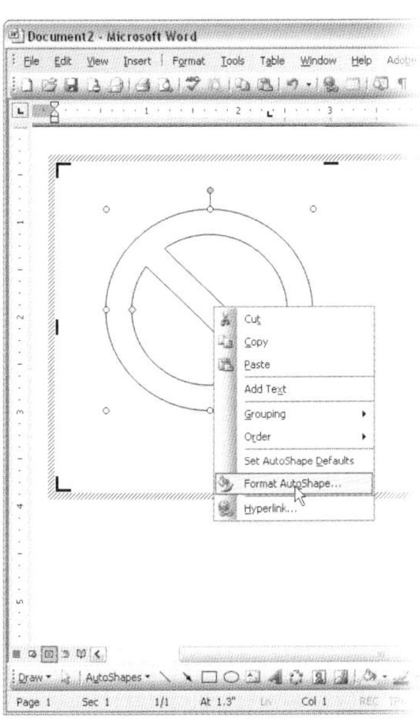

If you need to assign a precise size for your AutoShapes, right-click a shape that you've placed (see previous tip) and click Format AutoShape in the shortcut menu, then click the Size tab in the Format AutoShape dialog. Now, simply enter your required dimensions and click OK. Word will instantly adjust the size of your AutoShape.

Bright Outlook

WORKING
WITH
OUTLOOK

Does Outlook make you feel powerful? I don't mean take-over-a-country powerful, or bench-press 400 lbs powerful, but in-control powerful. It does? Good, I thought it

Bright Outlook

working with outlook

was just me. There's something about being in constant communication with friends, family, and business colleagues that just makes me feel powerful. Okay, maybe I'm getting a little carried away, but I'm literally sitting here, right now, receiving email, sending email, Instant Messaging, and video conferencing with my sister Julie (hey Julie!)—all at the same time. Man, I've really got it going on. I'm the master of information, the Great Communicator —a powerful, powerful man. I should be stopped. I might be getting a little carried away, but it's not my fault. It's Outlook's. It's like a drug. It's the first application I open and the last I close. Hmm...maybe I'm not powerful, maybe Outlook's powerful and it's just using me to do its dirty work...hmm.

 PROTECT YOUR PERSONAL FOLDERS

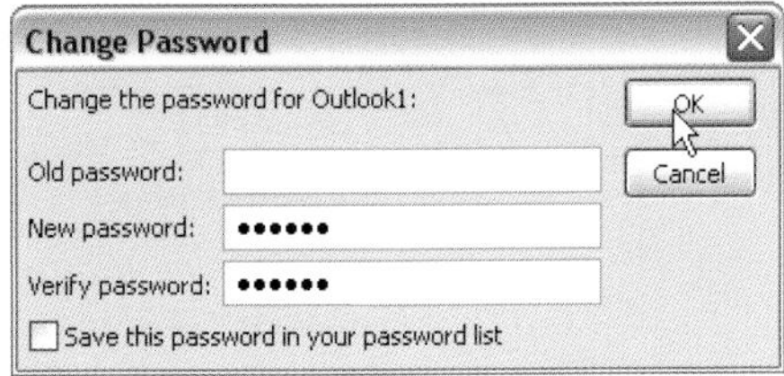

I love password protection and use it for just about everything. I even use it for my refrigerator's ice dispenser (seriously—it's sad). So, password protecting my email folders is a given. To password protect your email folders, right-click Personal Folders in the Navigation pane and click Properties for "Personal Folders" in the shortcut menu. Next, click the Advanced button in the dialog, then click the Change Password button. Type a password in the New Password field, then type it again in the Verify Password field. Make sure that "Save this password in your password list" is unchecked so that you're always required to supply a password when Outlook is launched. Click OK when finished. The next time you launch Outlook, you'll be prompted for a password before you can access Outlook's mail folders.

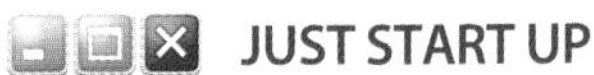 JUST START UP

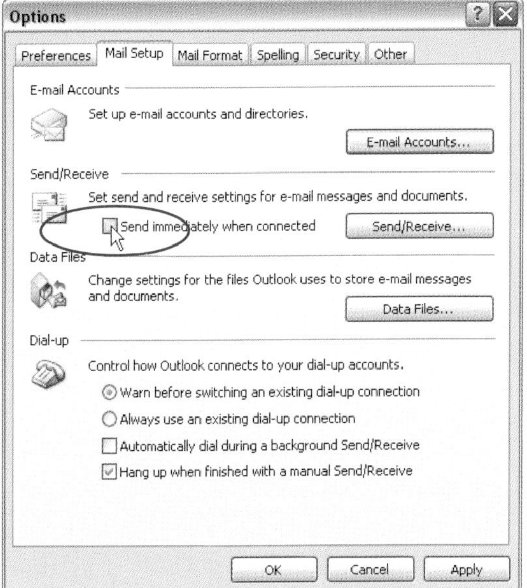

I'm not sure why "Send and receive at startup" is set up as the default. I personally think this is the most annoying thing ever. I mean, sometimes I just want to open Outlook and type an email or read an email or just look at my email. Unfortunately, there's not a kill option for this feature—only off. Here's how to do it: Click Tools>Options in the menu bar, then click the Mail Setup tab in the Options dialog. Next, uncheck Send Immediately When Connected, then click OK.

 SAME EMAIL...DIFFERENT COMPUTERS

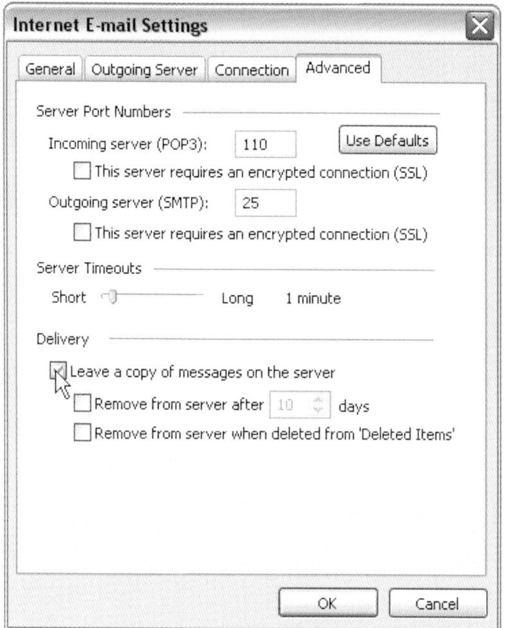

It's pretty convenient to be able to check your email on the road using your laptop, PDA, or another computer, but what's not convenient is that the mail is removed from your server. By default, incoming messages are automatically deleted from your server when received. So, what can you do to be able to read the received messages from other computers and not delete them? Just leave copies of your email on the server, which allows you to download them again later from another location. Here's how: Click Tools>Options in the menu bar, then click the Mail Setup tab in the Options dialog. Next, click the E-mail Accounts button, select "View or change existing e-mail accounts," and click Next. Now, double-click your POP account to open its email account settings. In the E-mail Accounts dialog, click the More Settings button, click the Advanced tab in the Internet E-mail Settings dialog, check "Leave a copy of messages on the server" under the Delivery category, and then click OK. You'll now be able to download your POP account's email messages from different computers.

BE CHOOSY WITH FIELD CHOOSER

You can organize Outlook's Inbox folder's details (headers) the same as in other folders. You can add columns by right-clicking any column header in the Inbox window and clicking Field Chooser in the shortcut menu. Next, simply drag-and-drop any available field onto the column header in any order you like.

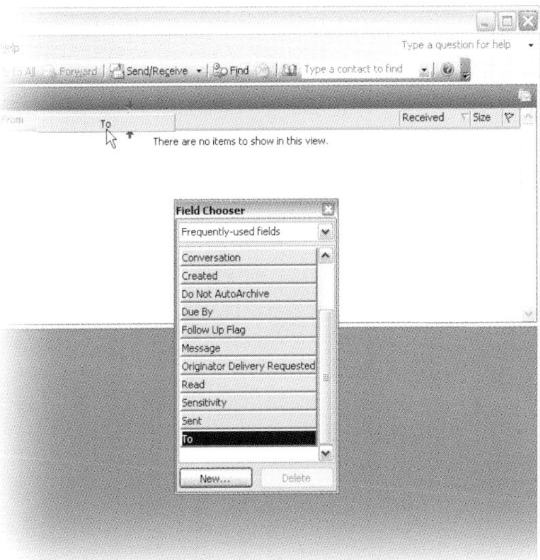

SORT YOUR MAIL

Click on any column header to quickly sort your messages in the Inbox folder. For example, click the Received header to list your messages by the date and time they were received or click Subject to sort messages by their subject lines. If you have multiple accounts set up, you might want to sort by using the Accounts column. This will quickly tell you which accounts received messages.

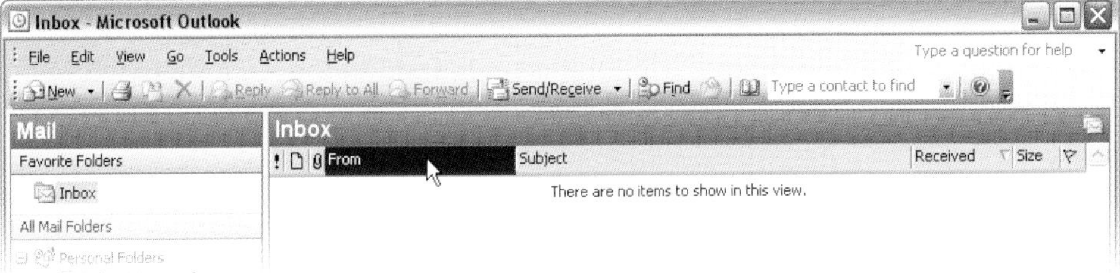

EMAIL SHORTCUT

Do you have someone that you email a lot—a friend, family member, or co-worker? If you do, this tip will make your life a bit easier. Right-click on your desktop and point to New and click Shortcut in the shortcut menu. In the "Type the location of the item" field, type "mailto:" (without the quotes) followed by your friend's email address (for example, mailto:friend@mydomain.com), then click Next. Give your shortcut a name and click Finish. Now, when you double-click your Outlook email shortcut icon on your desktop, a new mail message window will open with your friend's email address already in the To field—just type your message and click the Send button.

I'VE GOT THINGS TO DO

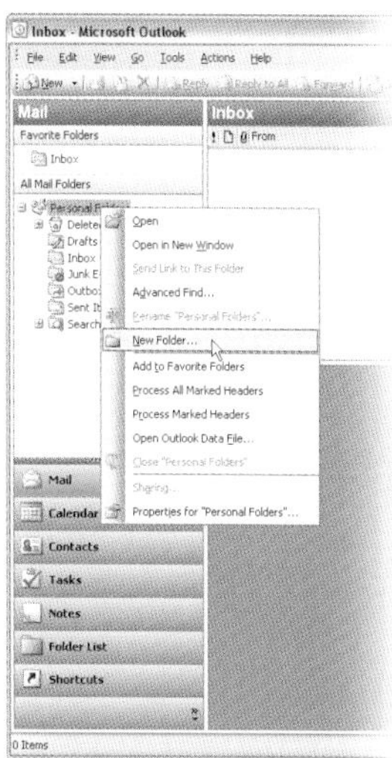

It's a good thing that you can add folders to Outlook because I get way too much email for the default folders to handle. When I opened Outlook for the first time, I created a Things To Do folder, where I can store email to work on later. You can also create folders to keep your email organized—it's easy. Here's how: Click the Mail button in the Navigation pane, right-click Personal Folders in the Mail pane, and click New Folder in the shortcut menu. Give your new folder a name, then click OK. Now you'll see your new folder listed under Personal Folders in the Navigation pane.

 FAST TRACK TO THE INBOX

I always go to my Inbox when launching Outlook because I'm usually opening the program to check for new email, and it just saves time to start there. To take the fast track to your Inbox, click the Shortcuts button at the bottom of the Navigation pane, then click Outlook Today under the Shortcuts link near the top of the pane. Next, click the Customize Outlook Today button at the top-right corner of the Outlook Today window. Now uncheck "When starting, go directly to Outlook Today" and click the Save Changes button at the top right of the pane. Now Outlook will automatically open your Inbox upon launch.

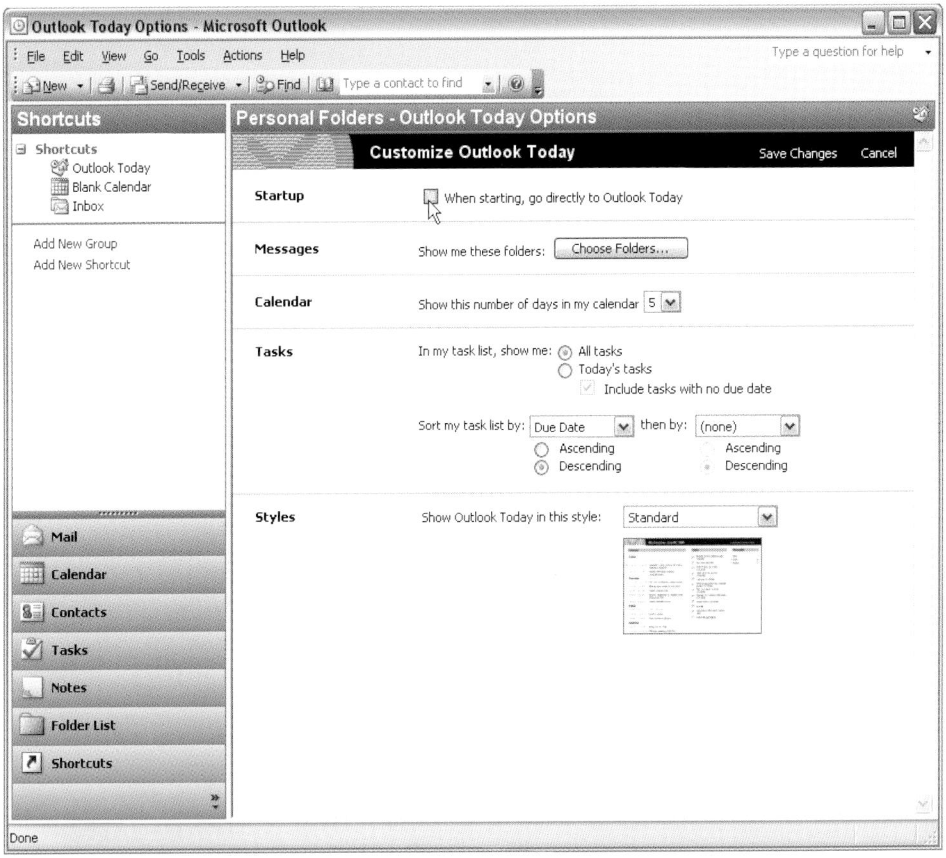

ORGANIZE YOUR MESSAGES QUICKLY

Now that you've added folders to organize your email, it's time to start using them. To move email, simply drag-and-drop your messages to any folder listed under Personal Folders.

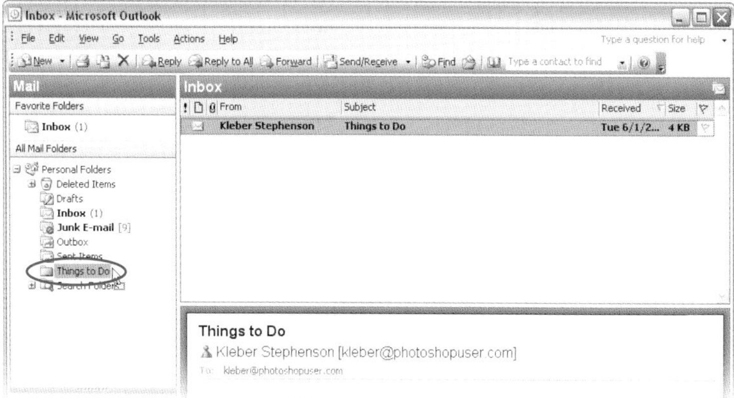

EASY EDIT

If you want to save an email message as a text file, try this: Open WordPad or Word, highlight the text of your email in the Reading pane in Outlook, then drag-and-drop the text into your text editor using your mouse. Now you can edit and save the message.

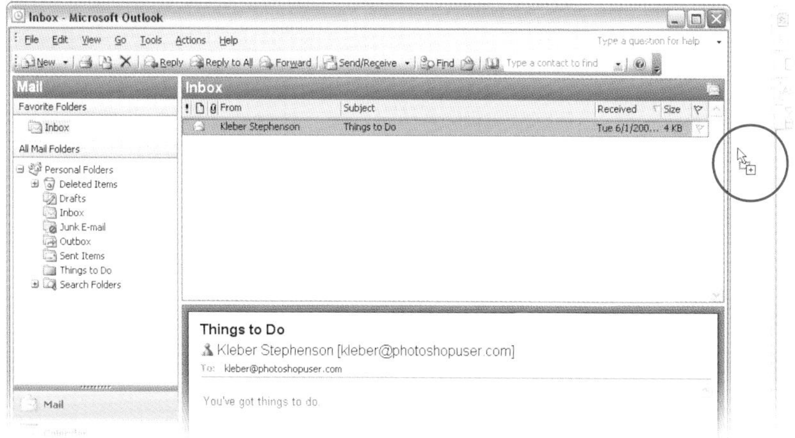

 KEEP EMAIL CONSISTENT

It's good that you can customize the text of incoming email, because I have to tell you, some people have a real twisted sense of which fonts look good. You can receive email with so many different typefaces and sizes that you're not even sure if they're written in English. Well, you can customize your incoming email so that it displays the same typeface and font size. To do this, click Tools>Options, click the Mail Format tab in the dialog, and click the Fonts button. Then, individually click the three Choose Font buttons to select your default font options for composing and replying to email, and click OK. Now all of your incoming and outgoing messages will have the same look.

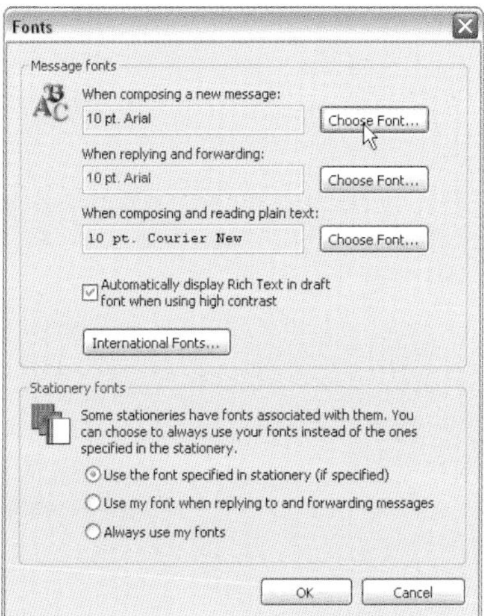

DRAG-AND-DROP YOUR ATTACHMENTS

If you're attaching files to an email, you can simply drag-and-drop them onto the email's Message window. This will instantly attach your files.

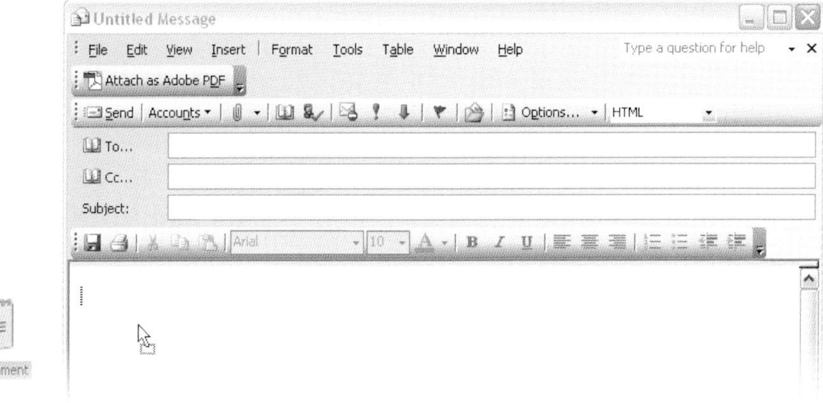

CONTROL-CLICK HYPERLINKS

By default, when inserting hyperlinks into a new email message or a reply, you can't simply click on a hyperlink to test it; however, you can get around this and test your hyperlinks by pressing-and-holding the Control key while clicking on the hyperlink. This will launch your Web browser, which will bring up the site.

EMAIL YOUR NOTES

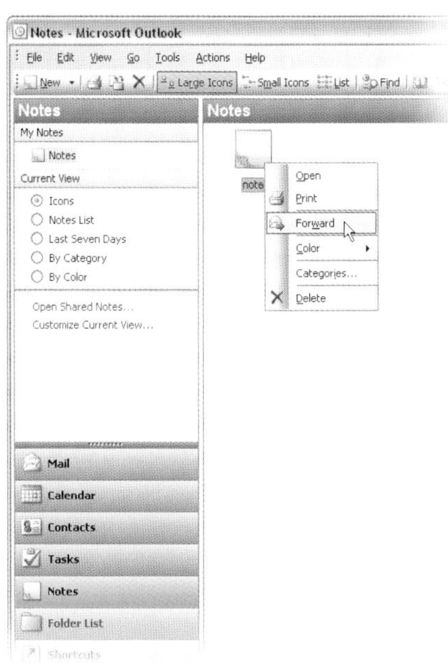

I use Outlook Notes all the time, and I often email my notes to people. You can quickly email your Outlook Notes by clicking on the Notes icon at the bottom of the Navigation pane. In the Note window, right-click any note and click Forward in the shortcut menu. This will open a new email message with your note attached. Simply provide a recipient in the To field, along with any comments, then click the Send button. You just emailed a Note document.

STICKY NOTES…REALLY!

When using Notes, keep in mind that they're sticky. You can use them just about anywhere. Drag-and-drop a note on your desktop or add them to Outlook's Shortcuts link for quick access (click the Shortcuts button at the bottom of the Navigation pane, right-click the Shortcuts link at the top of the pane, and select Notes in the resulting dialog). Just keep in mind that if you edit a note, changes may alter the name of the note, possibly making its shortcut unusable. You can also quickly change the color of your notes by right-clicking any note, pointing to Color in the shortcut menu, and picking a new color.

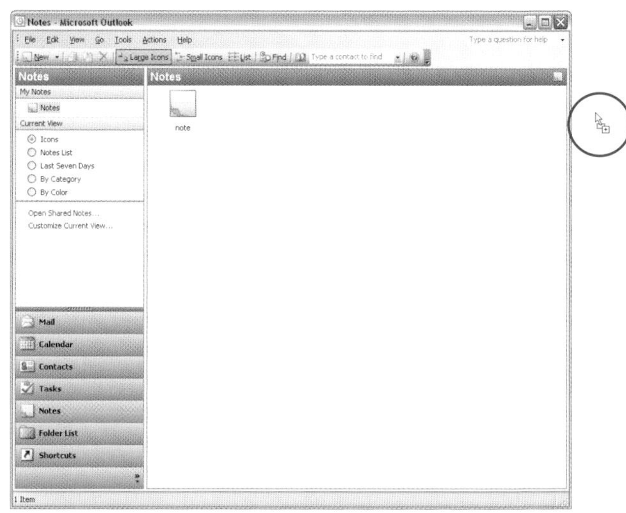

CHOOSE AN ACCOUNT

If you've set up Outlook to use multiple email accounts, then you'll need to select the account from which to send email messages. To do this, click File>New>Mail Message and simply click the Accounts button on the Email toolbar, then select the account that you want to use. The email account's server address will appear above the To field.

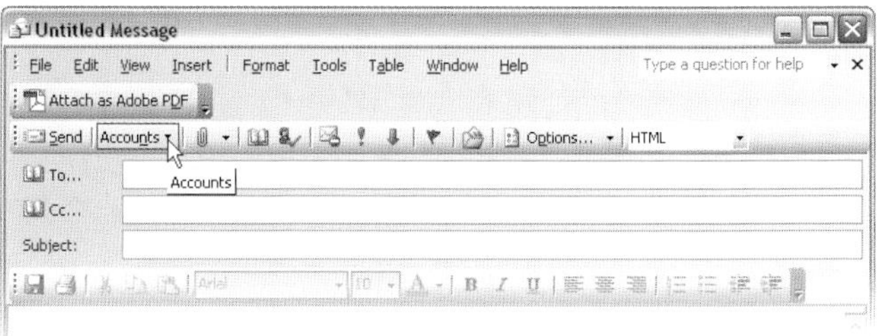

 TRACK DOWN THE PERSONAL FOLDERS

To view the location on your hard drive of your Personal Folders, with the Mail pane open, right-click Personal Folders and click Properties for "Personal Folders" in the shortcut menu. Next, click the Advanced button in the dialog. The location is displayed in the Filename field.

 PERSONALIZE PERSONAL FOLDERS

If you don't necessarily care for the name that Outlook has given your folders (Personal Folders), then change it to something a little more personal. To do this, right-click Personal Folders in the All Mail Folders pane, then click Properties for "Personal Folders" in the shortcut menu. Next, click the Advanced button in the dialog, type a new name in the Name field, and click OK. Your Personal Folders folder is now renamed.

 UN-JUNK EMAIL

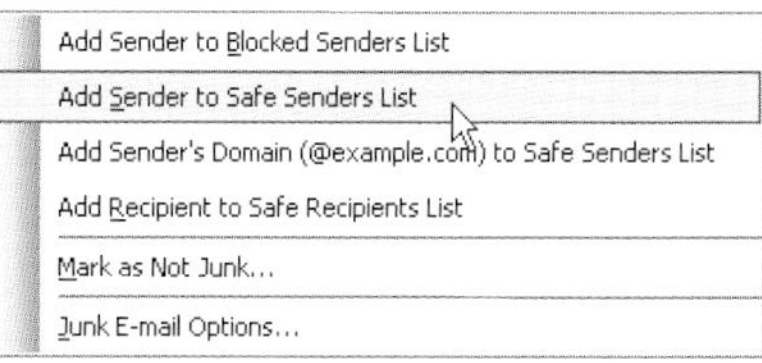

I get hundreds of junk emails a day and occasionally, as I'm blasting junk email left and right, I'll unintentionally drag-and-drop good email from my Inbox into my Junk E-mail folder. Well, you can quickly fix this by finding the email that you want to recover in your Junk E-mail folder, then right-clicking the email and clicking Junk E-mail>Add Sender to Safe Senders List in the shortcut menu. Now you'll be able to once again receive email from the sender (but you'll still have to drag-and-drop the email back into your Inbox or another folder for safekeeping).

CAN'T SPELL?

Let's face it, most of us can't spell (I can, but I can do everything...it's a burden). Well, Outlook can help. You can set up Outlook to automatically check your spelling before you send messages. To do this, click Tools>Options, then click the Spelling tab. Next, check "Always check spelling before sending" and click OK. You're feeling smarter already, aren't you?

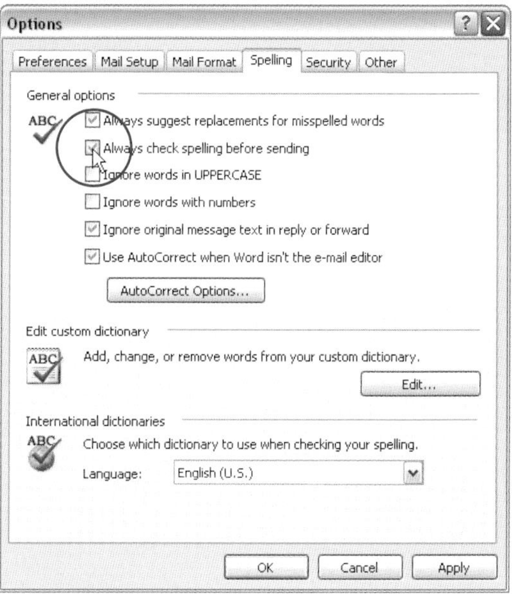

SAVE YOUR SEARCHES

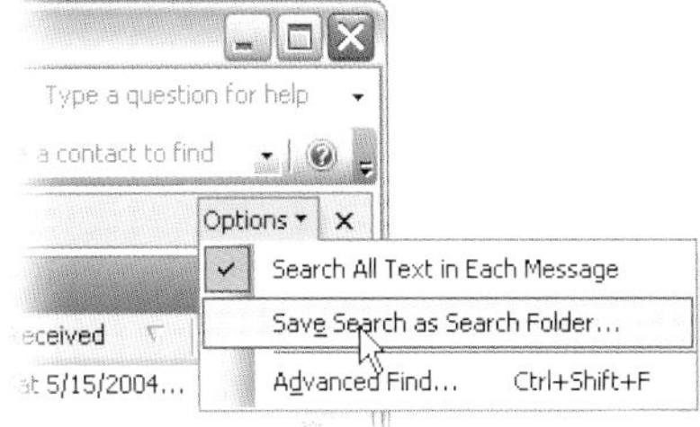

If you find yourself performing repeated searches for a particular word or term, you should save your search results by creating a search folder; that way you don't have to repeat the search in the future. To open Find in Outlook, press Control-E or click the Find button in Outlook's Standard toolbar. Next, type your search term in the Look For field, select your search location using the Search In drop-down menu, and click Find Now. When your search is finished, click the Options drop-down menu in the right corner of the window and select Save Search as Search Folder. Type a name for your search folder in the resulting dialog, then click OK. The folder will appear under Search Folders in the All Mail Folders pane. Now, the next time you need to view the results of the search, simply double-click the Search Folder to access your saved search folder.

COLLAPSIBLE GROUPS

Outlook automatically groups your messages in your mail folders by when they were received (today, yesterday, last week, last month). To make groups easier to navigate, you can collapse them to view only the group's heading by clicking any group heading, then press the Left Arrow key on your keyboard (or press the Right Arrow key to expand the group).

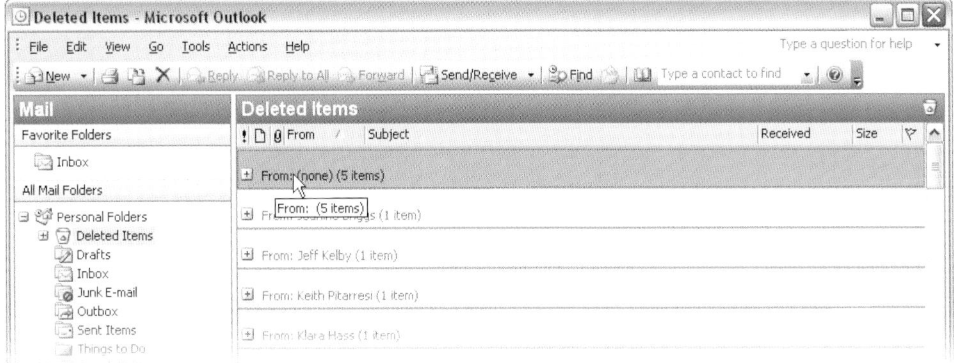

EVEN A FOLDER NEEDS A HOME (PAGE)

Here's a pretty cool little trick you can do with your mail folders: Add a home page to them. This is useful for reminding you of a folder's contents or to quickly view a frequently visited webpage. You can add a home page to some folders by right-clicking the folder in the All Mail Folders pane and clicking Properties in the shortcut menu. Next, click the Home Page tab in the dialog and type a URL in the Address field or click the Browse button to browse your hard drive. If you want the webpage to appear by default each time you open the folder, check "Show home page by default for this folder." When you're finished, click OK. If you've selected to show a webpage by default, then you should see your folder's home page displayed when you go to that folder.

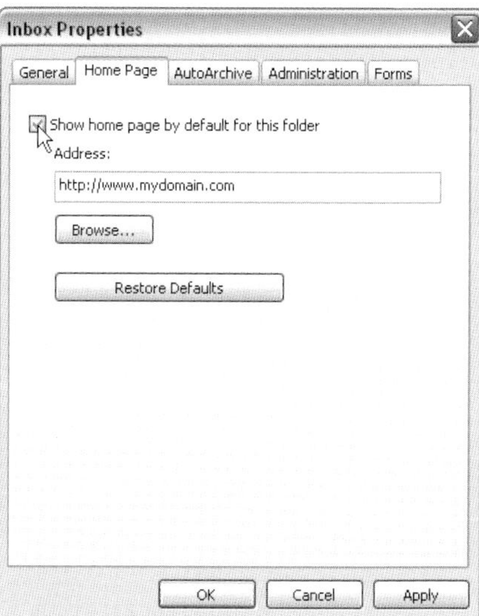

MAXIMUM VIEW

I honestly get about 900 emails a day (of course 875 of them are spam), but I still like to see as many messages as possible in my Inbox. A bigger view just makes sorting the good email from the bad quicker. To view more messages in your Inbox, be sure the Mail pane is active, then click View>Arrange By>Custom in the menu bar, click the Other Settings button, and uncheck "Use multi-line layout in widths smaller than [100] characters" listed under the Other Options category (near the bottom of the dialog), then click OK.

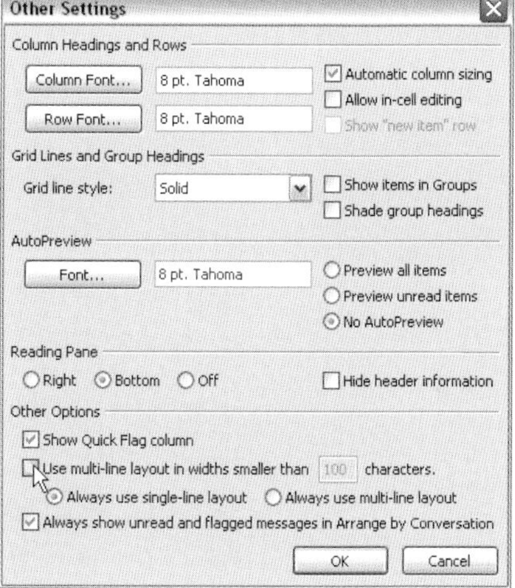

START UP WHERE YOU WANT

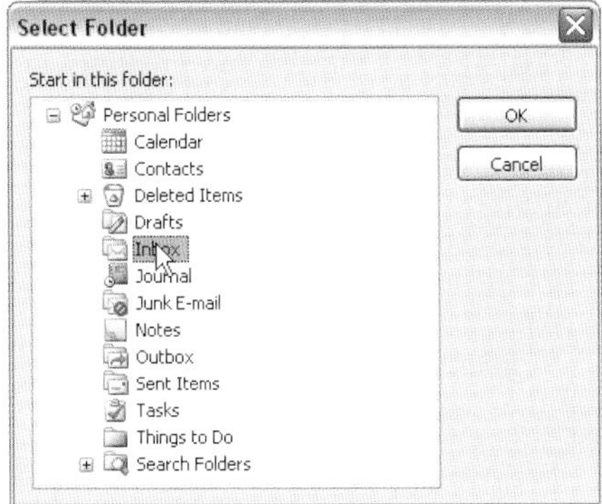

I always go to my Inbox when opening Outlook; however, you may not. You can set up Outlook to open automatically in any folder. Here's how: Click Tools>Options in the menu bar, then click the Other tab in the dialog. Next, click the Advanced Options button and click the Browse button in the top-right corner of the dialog. Now, select a folder to start up in, click OK, and close Outlook. When you reopen Outlook, it will now automatically open the folder you selected.

LAUNCH OUTLOOK AT STARTUP

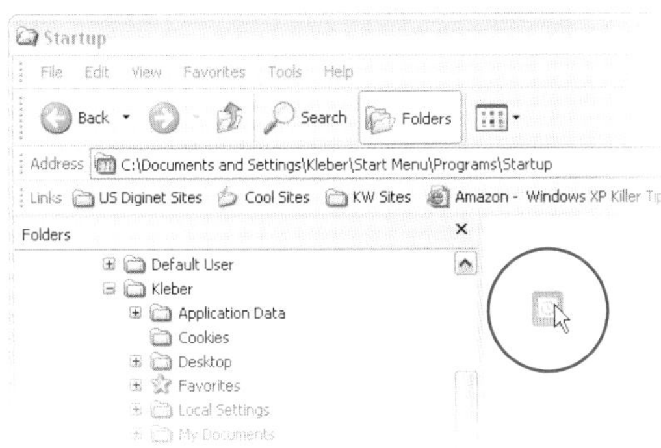

Wouldn't it be nice if Windows could just open Outlook for you automatically at startup? You, my friend, are in luck because Windows can. Right-click Start in the Windows Taskbar and click Explore in the shortcut menu. Navigate to your Startup folder (usually located in C:\Documents and Settings\<*user*>\Start Menu\Programs\Startup). Now, just press-and-hold the Control key as you drag-and-drop Outlook's application icon from your desktop into your Startup folder to create a shortcut to it. When Windows starts up, the program will launch automatically. You can also put shortcuts to your favorite folders in Startup to have them launch instantly as well.

 DON'T DUMP IT, ARCHIVE IT INSTEAD

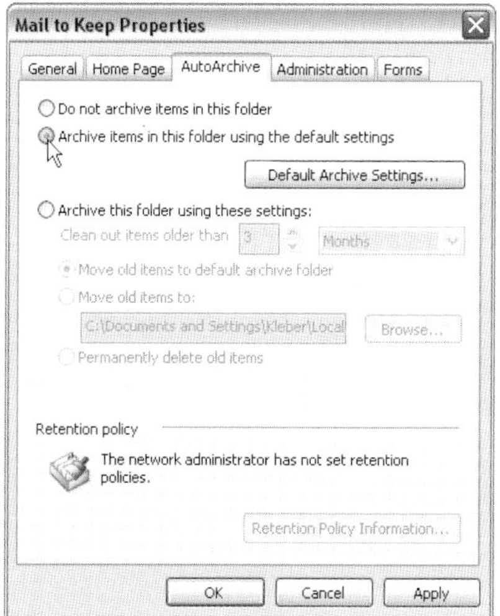

If you're the kind of person who never throws anything away, including your email, then do yourself a favor and archive your old email messages. This will boost the performance of Outlook when opening and searching folders. To archive a folder, right-click it and click Properties in the shortcut menu. Next, click the AutoArchive tab in the dialog, select "Archive items in this folder using the default settings," then click OK. Once you've created archive folders, you can add to them by simply dragging-and-dropping messages into them. *Note:* Items stashed in saved search folders can't be archived.

SNAG STATIONERY

Someone just sent you an email, and it has the coolest stationery attached that you've ever seen. Wouldn't it be great if you could snag it for yourself? You're in luck—you can. Here's how: Double-click the message containing the stationery to open it in its own preview window. Next, click File>Save Stationery in the menu bar, name the stationery, and then click OK. Now, when you apply stationery to new messages (by choosing Actions>New Mail Message Using>More Stationery), you'll see your new stationery listed in the Select a Stationery dialog. By the way, when you save stationery in Outlook, it's also saved to Word's stationery. *Note:* If you're not able to save stationery that you've received, it's probably because it's actually a Microsoft Word theme and not stationery. Outlook can't save Word themes.

COMPARE FOLDERS

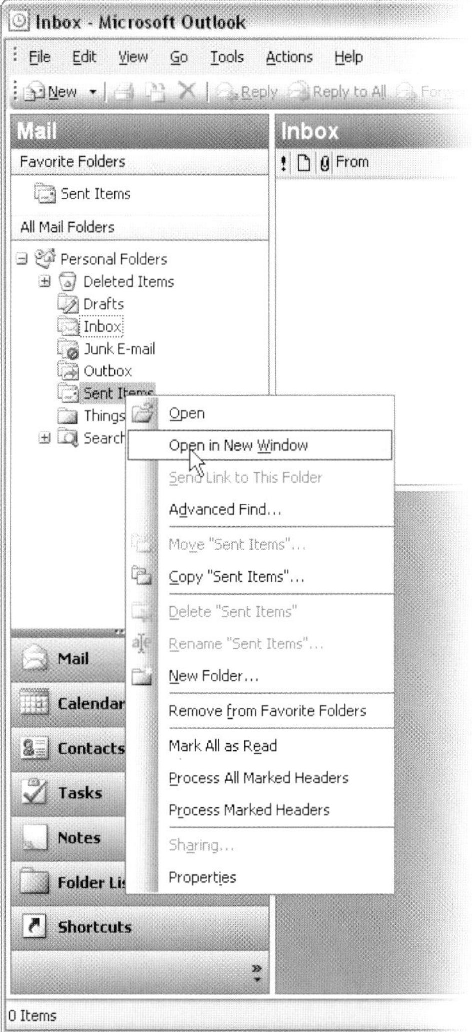

If you need to compare the contents of folders in Outlook, you can. Simply open the folders in their own windows. To do this, right-click any folder other than the one that's currently open, then click Open in New Window in the shortcut menu. This opens the folder in its own window.

GET RID OF THE JUNK

If you're plagued by spam (who isn't?), you can let Outlook get rid of most of it for you. Click Tools>Options in the menu bar, then click the Preferences tab in the Options dialog. Next, click the Junk E-mail button, select "High: Most junk e-mail is caught, but some regular mail may be caught as well. Check your Junk E-mail folder often," and click OK. Outlook does a fantastic job of detecting and removing junk email. You'll be surprised how well it works. Also, as recommended, be sure to check the Junk E-mail folder occasionally to ensure that good mail isn't being placed there accidentally.

OUTLOOK'S HIDDEN HELP

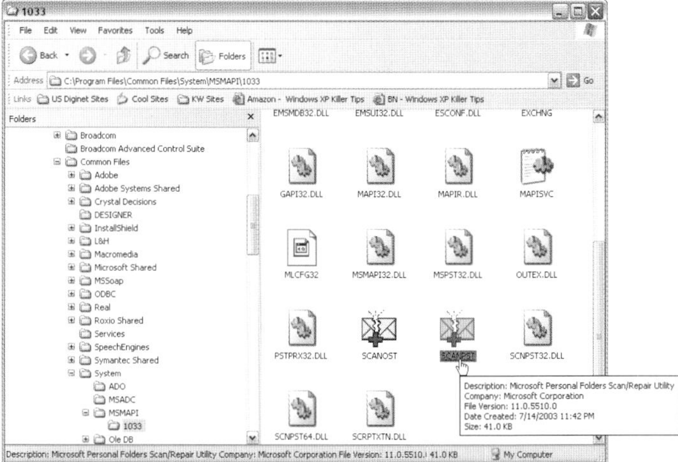

I get all giddy over hidden apps, and Outlook has one of the best-hidden apps out there. If Outlook's Personal Folders ever start causing you grief, and you begin receiving error messages while using your Personal Folders, then there's a hidden app that can probably help. Right-click Start on the Windows Taskbar, then click Explore in the shortcut menu. Now, use Windows Explorer to navigate to C:\Program Files\Common Files\System\MSMAPI\1033. Next, double-click the SCANPST file to open the Inbox Repair Tool dialog. Now, browse your hard drive to locate the PST file you want to scan, then click Start. (*Tip:* If you're not sure where your PST files are stored on your hard drive, do a search by choosing Start>Search in the Windows Taskbar.) Follow the prompts in the dialog to complete your scan.

 AUTO-SORT EMAIL

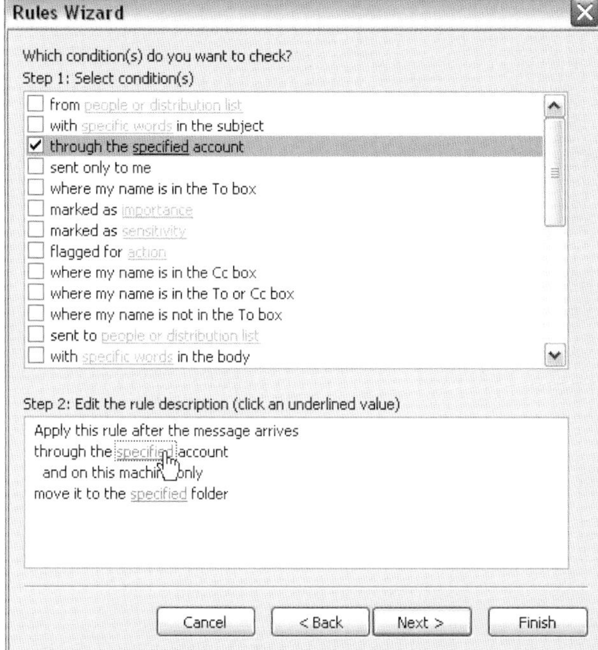

A super-fast way to keep your email organized is to move it to the correct folder when receiving it. For example, you may want to move all email sent to your office email address to a "Things To Do" folder when they're received. This can help keep messages organized and speed up archiving. To do this, click the down-facing arrow next to New in the menu bar and select Folder. Name your folder and click OK. Now click Tools>Rules and Alerts in the menu bar, then click the E-mail Rules tab in the Rules and Alerts dialog. (*Note:* Outlook can't filter HTTP email accounts, so you may get a warning dialog. Just click OK.) Next, click New Rule at the top left of the dialog, then select "Move messages from someone to a folder" under the Stay Organized category, and click Next. Now under Step 1, uncheck "from people or distribution list" and check "through the specified account." Under Step 2, click the word "specified" in the "through the specified account" and choose the email account in the Account drop-down menu. Then, click the word "specified" in the "move it to the specified folder" description under Step 2, and choose the folder to move the email to. Click Finish when you're done.

 WEB BROWSING WITH OUTLOOK

To browse the Web using Outlook, right-click the Standard toolbar and click Web in the shortcut menu to display the Web toolbar. Next, click the Start Page button (it looks like a tiny house) to open your home page in Outlook's Reading pane. Use the Web toolbar to browse, navigate, or search the Web.

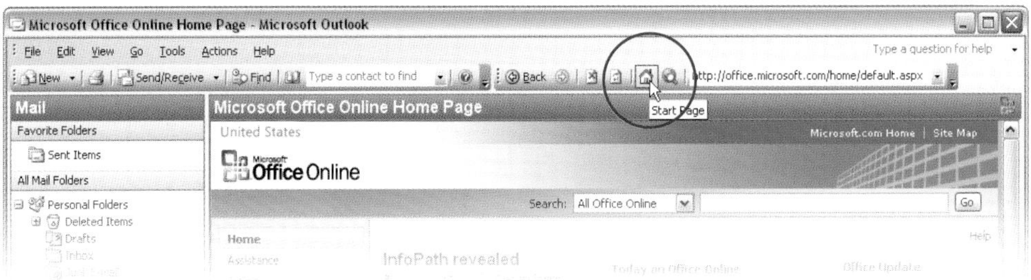

 SINGLE TASK, MULTIPLE CATEGORIES

If you've created a task and would like to associate it with several categories, there's no need to re-create the same task for each category. There's a faster way: Click Tasks in the Navigation pane and select By Category in the Current View category of the Tasks pane, then simply drag-and-drop the task into any new category.

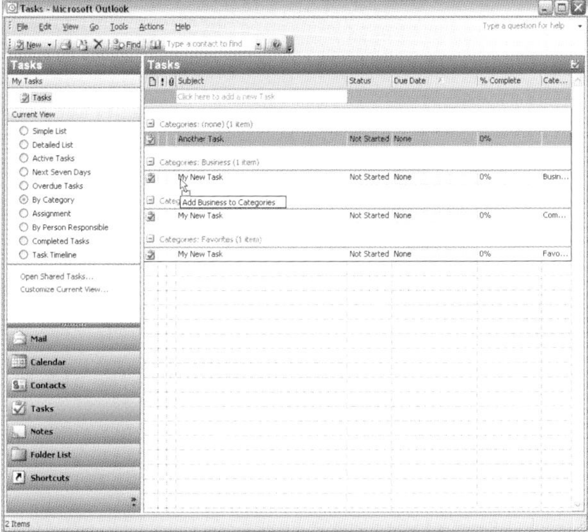

 A READING PANE YOU CAN ACTUALLY READ

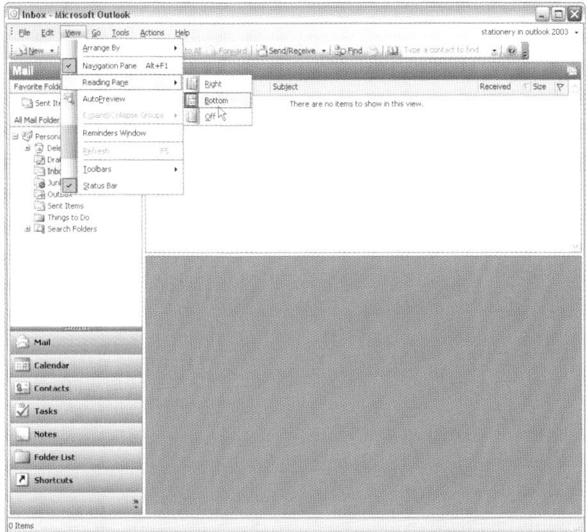

Outlook's Reading pane is displayed by default to the right of the Inbox pane, which makes total sense…I don't actually want to be able to read my messages. Yeah, that works well (kidding, that doesn't work well at all). Fortunately, we can move the Reading pane just in case you actually do want to read your email. Here's how: Click View>Reading Pane>Bottom in the menu bar. Now your Reading pane appears below the Inbox window, actually giving you enough room to read your messages.

 A REMINDER TO TURN OFF REMINDERS

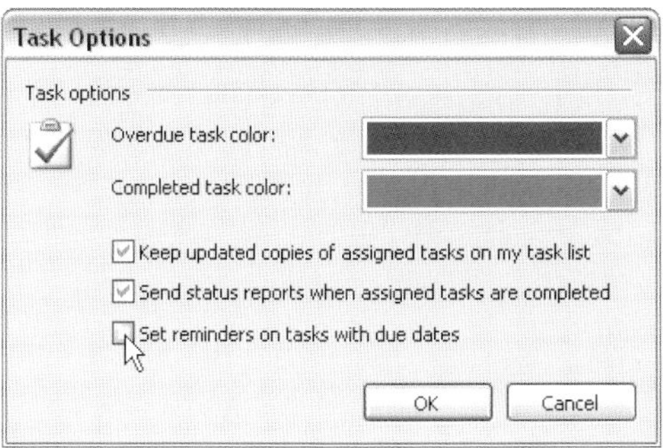

By default, Outlook will set a reminder automatically for every new task, which is just annoying, and because we don't like anything annoying, we're gonna turn this off. Click Tools>Options in the menu bar and in the Preferences tab, click the Task Options button. Uncheck "Set reminders on tasks with due dates," then click OK. I'm feelin' much less annoyed!

USING SHORTCUTS IN OUTLOOK

Outlook 2003 is the most user-friendly and customizable Outlook yet—a good example of this is Outlook's shortcuts. You can add URLs, application shortcuts, or even links to documents, putting all of your most-used tools just a click away. First, click Shortcuts in the Navigation pane. Now simply drag-and-drop any webpage icon, application shortcut, or document shortcut into the Shortcuts link at the top of the Shortcuts pane. Click any shortcut to use it.

GET RID OF J

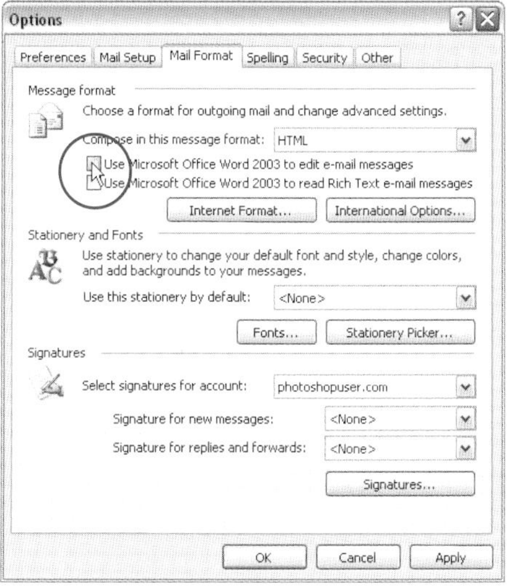

If you type a smiley :-) emoticon and Outlook replaces it with a "J" symbol, then Outlook is using Word to edit your email messages. Well, you can get your smileys back by using Outlook's editor instead. To use Outlook's text editor, click Tools>Options in the menu bar, then click the Mail Format tab in the Options dialog. Next, uncheck "Use Microsoft Office Word 2003 to edit e-mail messages" and click OK. Now, create a new message and type a smiley. There ya go.

YOU'VE GOT MAIL...SOUNDS

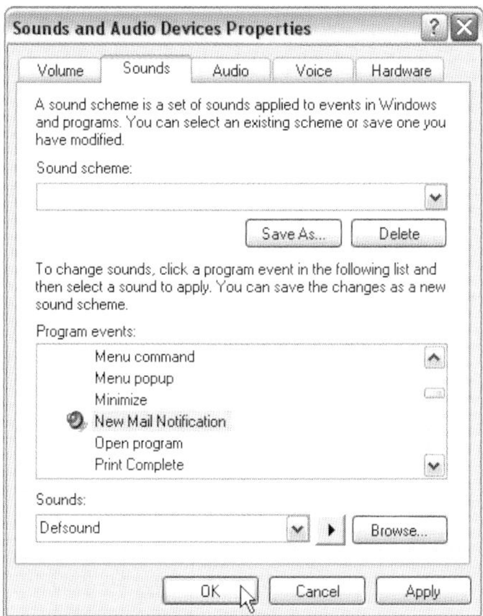

By default, Outlook uses the Windows XP System Notification sound, which sounds kind of like every other XP sound. You can, however, make the notification sound a little more distinguishable if you'd like to know that you've received new email. Here's how: In the Windows Taskbar, click Start>Control Panel>Sound, Speech, and Audio Devices>Sounds and Audio Devices. Next, click the Sounds tab in the dialog and scroll in the Program Events category to select New Mail Notification. Now, select a new sound from the Sounds drop-down menu at the bottom of the dialog or browse your hard drive to choose a new sound that you've saved. When finished, click OK.

BACK UP THE BAD

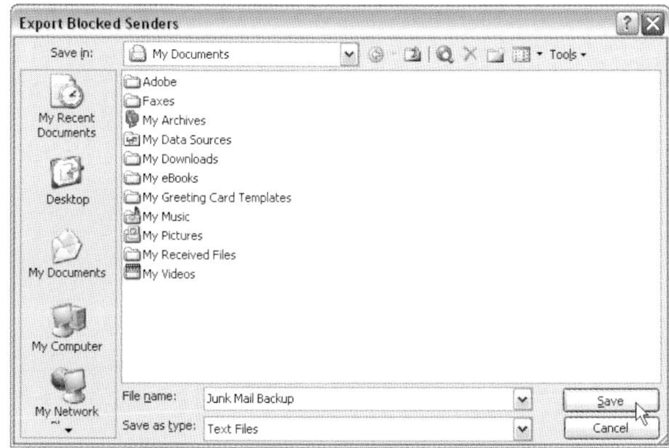

Okay, you've gone to a lot of trouble blocking spammers (or people you're just trying to avoid), and this is a list that you want to keep backed up. If anything ever happens to Outlook, you'll want to be able to replace your blocked senders list, or you may even want to share the list between computers. To back up your list, click Tools>Options in the menu bar, then click the Junk E-mail button. Next, click the Blocked Senders tab in the Junk E-mail Options dialog and click the Export to File button. Now, choose a location to save the file to, give your backup file a name, and click Save. Click OK to close out of the open dialogs. If you want to import your backed-up blocked senders list, click the Import from File button in the Junk E-mail Options dialog.

SIGN IT

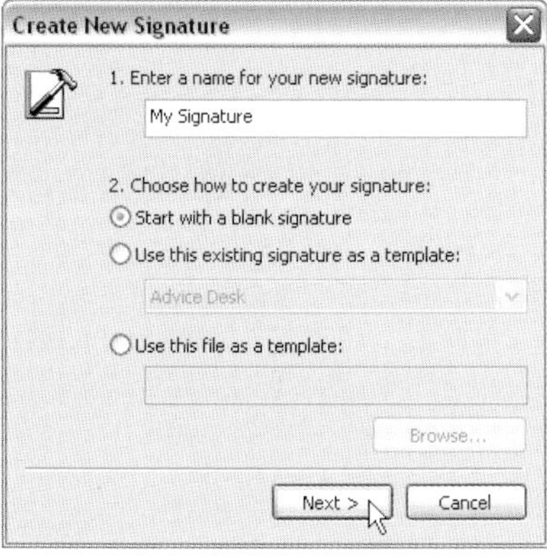

For most accounts, especially business accounts, you'll almost always have the same signature—ending your messages with the same name and any contact information. You don't have to type this information each time you send an email (unless you really like typing). Instead, you can create a signature just once for each email address (POP account) and Outlook will automatically add it to your messages. Here's how: Click Tools>Options in the Standard toolbar, then click the Mail Format tab in the Options dialog. Next, click the Signatures button at the bottom of the dialog and click New in the Create Signature dialog. Follow the Create New Signature dialog to name and create your signature. When you're done, click Finish, and then click OK to close the Create Signature dialog. In the Options dialog, select the POP account (for which you just created the signature) from the Select Signatures for Account drop-down menu. Then, in the Signatures category, choose to use your signature for new messages, replies, and forwards, and then click OK.

FLAG IT

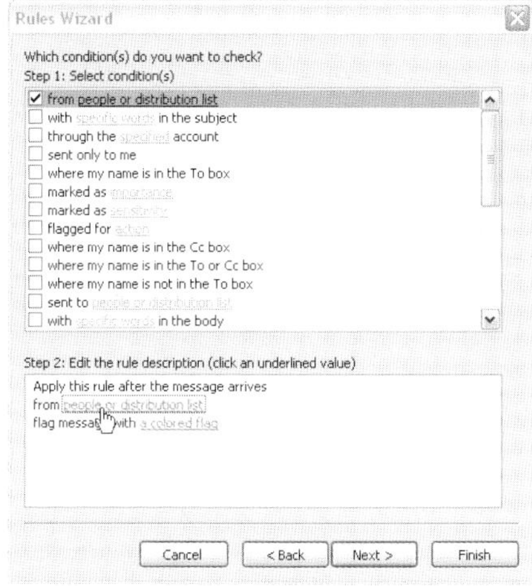

I receive a ridiculous amount of email throughout the day, and if I'm expecting an important email from someone, I'll set up a message rule to automatically flag it to notify me when it arrives. To automatically flag incoming messages, click Tools>Rules and Alerts in the menu bar and in the E-mail Rules tab, click the New Rule button and select "Flag messages from someone with a colored flag" under Step 1, then click Next. Now check "from people or distribution list" under Step 1, then click the "people or distribution list" link under Step 2, specify a contact, and click the From button or type an email address in the From field. Click OK to close the dialog. Next, click the words "a colored flag" in the "flag message with a colored flag" description under Step 2 and select a flag color in the resulting dialog. Click Finish when you're done. Now, when a message arrives from this person, it will immediately be flagged for easy recognition.

FOLLOW-UP FLAGS

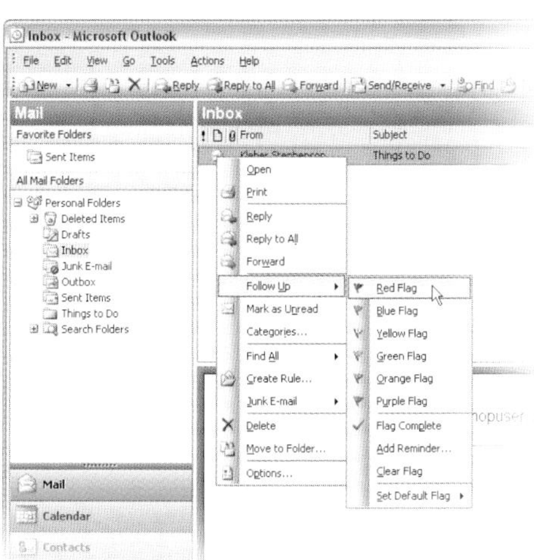

A quick way to add reminders to your email is to flag 'em; for example, you can flag important emails that require extra attention. To do this, right-click any email message, point to Follow Up, and click a flag color in the shortcut menu to identify your email. Your message will be flagged immediately. To remove a flag, right-click the message, point to Follow Up, and click Clear Flag. Another way to quickly flag an email is to select the message and press the Insert key on your keyboard. This shortcut instantly flags your message with a red-colored flag.

 COLOR-CODE MESSAGES

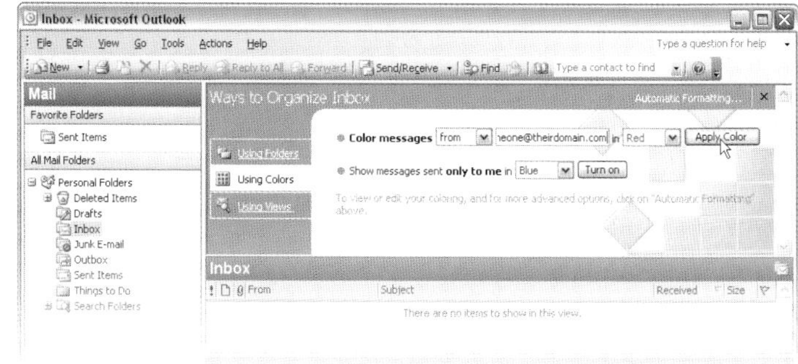

Another way (and probably my favorite) to highlight email from individuals is to color-code entire messages. To color code a message from individual addresses, click Tools>Organize and click the Using Colors link under Ways to Organize Inbox. Choose "from" in the Color Messages drop-down menu, type an email address in the field, and choose a color in the drop-down menu. When finished, click Apply Color. Now any message received from the email address you specified will be colored, making it very easy to recognize.

 BCC GROUPS

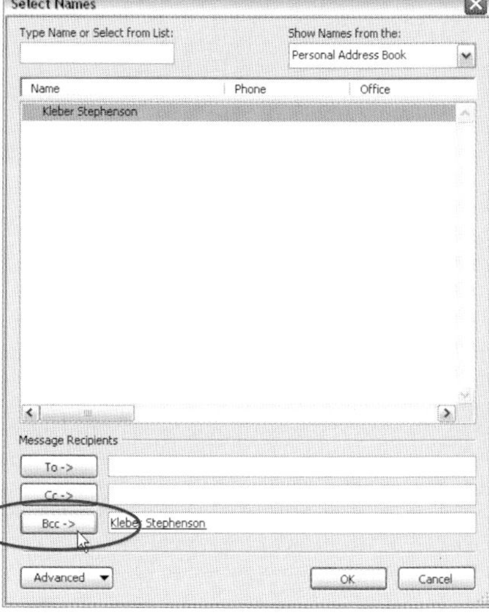

Something to keep in mind when sending email to groups is that everyone receiving the message will see the email address for each member on the list. Members of your group might not be crazy about this. There's a clever way around this problem, however. On a new message window, click the To button to select the recipients, but instead of adding your group to the To field, add it to the Bcc (Blind Carbon Copy) field near the bottom of the Select Names dialog. Just click a name or group in the window and click the Bcc button. Now when you send messages to the group, members will only know who sent the message, not who all of the recipients were.

 DON'T REPLY THERE

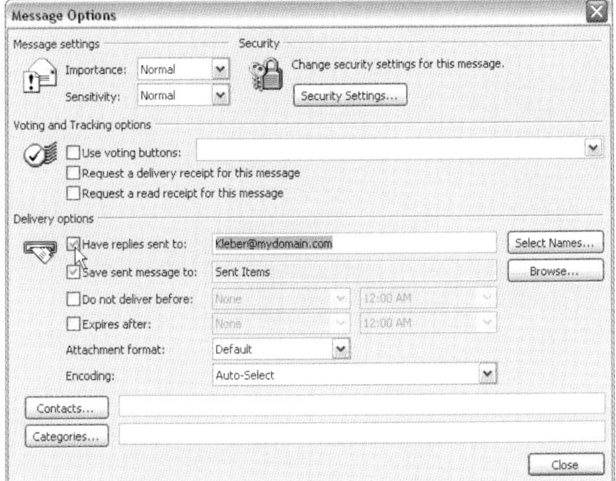

If you send email from someone else's computer, using his or her email address, then you probably don't want any replies sent back to your friend's account (it doesn't belong to you). Well, there's a way around this. Outlook can actually forward replies to a different email account than the one you sent the email from. To do this, create a new message, click the Options button on the Message toolbar, and check "Have replies sent to" under the Delivery Options category. Type an email address in the "Have replies sent to" field, then click Close. Now any replies to your message will be sent to the email account you specified.

 REQUEST A RECEIPT

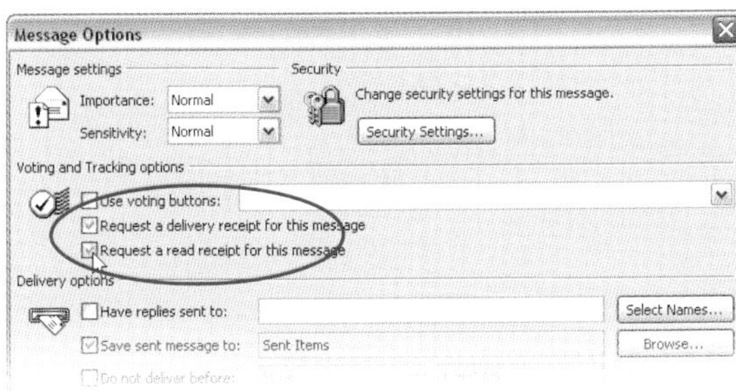

Don't you hate not knowing if someone received your email? I mean, you asked for a reply but of course one was never sent. So, you're just left hanging. Did the person get it? Did your server eat it? You don't know and because the person won't reply, you may never know. Stressful, isn't it? Well, there's a way that you can encourage the recipient to acknowledge that your email was received. Here's how: Create and compose a new message, then click the Options button in the Message toolbar. Next, check "Request a delivery receipt for this message" and/or "Request a read receipt for this message" under the Voting and Tracking Options category. Click Close when finished. Now, when recipients receive your message, they'll be prompted to acknowledge that they received it. If they do, you'll receive notification that it was received. If they don't, then subscribe their email address to every spammer on the Web. That'll teach 'em.

SHOW ONLY THE UNREAD

Is your Inbox getting a little crowded? Well, if it is, you can hide messages that you've read to help you quickly identify incoming (unread) email. Here's how: Click the Inbox in the All Mail Folders pane, click View>Arrange By>Custom in the menu bar, then click the Filter button in the dialog. Next, click the More Choices tab in the Filter dialog and check "Only items that are" and select "unread" from the drop-down menu. Click OK when finished, and you'll no longer see messages that you've already read.

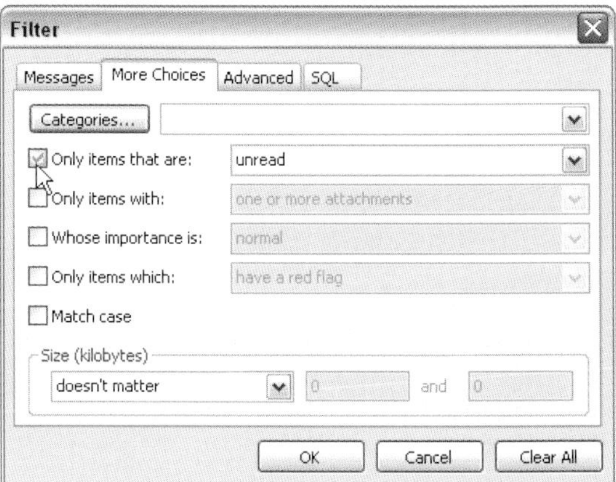

OOPS, I DIDN'T MEAN TO SEND THAT

Don't you wish there was an Undo button for sent email? Well, actually, there is. You can recall email sent from Outlook by first double-clicking the sent email in the Sent Items folder to open it in its own preview window, then clicking Actions>Recall This Message in the menu bar. You'll then see a pop-up dialog asking whether to delete the email or to replace the email with a new message. Choose which works best for you, then click OK. Now, before you start firing off an email to your employer telling him exactly what you think, there's a catch. The recipient has to be logged on to the Internet and the message must be received but not read. Yeah, pretty big catch, huh? Well, if you're able to successfully retrieve a message, Outlook will notify you and let you know that you just avoided a very close call.

 ZIP IT!

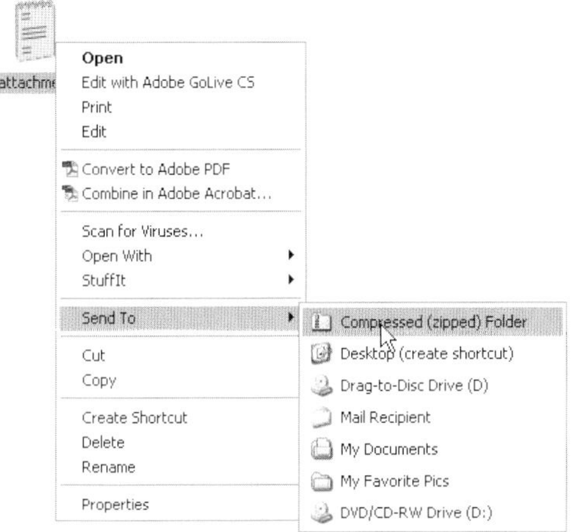

By default, Outlook doesn't allow you to view attachments that it determines may be harmful—containing viruses, for example. This is helpful until Outlook starts removing your attachments sent to others or removing attachments received from contacts that you know are perfectly fine. To prevent Outlook from removing your attachments, Zip them first by right-clicking the file and selecting Send To>Compressed (zipped) Folder. Now attach your file to your email message. Outlook doesn't filter zipped files, so you can send and receive zipped files without Outlook taking any action.

 QUICK, SEND WEBPAGES

You can quickly email a webpage to someone using Outlook. First, open the webpage in Outlook by entering a website in the Address field of the Web toolbar (which you can access by right-clicking any toolbar and selecting Web in the shortcut menu). Now click Actions>Send Web Page by E-mail. A new message window will open with the webpage and URL attached. Simply type a recipient in the To field, enter a message if you'd like, and then click the Send button.

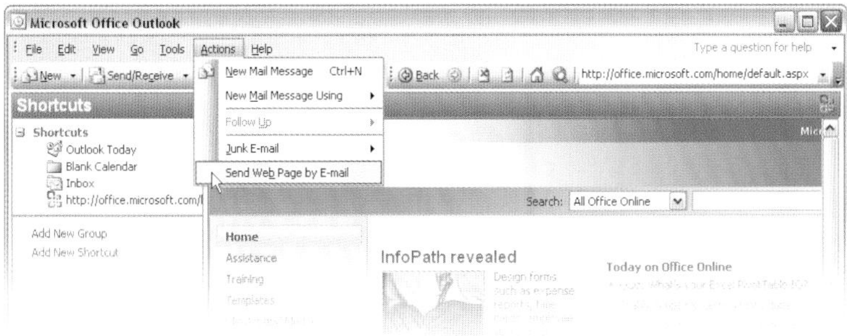

YOU'VE ALWAYS GOT MAIL

If you check your email throughout the day and have a constant connection to the Internet, there's no need for you to check manually for new messages. Let Outlook automatically check for you. First, click Tools>Options in the menu bar, then click the Mail Setup tab in the Options dialog. Next click the Send/ Receive button, check "Schedule an automatic send/receive every [ ] minutes," and type a number in the field for how often Outlook should check for new messages, then click Close. Now, minimize Outlook by clicking on the Minimize button in the top-right corner of Outlook's window, and it will automatically check for new messages while it's docked in the Windows Taskbar.

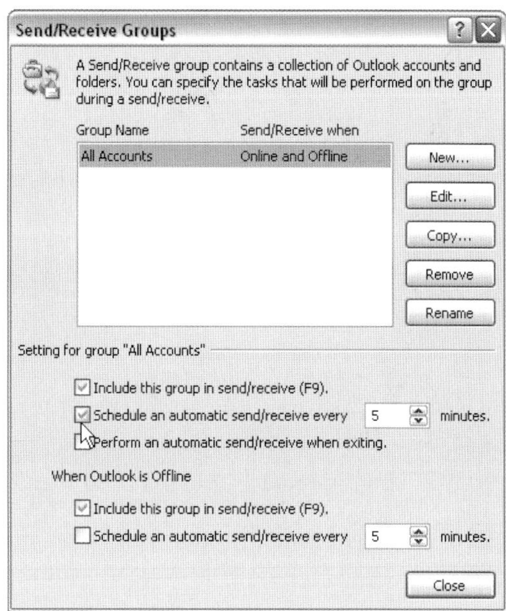

YOU'VE BEEN NOTIFIED, YOU'VE GOT MAIL

Now that you've minimized Outlook (see previous tip), how do you know if you've received new messages? The Window's Taskbar knows. When new messages arrive at your Inbox, the "You have new unopened items" icon will appear, informing you that you've received new email.

NO OFFICE? NO PROBLEM!

Believe it or not, there are people out there who don't use Office...shocking, isn't it? Well, just because they don't use Office, it doesn't mean that you can't share your documents. Outlook lets you send Office documents, such as Access, Excel, Publisher, and Word files, via email without the recipients having those programs installed on their computers. For example, to share a Word file, go to the Standard toolbar and click Actions>New Mail Message Using>Microsoft Office>Microsoft Word Document in the menu bar. A Word document opens that is ready to be created and emailed. Now, create your document (or copy-and-paste text from an Office file), type an email address in the To field, then click Send a Copy. Your Word document will be emailed, and you'll then be prompted to save the Word document that you just created.

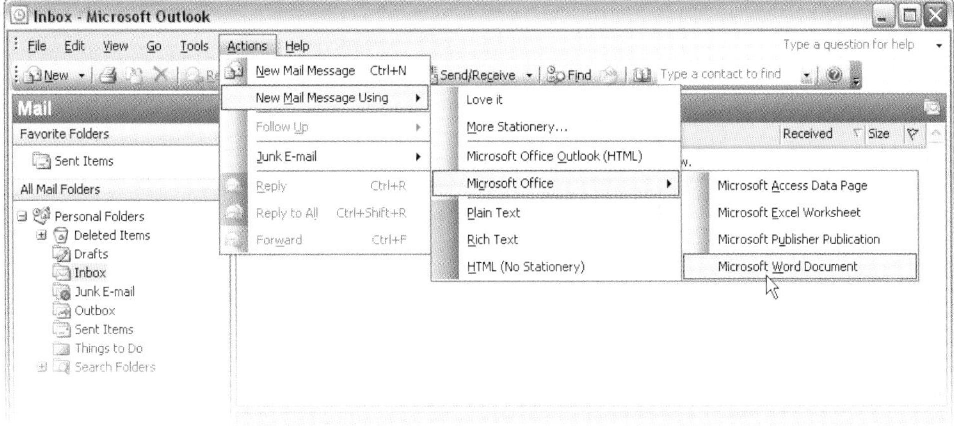

RIGHT-CLICK CONTACTS

Here's a quick way to send email to contacts. Click the Contacts button in the Navigation pane. With your contacts visible in the Contacts window, right-click a contact header (name) and click New Message to Contact in the shortcut menu.

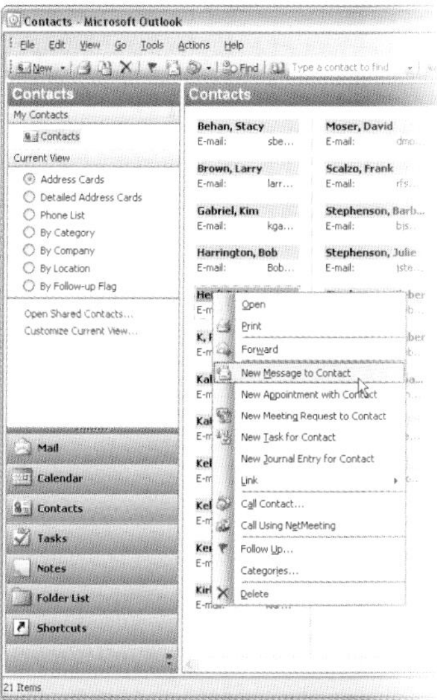

RIGHT-CLICK ATTACHMENTS

This whole right-clicking thing is really catching on—you can even use it to send files (attachments) via email. Try this tip the next time you need to send a file to someone. Locate the file you want to email, then right-click it and click Sent To>Mail Recipient in the shortcut menu. This will open a new Outlook message window with your file attached and ready to be sent. Now, just type the recipient's email address in the To field, type a message if you'd like, and then click Send.

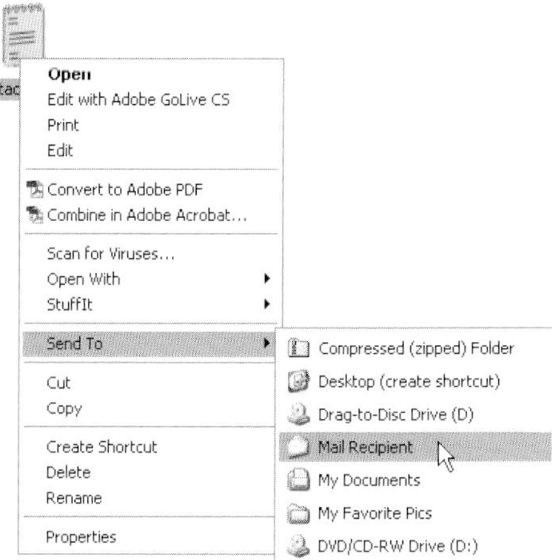

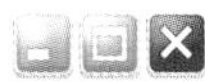

YOU'RE ANNOYING

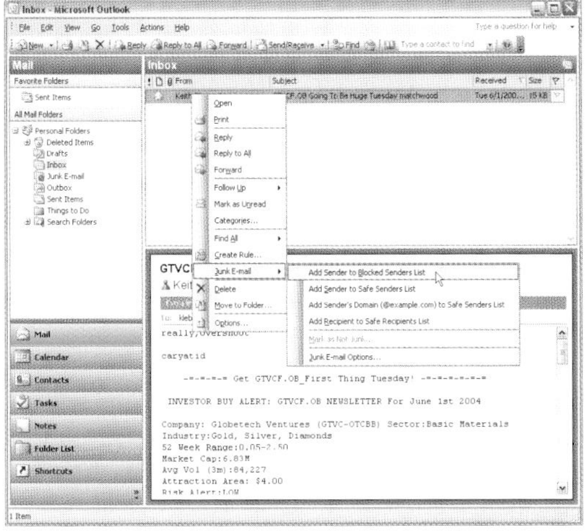

Are you getting email from someone who's really annoying? If you are, you can block that person's email address so that you won't see messages received from him or her. I do it all the time just for fun, but that's me. I'm just mean. Anyway, when you block an email address, any mail received from the address is automatically placed in your Deleted Items folder. You don't ever have to see it. To block a sender, right-click the email message and click Junk E-mail>Add Sender to Blocked Senders List in the shortcut menu. To remove someone from the list, click Tools>Options in the menu bar, and in the Preferences tab, click the Junk E-mail button under the E-mail category. Next, click the Blocked Senders tab and locate the person's email address, then select it and click Remove. Click OK when finished.

YOU'RE SAFE

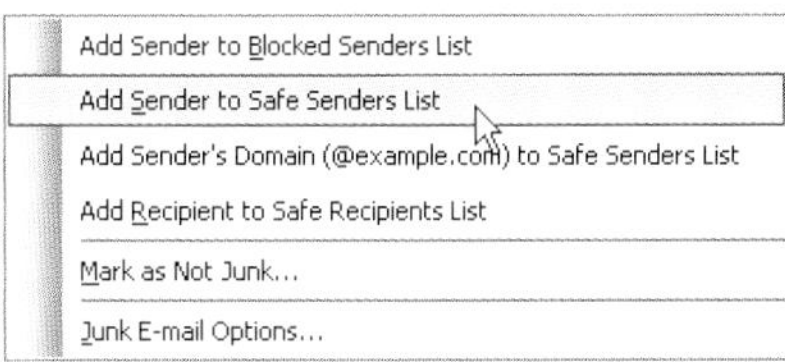

If you've set up Outlook to filter your email for spam, and you're worried that important email might get removed by mistake, you should add your contacts to your Safe Senders list. This gives your contacts a free pass with Outlook. No matter what they send you, it'll breeze right through untouched by Outlook. To add a contact to your Safe Senders list, simply right-click any message that person has sent you and click Junk E-mail>Add Sender to Safe Senders List in the shortcut menu. To remove this person from the list, click Tools>Options, click the Junk E-mail button, and in the resulting dialog, click the Safe Senders tab. Choose your sender from the list, click Remove, and then click OK.

QUICK JUNK BUTTON

The quickest way to whack spam the second it appears in your Inbox is to add the Junk E-mail button to Outlook's Standard toolbar, then you can get rid of spam in just one click. To do this, click Tools>Customize in the menu bar, then click the Commands tab. Select Actions listed under Categories, then click-and-drag Add Sender to Blocked Senders List from the Commands category to any location on Outlook's toolbar. Now anytime you get spam, you're only a click away from blocking that sender's address from ever sending you email again. To remove the button, click Tools>Customize in the menu bar, then simply drag the button off the toolbar until an "x" appears below your mouse pointer, then release your mouse button.

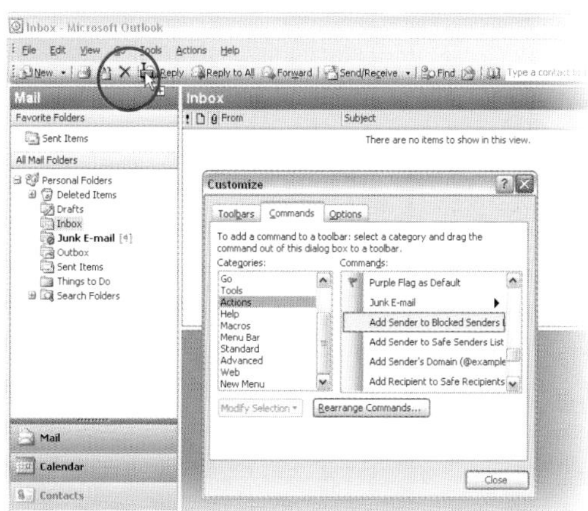

TURN OFF THE READING PANE

We all get spam—some worse than others—for example, junk mail containing adult images. And, if you work around children or co-workers who can see your monitor, then you need to be careful when checking your email. Well, fortunately, you can avoid displaying images by turning off the Reading pane. To do this, click View>Reading Pane>Off in the menu bar. Now received messages won't display their contents. You can quickly view any email, however, by right-clicking the message and clicking Open in the shortcut menu.

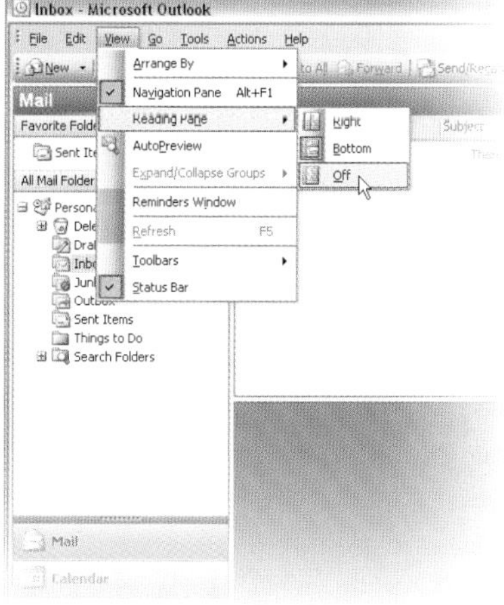

SORT THE JUNK WITH AUTOPREVIEW

Another great way to censor your email is to use Outlook's AutoPreview. Try this: Close the Reading pane by clicking View>Reading Pane>Off in the menu bar. Now, click View>AutoPreview in the menu bar. Messages in Outlook will now display the first few lines of an email's message. This helps you to quickly separate the valid email from the spam.

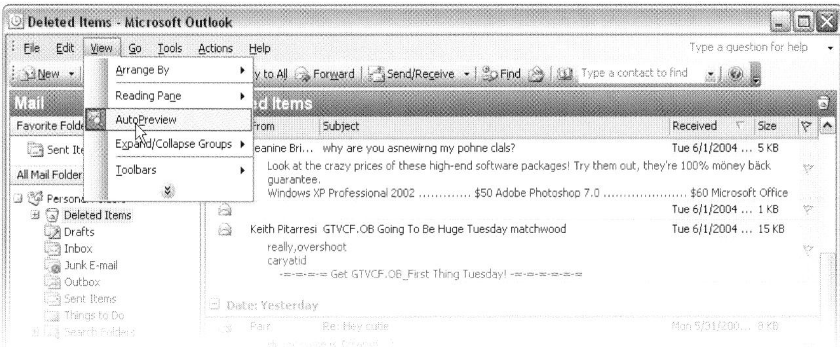

STOP DESKTOP ALERTS

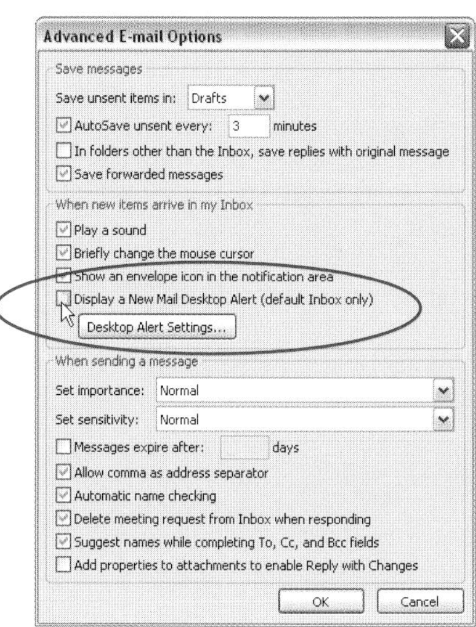

The first thing I do when I fire up my computer is open Outlook, check my email, then minimize Outlook, which I've set up to check my email continuously. Now, I'm receiving email just about every minute of the day, and Outlook's new email desktop alerts start to get really annoying by the 16th or 17th one. This is supposed to be helpful, but it's not—it's just annoying. Fortunately, we can stop Outlook from being so helpful by clicking Tools>Options in the menu bar. In the Preferences tab, click E-mail Options under the E-mail category, and then click Advanced E-mail Options in the dialog. Now, uncheck Display a New Mail Desktop Alert (default Inbox only) under the "When new items arrive in my Inbox" category, then click OK.

 LET 'EM VOTE ON IT

A great way to get instant feedback about an email is to poll the recipient. You can request that the recipients use voting buttons to provide quick answers to questions or proposals. For instance, if you're sending a proposal that requires someone's approval or rejection, you can send an email to request that the recipient replies with a response of, well, approval or rejection. Here's how: On a new message window, click Options in the Standard toolbar, then check Use Voting Buttons under the Voting and Tracking Options category. Next, choose the type of available responses from the drop-down menu (Approve;Reject, Yes;No, etc.), then click Close when finished. Now the recipient will be requested to respond using the voting dialog. Once the recipient responds, you'll receive a confirmation email displaying the results of your poll.

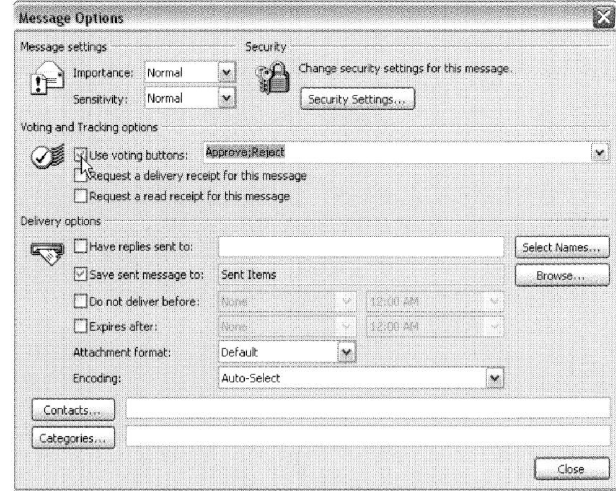

 PRINT YOUR CONTACTS

Now that you've gone to all the trouble of putting every person you've ever known into Outlook's Contacts list, you should print a directory to keep handy around your office or home. To print a copy of your contacts, click the Contacts button in the Navigation pane and click File>Print in the menu bar. Next, select Phone Directory Style under the Print Style category and click OK. You now have a printed copy of your contacts.

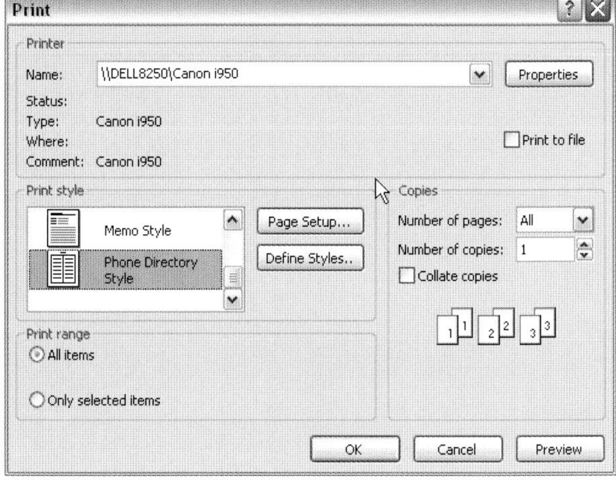

I PREFER NICKNAMES

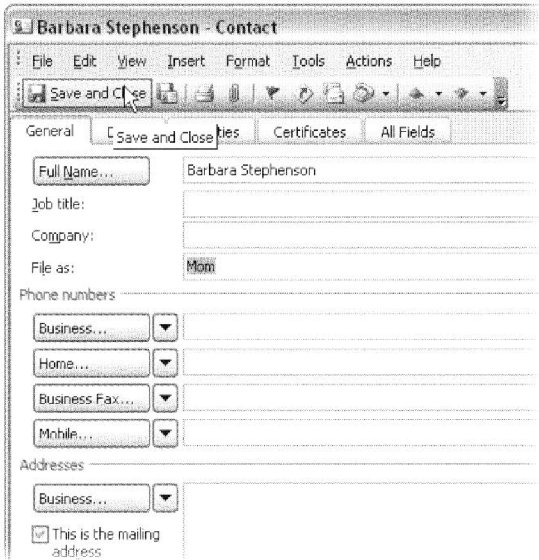

When looking up contacts, you may find it better to use nicknames or initials; for example, I like to find my mother by looking up "Mom." To look up contacts using nicknames or initials, double-click any contact in your Contacts list, then in the General tab, type a nickname or initials in the File As field, and click the Save and Close button. Now type the nickname or initials into the "Type a contact to find" search field in the toolbar to display the contact's info.

CHECK A CONTACT'S ACTIVITIES

To view all messages sent to you by a contact, click Contacts in the Navigation pane and double-click a name in the Contacts list to open a contact. Next, click the Activities tab on the contact's window and select All Items from the Show drop-down list. Now all messages from this contact in every Outlook folder will appear in the window. You can simply scroll the list to locate a particular message.

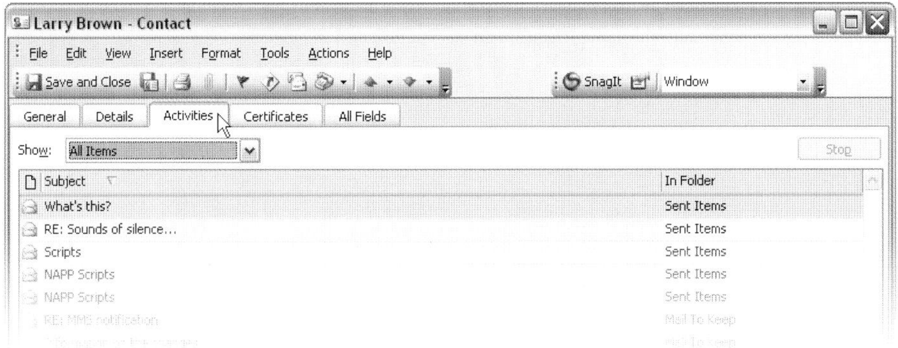

FIND A GROUP OF CONTACTS

The "Type a contact to find" field in the Standard toolbar of the Contacts pane is another great way to locate a group of contacts. If you need to locate all contacts from the same domain to send email to the group or to change the group's domain, type the domain name (e.g., msn) and press Enter on your keyboard. You'll be shown a list of everyone in your Contacts list who has that domain in his or her email address.

GET DIRECTIONS

Do you need directions to a contact's street address? You can get it right in Outlook. With the Contacts list open, double-click any contact for which you've saved an address and click the Display Map of Address button (it looks like a yellow street sign) in the toolbar. This will launch your Web browser, taking you to Microsoft's MapPoint website. Click the Get Map button on the webpage to display a map of the address.

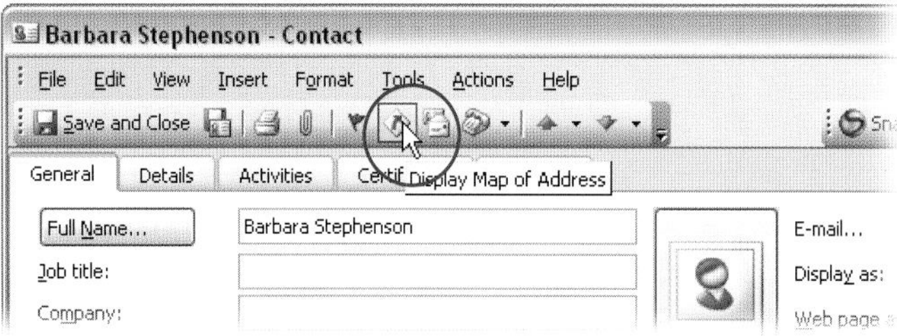

YOU CAN PICTURE IT

Your contacts just aren't complete until you give 'em a picture. This could be a picture of the actual person or any graphic that reminds you of that person (use your imagination). To add a picture to a contact, open any contact by double-clicking the name in the Contact list, then click the Add Contact Picture icon (it looks like a generic person in the dialog). Now, browse your hard drive using the Add Contact Picture dialog and click OK once you've selected your picture. The picture is now displayed in place of the Add Contact Picture icon. To remove a contact's picture, double-click the name in the Contacts list and then click Actions>Remove Picture in the Contact window's menu bar.

QUICKLY ADD TO CONTACTS

Here's a quick way to add an email sender's name to your Contact list. Drag-and-drop the message onto the Contacts button in the Navigation pane, which will open a new Contact window, including all of the contact's info. Now, make any changes or additions to the contact's info, then click the Save and Close button.

CATEGORIES CAN REMIND YOU

I have about 80 contacts listed in my Outlook's Contacts list at any given time, and sometimes it's difficult for me to remember why they're there. A quick way to remind yourself of who these contacts are is to categorize them. To do this, click Contacts in the Navigation pane and double-click a contact's name. Next, click the Categories button at the bottom of the Contact window. Now, simply check all the categories that describe the contact, click OK in the dialog when finished, and then click the Save and Close button in the Contact window. Now, you can just check the Categories field in the contact's info the next time you forget exactly who a contact is.

DON'T JUST REPLY, SEND AN INSTANT MESSAGE

If you receive an email from a contact and you want to respond so urgently that only an instant message will do, then click the contact's Personal Names Smart Tag. When you receive an email from someone that you've set up as a Microsoft Messenger contact (i.e., you've entered the person's IM name in the IM Address field in the General tab of the Contact window for that contact), you'll see a Smart Tag next to the person's name in the From field, as long as his or her online status is anything other than offline. To reply with an instant message, click the Smart Tag and click Send Instant Message in the shortcut menu. This will open the Messenger Conversation window, where you can type your message and click Send.

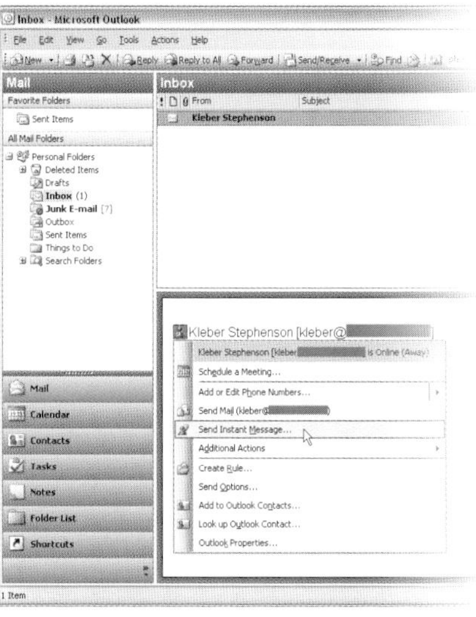

FORWARD A VCARD

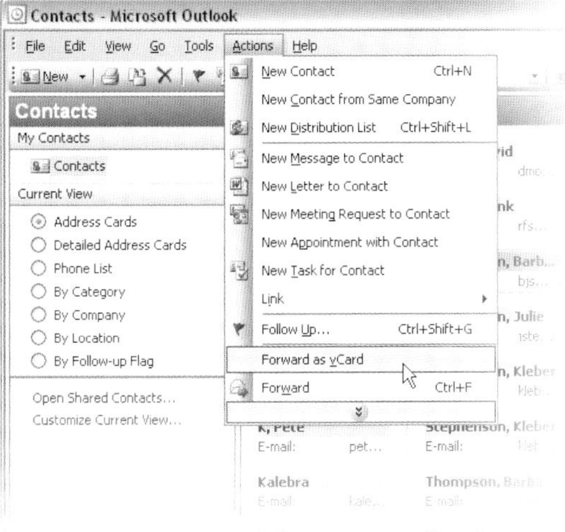

To share a contact's complete information with others or between computers, just attach a contact's vCard to an email. To do this, click Contacts in the Navigation pane, open a contact from your Contacts list, and click Actions>Forward as vCard in the Contacts menu bar. Next, type the recipient's email address in the To field, include any message, and then click the Send button.

SNAIL MAIL YOUR CONTACTS

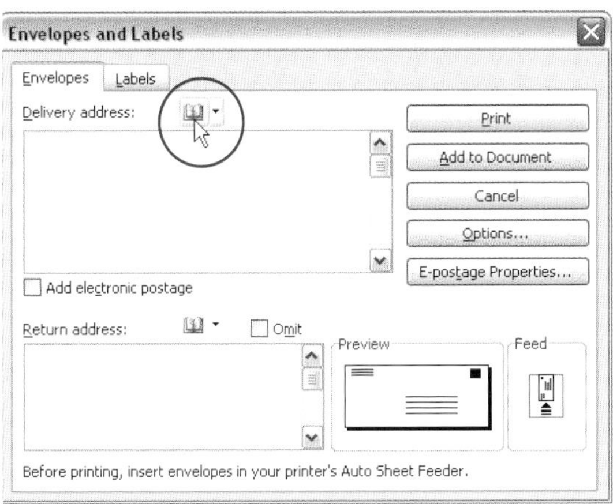

You can use Word's Envelopes and Labels dialog if you need to print a contact's address onto an envelope or label. Here's how: Launch Word and click Tools>Letters and Mailings>Envelopes and Labels in the menu bar. With the Envelopes tab open, click the Insert Address button (it looks like a book) next to the Delivery Address field to open Outlook's Contacts list. Now, simply select a contact from the list and click OK. The contact's name and mailing address will appear in the Delivery Address field. Click the Print button when finished.

QUICKLY CREATE APPOINTMENTS

You can easily turn any message into an appointment by dragging-and-dropping it from a folder or your Inbox onto the Calendar button in the Navigation pane. This will open a new Appointment window. Now make any changes, set the appointment's start and end times, then click the Save and Close button when you're finished. To turn your appointment into a meeting, click the Scheduling tab in the Appointment window, add anyone who's invited to the meeting in the All Attendees list on the left-hand side of the window, then click File>Save. Now click the Send button to email meeting invitations to those attendees who are saved in your Contacts list.

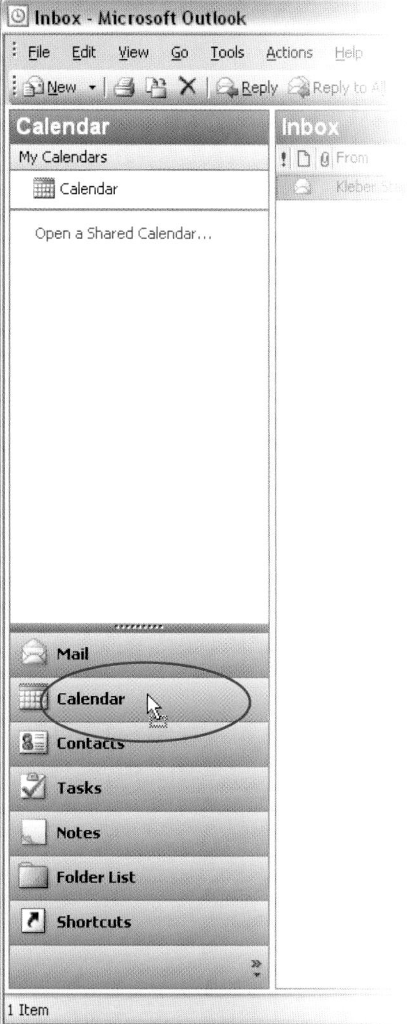

PRINT BLANK CALENDARS

My Outlook calendar fills up pretty quickly, making it impossible for me to print a blank calendar for other purposes. Well, there is a way in Outlook to print a blank calendar: Click the Calendar button in the Navigation pane, click the Month button in the toolbar to display your calendar in Month view, select the month that you want to print by clicking on the top month's name in the Calendar pane, then choose your month from the shortcut menu. (*Tip*: Click-and-drag in the pane to highlight any extra dates that you want to add to your calendar.) Next, click File>New>Folder and type a name for your new folder (e.g., My Blank Folder), then click OK. Now click the checkbox to the left of your new folder under My Calendars in the Calendar pane to open your calendar (be sure to uncheck any other calendars). Next, click File>Page Setup>Monthly Style in the menu bar, click the Print button in the dialog, and click OK in the Print dialog.

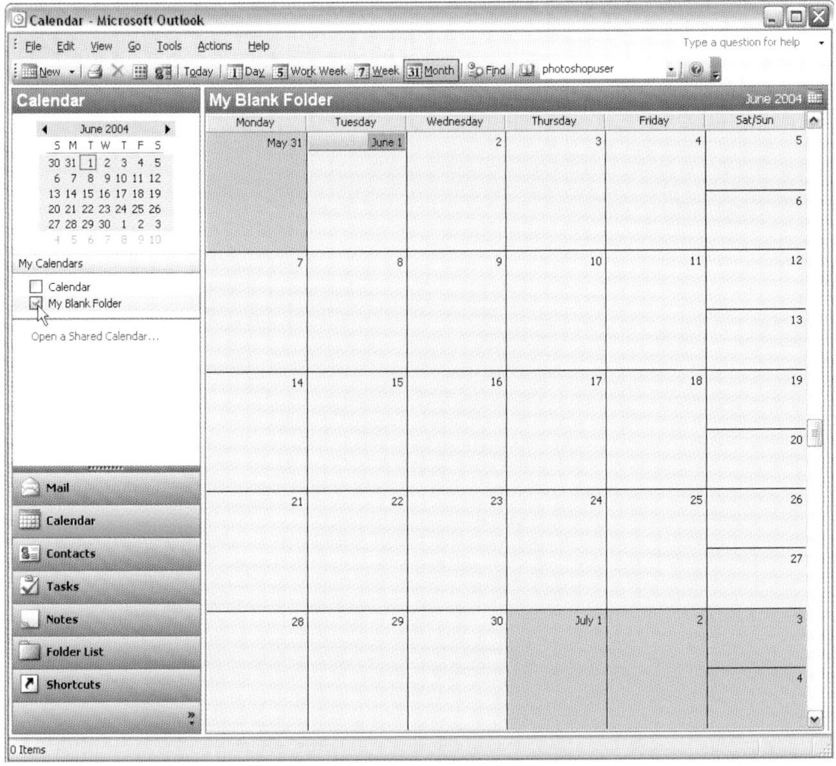

SHARE YOUR CALENDARS

The easiest way to share your Outlook calendars with others is to save them as webpages. To do this, click Calendar in the Navigation pane, then click File>Save as Web Page in the menu bar. Next, choose a start and end date for your calendar on the Save As Web Page dialog. You can also choose to include a background graphic and include appointment details. Click the Browse button to the right of the File Name field to give your calendar webpage a name and to choose where you want the file saved on your hard drive, then click Select. Now click Save in the Save As Web Page dialog.

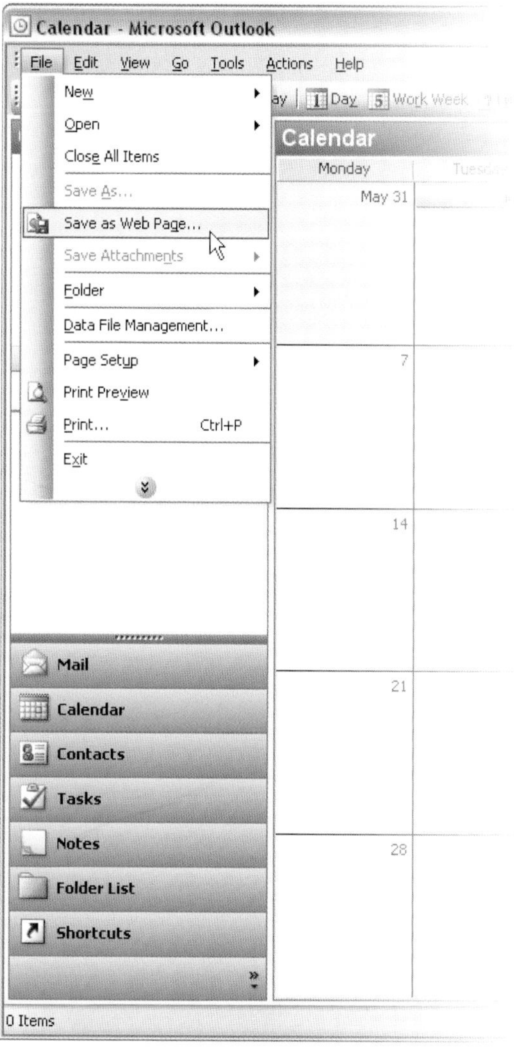

I NEED MY WEEKENDS

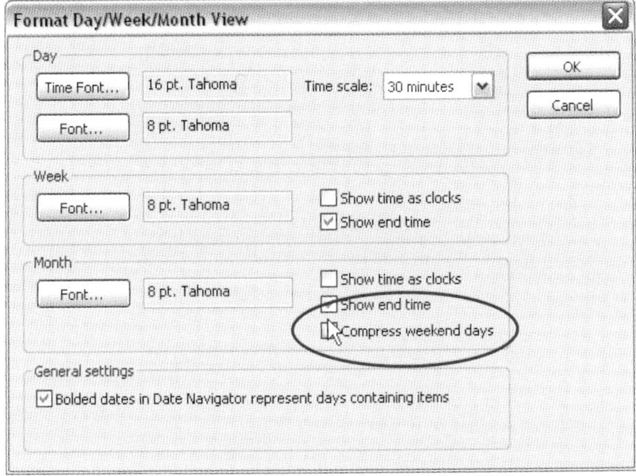

For some reason, Outlook calendars just don't think weekends are important; they're not even represented with their own boxes. They're lumped together (Sat/Sun). Well, I work all the time and my weekends are just as busy as my weekdays, so I need a full-sized box for my weekend days. To make an Outlook calendar show weekend days in their own fields, right-click your calendar while in Month view (View>Month), then click Other Settings in the shortcut menu. Next, uncheck Compress Weekend Days and click OK. Saturday and Sunday now appear in separate fields on the calendar.

MASTER TIME ZONES

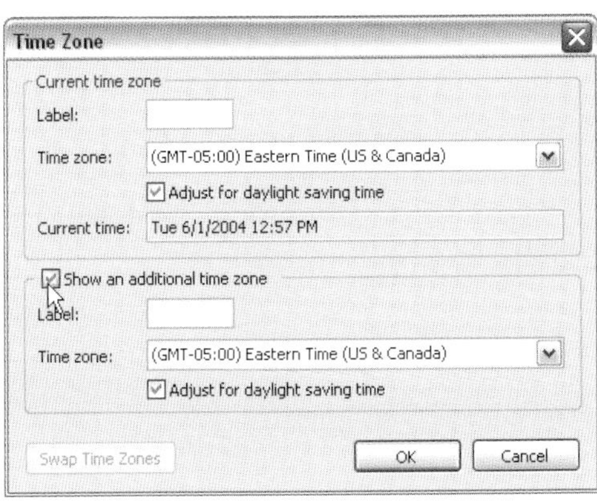

If you're traveling overseas or even to different time zones, you can always keep your time differences straight by adding two time zones to your calendars. To display two time zones while you're in Day or Work Week views (which you can select in the Calendar toolbar), click Tools>Options in the menu bar. In the Preferences tab in the Options dialog, click Calendar Options, then click the Time Zone button near the bottom of the dialog. In the Time Zone dialog, check Show an Additional Time Zone and choose the time zone to be displayed from the Time Zone drop-down menu. You can also give a name to your time zones using the Label fields. Click OK when finished, and you're now the master of two time zones.

Power(ful) Point of View

WORKING
WITH
POWERPOINT

I apologize for the fact that I'm a little distracted as I'm writing this. The Tampa Bay Lightning, the "Bolts," are ten minutes and twel...eleven seconds from winning the Stanley

Power(ful)Point of View

working with powerpoint

Cup! Is Tampa the mecca of the sports world or what? If we could only get the Devil Rays (MLB) going, there would be no doubt. The Calgary Flames just scored a point off a power play that should have never happened...BAD CALL! The ref called a bad penalty that set up the point. We're still up with a score of 2 to 1, though. Anyway, PowerPoint is a great application that everybody who creates presentations should use. This chapter will show you how to do all kinds of cool things in PowerPlay, I mean PowerPoint. "Habi" (Nikolai Khabibulin, the goalie) is playing lights-out hockey—we should take this. I'll let you know how it turns out...WE WON! WE WON THE STANLEY CUP! STANLEY'S GETTING A TAN!

CHANGING COLORS

Have you ever found the perfect clip art picture, but couldn't use it because it didn't match the color theme of your presentation? If you have, then you're gonna love this. Insert a clip art image by clicking Insert>Picture>Clip Art, then search for an image that you like, and drag-and-drop the image from the Clip Art task pane onto a slide. Next, double-click the image to open the Format Picture dialog, and in the Picture tab, click the Recolor button, and there it is...the coolest tool in PowerPoint. Using the Recolor Picture dialog, you can change any color in the clip art image. Just look for the image color you want to replace by selecting that color's checkbox under the Original category to the left, then select a new color to replace it using the corresponding color's New drop-down menu. Click OK when finished.

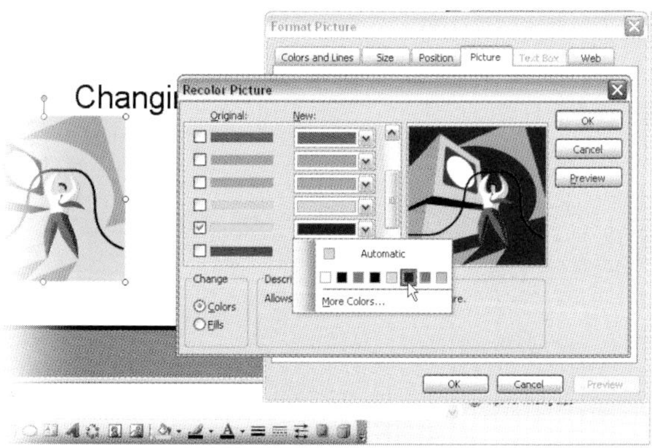

SNAG SLIDES

If you've ever thought it would be great to insert slides from an existing presentation into your current presentation, then you're not alone. This is a great idea and you can have PowerPoint do it for you. Here's how: Navigate in your existing presentation using the Slides tab to where you'd like to insert the new slide, then click Insert>Slides from Files in the menu bar. (*Note:* PowerPoint will insert the slides underneath the slide you're working on.) Under the Find Presentation tab in the Slide Finder dialog, click Browse to locate the presentation that you want to snag a slide from. When you find the presentation and click Open, check out the Select Slide window in the dialog. There are all of your slides. Now simply click the slide(s) to insert, and click Insert. The slide(s) now appears in your current presentation...sweet!

DELIVER THE PACKAGE

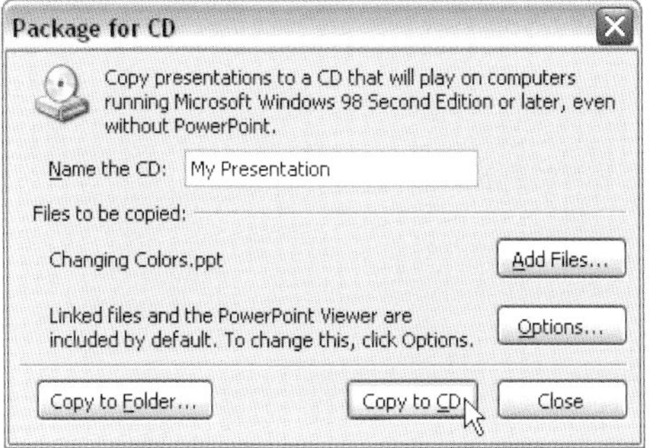

PowerPoint's new Package for CD feature is great for distributing corporate presentations to customers; sending animated holiday greetings to family, friends, and associates; and even for storing (backing up) your presentations. To package your presentation to CD, click File>Package for CD in the menu bar. Follow the Package for CD dialog to give your presentation a name, add files to the CD, and choose additional options to save with your presentation. Click the Add Files button to add any media files included in your presentation. Click the Options button to include the PowerPoint Viewer (which allows the viewer who doesn't have PowerPoint to play a presentation), play the presentations automatically when the CD is inserted, and to embed TrueType fonts. In the Options dialog, you can even password protect the presentation if it contains sensitive information. When you're finished packaging your presentation, click Copy to CD, and PowerPoint will prompt you to insert a blank CD (if you haven't already done so) and will begin copying your presentation to a CD.

BEGIN OR END IN A FLASH

While in Slide Show view (View>Slide Show or press F5), you can quickly jump to the end (last slide) of your presentation by pressing the End key on your keyboard. You can also jump back to the beginning (first slide) of your presentation by pressing the Home key on your keyboard.

TAB A BULLET

If you need to insert a Tab character into a bulleted list, don't press the Tab key—it won't work. Instead press Control-Tab on your keyboard. This will insert the Tab character without messing with your bulleted list.

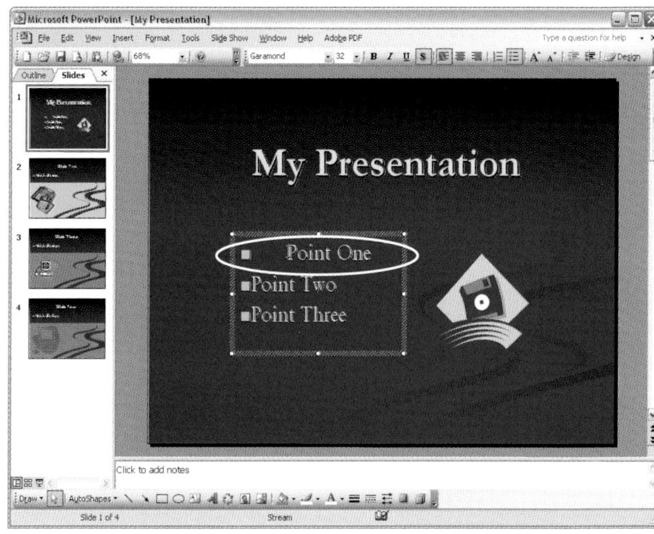

SHIFT TO SLIDE MASTER

The only thing that could make the Slide Master better is if we could access it more quickly. Fortunately, we can by using this little trick: To quickly change to PowerPoint's Slide Master view, Shift-click the Normal View button beneath the Slides pane. This changes Normal view to Slide Master View. Use the same technique for the other views' buttons for additional view options. Hey, and keep the fun going by also pressing Shift-Control and clicking the view buttons for even more options.

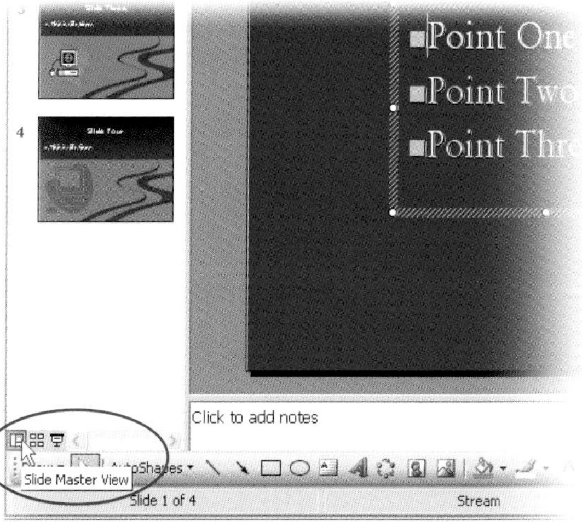

MASTER YOUR PRESENTATION

When designing a presentation that has several repeating objects, such as your company logo, located in the same positions, use the Slide Master to insert them. This ensures that the look of your presentation is consistent and objects are always placed in the same spot on each slide. Besides, if you need to move your logo, moving it on the Slide Master will move it to the exact same spot on each slide simultaneously. To do this, click View>Master>Slide Master. Next, click Insert>Picture>From File (or click Insert>Picture>Clip Art, as I did here). Use the Insert Picture dialog to browse for your logo on your hard drive, clicking Insert to place the logo (or just drag-and-drop a clip art image onto your document). Position the image wherever you'd like. Now click the Close Master View button in the Slide Master View toolbar, and you can see that your logo appears in the same location on each slide.

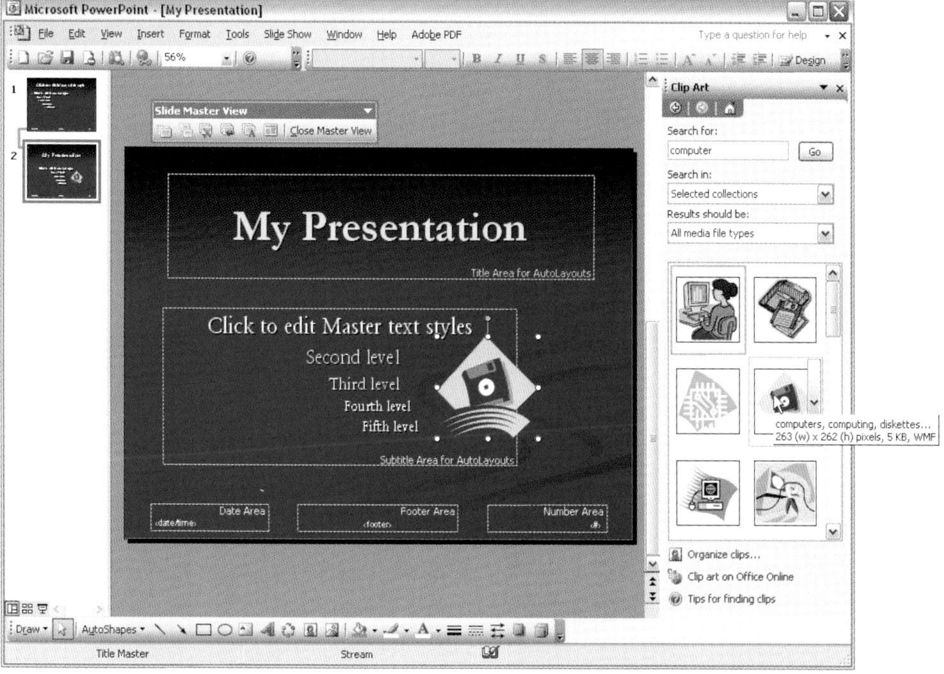

DON'T PRINT, YOU'RE HIDDEN

I often print my presentation, usually just for a different visual perspective, but I don't always need to print all of the slides to accomplish this. So, I hide the slides that I don't want to print. To hide slides, right-click any slide in the Slides tab and click Hide Slide in the shortcut menu. Now before you print the presentation (File>Print), be sure to uncheck Print Hidden Slides in the bottom right-hand corner of the Print dialog, then click OK.

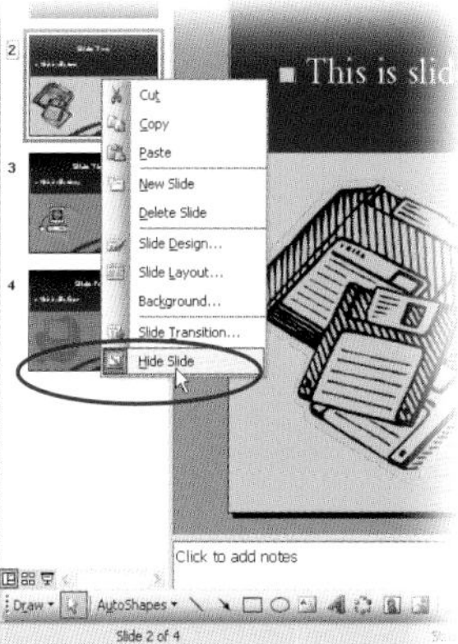

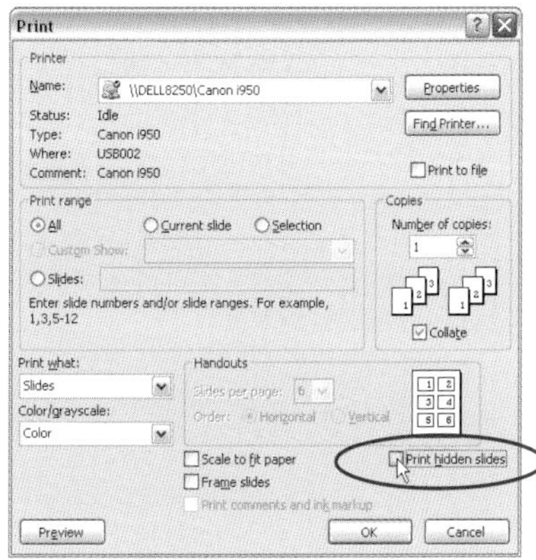

QUICK COPY

To quickly copy a slide in PowerPoint, drag-and-drop any slide within the Slides pane using your right mouse button. When you drop the slide where you want to place the copy, choose Copy from the shortcut menu. You've just copied a slide.

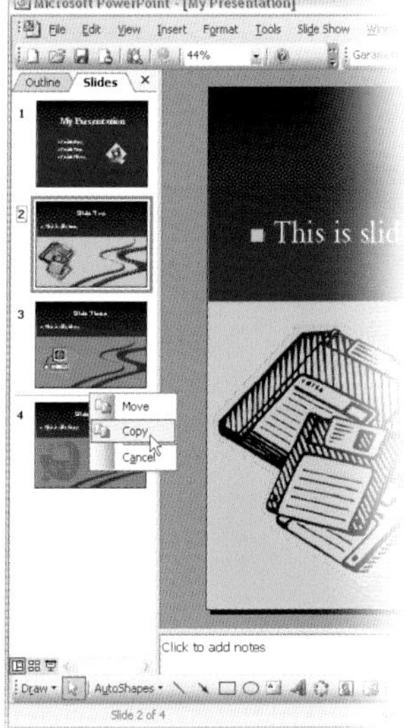

WEB IT

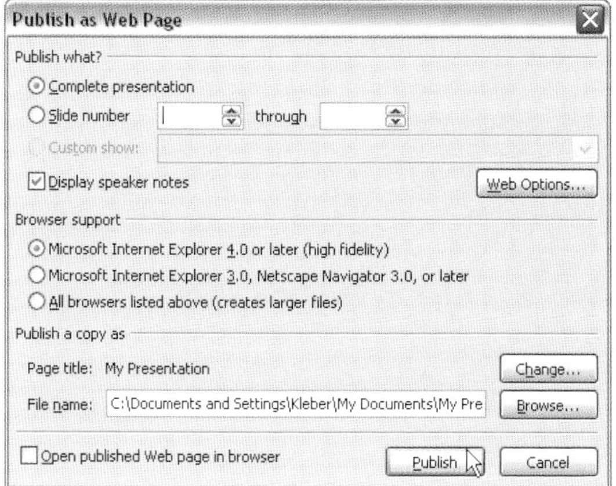

If you need to share your PowerPoint presentation on the Web, then you're in luck—PowerPoint makes it easy. When you're ready to share your presentation, click File>Save as Web Page in the menu bar, then click the Publish button on the Save As dialog. Next, choose whether to publish the entire presentation or only certain slides, whether to display speaker notes (if any), which browser to support, and where to save your file. When finished, click Publish and your presentation is packaged and ready to post to the Web.

DON'T FORGET TO EMBED

Don't assume when you share your presentations that others will have the same fonts installed on their computers that you've used in your presentation. To ensure that others view your presentation as you've intended and with the fonts you've used, you'll want to embed your fonts when you save. To do this, click File>Save As in the menu bar, then click Tools>Save Options on the Save As dialog. Next, check Embed TrueType Fonts in the Save Options dialog and click OK. Now your fonts will be included with your presentation.

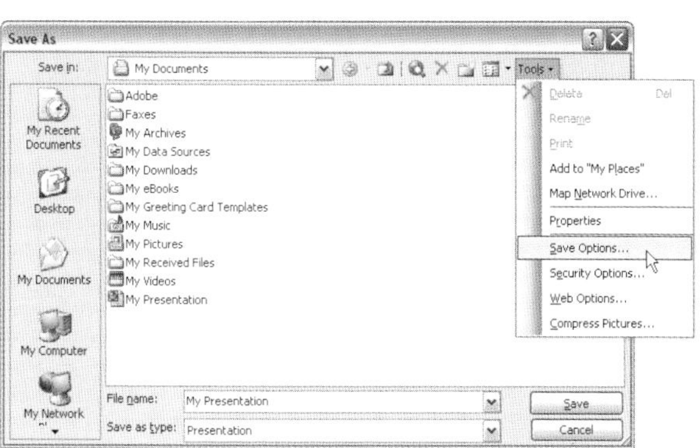

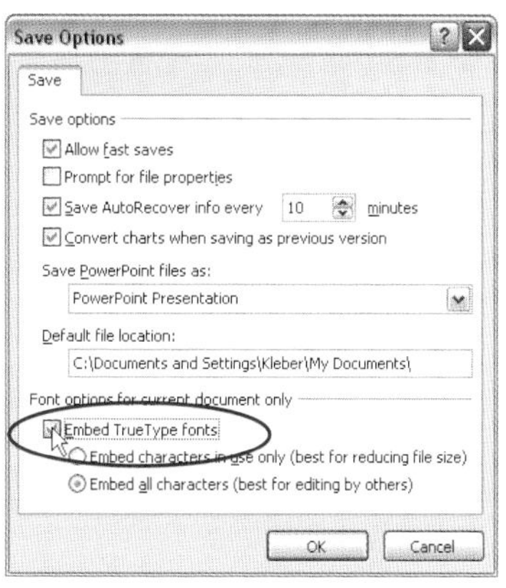

THAT'S PERFECT!

The two most common shapes drawn in PowerPoint are an oval and a rectangle. The PowerPoint developers knew this—that's why each shape has its own shape button on the Drawing toolbar. Now, ovals and rectangles are great, but what I really need are perfect circle and square buttons. If you went looking, you might think PowerPoint doesn't have them, but they're there: You just have to know how to access them. Make sure the Drawing toolbar is open by right-clicking any toolbar or menu and clicking Drawing. Press-and-hold the Shift key on your keyboard while drawing with the Oval tool to create a perfect circle (as I did here). Press-and-hold the Shift key while drawing with the Rectangle tool to create a perfect square. You can also use the Shift-key trick to create perfectly straight lines in PowerPoint using the Line tool.

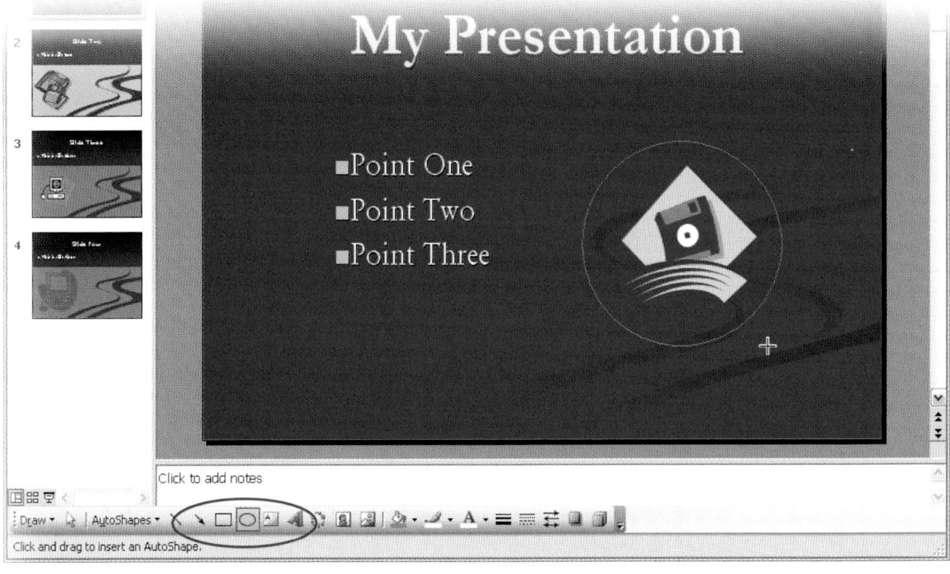

GLOBAL FONT REPLACEMENT

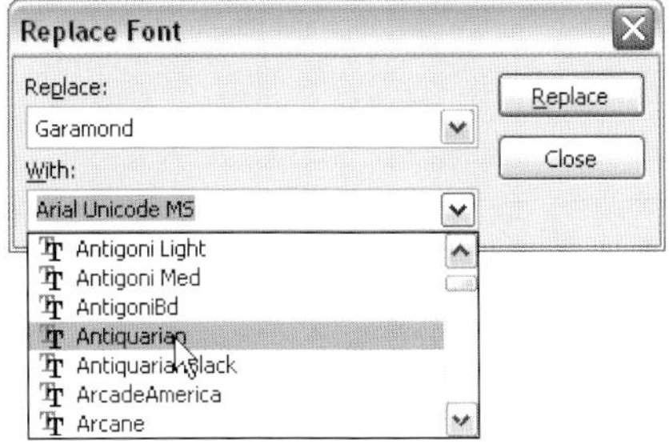

We all make bad judgment calls when it comes to fonts, and realizing that Comic Sans just won't cut it for your corporate presentation can be a painful experience, especially when faced with the prospect of manually changing the font throughout your entire presentation. This is just bad. To quickly fix your font disaster, click Format>Replace Fonts in the menu bar. This opens the Replace Font dialog. Use the Replace drop-down menu to select the font you want to change in your document, then choose the replacement font using the With drop-down menu. Click Replace when finished and all of the selected fonts are instantly changed, then click Close.

SUPER-FAST SHAPES

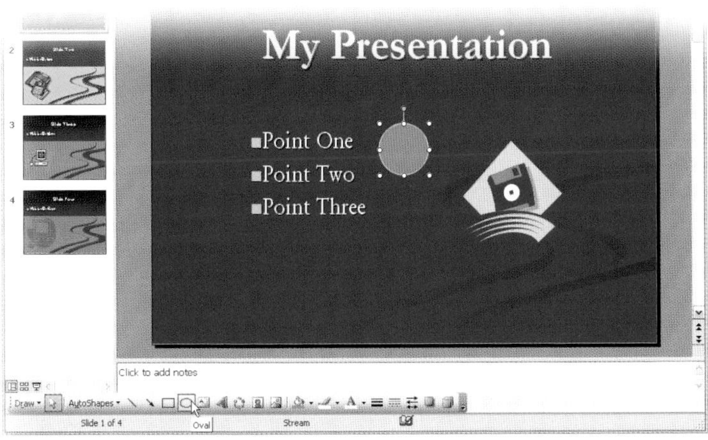

When creating shapes, most PowerPoint users draw a shape manually (using their mouse) and then use the shape's resize handles to adjust its size and positioning. Well, there's a faster way to create shapes: Press-and-hold the Control key on your keyboard, then simply click the shape tool's button in the Drawing toolbar (I Control-clicked the Oval button). This will instantly create the shape and place it in the center of your slide. Now, go ahead and resize and reposition your shape.

 MORE AND MORE SHAPES MADE EASY

If you need to draw the same shape multiple times, first double-click any shape's button on the Drawing toolbar before you begin (I chose the Rectangle tool in this example). Double-clicking the button will leave it active, meaning that you can continue to draw using that shape until your hand cramps up and you black out from exhaustion. When you come to, click the shape button once more to deactivate it.

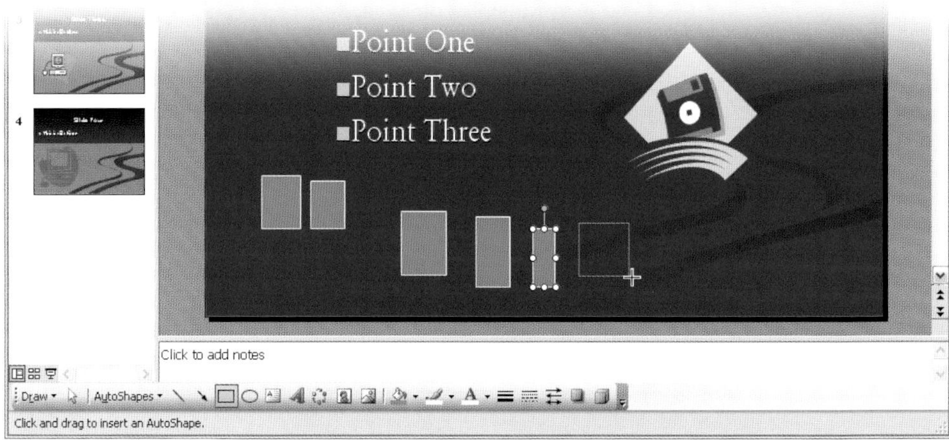

PERFECTLY SPACED SHAPES

Spacing shapes evenly can be a pretty tricky proposition. I once had 15 objects to line up—it took me three hours and a shot of Demerol and they still weren't quite right. So, I took some more Demerol, shut down my computer, and became a pharmaceutical salesman (kidding). Actually, I found a better way to line up my shapes. Click any shape tool and draw your shape, then press Control-D on your keyboard to duplicate the shape. Drag the duplicated shape to the exact spacing for your additional shapes, then press Control-D again and again to space them exactly the same distance apart.

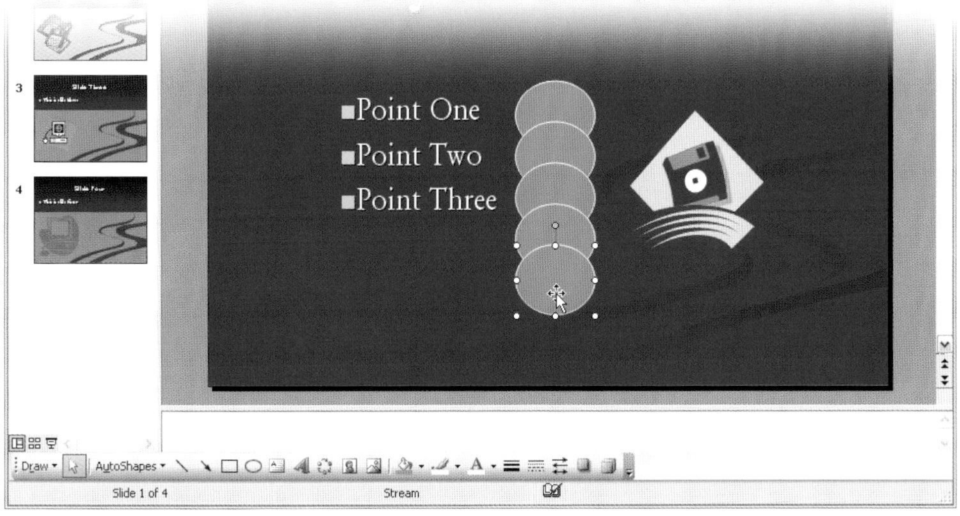

GIVE ME MORE GUIDES

When creating presentations, I use several guides to help lay out my slide's objects. You can view guides by pressing Control-G on your keyboard while you're in Normal view (View>Normal). Next, check "Display drawing guides on screen" in the Grid and Guides dialog, and uncheck any Snap To or Grid Settings options if you don't want to display a grid, then click OK. This will display two intersecting guides on your slides, which is great, but I need more. To create additional guides, press-and-hold the Control key on your keyboard while dragging an existing guide. Release your mouse button to drop the new guide into place. Repeat this to create as many guides as you want. To delete a guide, drag-and-drop it off any edge of your slide.

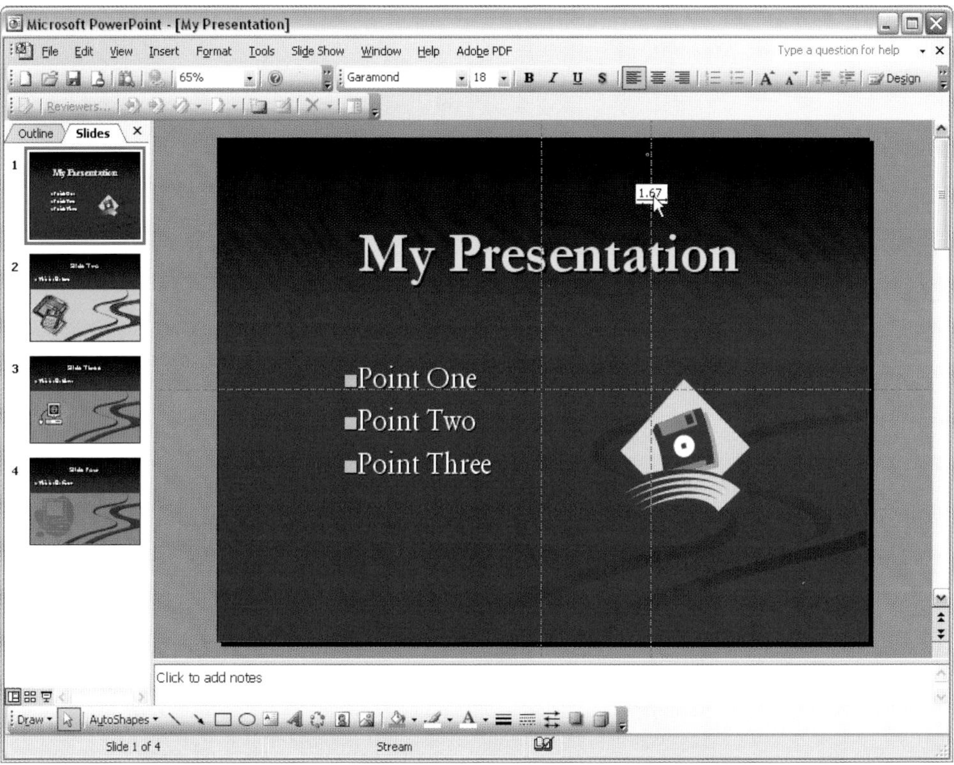

PICTURE THIS!

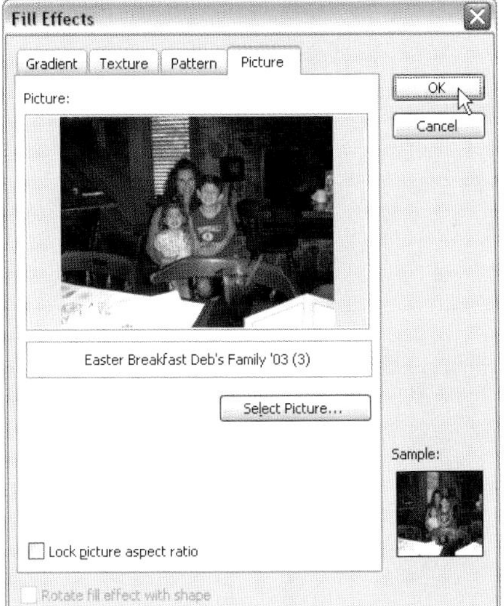

Pictures say a lot, and if you want to say a whole lot, then use one as the background for your entire presentation or individual slides. Here's how: Right-click any blank space on a slide and click Background in the shortcut menu. Next, click the drop-down menu under Background Fill and click Fill Effects. Then click the Picture tab in the Fill Effects dialog and click the Select Picture button. Browse your hard drive to locate your picture, click Insert, and then click OK in the Fill Effects dialog. Now, in the Background dialog, click Apply to All to apply the picture to every slide in your presentation or click Apply to affect only the slide you're currently working on.

OPTIONS ARE GREAT!

I'm an options kind of guy…I need 'em and lots of 'em, because I'm never completely sure what I'm doing. I found a great option in PowerPoint that adds real flexibility when designing presentations. Try this: View your presentation in Slide Show view by clicking View>Slide Show in the menu bar or simply press F5 on your keyboard. Next, right-click anywhere on the current slide and check out all of the great options available in the shortcut menu. You can navigate your presentation, change the appearance of your screen, jump to different slides (as shown here), and change your mouse pointer to draw or highlight objects. I love options!

WORD PRESENTATIONS?

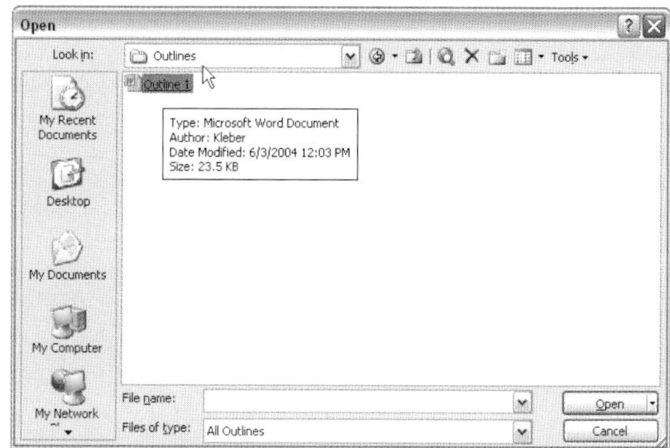

The truly great thing about Office is how everything works so amazingly well together. For example, did you know that you could convert a Word outline into a PowerPoint presentation? Yep, you sure can. To do this, you first must have created an outline in Word using Word's headings in the Styles and Formatting task pane (see Word Help for formatting a document if you need assistance). PowerPoint interprets Word's Heading 1 paragraph style as an individual slide, Heading 2 as a top-level bullet point, and Heading 3 as a second-level bullet point. So, once you've set up your outline in Word, launch PowerPoint, click File>Open in the menu bar, and then choose All Outlines in the Files of Type drop-down menu in the Open dialog. Next, browse your hard drive for the outline you created in Word, click Open, and PowerPoint opens the outline and converts it into a presentation.

LINK 'EM

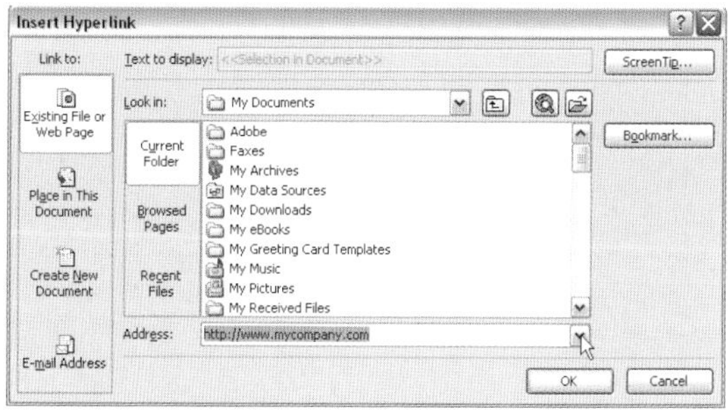

PowerPoint has the capability to create hyperlinks from just about any object to just about anything, and one great use for this is to launch a webpage during your presentation. Here's an example: You're giving a presentation and at a certain point you'd like to open your Web browser (this requires an active Internet connection) to visit your corporate website, provide additional information, or to highlight services. Just select the text or object that you want to link from and press Control-K to open the Insert Hyperlink dialog. Next, type the URL in the Address field at the bottom of the dialog and click OK. You can test your hyperlink in Slide Show view by pressing F5 on the keyboard. Now, click the hyperlink to launch your Web browser, which will launch your website.

SIZE DOWN

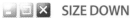

By default, if you open multiple presentations, they're displayed in Normal view, one on top of the other, forcing you to close each presentation to view the others—that bites! I want to view all of my open presentations at once...and you can. Here's how: First, open several presentations (File>Open), then press Control-F5 on your keyboard. This sizes down all of your presentations within the PowerPoint window. Now maximize any presentation you want. Repeat this keyboard shortcut to quickly minimize any open presentation.

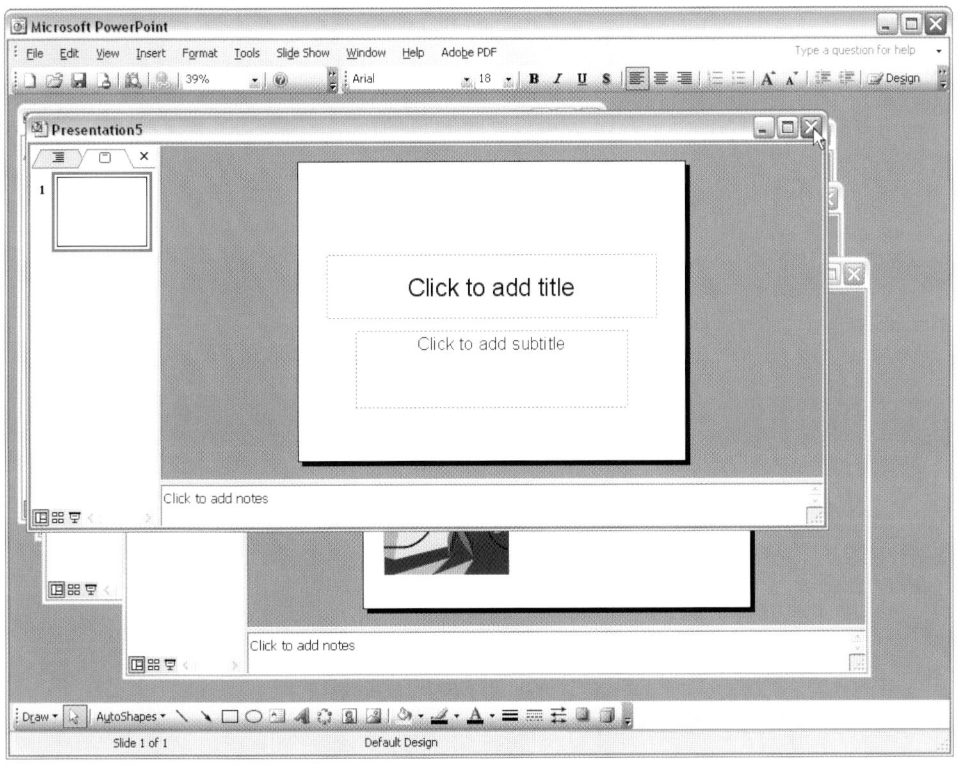

TAKE A PICTURE

Here's a really slick trick for saving an entire slide as a graphic. It's great for when you need to create screen shots of your presentations to use on the Web. First, switch your view to Notes Page by clicking View>Notes Page in the menu bar, then right-click anywhere on the slide and click Copy in the shortcut menu. Now switch back to Normal view (View>Normal), right-click anywhere on a slide, and click Paste in the shortcut menu. Next, right-click the pasted picture and click Save as Picture in the shortcut menu. Using the Save as Picture dialog, select a location to save the picture on your hard drive and select your image's format using the Save as Type drop-down menu (e.g., JPEG or GIF for the Web), then click Save.

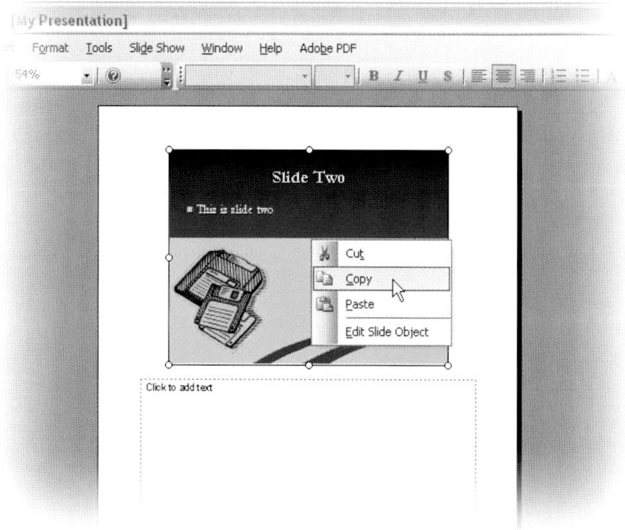

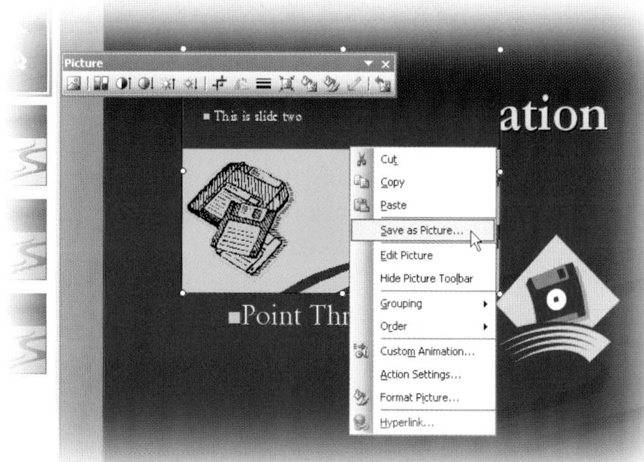

CONTROL THE SHADOWS

Shadowed text just looks cool! I personally think all text should have a drop shadow, but that's just me. Unfortunately, PowerPoint's default text shadowing isn't great, but that doesn't mean you shouldn't use drop shadows for your text—you just have to find a better way. To apply drop shadows to text, never use the text shadow formatting command. Instead, do this: Select the text you'd like to add a drop shadow to, click the Shadow Style button on the Drawing toolbar, then click Shadow Settings to display the Shadow Settings toolbar, and click any Nudge Shadow button to create a drop shadow for your text. Now you have complete control over your drop shadow: You can move the shadow in any direction by clicking the Nudge Shadow buttons or give it any color you like by pressing the Shadow Color button in the Shadow Settings toolbar.

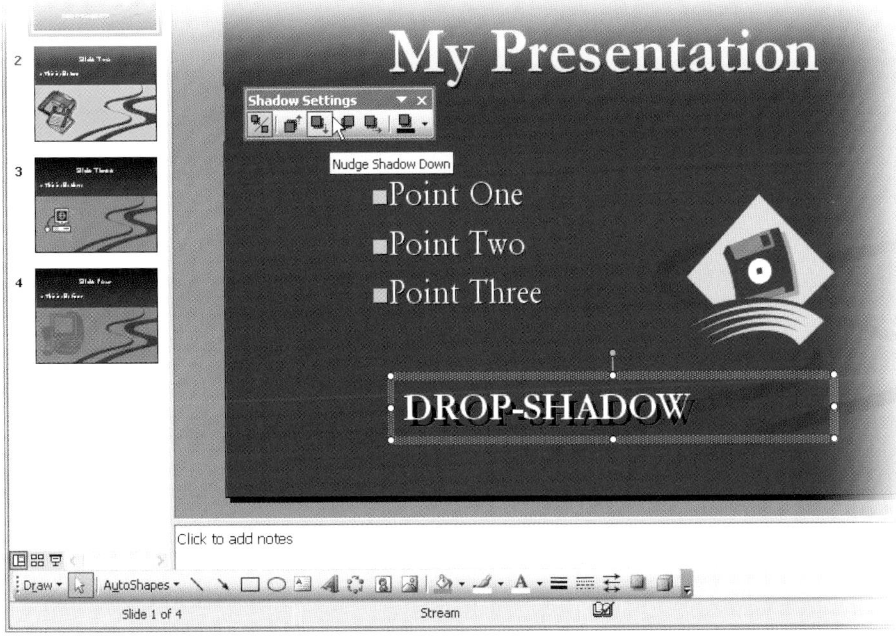

SUPER-FAST SYMBOLS

There are three characters that you're going to use repeatedly in presentations, especially when giving corporate presentations: They're the ©, ™, and ® symbols. Fortunately, there are quick keyboard shortcuts for inserting each of them. Next time you need to use one of these symbols, try these shortcuts: Type "(c)" for ©, "(tm)" for ™, and "(r)" for ® (all without the quote marks). PowerPoint will immediately replace the text with the symbols.

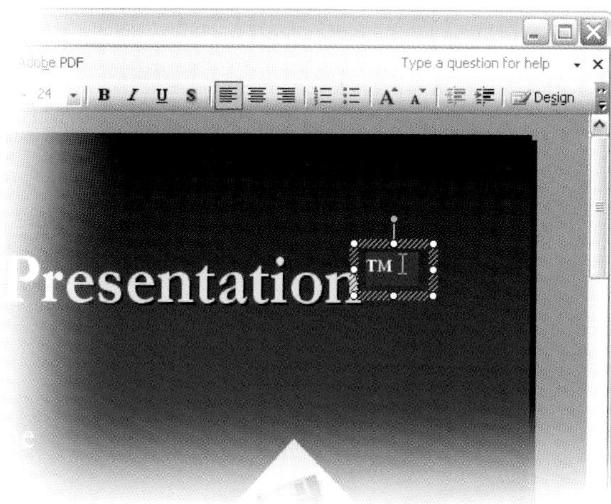

KIOSK COOL

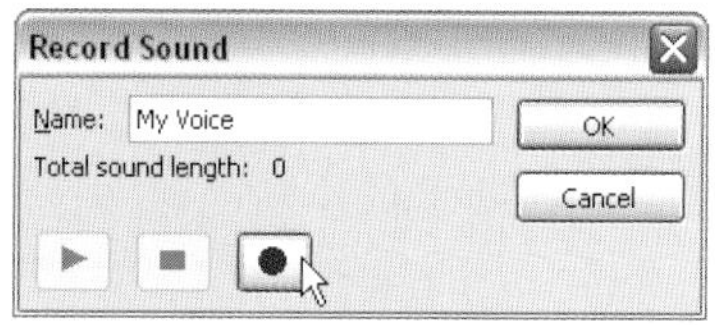

Presentations don't have to always be in person. You can create a self-running presentation, complete with voice recordings—ideal for kiosk presentations. To add voice recordings to your presentation, select the slide to which you want to add voice recordings, then click Insert>Movies and Sounds>Record Sound in the menu bar. Name your recording in the Name field, then click the Record button (the button with a red circle) in the Record Sound dialog. When finished, click the Stop button, then click OK. A small speaker icon will appear on your slide. To preview your recording, double-click the speaker icon on the slide in Normal view (View>Normal) or right-click the icon for more options.

 MIX IT UP

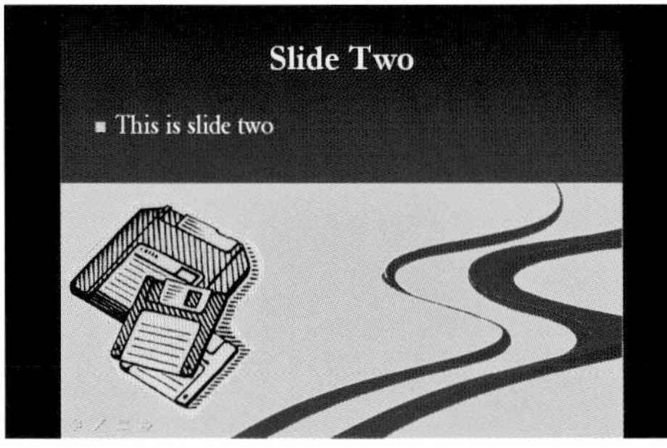

If you're giving a presentation and need to skip ahead to a slide or jump back to a previous slide, this is how to do it—all the while looking like a PowerPoint pro: While you're in Slide Show view (press F5), type the number of the slide that you want to open (making sure that the Number Lock key is on), then press Enter on your keyboard. This opens the slide, making you look magical and even a little better looking. You can of course always right-click any slide during a presentation and click Go to Slide and select your slide's number on the shortcut menu, but that won't look magical or better looking at all.

 CAN'T MISS THAT LOGO

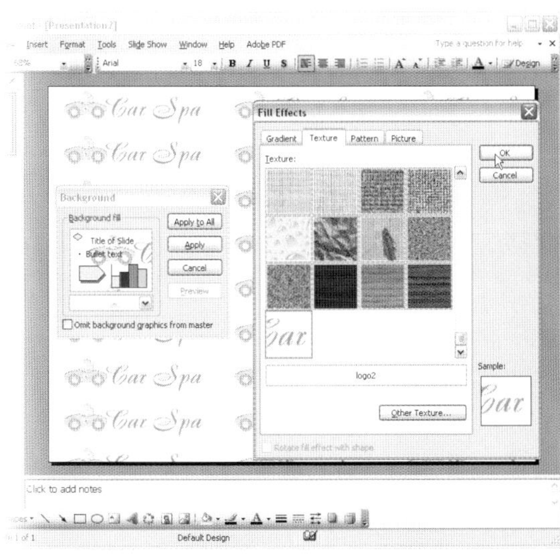

If you want people to remember your company logo, put it where they can't miss it: Tile it on the background of your presentation. To do this, right-click your slide and click Background on the shortcut menu, then click the drop-down menu under Background Fill and click Fill Effects. Next, click the Texture tab on the Fill Effects dialog and click Other Texture. Now browse your hard drive for your logo, click Insert, and then OK on the Fill Effects dialog. Now, click Apply to All to tile your logo on every slide in your presentation or click Apply to add your logo to the current slide only. Now that's a hard-to-miss logo.

IT'S GOOD TO TAKE NOTES

When giving an informational presentation, you may find it useful to provide handouts for note-taking. While you can create handouts (aka: speaker's notes) in PowerPoint, there's a better option: Export your handouts to Word, which gives you greater control of the handout's formatting and design. To do this, open the PowerPoint presentation for which you want to create handouts, then click File>Send To>Microsoft Office Word. Select the page layout for your notes ("Blank lines next to slides" works best for note-taking), then click OK in the dialog. Word will launch, showing your slides in tables, which you can quickly edit and print (File>Print).

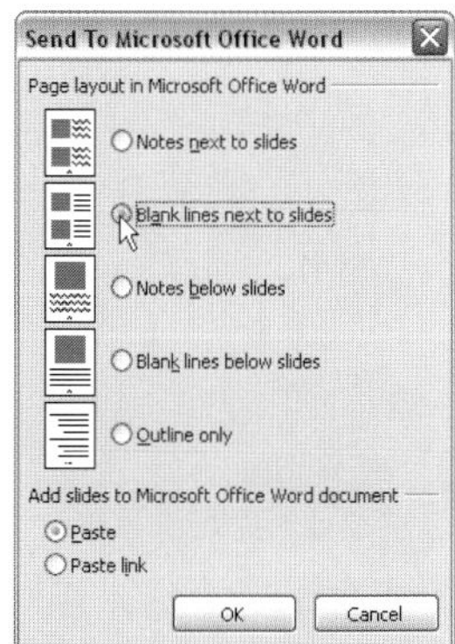

GIDDYAP

You can save a PowerPoint presentation so that it starts automatically when opened, bypassing the program window. This only works when you haven't launched PowerPoint yet. First, save your presentation as a PowerPoint Show (.pps). Click File>Save As in the menu bar, select PowerPoint Show from the Save as Type drop-down menu on the Save As dialog, and then click Save. Now, whenever you double-click the document's icon to open the presentation, it will automatically launch PowerPoint and begin to play.

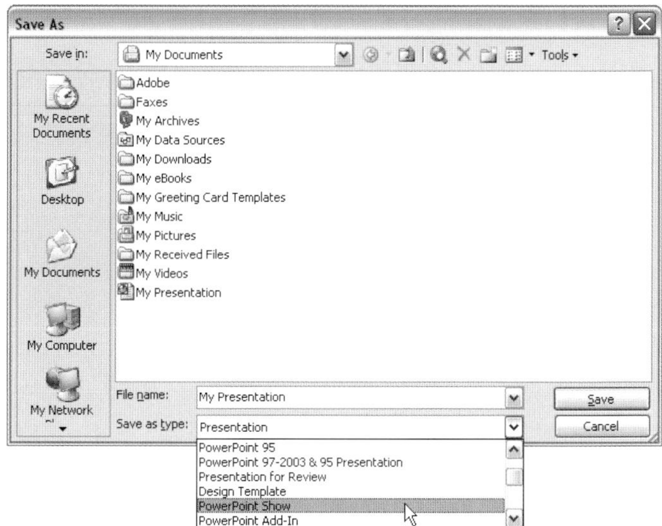

DON'T JUST FLIP, TRANSITION

Don't just flip slides, add a little flair to your presentations with transitions. To add a transition to any slide, make sure you're in Normal view (View>Normal), then right-click a slide in the Slides tab, and click Slide Transition in the shortcut menu. This opens the Slide Transition task pane. Next, choose a transition from the list. Select the transition's speed (how quickly it displays) by using the Speed drop-down menu, then select any sound to accompany the transition in the Sound drop-down menu. To apply the transition to just the selected slide, simply close the Slide Transition task pane; to apply the transition to all slides, click the Apply to All Slides button. Click the Play button to preview your transitions.

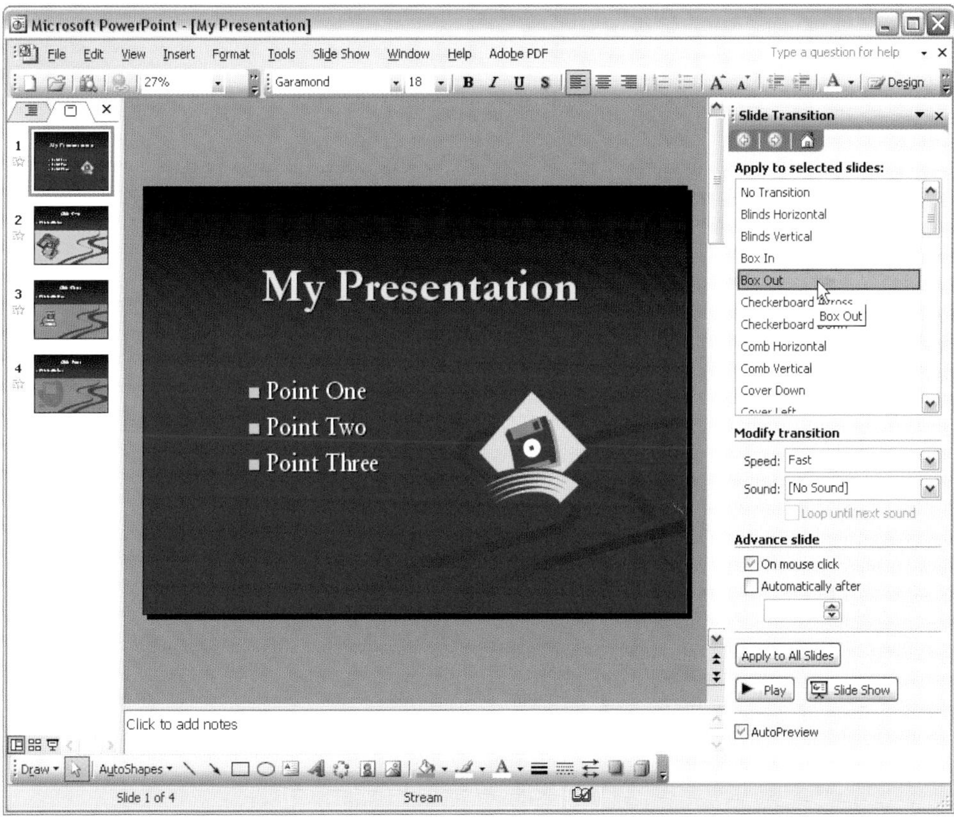

PIXEL PUSHING

Do you need to move your object a single pixel or just 1/12th of an inch? When you need to be exact, you need to be exact, and when you need to be that exact, remember this: By default, you can nudge your objects 1/12th of an inch—with or without the rulers visible (View>Ruler)—by using the arrow keys on your keyboard. But if you live in a pixel world, press-and-hold the Control key, then press the Left or Right Arrow keys to move your object a single pixel in either direction (as I did here with the computer logo).

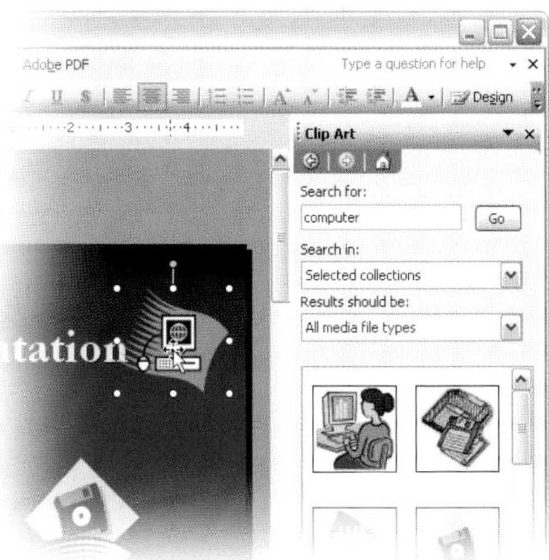

POWER ALBUMS

PowerPoint is perfect for sharing your digital photo albums. What, you haven't used PowerPoint to create digital photo albums and then sent them to your family and friends? I'm shocked! Well, you will now, once you learn how to do it. Click Insert>Picture>New Photo Album in the menu bar, which opens the Photo Album dialog. Next, click File/Disk to browse your hard drive or click Scanner/Camera to import your pictures from a digital camera or scanner. Continue to click File/Disk to insert all of your images, then choose your album layout options from the Picture Layout drop-down menu, and click Create when finished. PowerPoint creates your photo album and lays it out in a new presentation window. To update your album, click Format>Photo Album in the menu bar.

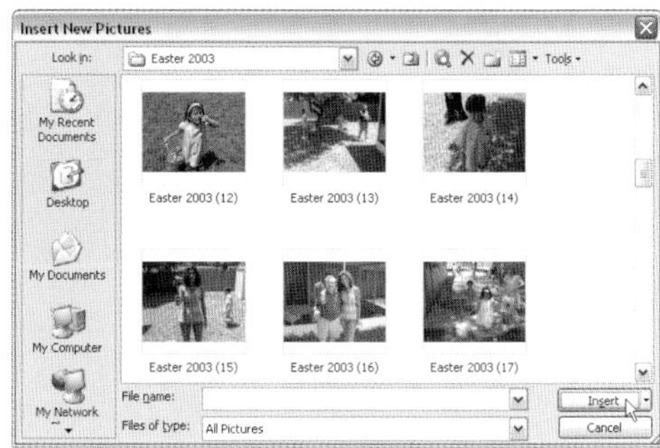

SUMMARY SLIDE

To create a summary slide of your PowerPoint presentation, Control-click to select the slides in the Slides pane that you want to include in your summary, then press Alt-Shift-S on your keyboard. This will create a summary slide and place it at the top of the slide order. Creating a summary slide can be used effectively to highlight topics that will be covered during your presentation or to recap your presentation at the closing.

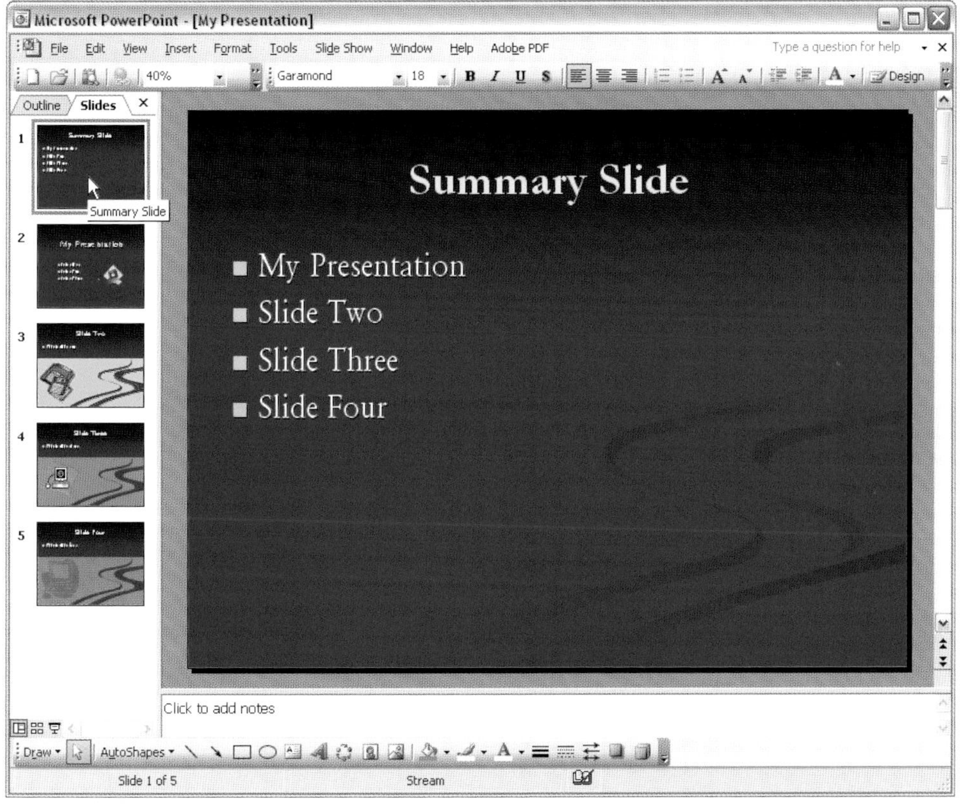

 BLACKOUT

There will be times during a presentation when you'll want to "black out" your display—useful before beginning a presentation or when pausing to answer questions. To black out your display while in Slide Show view (press F5), press the "b" key on your keyboard. Press the "b" key again to show your display again.

 OBJECTS TOO SMALL?

We probably all have too much stress in our lives, and selecting objects in PowerPoint really shouldn't push anyone into having a psychotic episode, but trying to select small objects that are buried by a pile of other objects can just about do that. Here's a tip to help you avoid freaking out at your desk. First, press the Escape (Esc) key on your keyboard to ensure that nothing is selected. Next, repeatedly press the Tab key to jump from object to object until you've selected the freakishly small object, then press the Backspace key to delete it. You really shouldn't be using freakishly small objects anyway.

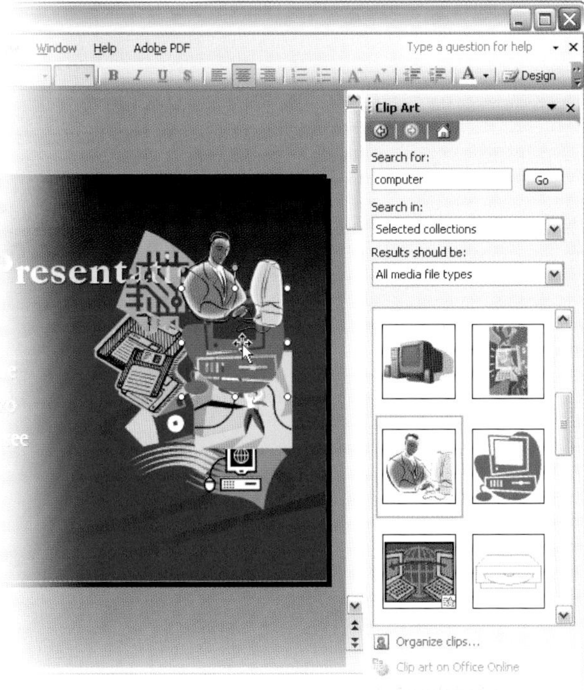

GIVE CREDIT

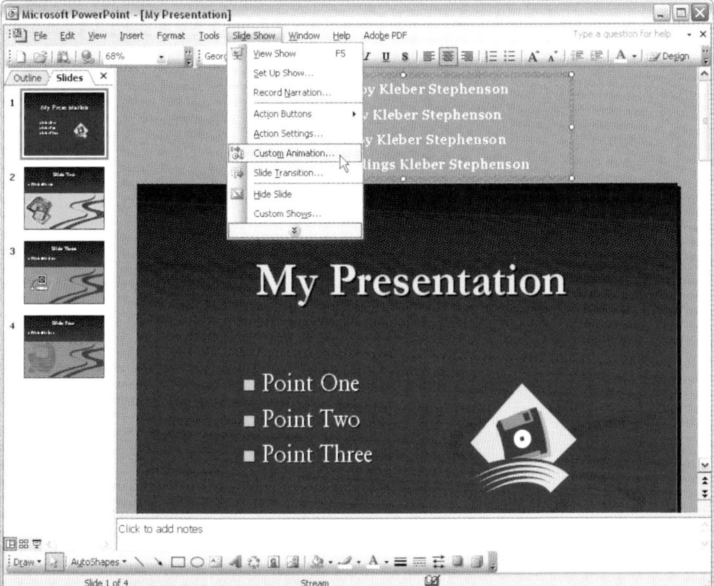

Want to throw in some closing credits? Here's how: Create a text box on your final slide by selecting your slide in the Slides tab and clicking Insert>Text Box in the menu bar. Click-and-drag to create your text box and then type your credits (names and titles). Next, select the text box and drag it off the top of the slide. Now, click Slide Show>Custom Animation in the menu bar and, with the text box still selected, click the Add Effect drop-down menu in the Custom Animation task pane. Now click Entrance>More Effects and select Crawl In, then click OK. Click Play to preview your credits. To edit your effect, click the down-facing arrow next to your effect in the Custom Animation task pane and choose Effect Options in the shortcut menu. *Note:* You may need to change the color of your text to ensure that it doesn't blend in with your slide's background by selecting the text and clicking the Font Color button in the Formatting toolbar.

CAN YOU SPELL BUSINESS?

There's nothing worse than poor spelling in a presentation. Honestly, if you can't spell business, then you're probably not going to get mine. So, do yourself a favor and always check your spelling before you give a presentation. You have no excuse not to—PowerPoint makes it easy. Press F7 on the keyboard and PowerPoint will check the spelling on each slide. If any misspellings are found, PowerPoint will open the slide, launch the Spelling dialog, and highlight the incorrect text so you can fix it.

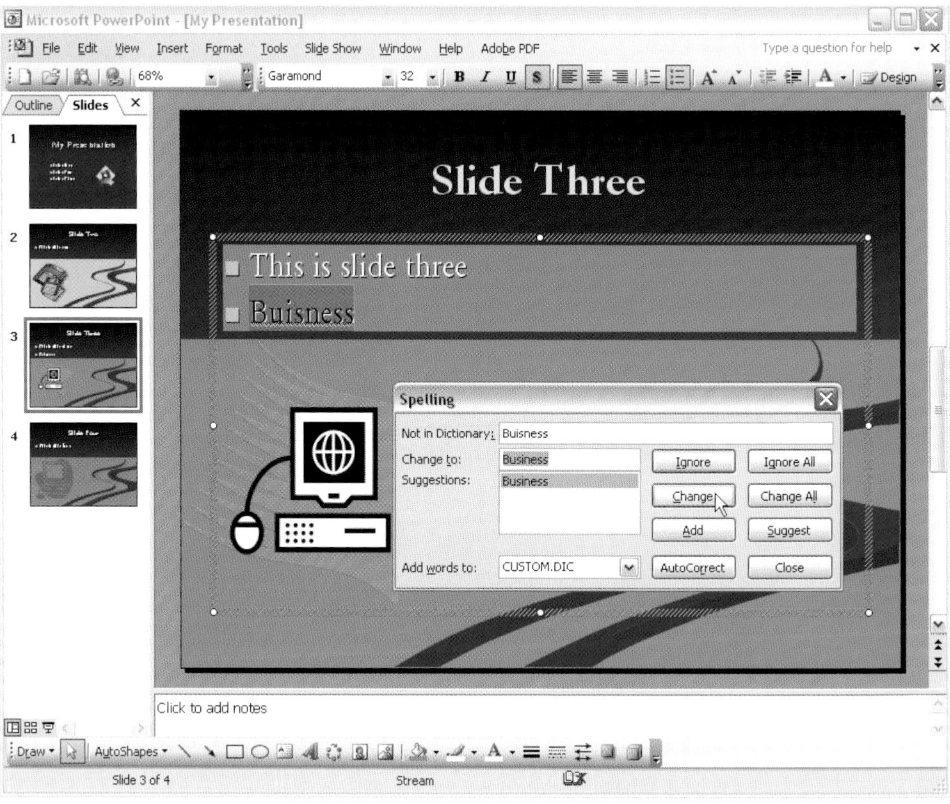

BECOME A TEMPLATE DESIGNER

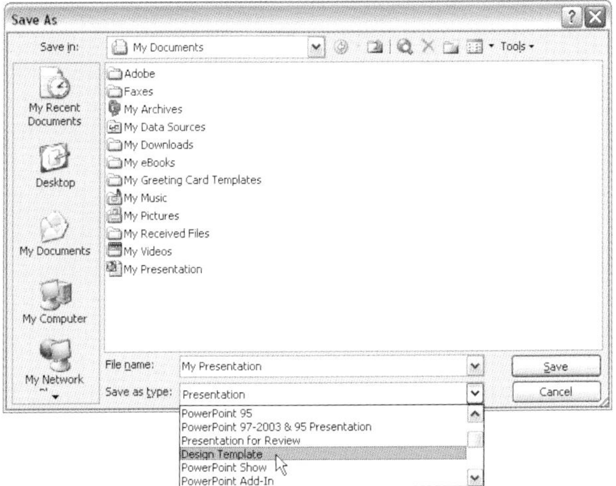

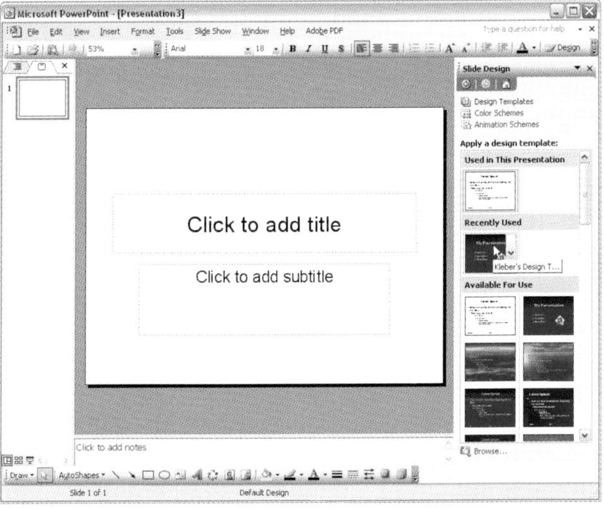

Creating really good presentations takes time and effort, and once you've completed your work of art, be sure to put it to good use by making it into a design template so you can use it again. To save your presentation as a template, click File>Save As in the menu bar, select Design Template from the Save as Type drop-down menu in the Save As dialog, then click Save. To use your design template, click File>New in the menu bar, then click the From Design Template link on the New Presentation task pane. Your saved templates will appear at the top of the Available for Use category in the Slide Design task pane. Click your template icon to apply it to your new presentation. *Note:* If your design template doesn't show up in the Slide Design task pane, try re-launching PowerPoint.

DON'T CUT, CROP INSTEAD

Sometimes the whole picture just won't do; maybe you just want to emphasize a portion of a picture. Well, you can hide a portion of a picture in PowerPoint by using the Crop tool. To crop a picture, first select the object and then click the Crop button in the Picture toolbar. (If you don't see the Picture toolbar, right-click any toolbar or menu and click Picture.) Next, click-and-drag any resize handle to crop the picture. If you crop too much of your picture, don't worry, it's not deleted. Simply drag the handle out while using the Crop tool to reveal cropped portions of the picture.

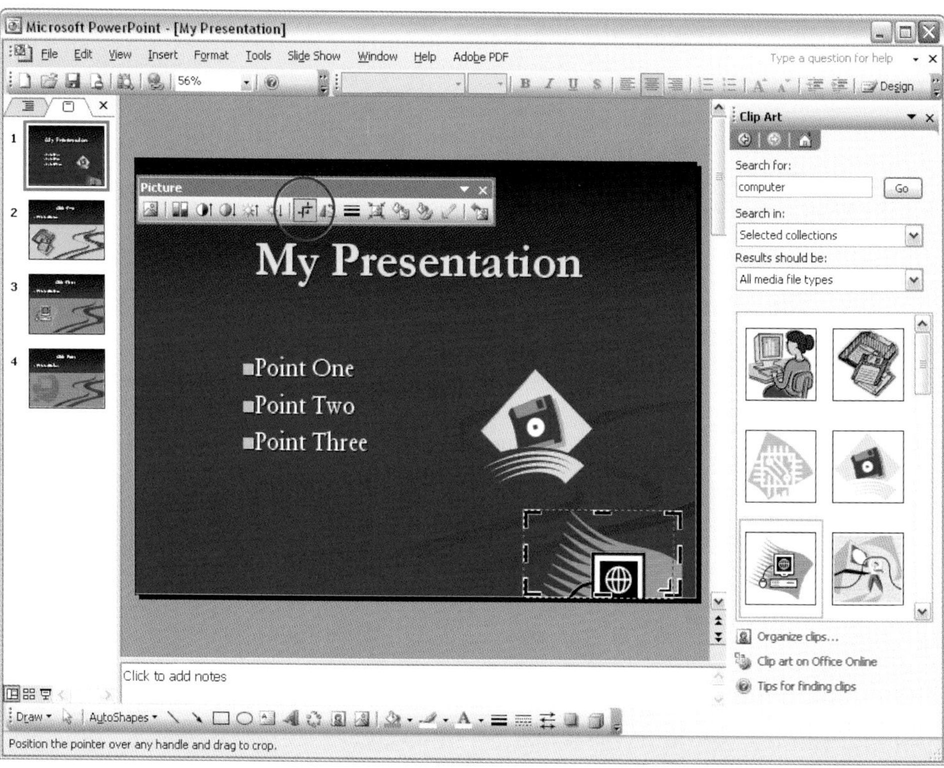

WE'RE CONNECTED

When I was a kid, I loved to play connect-the-dots—actually, I rocked at connect-the-dots. If there had been a connect-the-dots circuit, I'd have a different career. Unfortunately, not everyone shares my love of dots, but I'm pretty sure there's a fellow connect-the-dotter on the Office development team, because they dedicated an entire AutoShapes collection to connecting things. If you have two or more objects that you'd like to connect in PowerPoint—such as a text box to a graphic—do this: Click AutoShapes>Connectors in the Drawing toolbar to select a style for your connector line. Next, place your mouse pointer over one of the objects and click any anchor point that you'd like to connect to. Then, move your mouse pointer to the second object and click any anchor point to create the connector line. You can customize your connector line by double-clicking on the line (avoiding the line's anchor points) to open the Format AutoShape dialog.

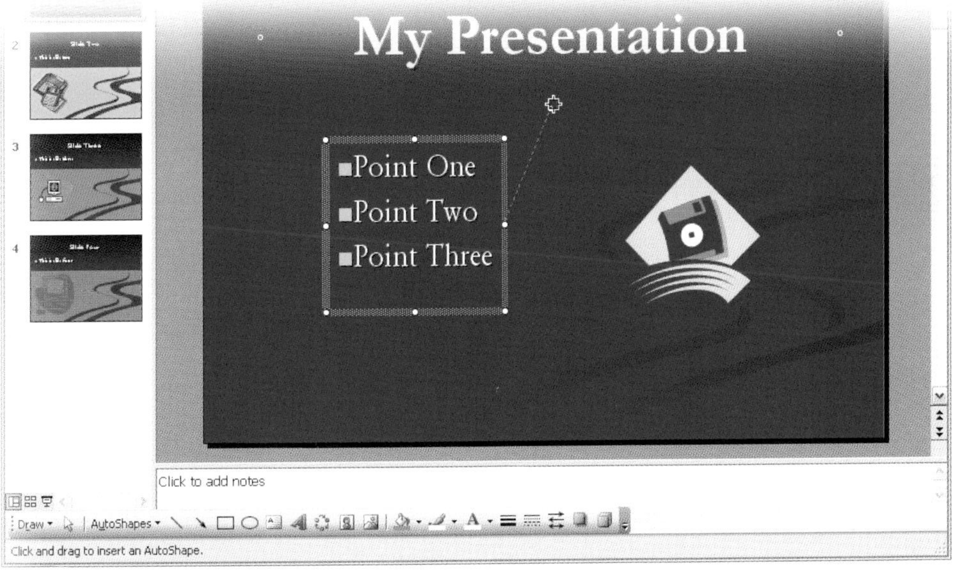

I'D LIKE TO COMMENT

Adding comments to your presentations is a perfect way to remind yourself of ideas or to offer suggestions when designing a presentation with others. To insert a comment, first make certain you're in Normal view by clicking View>Normal in the menu bar, then click Insert>Comment. This will insert a comment into your slide. Type your comments in the text box, then click anywhere outside the comment box to close it. Simply click the comment's icon to view it again. To delete a comment, right-click the comment's icon and click Delete in the shortcut menu.

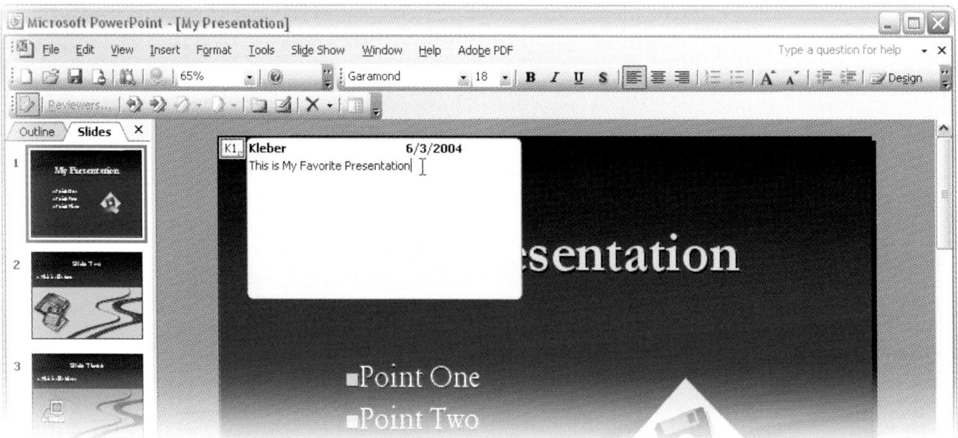

QUICKLY ANIMATE OBJECTS

Adding animations to text and objects is what PowerPoint is all about. Yep, it's all about the animations. To add animations to just about anything (text blocks, graphics, shapes, etc.), first select the object, then right-click it and click Custom Animation in the shortcut menu. Now click the Add Effect drop-down menu in the Custom Animation task pane to choose an effect. PowerPoint will preview the effect when the AutoPreview checkbox is selected. When finished, click Play at the bottom of the Custom Animation task pane to preview your animation.

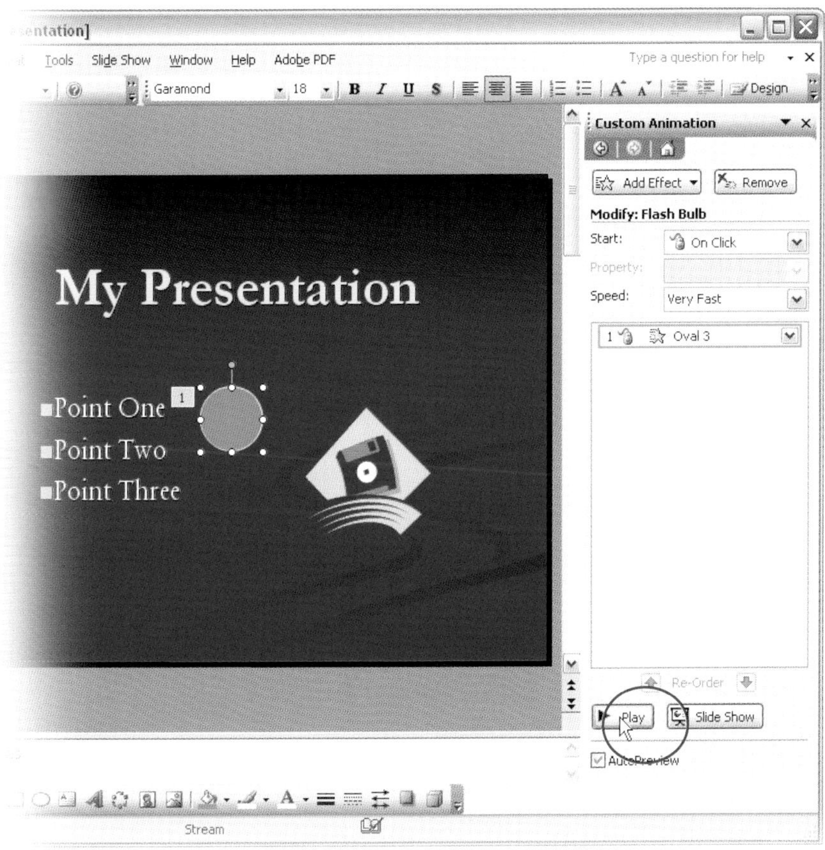

MORE TEMPLATES

About the only thing that's better than PowerPoint's design templates are more templates. And you can get a ton for free, if you know where to look. Open PowerPoint's Startup task pane by pressing Control-F1. Then click the down-facing arrow to the left of the Close button on the task pane's header and choose Site Design to display the Site Design task pane. Scroll to the bottom of the available templates and click the last thumbnail, named Design Templates on Microsoft Office Online. This will launch your Web browser and take you to PowerPoint template heaven. Go nuts, there's a ton of 'em.

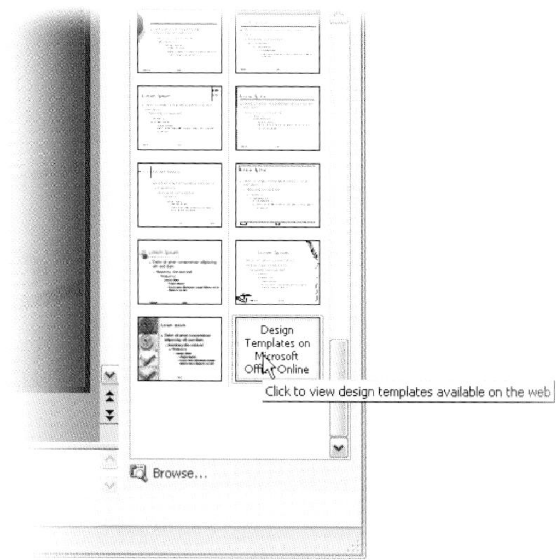

I'M COMPRESSED!

It's time to knock PowerPoint down to size—PowerPoint's graphics anyway. Graphics can really add up in a presentation, especially if you're using stock photography. And, if you're not able to save your presentation to CD because it's the size of your MP3 collection, then you may have a problem. You could try to compress your graphics one at a time, but that would take way too long. Try this instead: Right-click the Standard toolbar and click Picture to open the Picture toolbar, then click the Compress Pictures button. Select the All Pictures in Document option in the Compress Pictures dialog, choose a Resolution, and whether or not to "Delete cropped areas of pictures," then click OK. Now, you can save your presentation to a disc. *Note:* This may alter the way graphics print or look onscreen.

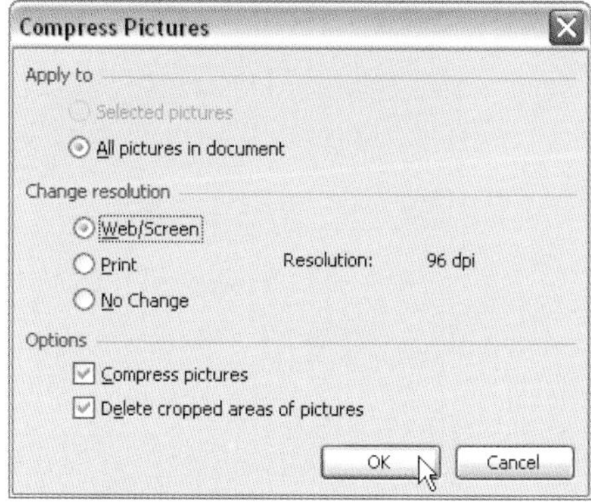

PREVIEW AND EDIT

Viewing your presentation in Slide Show view has its limitations—most obviously, you can't edit your presentation. Unless of course you know this trick: Press-and-hold the Control key on your keyboard and click View>Slide Show in the menu bar. This opens a mini preview window. Now you can compare your presentation in Slide Show view and Normal view (although you may have to adjust your PowerPoint window to see both views, as I did here). Make any changes to your presentation in Normal view while you're viewing the presentation in Slide Show view. To close the mini Slide Show view, click on it to make it active and press the Escape key. Pretty cool!

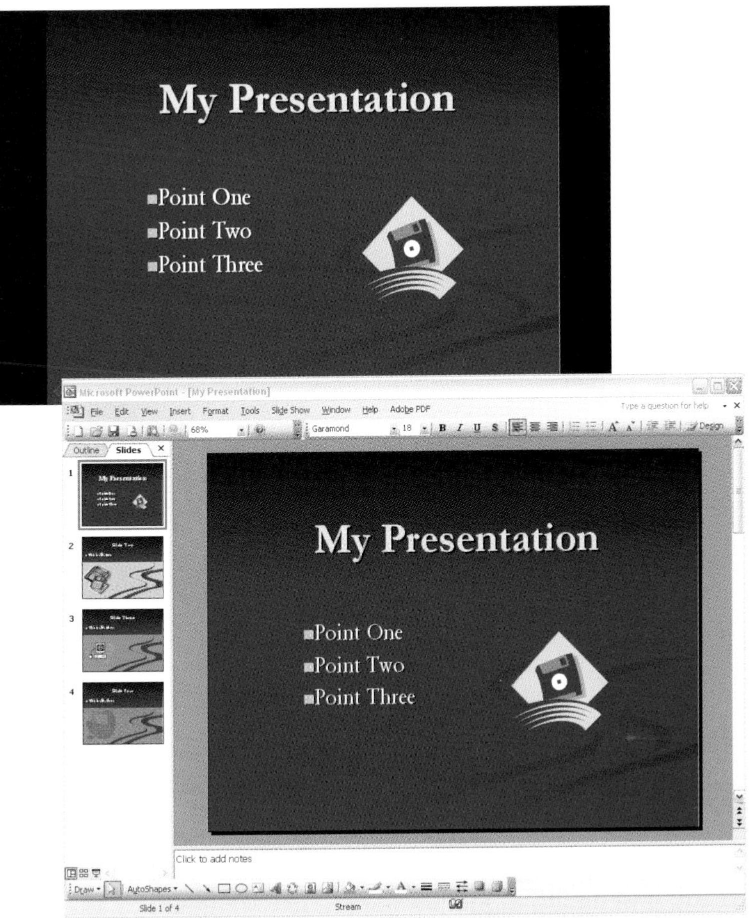

QUICK NOTES

I typically take a lot of notes, simply because I can't remember anything. Hold on, what was I writing about?...see, it's bad. Fortunately, PowerPoint comes to the rescue for all of us memory-challenged folks. As I'm designing a slide for a presentation, I may have several great ideas (and even more bad ones) that I want to share, or I may want to record some comments (called speaker notes) to help during my presentation. To save your ideas and comments for any particular slide, type them into the Notes pane located directly beneath your slide in Normal view (View>Normal). This is your notes page. If you need more room for your notes, place your cursor over the divider bar until the cursor changes to the horizontal move tool and just drag the bar upward to expand the Notes pane. Now you won't forget a thing, I think...I can't remember.

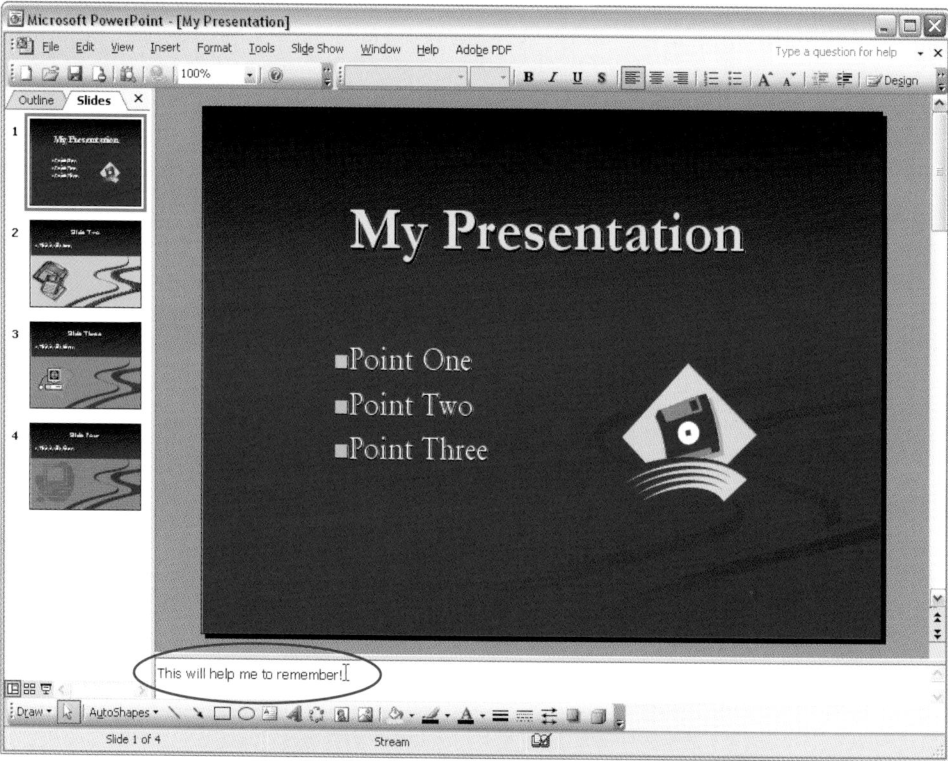

 CUSTOMIZE YOUR CUSTOMERS

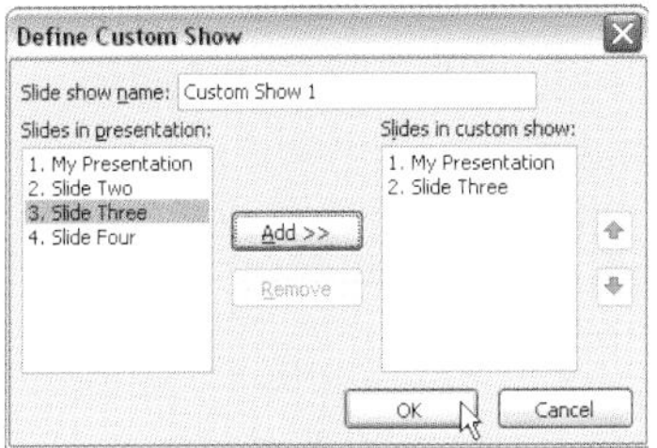

You've created the perfect presentation, worked weeks on getting it just right, and now you just have to figure out how to make it work for all of your potential customers. Well, you don't have to create a new presentation for each customer; create a custom show instead. Open your presentation, then click Slide Show>Custom Shows in the menu bar. Next, click the New button in the Custom Shows dialog, name your custom show, then select which slides to add by selecting them in the left column and clicking Add in the Define Custom Show dialog. When finished, click OK, then click the Show button to see what your presentation will look like. Use the Custom Show feature to create as many variations of your presentation as you want. When you're ready to use your custom shows, click Slide Show>Custom Show in the menu bar, click a saved custom show in the dialog, and then click the Show button.

 DON'T HAVE TRANSITIONS FOR THE WEB?

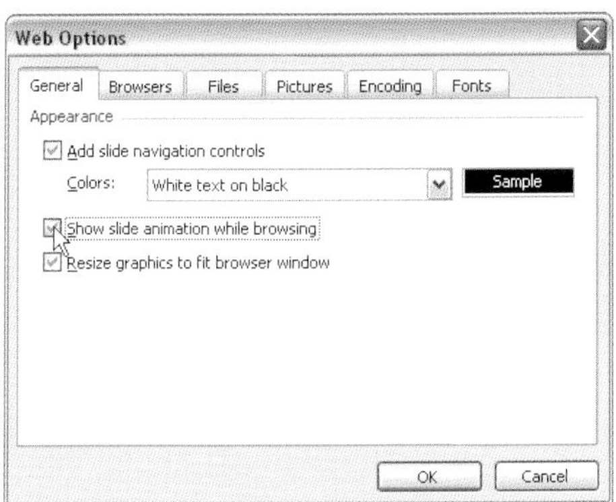

Transitions and animations are really cool, but if you've ever saved a presentation for the Web, you might have noticed that your transitions and animations weren't included. For whatever reason, you've got to tell PowerPoint to include these when saving for the Web. Here's how: Click Tools>Options in the menu bar, then click the General tab in the Options dialog. Next, click Web Options and in the dialog, check "Show slide animation while browsing." Now when you save your presentation for the Web (File>Save As Web Page), your transitions and animations will be included.

QUICK DEFAULTS

PowerPoint's default colors for shapes just don't work. Have you ever seen the default light-blue shapes in any PowerPoint presentation? Probably not. To avoid the light-blue blues, create a shape (I used the Oval tool from the Drawing toolbar), then click the down-facing arrow next to the Fill Color button, and change its stroke color by clicking the down-facing arrow next to the Line Color button (both found in the Drawing toolbar). Next, right-click the shape and click Set AutoShape Defaults in the shortcut menu. Now anytime you draw the shape, it'll be created using your new default colors.

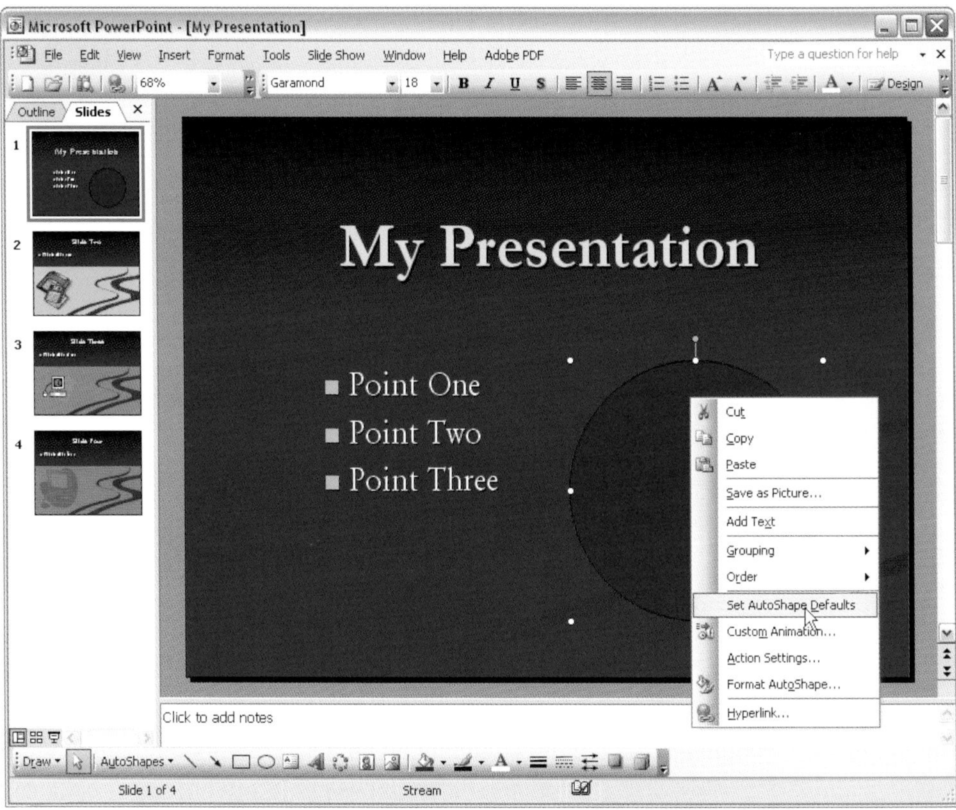

Time to Excel

My chapter description for Word contained an inaccuracy. I stated that Word finally gave computer users something to do with their computers. Well, that's not entirely

Time to Excel

working with excel

true. Believe it or not, the program that gave rise to the computer was a spreadsheet application. Yeah, a spreadsheet application. It was named VisiCalc and was created by Dan Bricklin and Bob Frankston in 1979. People who never had a use for computers finally did. Although I hate to admit it, Excel is my favorite Office application. I hate to admit it because I get so geeky with it. The true computer geek comes out in me when I'm using Excel. It's just so powerful, and when mastered, it's amazing what you can make it do. So, let's get geeky and jump right in. Turn the page.

STOP FLINCHING

Let's face it, Excel's an ugly program; it just is (please don't email me about this, you won't change my mind). Every time I open it, I flinch. It could be the mass of gray grid lines…yeah I'm pretty sure it's the mass of gray grid lines. Gray is an ugly color. So let's change the color. Click Tools>Options in the menu bar, then click the View tab in the Options dialog. Next, select a new color from the Gridlines Color drop-down menu (anything other than gray will do), and click OK. That's slightly better!

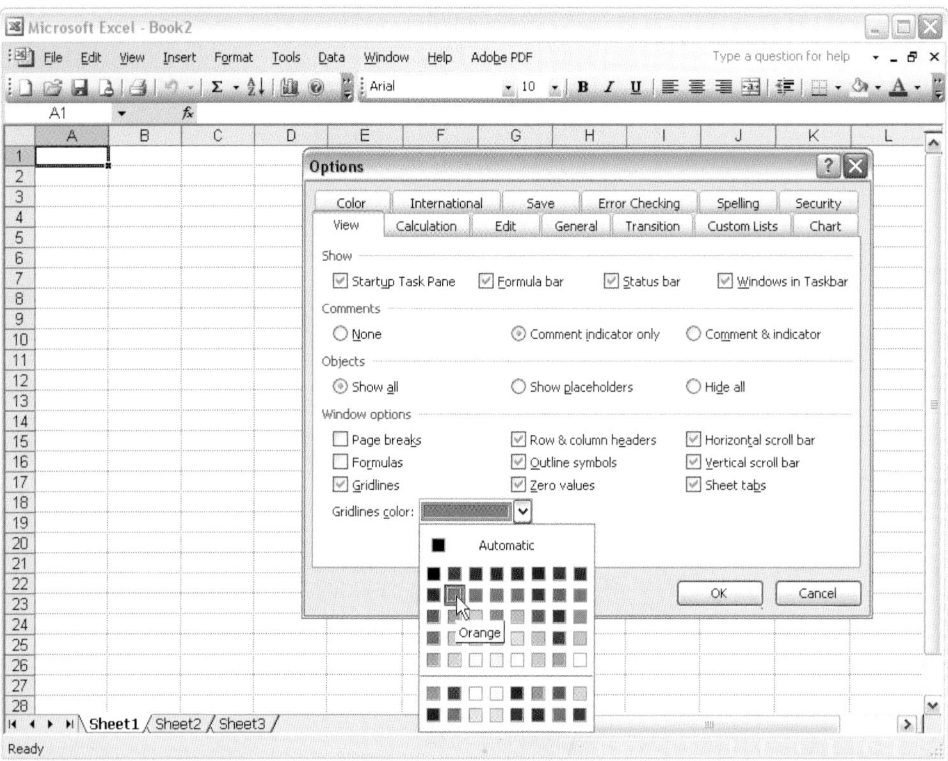

GETTIN' CRAZY WITH BACKGROUNDS

Now, I know that coloring your grid lines might be about all the excitement the average Excel user can take, but let's push the envelope and get really daring. Let's add a little more personality to your worksheets by adding a background picture. I know, take a couple deep breaths and we'll start when you're ready. Ready? Good! Click Format>Sheet>Background in the menu bar. Next, browse your hard drive using the Sheet Background dialog to locate a picture, and then click Insert. To remove the image, go to Format>Sheet>Delete Background. It's almost more than you can handle, isn't it?

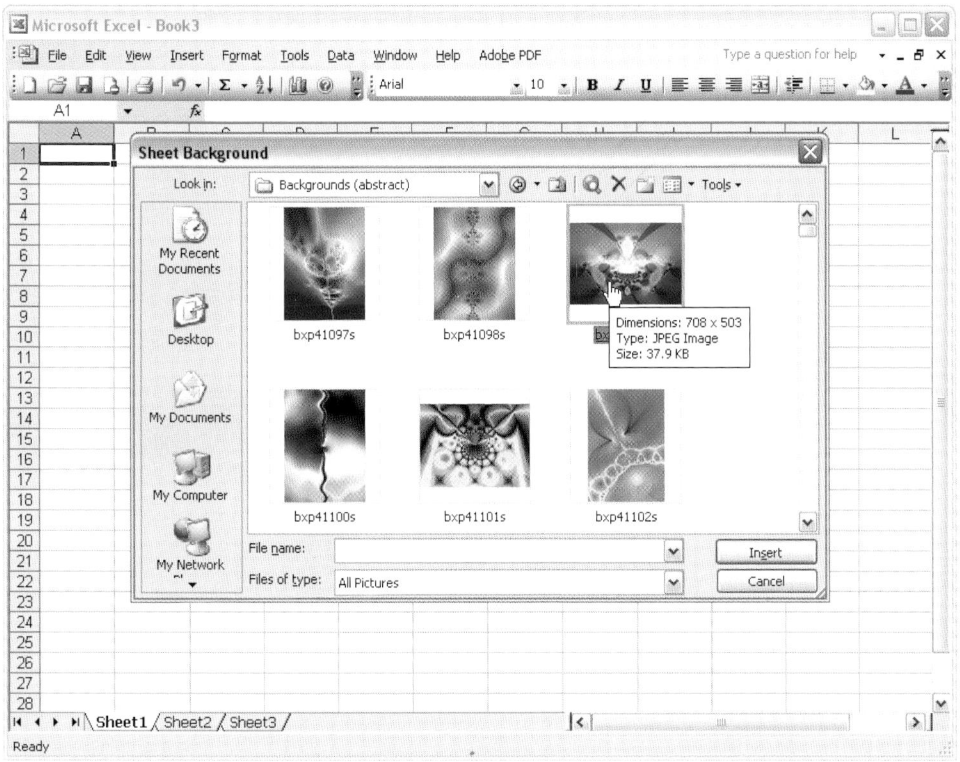

 WHOA, THAT'S A DIFFERENT WORKSHEET

If you're really sick of looking at Excel's grid lines—regardless of their color—then get rid of 'em. You think I'm getting carried away…well, maybe, but I can't stop doing it. I'm this close to getting comfortable with working in Excel with no grid lines and headers. Try it; maybe it'll catch on. Click Tools>Options in the menu bar, then click the View tab in the Options dialog. Next, in the Window Options category, uncheck Gridlines, Row & Column Headers, and anything else that you can live without, and then click OK. Whoa, that's different!

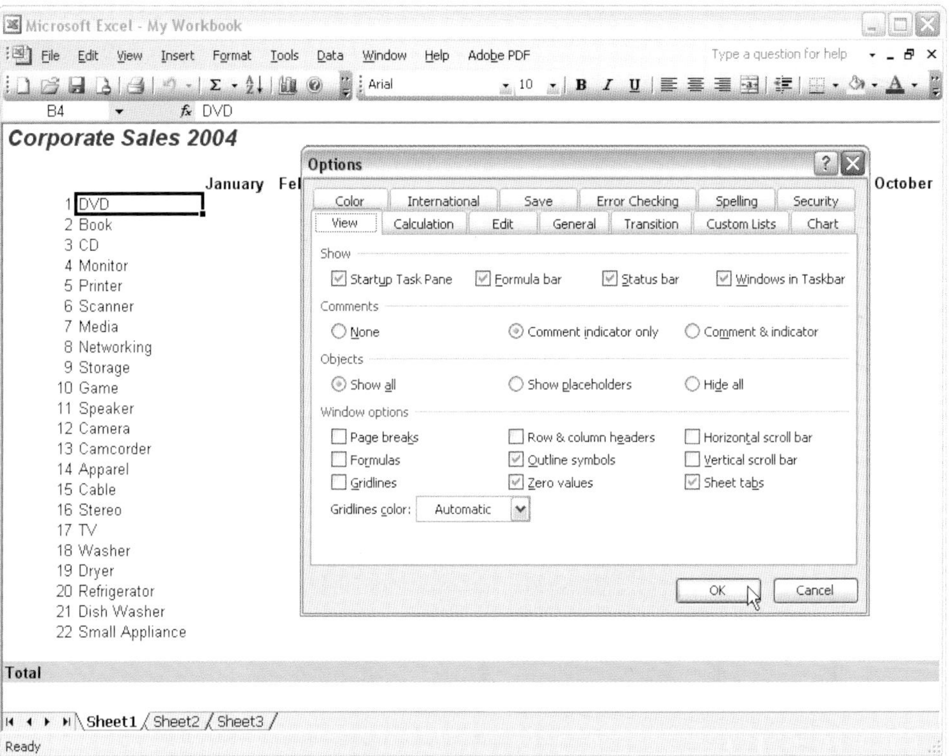

CENTERING TEXT

Excel may not offer Word's formatting capabilities, but you can still get your worksheets to look good. Centering a row's text inside columns to create a page header is a start. On line 1 type a heading, then click-and-drag to select as many cells as necessary in line 1, which will create headings over the worksheet's data (and if you use a month, as I did here, Excel will automatically enter the following months in the selected cells as you drag). Next, right-click a selected cell and click Format Cells in the shortcut menu. Then, click the Alignment tab in the Format Cells dialog, select Center Across Selection in the Horizontal drop-down menu, and click OK. Your text will now be centered in the selected cells.

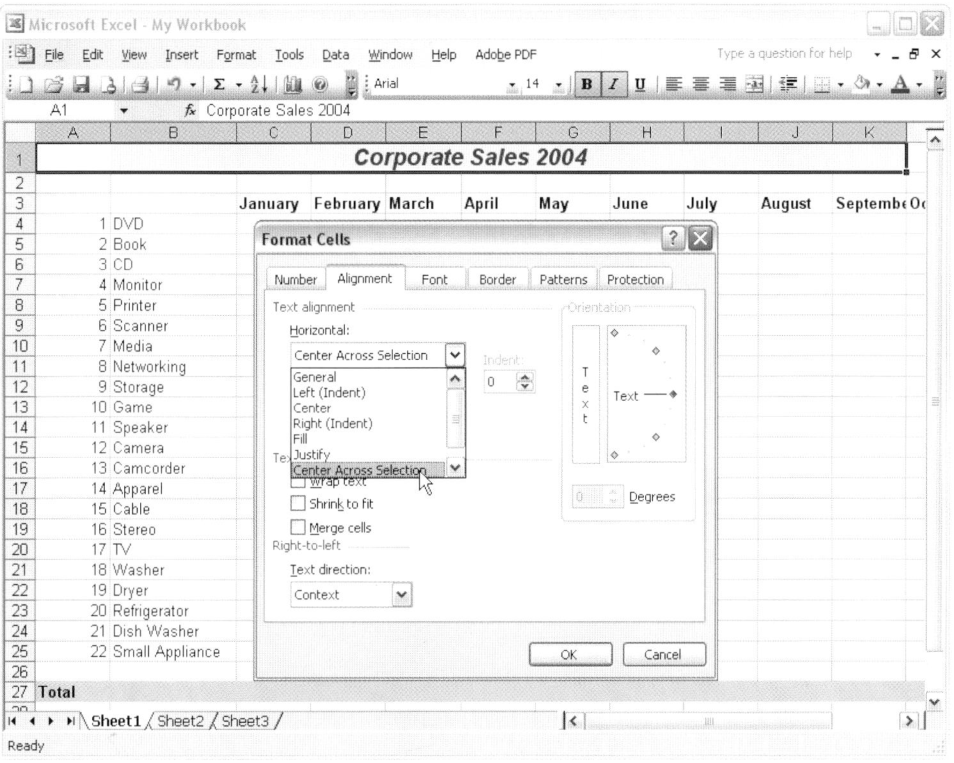

A QUICKER CALCULATOR

The tool that you'll probably use most frequently in Excel is the calculator, and when you get tired of going to your Start menu in Windows Taskbar every time you need it, you can add it to any Excel toolbar or even add it to the menu bar. Here's how: Click Tools>Customize in the menu bar and click the Commands tab in the Customize dialog. Next, select Tools under Categories, then drag-and-drop the Custom Calculator command from the Commands list onto the menu bar or any toolbar, and click Close. Now, anytime you need a calculator it's only a click away.

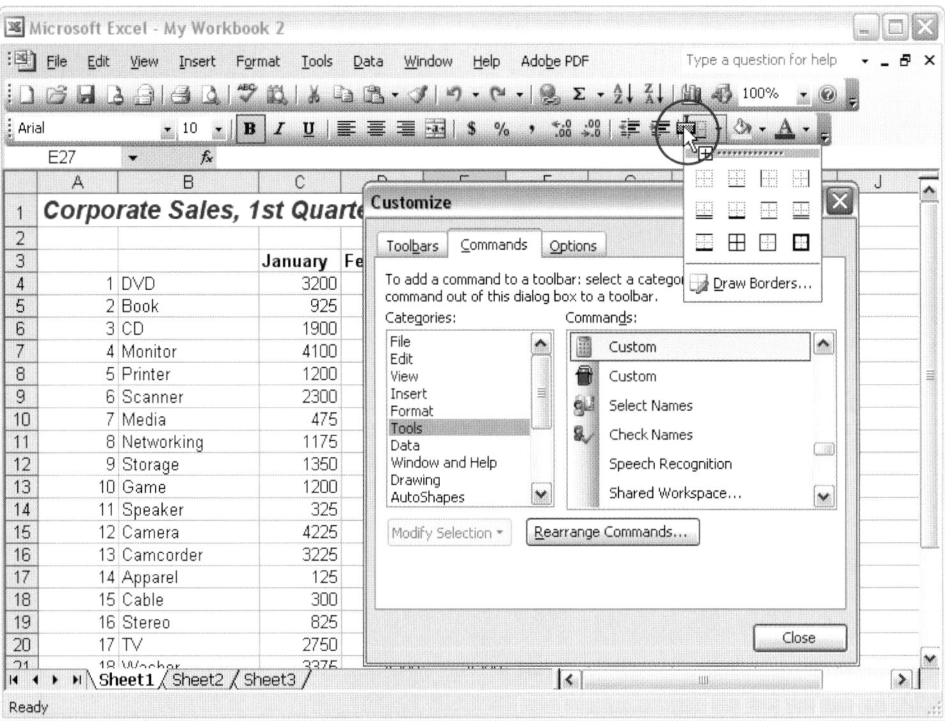

IT'S PICTURE TIME

Excel has the ultimate camera. It allows you take pictures of data on any worksheet then place the picture onto any other workbook's worksheet. Not impressed yet? You're about to be. What makes Excel's camera so cool is that the picture is live, meaning that whenever you make any changes to the photographed worksheet's data, the picture is updated simultaneously. Told ya you'd be impressed. To do this, first add the camera to your toolbar by clicking Tools>Customize in the menu bar and click the Commands tab in the Customize dialog. Next, select Tools under Categories, then drag-and-drop the Camera from the Commands list onto any toolbar, and then click Close. Now, Shift-click or click-and-drag to select the cells that you want to take a picture of, and then click the Camera button on the toolbar—the cells will be outlined by "marching ants" (an animated dashed line). Open any worksheet and click anywhere with your mouse pointer to paste the picture automatically. Now the data is always available to you. Anytime the data is changed on the original worksheet, it will be updated in the "picture" as well. To remove the picture, simply select it, then press Delete on your keyboard.

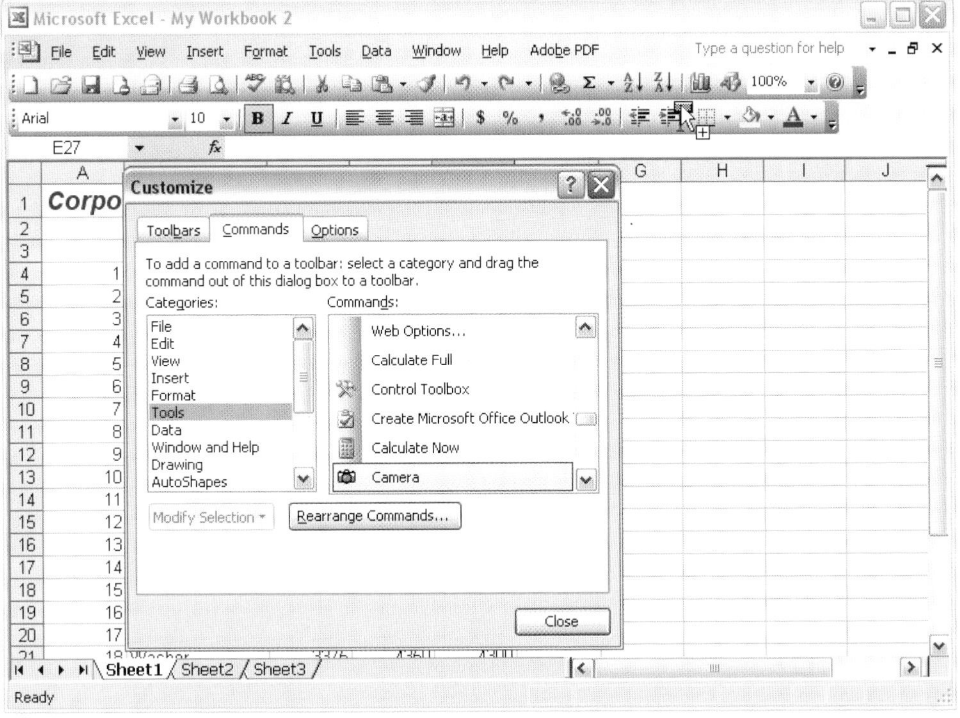

TAKE A (REAL) PICTURE

Okay, I'm sure you're thoroughly impressed with Excel's Camera tool (see previous tip). But maybe you're wondering if it's possible to actually take a picture of your data that you can then paste into other Office applications, such as Word, PowerPoint, or Publisher. Boy, we really think alike (scary). You can, and here's how: Select the data that you want to create a picture of, then press-and-hold the Shift key on your keyboard and click Edit>Copy Picture in the menu bar. Select As Shown on Screen in the Copy Picture dialog, then choose a format, and click OK. This copies the picture to the Office Clipboard. Now, open Word, PowerPoint, Publisher, or any application that will accept Picture and Bitmap file formats, and press Control-V to paste the picture.

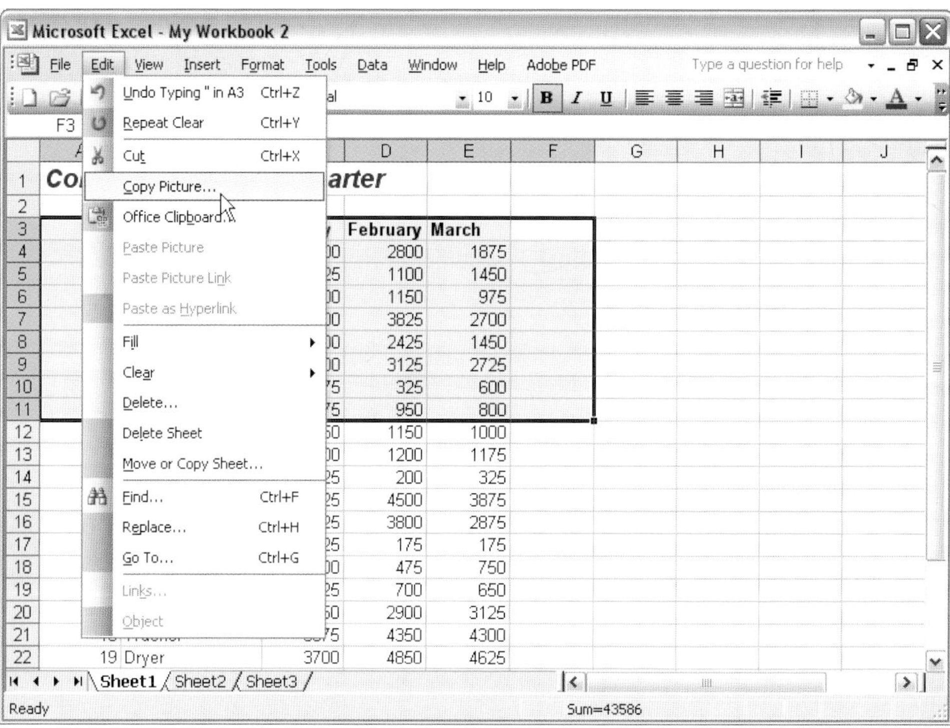

MY FAVORITE WORKBOOK, RIGHT AWAY

Did you know that you could automatically open your favorite workbook each time you launch Excel? You can! Do this: Open your workbook, then click File>Save As in the menu bar. Next, use the Save In drop-down menu in the Save As dialog to navigate to the XLSTART folder (don't you just love how Microsoft names stuff?) that's typically located in C:\Program Files\Microsoft Office\OFFICE11\XLSTART if you installed Office 2003 using the default setup (if not, perform a search for "XLSTART" by going to Start>Search from the Windows Taskbar). Now click Save. Now each and every time you open Excel, it will automatically open your favorite workbook. If you want to restore Excel to its default setup, simply remove the workbook from the XLSTART folder, and Excel will once again open a new, blank spreadsheet when launched.

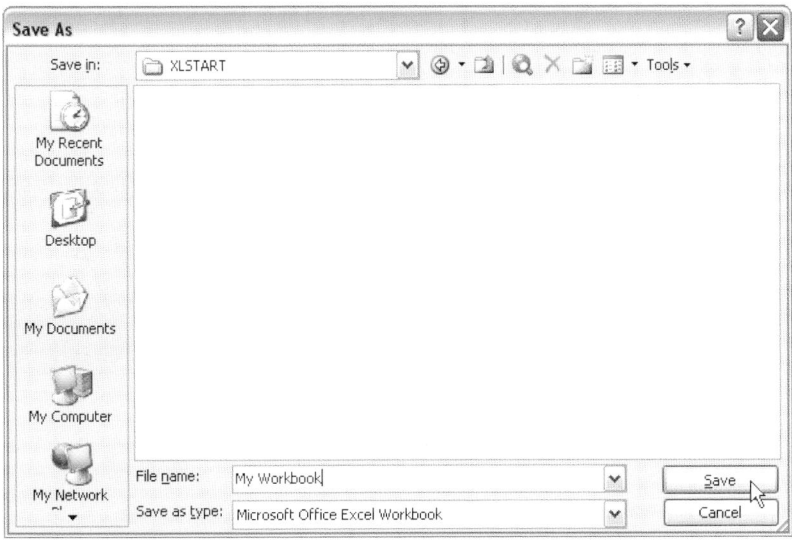

ABC'S TO 123'S

You don't have to use letters as your worksheet's column headings. Oh, Microsoft would like you to think that you have to because they named the option to change this "R1C1 reference style"—huh? Anyway, you can change your ABC's to 123's—despite Microsoft's attempts to deter you—by clicking Tools>Options in the menu bar and clicking the General tab in the Option dialog. Next, check "R1C1 reference style" (baffling) in the Settings category and click OK. Now your ABC's are 123's. *Note:* This may alter the way Excel performs functions.

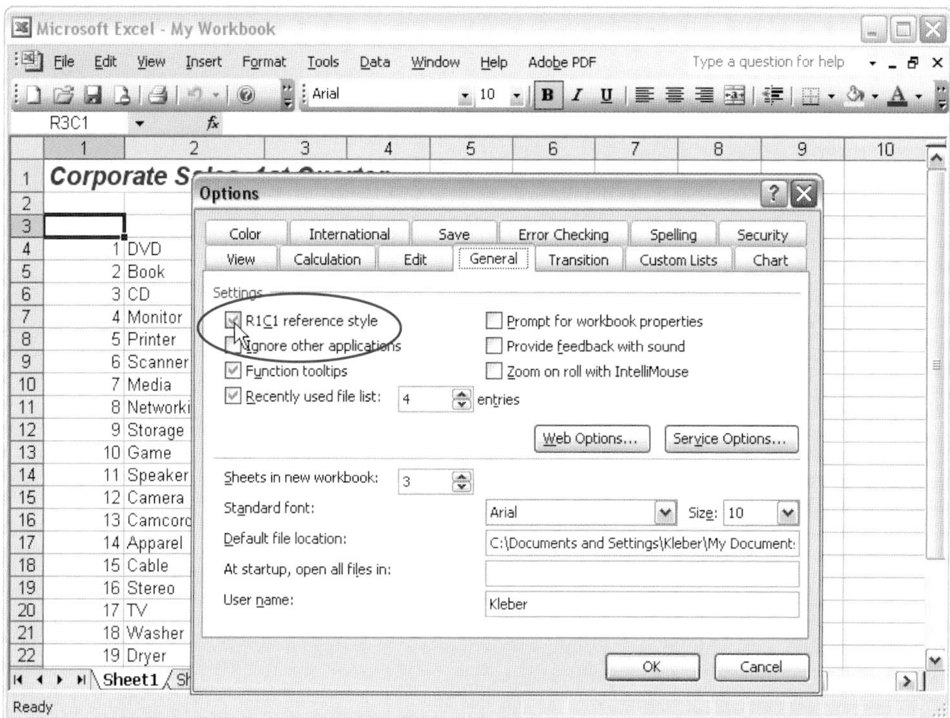

 BETTER PRINTS

By default, Excel prints workbook data starting from the top-left margin of each page, which is fine—I guess you have to set something as the default. But this doesn't always look best when distributing printouts. For instance, you may want to center your data, and I wouldn't blame you. Here's how to do it: Click File>Page Setup in the menu bar and click the Margins tab in the Page Setup dialog. In the Center on Page category, check Horizontally to print data centered at the top of the page or choose Vertically to print data centered along the left side of the page. Check both to center printed data directly in the center of the page.

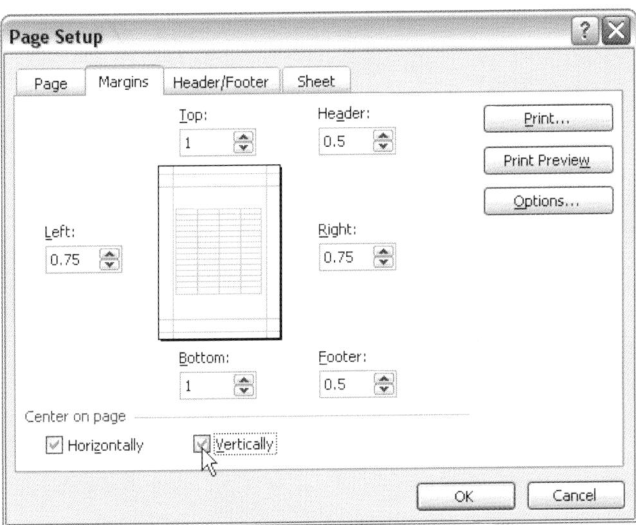

CONTROL YOUR PRINTS

If you need even greater control over how your worksheets print, then you're a control freak—you have issues, and you should seek counseling. But until you get help, you can use Excel's Print Preview to get your printed worksheets to look just right. Click the Print Preview button on the Standard toolbar, then click the Margins button at the top of the Print Preview window. Now, place your mouse pointer on any margin line and click-and-drag the margin line to any location on the worksheet. When finished, click Print.

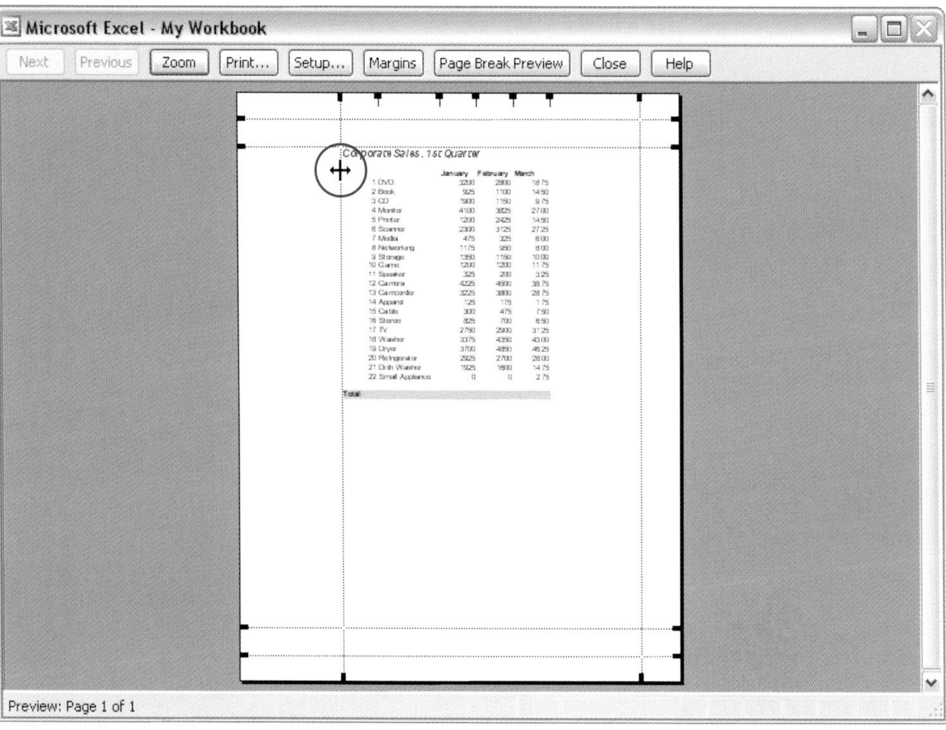

IT'S TIME TO BREAK UP

By default, Excel automatically creates page breaks for your worksheets, which break it into sections that will print on your printer's default paper size (typically 8.5"x11"). You can view a worksheet's page breaks by scrolling until you see a black dashed line, which indicates a page break. (*Note:* If you still don't see page breaks, go to File>Page Setup, then click the Sheet tab, check Gridlines, and click OK. This option prints your gridlines. If you don't want to print your gridlines but still want to see the page breaks, return to the Page Setup dialog and uncheck Gridlines under the Sheet tab. Your page breaks will still appear.) But, what do you do if you want to break your 8.5"x11" worksheet into two or more sections that will print on individual sheets of paper? You need to insert manual page breaks. To do this, select the cell at the bottom-right of the last cell that you want to appear on your page, and then click Insert>Page Break in the menu bar. A page break will appear above the selected cell. Now, click the Print button to print the pages. To remove the page break, select the same cell and click Insert>Remove Page Break in the menu bar.

Microsoft Excel - My Workbook

File Edit View Insert Format Tools Data Window Help Adobe PDF

F12

	A	B	C	D	E	F	G	H	I	J
3			January	February	March					
4	1	DVD	3200	2800	1875					
5	2	Book	925	1100	1450					
6	3	CD	1900	1150	975					
7	4	Monitor	4100	3825	2700					
8	5	Printer	1200	2425	1450					
9	6	Scanner	2300	3125	2725					
10	7	Media	475	325	600					
11	8	Networking	1175	950	800					
12	9	Storage	1350	1150	1000					
13	10	Game	1200	1200	1175					
14	11	Speaker	325	200	325					
15	12	Camera	4225	4500	3875					
16	13	Camcorder	3225	3800	2875					
17	14	Apparel	125	175	175					
18	15	Cable	300	475	750					
19	16	Stereo	825	700	650					
20	17	TV	2750	2900	3125					
21	18	Washer	3375	4350	4300					
22	19	Dryer	3700	4850	4625					
23	20	Refrigerator	2925	2700	2800					
24	21	Dish Washer	1925	1600	1475					
25	22	Small Appliance	0	0	275					

Sheet1 / Sheet2 / Sheet3 /

Ready

A FAMILIAR PRINT

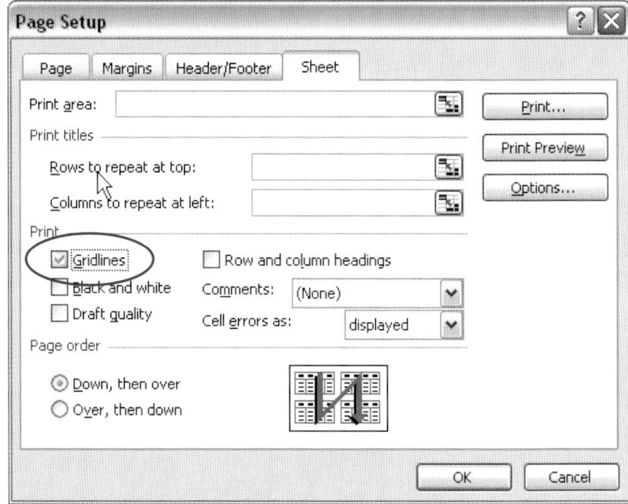

Have you ever noticed that a printed worksheet doesn't read as well as an onscreen worksheet? Do you know why? It's because Excel doesn't print gridlines. You get so used to seeing them that when they're not there, your printout almost looks confusing. You can, however, tweak Excel so that it prints the gridlines, which is a good thing because I really don't like being almost confused. Click File>Page Setup in the menu bar and click the Sheet tab in the Page Setup dialog. Next, check Gridlines under the Print category and click OK. Now when you print your workbook, Excel will also print the familiar grid lines.

PRINT A WORKBOOK RANGE

If you need to print a selected range of several or all worksheets in a workbook, here's how: First, select the worksheets that you want to print the same range for by pressing-and-holding the Control key on your keyboard, then click each worksheet's tab at the bottom-left corner of the Excel window. Next, select your print range on Sheet 1, then click File>Print in the menu bar. Now, choose Selection listed under Print What in the Print dialog and click OK. Each worksheet will now print only the selected range from Sheet 1.

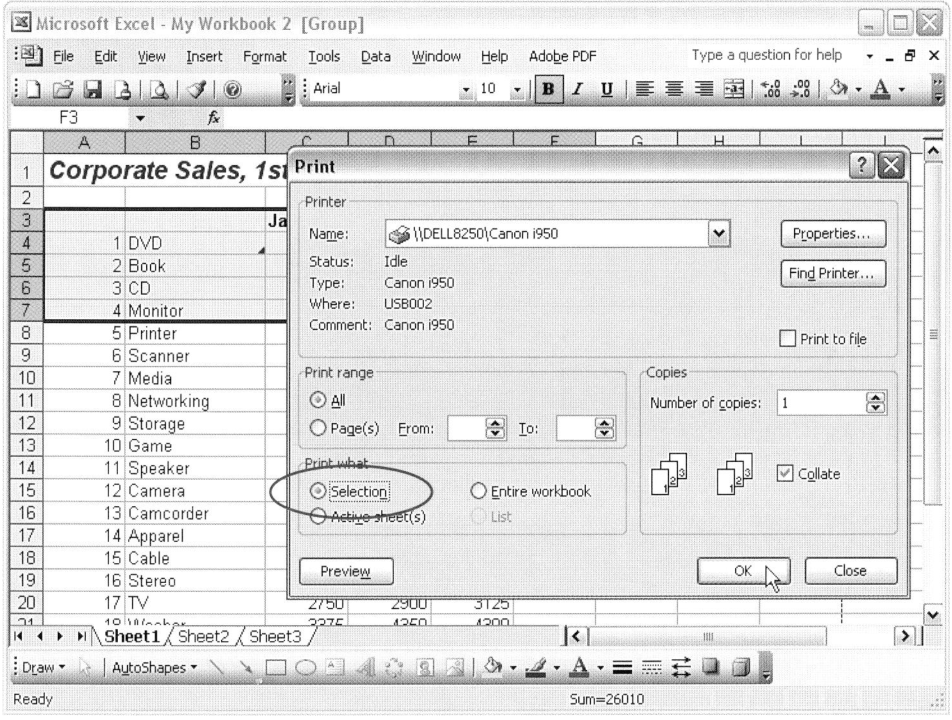

AM I RICH YET?

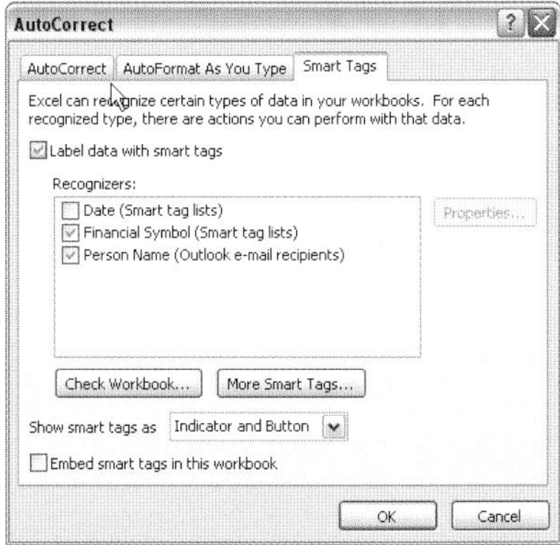

I love things that are live: football games, fireworks, Limp Bizkit (small venue), and adding live data to my Excel worksheets. I can't help you with football games, fireworks, or Limp Bizkit, but I can show you how to liven up your worksheets with live data. Excel uses Smart Tags to insert live stock quotes into your worksheets. All you need is an active Internet connection and your favorite stock symbol. By default, Smart Tags are not turned on, so let's do that first. Click Tools>AutoCorrect Options in the menu bar and click the Smart Tags tab in the AutoCorrect dialog. Next, check Label Data with Smart Tags, and under the Recognizers category check Financial Symbol (Smart Tag Lists) and any other Recognizers you wish, then click OK. Now, type your stock symbol into any cell using all capital letters, and then press Enter on your keyboard. You'll notice a small triangle in the bottom-right corner of the cell. Move your pointer over it to show the cell's Smart Tag, click the Smart Tag, and click Insert Refreshable Stock Price. Next, select where to insert the stock quote using the Insert Stock Price dialog (either on a new worksheet or starting in a particular cell on the current worksheet) and click OK. And, there it is—your favorite stock quote courtesy of MSN MoneyCentral. To control when the stock quote is refreshed, right-click anywhere over the stock quote and click Data Range Properties in the shortcut menu. In the dialog, check Refresh Every and change the minutes to any number you'd like or choose to Refresh Data on File Open, then click OK.

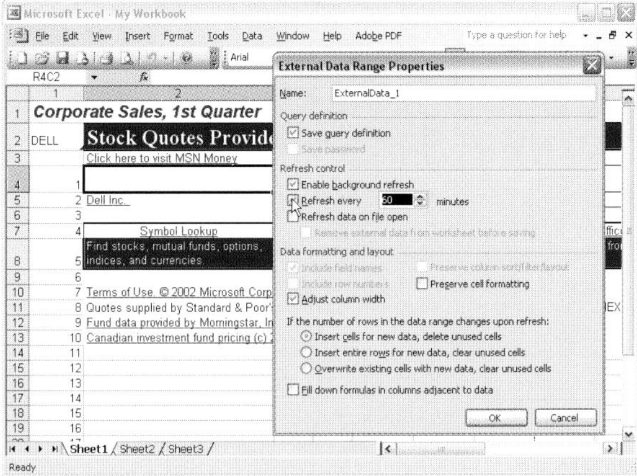

 YOU COULD SAVE A PENCE

That previous tip was fun, wasn't it? Live data always gets me going. So, let's keep the adrenaline pumping and add other live data without using Smart Tags. It just gets better and better, doesn't it? Anytime I travel overseas, I watch the currency exchange rates (I'll wait days to save a penny). And, with my laptop, Excel, and Wi-Fi, I'm always on top of what the dollar's doing at any given time. Do this: Select any cell on an existing or new worksheet and click Data>Import External Data>Import Data in the menu bar. Then, select MSN MoneyCentral Investor Currency Rates from the My Data Sources folder and click Open. Choose where to insert the data on your existing worksheet or choose a new worksheet in the Import Data dialog, and then click OK. Oh yeah, I'm a master of money.

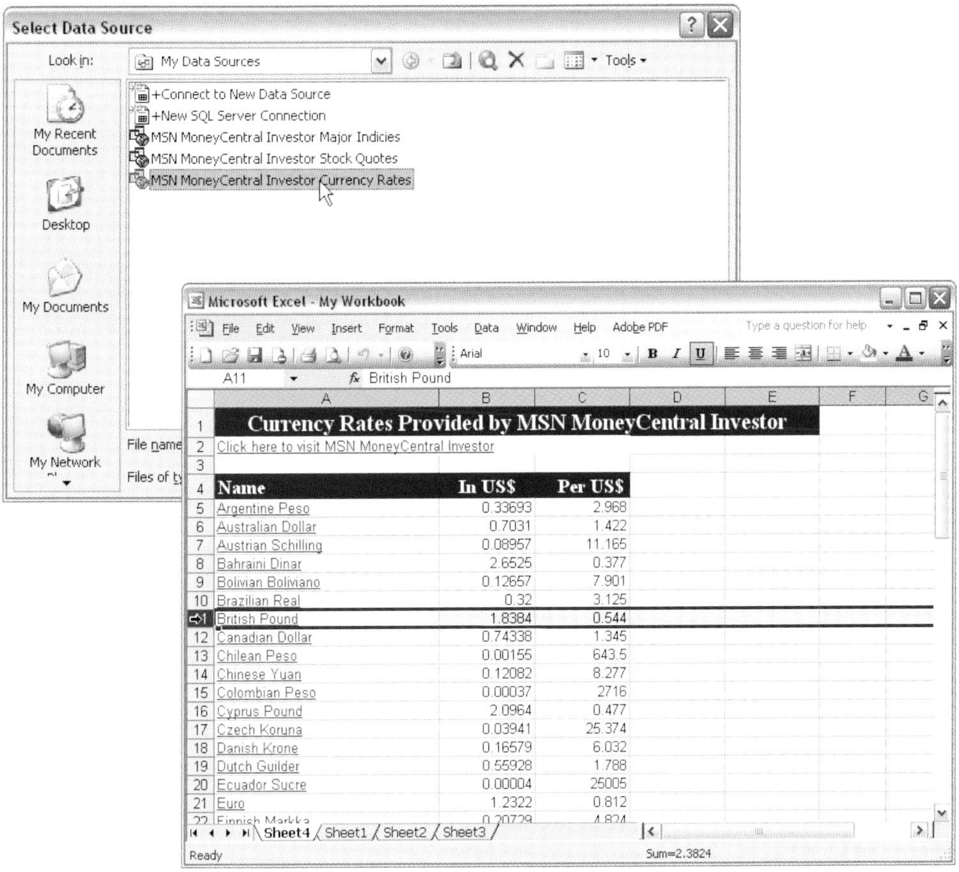

 IT'S A RANDOM THING

There are good random things (hugs, gifts, winning the lottery) and bad random things (violence, bee stings, hair loss), but adding random numbers to an Excel worksheet is somewhere in between. To add random numbers to your worksheets, select the cell that you want to add a random number function to, then type =rand()*50 (use any number you want), and press Enter on your keyboard. This places random numbers zero to 50 into the formula field. Now drag the field's fill handle (its bottom-right handle) to expand your random numbers to as many cells as you'd like (as I did here). By default, Excel will use the General number format to generate the numbers. If you want to display only whole numbers, Shift-click to select all of your cells, right-click the selection, click Format Cells in the shortcut menu, and then click the Number tab on the Format Cells dialog. Next, select Number under Category, choose 0 (zero) in the Decimal Places drop-down menu, and then click OK. Now, you'll see only whole numbers.

Microsoft Excel - My Workbook

File Edit View Insert Format Tools Data Window Help Adobe PDF

F4 =RAND()*50

	A	B	C	D	E	F	G	H	I	J
5	2	Book	925	1100	1450	4.547345	44.0751	25.64151		
6	3	CD	1900	1150	975	35.44887	24.62832	48.20423		
7	4	Monitor	4100	3825	2700	45.52643	0.53639	26.91065		
8	5	Printer	1200	2425	1450	7.534828	25.73961	15.12388		
9	6	Scanner	2300	3125	2725	41.31406	0.761965	4.159164		
10	7	Media	475	325	600	20.42733	32.04052	47.06695		
11	8	Networking	1175	950	800	9.287081	43.0901	28.92261		
12	9	Storage	1350	1150	1000	25.58892	29.30255	19.87352		
13	10	Game	1200	1200	1175	28.99266	32.52093	43.2724		
14	11	Speaker	325	200	325	10.03996	24.69657	7.959079		
15	12	Camera	4225	4500	3875	17.03413	10.23941	47.44989		
16	13	Camcorder	3225	3800	2875	49.3616	24.75804	49.66472		
17	14	Apparel	125	175	175	34.71285	28.38495	0.213509		
18	15	Cable	300	475	750	13.9209	22.64069	28.14285		
19	16	Stereo	825	700	650	34.21343	36.58277	46.28459		
20	17	TV	2750	2900	3125	16.26047	18.07141	20.65016		
21	18	Washer	3375	4350	4300	35.99612	28.06984	4.738346		
22	19	Dryer	3700	4850	4625	42.89456	20.79691	1.94924		
23	20	Refrigerator	2925	2700	2800	1.075767	12.09476	46.29169		
24	21	Dish Washer	1925	1600	1475	41.84987	45.21441	14.00736		
25	22	Small Appliance	0	0	275	2.997971	10.24669	47.75954		
26										
27	Total									

Sheet1 / Sheet2 / Sheet3 /

Ready Sum=1686.941947

.2989345?

Do your cells or range have too many decimal spaces? If there are more than two, then yes they do—at least they do for me. I don't even know what three decimals represent, much less 20 of them. Decimals make me feel stupid, so I delete them as quickly as possible. You can too by selecting your cell or range and clicking the Decrease Decimal button on the Formatting toolbar. If you're a freak, you can click the Increase Decimal button on the Formatting toolbar.

Microsoft Excel - My Workbook

F4 =RAND()*50 — Decrease Decimal

	A	B	C	D	E	F	G	H
1	Corporate Sales, 1st Quarter							
2								
3			January	February	March	April	June	July
4	1	DVD	3200	2800	1875	11.74		
5	2	Book	925	1100	1450	45.98		
6	3	CD	1900	1150	975	45.91		
7	4	Monitor	4100	3825	2700	18.65		
8	5	Printer	1200	2425	1450	11.47		
9	6	Scanner	2300	3125	2725	9.98		
10	7	Media	475	325	600	24.65		
11	8	Networking	1175	950	800	23.45		
12	9	Storage	1350	1150	1000	2.70		
13	10	Game	1200	1200	1175	0.70		
14	11	Speaker	325	200	325	23.78		
15	12	Camera	4225	4500	3875	15.87		
16	13	Camcorder	3225	3800	2875	3.92		
17	14	Apparel	125	175	175	26.81		
18	15	Cable	300	475	750	39.64		
19	16	Stereo	825	700	650	38.20		
20	17	TV	2750	2900	3125	19.93		
21	18	Washer	3375	4350	4300	31.67		
22	19	Dryer	3700	4850	4625	24.48		

Sheet1 / Sheet2 / Sheet3 — Ready — Sum=470.72

 SHARE YOUR FORMATTING

To add the same page formatting to multiple worksheets, press-and-hold the Control key on your keyboard, then click to select each worksheet's tab (along the bottom-left corner of the Excel window) that you want to apply the same page setup to. Next, click File>Page Setup in the menu bar and click the Page tab in the Page Setup dialog. Make any changes to the page setup, and then click OK. The settings are applied only to the selected worksheets. I use this tip when setting up pages within a workbook that should print landscape instead of the default portrait orientation. When finished, press the Shift key and click the current tab to deselect the grouped worksheets.

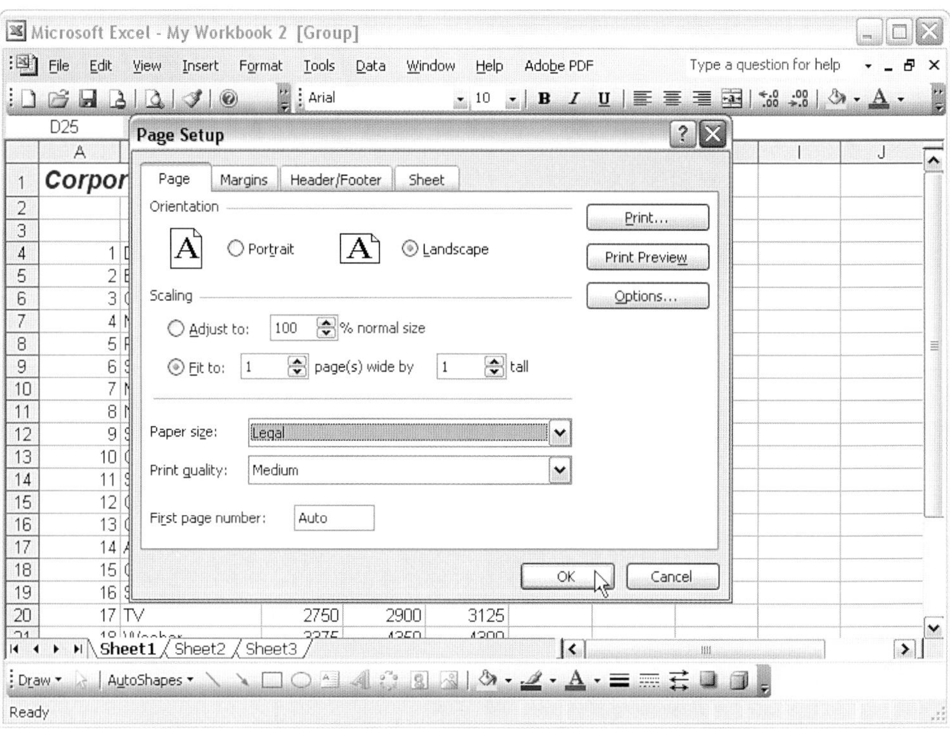

THE TITLE'S THE SAME

I often give each worksheet within a workbook the same title. Each worksheet may hold different data, but the report's title doesn't typically change from worksheet to worksheet. Giving each worksheet the same title manually can be a real chore, but you don't have to type or paste the title onto each worksheet; use this shortcut instead: First, group your worksheets by pressing the Control key on your keyboard and clicking each worksheet's tab (along the bottom of the Excel window) that you want to have the same title. Then click Sheet 1, select cell A1, and type your title (my title is "Corporate Sales 1st Quarter"). The title now appears on each worksheet in the same location. Repeat this to share any type of data among your worksheets. When finished, press the Shift key and click the current tab to deselect the grouped worksheets.

Microsoft Excel - My Workbook [Group]

File Edit View Insert Format Tools Data Window Help Adobe PDF

A1 Corporate Sales 1st Quart

	A	B	C	D	E
1	***Corporate Sales 1st Quart***				
2					
3			**January**	**February**	**March**
4	1	DVD	3200	2800	1875
5	2	Book	925	1100	1450
6	3	CD	1900	1150	975
7	4	Monitor	4100	3825	2700
8	5	Printer	1200	2425	1450
9	6	Scanner	2300	3125	2725
10	7	Media	475	325	600
11	8	Networking	1175	950	800
12	9	Storage	1350	1150	1000
13	10	Game	1200	1200	1175
14	11	Speaker	325	200	325
15	12	Camera	4225	4500	3875
16	13	Camcorder	3225	3800	2875
17	14	Apparel	125	175	175
18	15	Cable	300	475	750
19	16	Stereo	825	700	650
20	17	TV	2750	2900	3125
21	18	Washer	3375	4350	4300
22	19	Dryer	3700	4850	4625

Sheet1 / Sheet2 / Sheet3

Edit

 HOW LONG TIL MY BIRTHDAY?

Counting the number of days between two dates is harder than you might think. It's almost impossible to remember which months have 30 or 31 days (February's easy, unless it's a leap year, then it gets crazy). Even if you think you know, you're probably wrong. Well, you can use Excel to take the guesswork out of counting days. For example, if you need to know how many days there are between now and your next birthday (mine's January 21st), do this: Select any cell, then type: ="your next birthday's date"-"today's date". It should look something like this: ="1/21/05"-"5/6/04". Now press Enter on your keyboard. The number that appears represents the number of days between now and the blessed event—in this case, my birthday.

Microsoft Excel - My Workbook

SUM ="1/21/05"-"5/6/04"

	A	B	C	D	E	F	G
1	Corporate Sales, 1st Quarter						
2							
3			January	February	March		
4	1	DVD	3200	2800	1875		
5	2	Book	925	1100	1450		="1/21/05"-"5/6/04"
6	3	CD	1900	1150	975		
7	4	Monitor	4100	3825	2700		
8	5	Printer	1200	2425	1450		
9	6	Scanner	2300	3125	2725		
10	7	Media	475	325	600		
11	8	Networking	1175	950	800		

Microsoft Excel - My Workbook

G5 ="1/21/05"-"5/6/04"

	A	B	C	D	E	F	G
1	Corporate Sales, 1st Quarter						
2							
3			January	February	March		
4	1	DVD	3200	2800	1875		
5	2	Book	925	1100	1450		260
6	3	CD	1900	1150	975		
7	4	Monitor	4100	3825	2700		
8	5	Printer	1200	2425	1450		
9	6	Scanner	2300	3125	2725		
10	7	Media	475	325	600		
11	8	Networking	1175	950	800		

 QUICK CALCULATIONS

The previous tip works great for calculating the days between two dates; however, what if you want to calculate the days between two existing dates? For example, cell A9 already contains the date of your next birthday (1/21/2005) and cell B9 contains today's date (5/6/2004). Do this: In cell C9, type =A9-B9, then press Enter on your keyboard. Next, right-click the cell containing the results (C9) and click Format Cells in the shortcut menu. Click the Number tab in the Format Cells dialog and click General listed under Category, and then click OK. Cell C9 displays the results—260. That's quick!

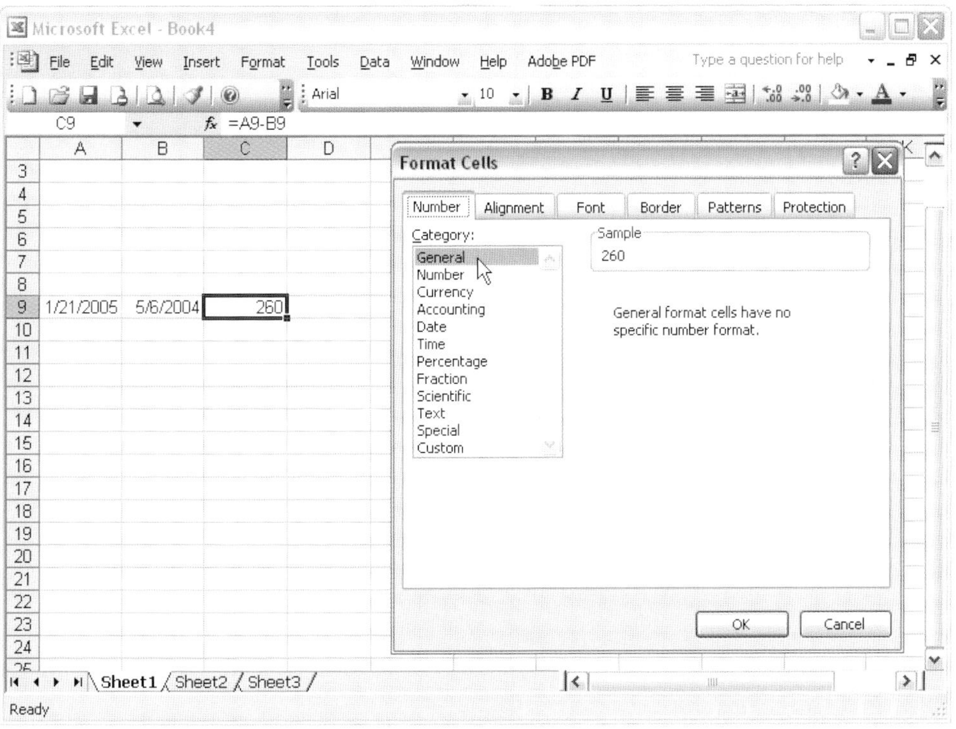

TOTAL YOUR WORKSHEETS

There are certain circumstances that require adding sums from several worksheets to compare data. This is very common when comparing monthly, quarterly, and annual sales reports. And, you can do this easily as long as each worksheet shares the same layout. To demonstrate this, open a new Excel workbook (File>New and click Blank Workbook in the New Workbook task pane). Next, type "Sales" in cell A3, and type "10,000" in cell B3 (both without the quotes). Then type "10,000" in cell B3 on both Sheet 2 and Sheet 3. Now, type: =SUM(Sheet1:Sheet3!B3) into cell A5 on Sheet 1, and then press Enter on your keyboard. Cell A5 on Sheet 1 displays the result of 30,000.

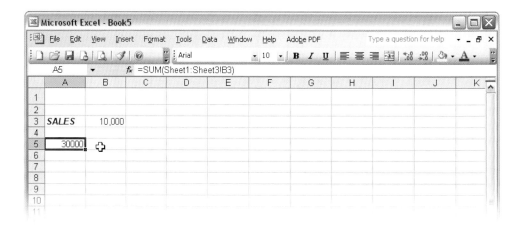

ANOTHER QUICK CALCULATION

This is the best quick sum tip, and it's so obvious I bet you've never noticed it. Select several cells on your worksheet containing numbers that you'd like to sum, then look at the bottom of Excel's window. The sum of the selected cells (SUM="total") appears along the bottom-right side of the status bar. Now, right-click anywhere on the status bar for additional options. Very quick!

Microsoft Excel - My Workbook

E4 | 1875

	A	B	C	D	E
1	Corporate Sales, 1st Quarter				
2					
3			January	February	March
4	1	DVD	3200	2800	1875
5	2	Book	925	1100	1450
6	3	CD	1900	1150	975
7	4	Monitor	4100	3825	2700
8	5	Printer	1200	2425	1450
9	6	Scanner	2300	3125	2725
10	7	Media	475	325	600
11	8	Networking	1175	950	800
12	9	Storage	1350	1150	1000
13	10	Game	1200	1200	1175
14	11	Speaker	325	200	325
15	12	Camera	4225	4500	3875
16	13	Camcorder	3225	3800	2875
17	14	Apparel	125	175	175
18	15	Cable	300	475	750
19	16	Stereo	825	700	650
20	17	TV	2750	2900	3125
21	18	Washer	3375	4350	4300
22	19	Dryer	3700	4850	4625

Sheet1 / Sheet2 / Sheet3

Ready Sum=7875

None
Average
Count
Count Nums
Max
Min
Sum

QUICK LISTS

To create a numbered list in Excel, first select the cell that you want to be your first numbered cell and type the numeral one (1). Now, press-and-hold the Control key on your keyboard and drag the fill handle downward to create a numbered list that increases by one number for each cell selected.

Microsoft Excel - My Workbook

File Edit View Insert Format Tools Data Window Help Adobe PDF

G4 fx 1

	A	B	C	D	E	F	G
1	Corporate Sales, 1st Quarter						
2							
3			January	February	March		
4	1	DVD	3200	2800	1875		1
5	2	Book	925	1100	1450		2
6	3	CD	1900	1150	975		3
7	4	Monitor	4100	3825	2700		4
8	5	Printer	1200	2425	1450		5
9	6	Scanner	2300	3125	2725		6
10	7	Media	475	325	600		7
11	8	Networking	1175	950	800		8
12	9	Storage	1350	1150	1000		9
13	10	Game	1200	1200	1175		10
14	11	Speaker	325	200	325		11
15	12	Camera	4225	4500	3875		12
16	13	Camcorder	3225	3800	2875		13
17	14	Apparel	125	175	175		14
18	15	Cable	300	475	750		15
19	16	Stereo	825	700	650		16
20	17	TV	2750	2900	3125		17
21	18	Washer	3375	4350	4300		18
22	19	Dryer	3700	4850	4625		

Sheet1 / Sheet2 / Sheet3

Ready Sum=171

MORE QUICK LISTS

The previous technique works great for creating numbered lists, but don't stop there. Try this: Select a cell and type "Sunday" (without the quotes), drag the fill handle downward to create a daily calendar. This also works for months, years, and other sequential data. Go nuts! If the list doesn't appear sequentially, then click the Auto Fill Options Smart Tag that appears at the bottom of the last cell selected and click Fill Series.

Microsoft Excel - My Workbook

File Edit View Insert Format Tools Data Window Help Adobe PDF

G4 Sunday

	A	B	C	D	E	F	G
1	***Corporate Sales, 1st Quarter***						
2							
3			**January**	**February**	**March**		
4	1	DVD	3200	2800	1875		Sunday
5	2	Book	925	1100	1450		Monday
6	3	CD	1900	1150	975		Tuesday
7	4	Monitor	4100	3825	2700		Wednesday
8	5	Printer	1200	2425	1450		Thursday
9	6	Scanner	2300	3125	2725		Friday
10	7	Media	475	325	600		Saturday
11	8	Networking	1175	950	800		Sunday
12	9	Storage	1350	1150	1000		Monday
13	10	Game	1200	1200	1175		Tuesday
14	11	Speaker	325	200	325		Wednesday
15	12	Camera	4225	4500	3875		Thursday
16	13	Camcorder	3225	3800	2875		Friday
17	14	Apparel	125	175	175		Saturday
18	15	Cable	300	475	750		Sunday
19	16	Stereo	825	700	650		Monday
20	17	TV	2750	2900	3125		Tuesday
21	18	Washer	3375	4350	4300		
22	19	Dryer	3700	4850	4625		

Sheet1 / Sheet2 / Sheet3

Ready

 MY OWN QUICK LISTS

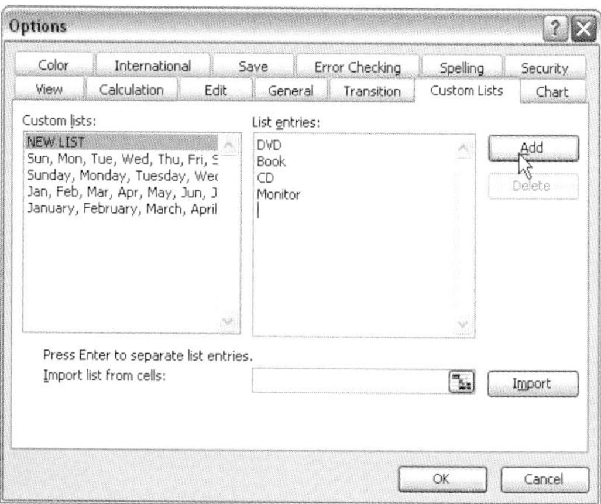

The previous few tips work great for adding lists to Excel, but it gets better. If you have your own sequential list that Excel doesn't recognize (such as your products listed in alphabetical order), add them to Excel's custom list, then you can quickly create entire lists of your products by simply dragging them onto your worksheet. Click Tools>Options in the menu bar and click the Custom Lists tab in the Options dialog. Next, select NEW LIST in the Custom Lists category and add your list in the List Entries field. Separate each entry with a comma and space (or simply press Enter after each entry) and then click Add. Click OK to close the dialog. Now your custom list is ready to be inserted at any time—just type the first word or number of your custom list and drag the cell's fill handle. If the list doesn't appear sequentially, click the Auto Fill Options Smart Tag that appears at the bottom of the last cell selected and click Fill Series.

 I WANT MORE

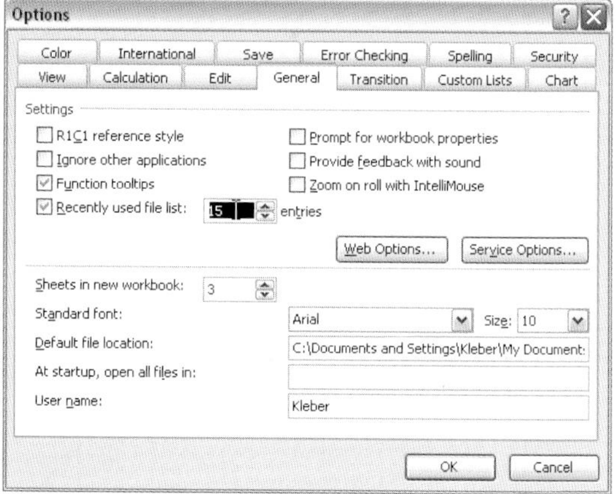

At the bottom of the File menu, Excel displays the four most recent documents you've worked on, which is helpful, but it's not enough. I'd like to see my last 10 or 15 files that I've worked on. To change this, click Tools>Options in the menu bar and click the General tab on the Options dialog. Type 10, 15, or whatever you prefer into the Recently Used File List, and then click OK. Now click File in the menu bar to view the new list of most recently viewed files.

MOVABLE DATA

Here's a slick trick to show field data in text boxes. This allows you to move data anywhere you'd like on your worksheet without affecting your fields. To do this, open the Drawing toolbar by right-clicking any toolbar and selecting Drawing. The Drawing toolbar appears at the bottom of the Excel window. Click the Text Box button and click-and-drag on your worksheet to draw a text box. Now, type "=" (without the quotes) in the Function bar, click the cell that contains the data you want to display in the text box, and then press Enter on your keyboard. The data appears in the text box. Now you can move the text field anywhere on the worksheet.

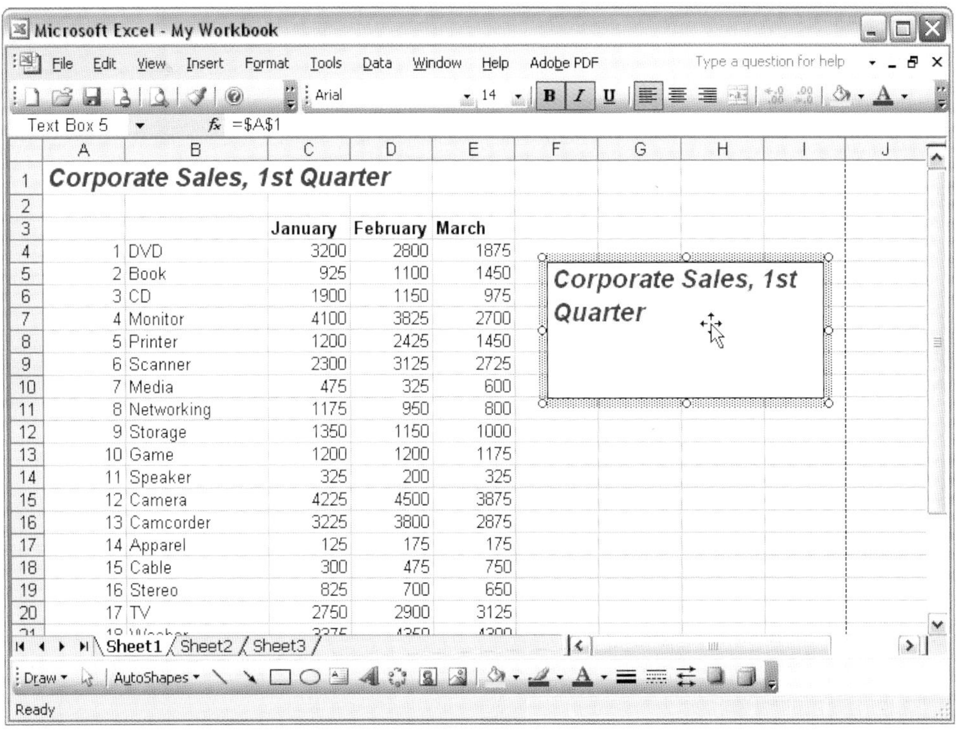

PROTECT YOUR WORKSHEETS

Protecting your worksheet's data in Excel is very difficult, so follow along closely. First, click Tools>Protection>Protect Sheet, and then type a password in the Password to Unprotect Sheet field. Next, select the various tasks that you want to allow users to perform without your permission and click OK. Reenter your password when prompted and click OK again (this isn't the hard part). Now for the hard part: Don't save your password to an Outlook sticky note and then email the note along with the worksheet to practically everyone in your address book (a pathetic, true story).

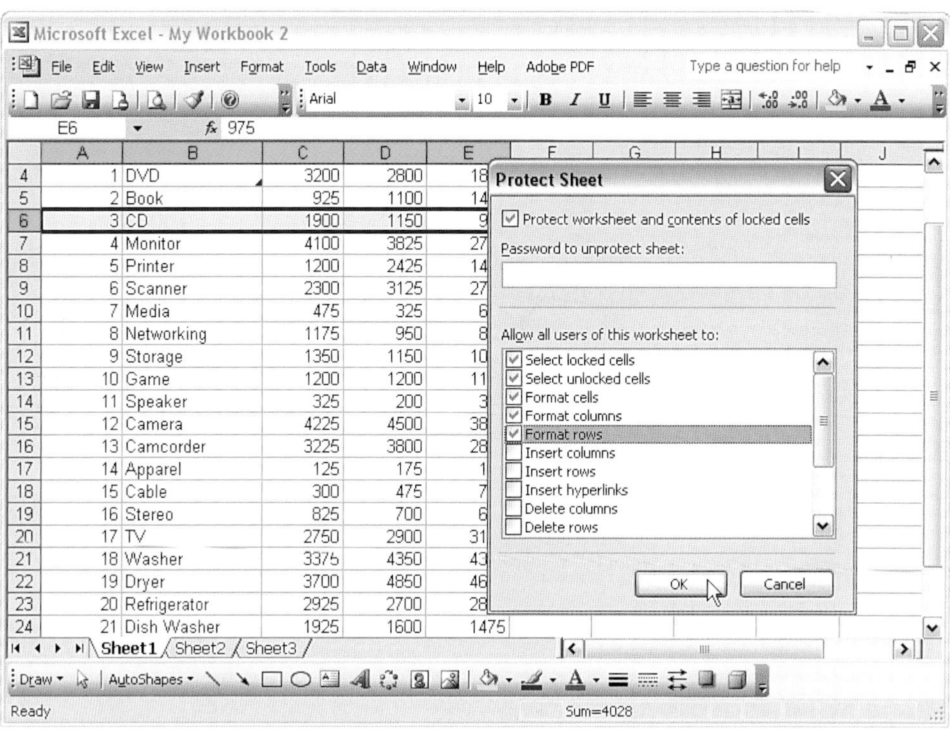

BE IMPATIENT

I've always been told that I'm impatient. It's true—traffic and low batteries on my TV remote freak me out—but sometimes impatience pays off. For example, I found a nice little trick to speed up AutoCorrect. When you begin typing in a cell, you'll notice that after a while, AutoCorrect begins to offer suggestions to complete your text. If you want to speed up this handy feature, right-click the cell and click Pick from Drop-Down List in the shortcut menu. A little pop-up menu listing available AutoCorrect words will appear directly beneath your cell. Now, find your choice and click it to place it in your document.

Microsoft Excel - My Workbook

File Edit View Insert Format Tools Data Window Help Adobe PDF

B26 Cam

	A	B	C	D	E	F	G	H	I	J
7	4	Monitor	4100	3825	2700					
8	5	Printer	1200	2425	1450					
9	6	Scanner	2300	3125	2725					
10	7	Media	475	325	600					
11	8	Networking	1175	950	800					
12	9	Storage	1350	1150	1000					
13	10	Game	1200	1200	1175					
14	11	Speaker	325	200	325					
15	12	Camera	4225	4500	3875					
16	13	Camcorder	3225	3800	2875					
17	14	Apparel	125	175	175					
18	15	Cable	300	475	750					
19	16	Stereo	825	700	650					
20	17	TV	2750	2900	3125					
21	18	Washer	3375	4350	4300					
22	19	Dryer	3700	4850	4625					
23	20	Refrigerator	2925	2700	2800					
24	21	Dish Washer	1925	1600	1475					
25	22	Small Appliance	0	0	275					
26		Cam								
27	Total									

Camcorder
Camera
CD
Dish Washer
Dryer
DVD
Game
Media

FREEZE!

This is a real problem for me. I can't remember the names of my column headings. It doesn't matter if I have 20 columns or just one—if it's out of sight, it's out of mind. But, I found a fix…I freeze my column headings. To do this, select the first cell on the left directly below the column headings and click Window>Freeze Panes in the menu bar. A thin black line appears directly below the column headings. Now, scroll your worksheet. The headings don't move; they're always in sight. To unfreeze your headings, click Window>Unfreeze Panes in the menu bar.

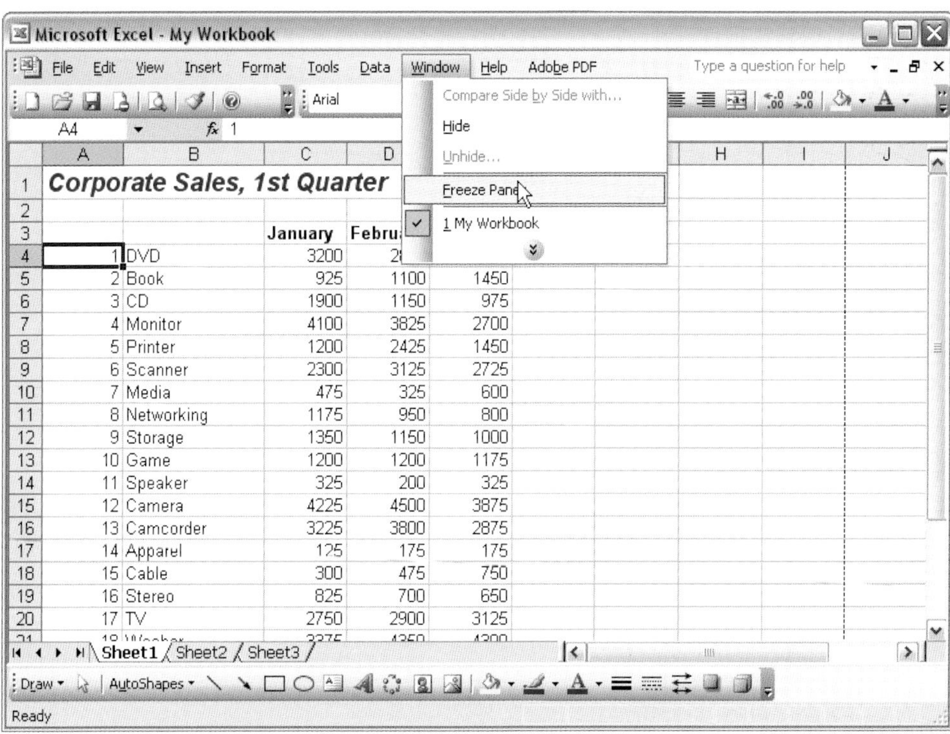

IN THE RED

Get back the red—as in "in the red." By default, negative currency numbers are displayed in black. But, when I'm in the red, I want to see it. If you do too, select your cells that use currency, click Format>Cells in the menu bar, and click the Number tab in the Format Cells dialog. Click Currency listed under Category, and then select a red format in the Negative Numbers field to display negative currency numbers in red. Now all negative currency numbers will be shown in red.

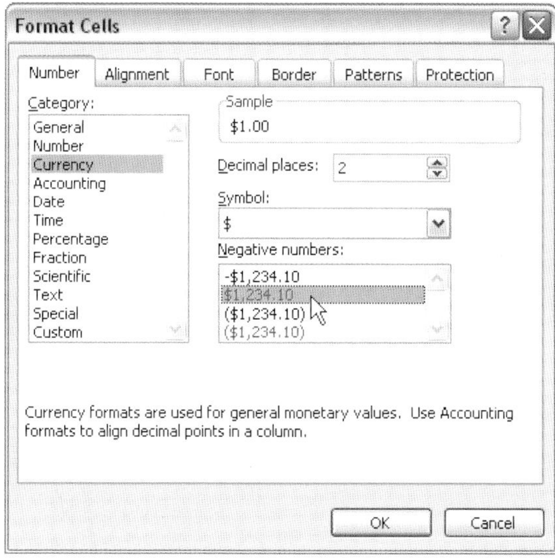

WRAP TEXT

For formatting's sake, wrap your text. By default, you can type text into a cell until your fingers fall off and all your text will still appear on one line. This wreaks havoc on your columns. You can avoid this, however, by wrapping your text within a cell. To do this, right-click any cell where you want to wrap the text, click Format Cells in the shortcut menu, and then click the Alignment tab in the Format Cells dialog. Next, check Wrap Text under the Text Control category and click OK. The text is now wrapped in the cell.

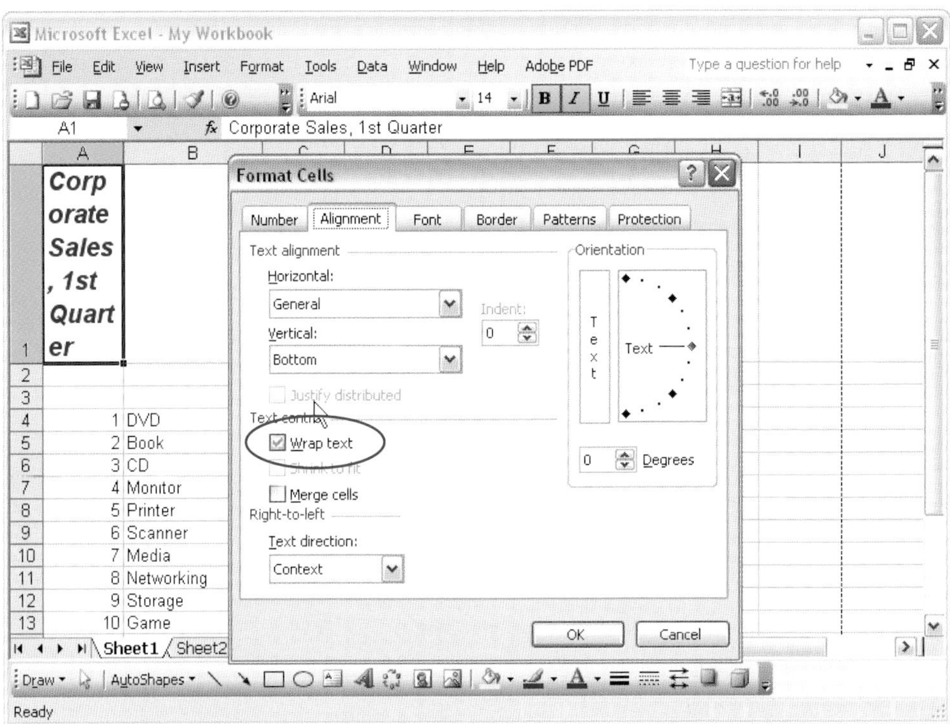

IT LOOKS COOL, SO IT MUST BE DONE

Here's a completely useless tip, which serves absolutely no purpose. But it looks cool and anything that looks cool in Excel must be done—because as we all know: Nothing in Excel looks cool (except for this). Select your column headings by pressing-and-holding the Control key on your keyboard and clicking each heading's cell. Next, click Format>Cells in the menu bar and click the Alignment tab in the Format Cells dialog. Be sure that the Horizontal drop-down menu in the Text Alignment category is set to General. Now, click any angle in the Orientation window to slant the column headings and click OK. Your text is now slanted to the orientation you selected. Hmm, a little flair. This is just so unexpected of Excel.

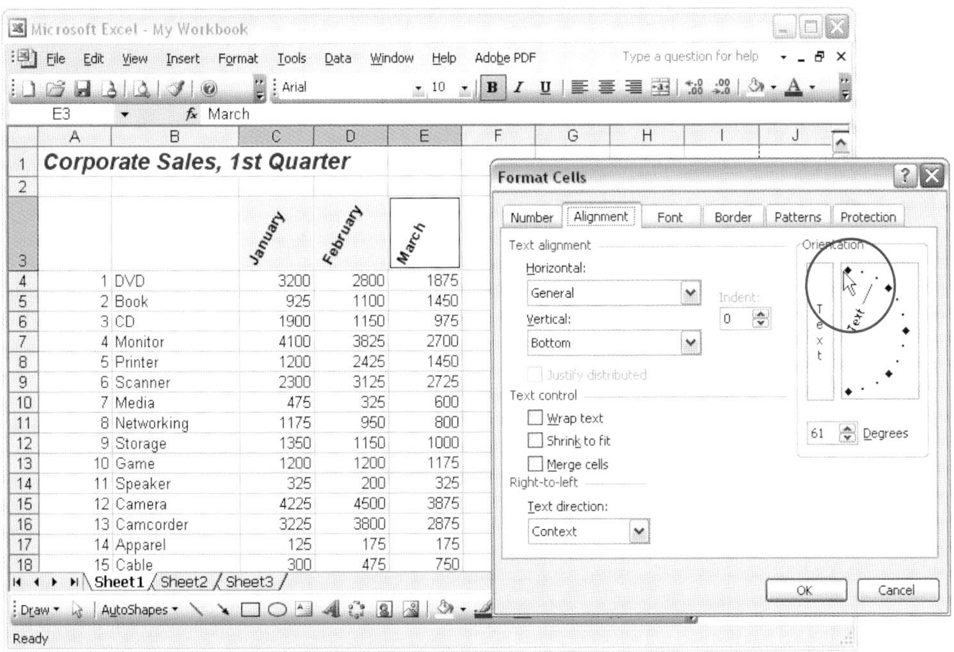

 SHARE (KIND OF)

Want to share just a little? I love to share just a little. I've never been an especially good sharer. In my family, I was the only boy and I had four sisters, so I never had to share anything. My sisters, on the other hand, had to share everything...they still resent me to this day (kidding, my sisters are wonderful, really). Anyway, here's a way to share your workbooks with others but prevent them from making changes (kind of like sharing). Open the workbook that you want to protect and click File>Save As in the menu bar. Next, click Tools in the top-right corner of the Save As dialog and click General Options. In the Save Options dialog, leave the Password to Open field blank (this allows anyone to open the workbook), but type a password in the Password to Modify field, and then click OK. You'll be asked to confirm your password. Click Save on the Save As dialog and you're finished. Now when anyone opens the workbook, they'll have the option to provide a password for unlimited access to your workbook or to open the workbook as Read Only. It feels good to share a little. To remove password protection, simply delete the password from the Save Options dialog, click OK, and then click Save in the Save As dialog.

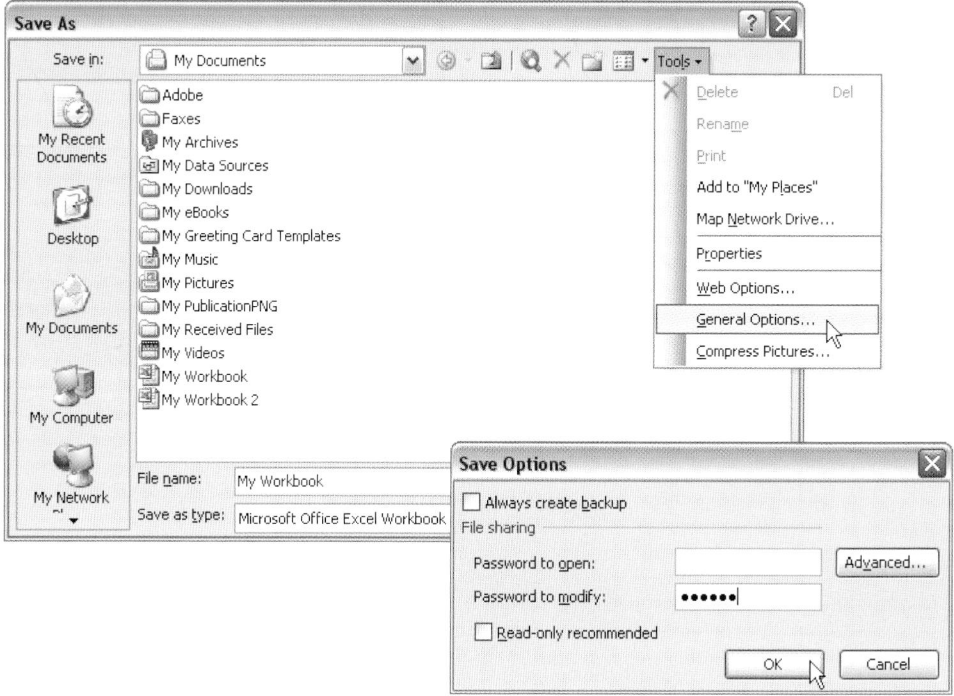

DO YOU VALIDATE?

It's always a good idea to assign data validation to cells that require very specific information. For instance, you may be gathering information about someone's shoe size (I'm sure shoe size is very important to someone out there), which requires a number. Well, if the person accidentally types "really big," that's not giving you the info you need. So, you can force the person to enter a number range. Here's how: Select the cell to which you want to add data validation, then click Data>Validation in the menu bar and click the Settings tab on the Data Validation dialog. Next, select Whole Number from the Allow drop-down menu and select Between from the Data drop-down menu. Type a Minimum number (e.g., 5) and a Maximum number (e.g., 14), and then click OK. Now the cell will only accept a number between 5 and 14. To remove validation from a cell, select the cell and click Data> Validation in the menu bar. Select the Settings tab, click the Clear All button, and click OK.

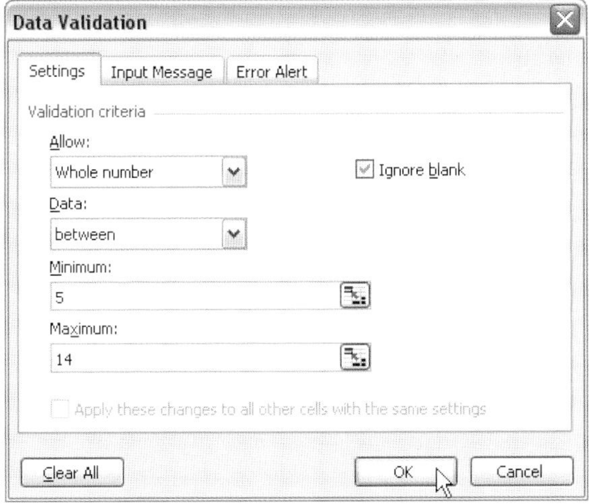

GIVE ME FRACTIONS

Go ahead—type a fraction into a cell (e.g., 1/12) and press Enter on your keyboard. Didn't work? Try it again. Still didn't work? Try it again. Hmm, you must be doing something wrong. Oh wait, it's not you, it's Excel. Excel interprets fractions as dates. Nice, huh? Actually you can make Excel recognize your fractions. Here's how: Type a zero followed by a space in front of your fraction (e.g., 0 1/12). I bet that'll work.

Microsoft Excel - My Workbook

E4 fx 0 1/12

	A	B	C	D	E
1	Corporate Sales, 1st Quarter				
2					
3			January	February	March
4	1	DVD	3200		0 1/12
5	2	Book	925	1100	1450
6	3	CD	1900	1150	975
7	4	Monitor	4100	3825	2700
8	5	Printer	1200	2425	1450
9	6	Scanner	2300	3125	2725
10	7	Media	475	325	600
11	8	Networking	1175	950	800

Microsoft Excel - My Workbook

E4 fx 0.0833333333333333

	A	B	C	D	E
1	Corporate Sales, 1st Quarter				
2					
3			January	February	March
4	1	DVD	3200	2800	1/12
5	2	Book	925	1100	1450
6	3	CD	1900	1150	975
7	4	Monitor	4100	3825	2700
8	5	Printer	1200	2425	1450
9	6	Scanner	2300	3125	2725
10	7	Media	475	325	600
11	8	Networking	1175	950	800

 CHECK ALL OF MY SPELLING

Yes, even Excel users need to check their spelling, and here's a quick trick to check the spelling for your entire workbook. Press-and-hold the Control key on your keyboard, then click each sheet's tab in your workbook to group them. Now, press F7 on your keyboard and the Spelling Checker will check each selected worksheet for misspellings, not just the current worksheet.

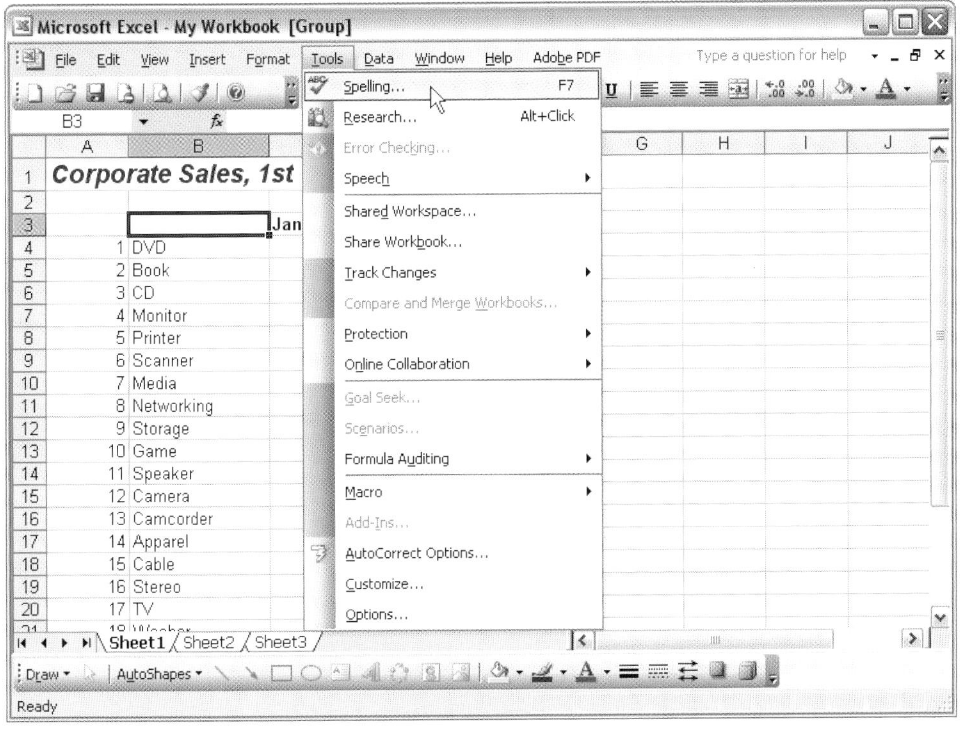

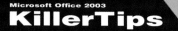

THE FORMULA TO COMMENTS

When developing workbooks with others, you may want to attach comments directly to your formulas as reminders, ideas, or explanations. To do this, click the cell containing the formula that you want to add a comment to, and then type: +N("your comment") (including the quotation marks) in the Formula bar. Press Enter on your keyboard when you're finished. This command applies the comment to the formula without affecting its results. To view the comment, just click the cell and look in the Formula bar.

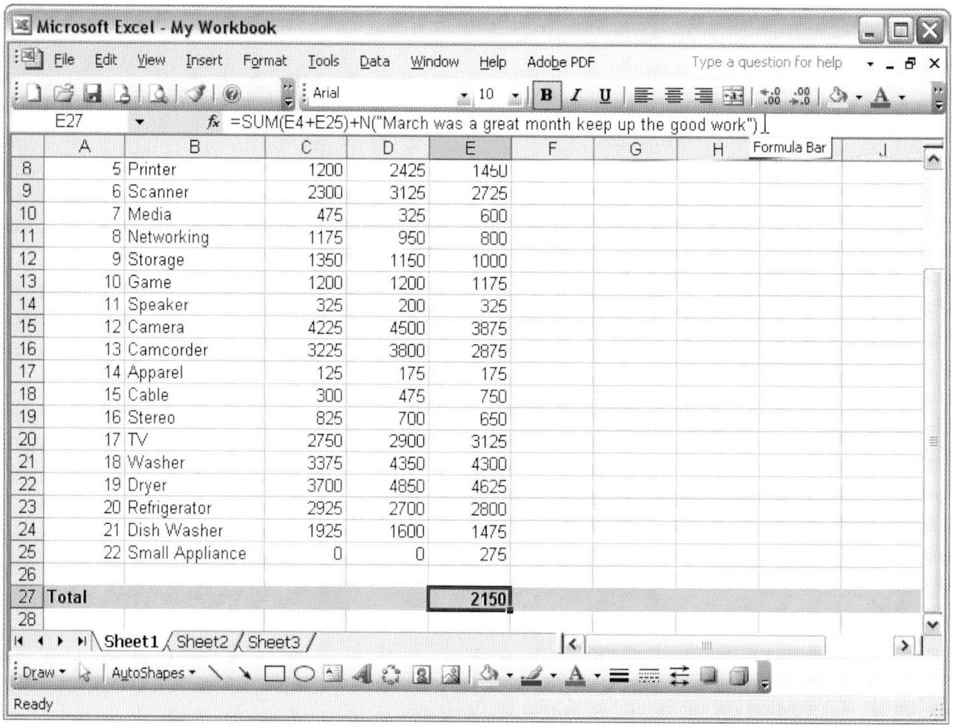

Microsoft Excel - My Workbook

E27 =SUM(E4+E25)+N("March was a great month keep up the good work")

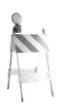

	A	B	C	D	E
8	5	Printer	1200	2425	1450
9	6	Scanner	2300	3125	2725
10	7	Media	475	325	600
11	8	Networking	1175	950	800
12	9	Storage	1350	1150	1000
13	10	Game	1200	1200	1175
14	11	Speaker	325	200	325
15	12	Camera	4225	4500	3875
16	13	Camcorder	3225	3800	2875
17	14	Apparel	125	175	175
18	15	Cable	300	475	750
19	16	Stereo	825	700	650
20	17	TV	2750	2900	3125
21	18	Washer	3375	4350	4300
22	19	Dryer	3700	4850	4625
23	20	Refrigerator	2925	2700	2800
24	21	Dish Washer	1925	1600	1475
25	22	Small Appliance	0	0	275
26					
27	Total				2150
28					

WINGDINGIN' IT

Comments are useful but they're not cool; you'd have to be able to place pictures into comments for them to be cool and you can't. But wait—Wingdings are kind of like pictures. Actually, they're exactly like pictures (type pictures), and we can place type into text boxes. Let's see if it works. Select any cell where you want to add a comment, then click Insert>Comment in the menu bar, and a comment box appears. Now highlight the text and change the Font field in the Formatting toolbar to Wingdings. Type until you find a character that expresses your comment (I pressed Shift-J to get a smiley face). You can also make the character as large as necessary by highlighting it and using the Font Size drop-down menu in the Formatting toolbar. Comments are now officially cool!

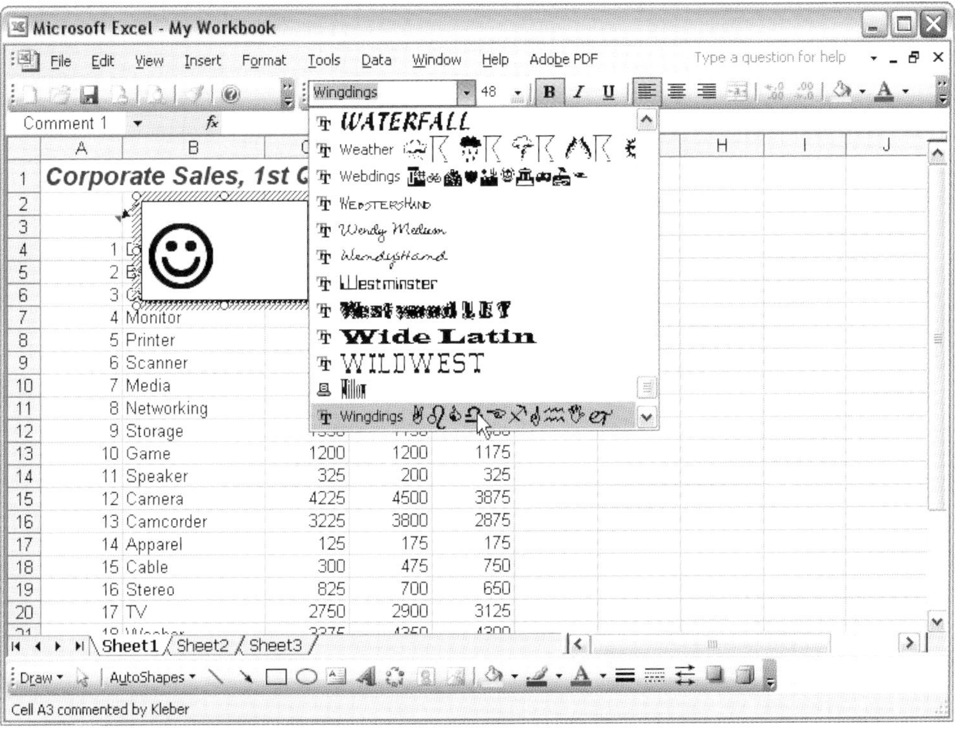

EXCEL CAN BE LONELY

Creating Excel worksheets is a lonely business. Most people avoid Excel users (our brilliance intimidates them). Well maybe your colleagues won't talk to you, but Excel will. First, open the Text to Speech toolbar by right-clicking any toolbar and clicking Text to Speech. Next, select the cells that you want Excel to read, then press the By Rows or By Columns button on the Text to Speech toolbar to tell Excel the order in which your cells should be read, then click the Speak Cells button. I feel so loved! To stop Excel from talking to you, click the Stop Speaking button on the Text to Speech toolbar.

Microsoft Excel - My Workbook

Corporate Sales, 1st Quarter

		January	February	March
1	DVD	3200	2800	1875
2	Book	925	1100	1450
3	CD	1900	1150	975
4	Monitor	4100	3825	2700
5	Printer	1200	2425	1450
6	Scanner	2300	3125	2725
7	Media	475	325	600
8	Networking	1175	950	800
9	Storage	1350	1150	1000
10	Game	1200	1200	1175
11	Speaker	325	200	325
12	Camera	4225	4500	3875
13	Camcorder	3225	3800	2875
14	Apparel	125	175	175
15	Cable	300	475	750
16	Stereo	825	700	650
17	TV	2750	2900	3125

Text To Speech

By Columns

Sum=41525

LET'S HOOK UP

If you need to join separate cells into a single text string, use the Concatenate function; =CONCATENATE(first cell," ",second cell). For example, you want to join the text from cell A4 through E4 into G4. To do this, type into cell G4 =CONCATENATE(A4," ",B4," ",C4," ",D4," ",E4,"") and then press Enter on your keyboard. The text from each field appears in G4. You can add any cell from your worksheet or add as many cells as you want to appear in the selected cell. You can also add formatting to separate the text—simply replace the space between the quote marks with commas, periods, hyphens, or whatever.

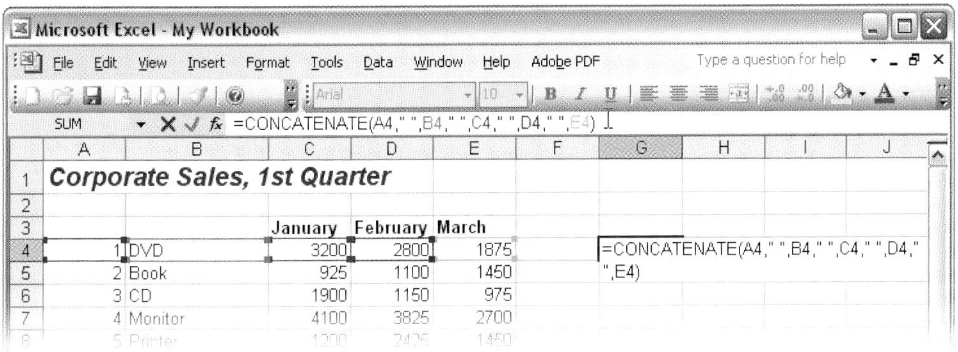

Microsoft Excel - My Workbook

File Edit View Insert Format Tools Data Window Help Adobe PDF

SUM =CONCATENATE(A4," ",B4," ",C4," ",D4," ",E4)

	A	B	C	D	E	F	G
1	Corporate Sales, 1st Quarter						
2							
3			January	February	March		
4	1	DVD	3200	2800	1875		=CONCATENATE(A4," ",B4," ",C4," ",D4," ",E4)
5	2	Book	925	1100	1450		
6	3	CD	1900	1150	975		
7	4	Monitor	4100	3825	2700		

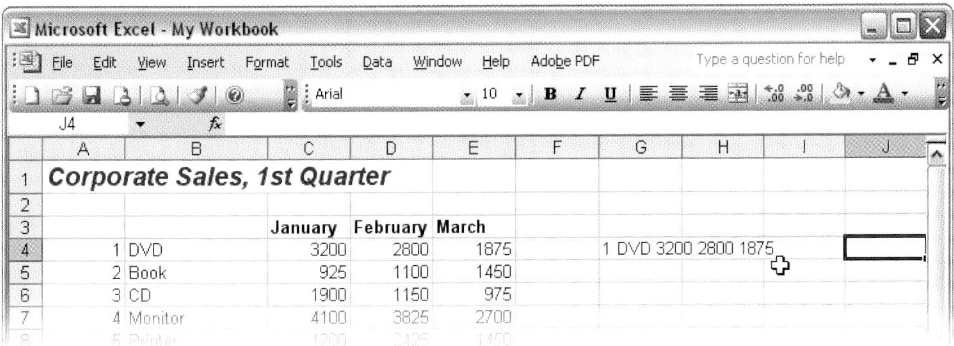

QUICK GRAPHS

The only thing better than graphs are quick graphs, and you can make one by first selecting a data range on your worksheet and then pressing the F11 key on your keyboard. Your new graph appears on its own worksheet. You can also change the chart type: Simply click the Chart Type button on the Chart toolbar (which opens automatically anytime a chart is created) and select a chart style in the Chart Type drop-down menu.

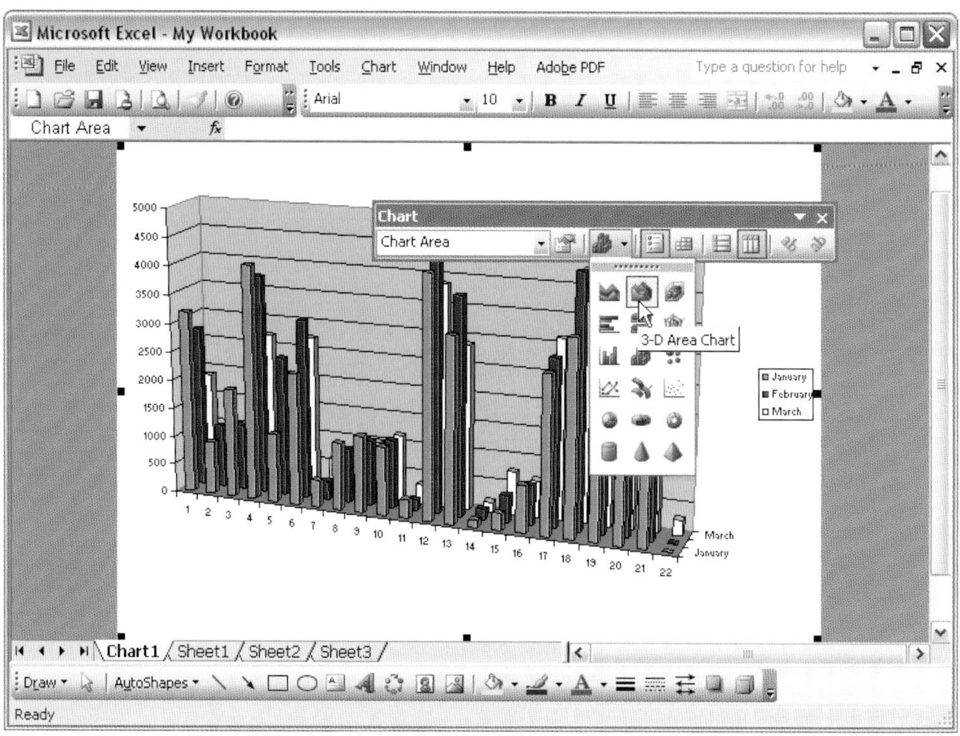

JUMPIN' HERE, JUMPIN' THERE

I'm always jumping back and forth between worksheets and I've found the quickest way to do this is by pressing Control-Page Down on the keyboard to move to the next worksheet to the right (as shown) or pressing Control-Page Up to jump to the next worksheet to the left.

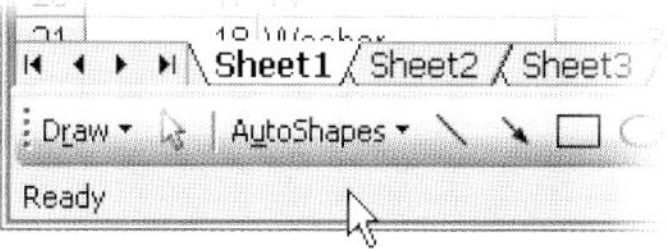

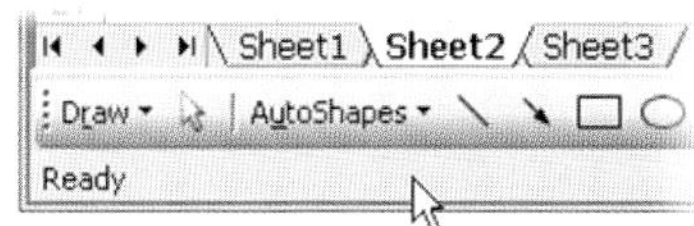

SMART NAVIGATION

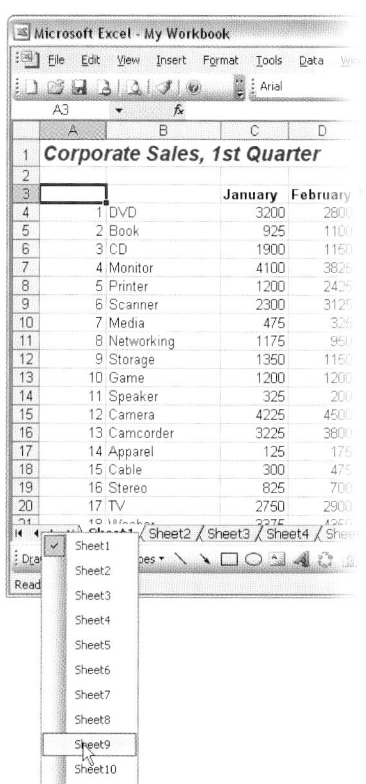

You may think you have to use the four arrow buttons at the bottom-left corner of your Excel workbook's window to jump to a worksheet in a large workbook. Well, you'd be right, but you don't actually have to click the arrows—you can right-click the arrows. This gives you a shortcut menu of all worksheets in your workbook. Now, simply click the worksheet in the shortcut menu that you want to view to instantly jump to it.

POWER SHARING

Excel makes sharing workbooks painless and even gives you the final "say-so" to any conflicting changes. This means that if two other users have a different idea about a formula or whatever, you'll be asked to determine who "wins." To share your workbook, click Tools>Share Workbook in the menu bar and click the Editing tab in the Share Workbook dialog. Next, check "Allow changes by more than one user at the same time. This also allows workbook merging." Now, click the Advanced tab and select Automatically Every and type 15 to save update changes every 15 minutes. This allows you to compare your changes with others'. Then click OK. You can tell when a workbook is shared by looking at the workbook's title bar—the word Shared appears in brackets: "[Shared]". To stop sharing your workbook, click Tools>Share Workbook in the menu bar and under the Editing tab uncheck "Allow changes by more than one user at the same time. This also allows workbook merging." Then click OK.

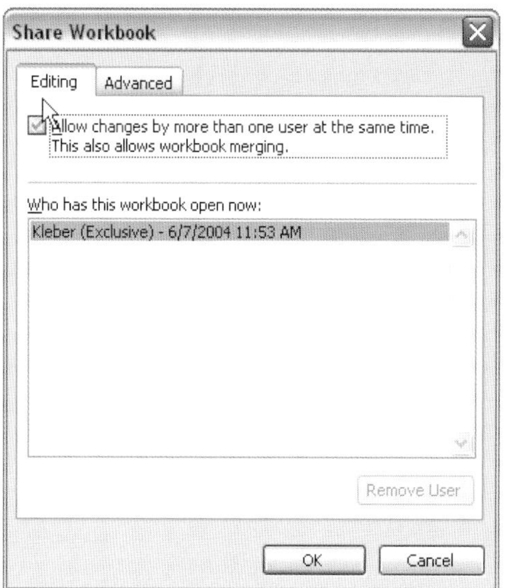

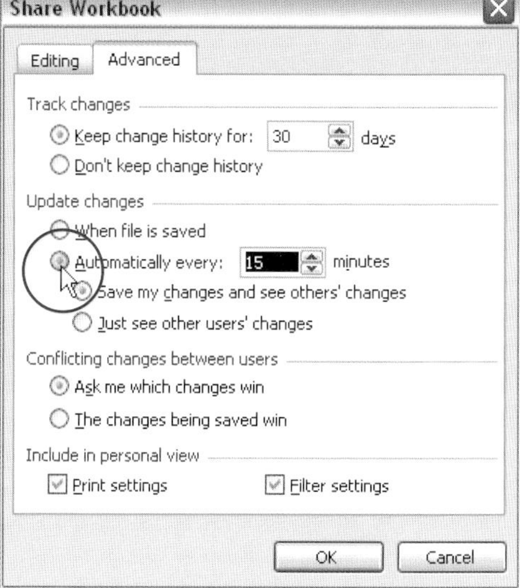

HIDE WORKSHEETS

Workbooks can get stupidly large, making them a little difficult to navigate. Many of mine are stupid and large. So, to make large workbooks a little easier to navigate, hide worksheets that you don't regularly use or that contain static data that very seldom (if ever) changes. To hide a worksheet, first select the worksheet you want to hide, then click Format>Sheet>Hide in the menu bar. It's gone! When you want to unhide your worksheets, click Format>Sheet>Unhide in the menu bar. Now, select the worksheet that you want to view using the Unhide dialog and click OK. It's back!

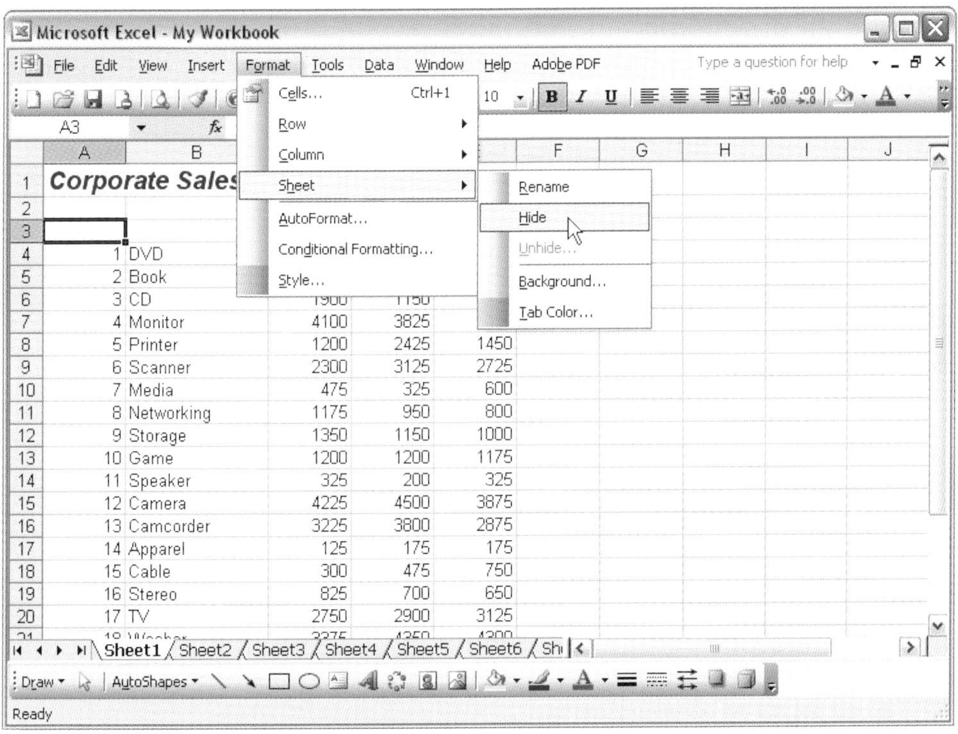

DON'T FORGET THE PIXELS

The Web is a world of pixels. Resolution is measured in pixels: 800x600, 1280x1024, and so on. So, when optimizing a worksheet for the Web, you should use this scale of measurement—and Excel's ScreenTips can help. When pressing-and-holding your mouse pointer to adjust column widths and row heights, check out the measurement ScreenTip—not only does it show Excel's standard measurements but also the pixel measurement to the right. As you adjust columns and rows, the pixel distance is also displayed.

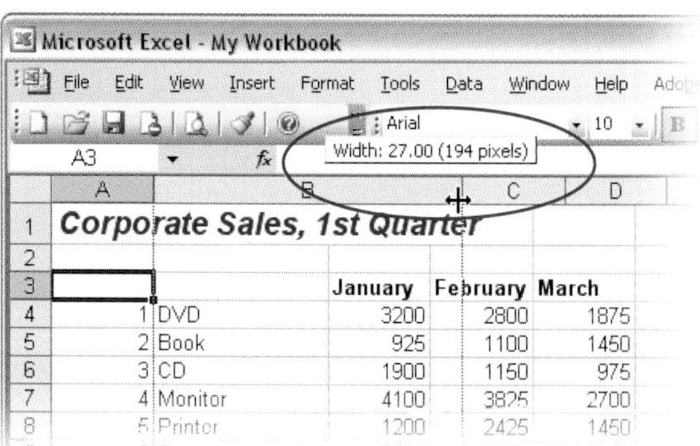

CASE-SENSITIVE SORTS

By default, when sorting data in Excel, it doesn't distinguish between upper- and lowercase letters, which may be a problem, especially if you want to sort by words using capital letters, for example. We can change this, though. Select your range, then click Data>Sort in the menu bar and click the Options button in the Sort dialog. Next, check Case Sensitive in the Sort Options dialog and click OK. Now Excel will recognize letter case when sorting.

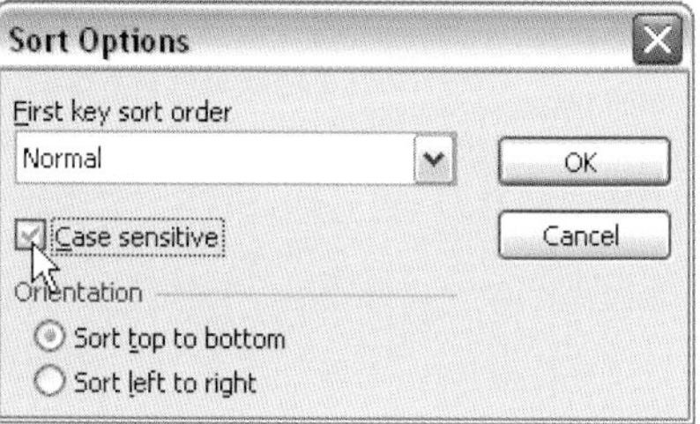

SELECT LARGE RANGES

There are many ways to select ranges in Excel, but the one I use most is the Shift-click shortcut. This shortcut really comes in handy when you have to select columns that don't appear onscreen. When this happens to you, click the first cell in your range (top-left cell) and use the scroll bar to navigate to the bottom-right cell of the range. Now, press-and-hold the Shift key on your keyboard and click the last cell in your range (bottom-right cell). Your range is now selected. Now delete it, ranges shouldn't be that big (just kidding).

Microsoft Excel - My Workbook

	A	B	C	D	E	F
7	4	Monitor	4100	3825	2700	
8	5	Printer	1200	2425	1450	
9	6	Scanner	2300	3125	2725	
10	7	Media	475	325	600	
11	8	Networking	1175	950	800	
12	9	Storage	1350	1150	1000	
13	10	Game	1200	1200	1175	
14	11	Speaker	325	200	325	
15	12	Camera	4225	4500	3875	
16	13	Camcorder	3225	3800	2875	
17	14	Apparel	125	175	175	
18	15	Cable	300	475	750	
19	16	Stereo	825	700	650	
20	17	TV	2750	2900	3125	
21	18	Washer	3375	4350	4300	
22	19	Dryer	3700	4850	4625	
23	20	Refrigerator	2925	2700	2800	
24	21	Dish Washer	1925	1600	1475	
25	22	Small Appliance	0	0	275	
26						
27	Total				2150	

Ready Sum=128228

 SHOW OFF YOUR FORMULAS

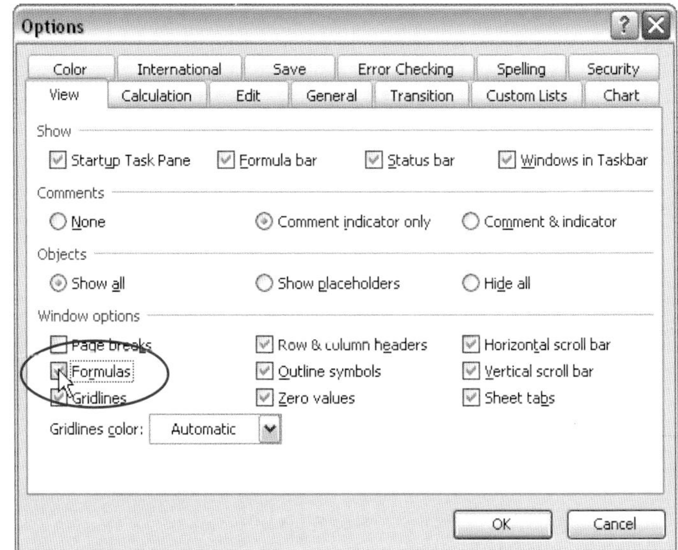

Are you a show-off? I am! It's so bad that I'm always catching myself trying to impress me. It's really very distracting. Here's a way to show off your formulas onscreen, or even print and share your formulas. Hold on, I know what you're thinking; you're thinking that Excel only displays and prints formula results, not the formula itself. Well, it does by default, but we don't believe in defaults. Click Tools>Options in the menu bar and click the View tab in the Options dialog. Next, check Formulas under the Window Options category, and then click OK. All your formulas are displayed, not the formula results. Now, display 'em, print 'em, and share 'em. It's fun to be a show-off!

REMEMBER TO COLOR CODE

We all need reminders and here's a great way to remind yourself of work that you need to complete on a worksheet or to highlight worksheets that contain special or important data. Right-click a sheet's tab at the bottom-left corner of the Excel window, then click Tab Color in the shortcut menu. Select a color (anything but gray) and click OK...instant reminder.

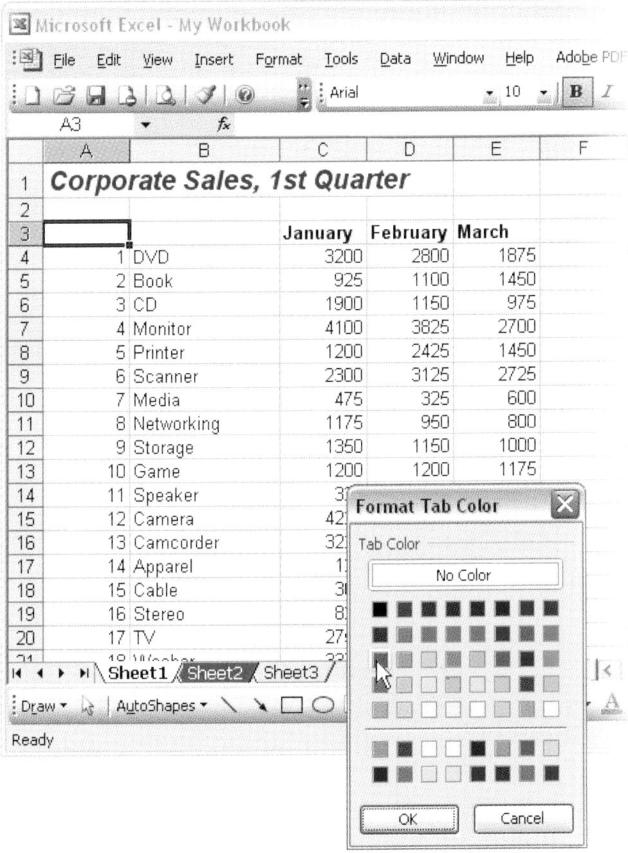

"WATCH" YOUR WINDOW

Excel's Watch Window is a clever idea and it's very useful. If you're not using it, you should be. As your worksheet becomes longer and longer, important data is shifted out of view in Excel's window. The Watch Window keeps important data always in view. To add a Watch Window, right-click a cell that you always want to view and click Add Watch in the shortcut menu. A Watch Window dialog appears listing your cell. To add additional cells to your Watch Window, select the cell and click Add Watch on the Watch Window dialog. The Watch Window dialog will sit on the worksheet's foreground as you work, always keeping your favored cells in view.

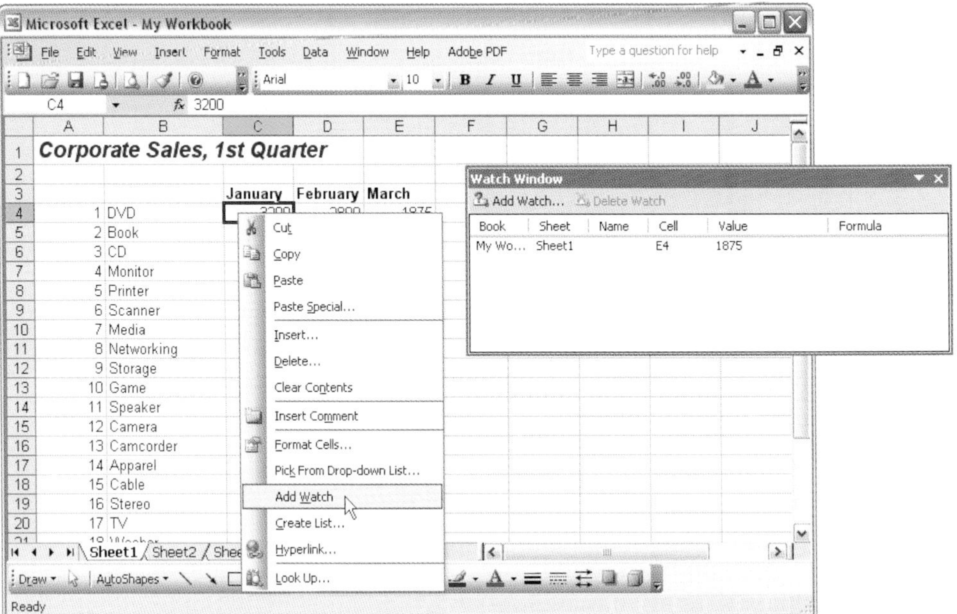

DON'T SAVE THE GEEK-SPEAK

Most Excel users don't give a great deal of thought to naming their workbooks. It's usually something like "Q1604R"—they're very creative people. Well, this may be effective geek-speak, but remember, when saving workbooks to the Web, most people don't understand geek-speak. So when saving, be sure to change the workbook's title to something that helps users to identify it. To change a workbook's title for the Web, click File>Save as Web Page in the menu bar, then click the Change Title button on the Save As dialog. Name your file in the resulting dialog, click OK, and then click Save in the Save As dialog. By default, if you don't change the workbook's title, the file name will appear as the webpage's title.

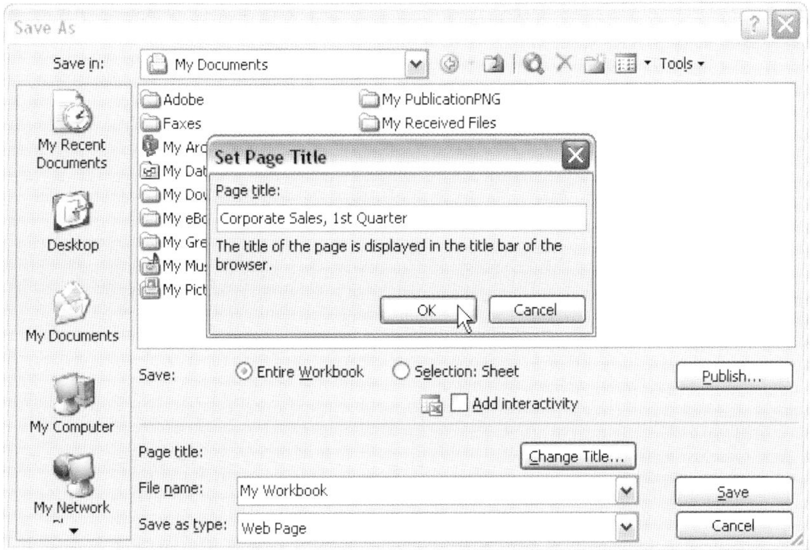

 PAINT COLUMNS AND ROWS

To copy a row's or column's formatting and apply it to other rows or columns, use Excel's Format Painter. Select the row or column with the formatting that you want to copy by clicking the row or column heading and then click the Format Painter button (it looks like a paintbrush) on the Standard toolbar. Next, click the row or column heading that you want to copy the formatting to (your mouse pointer will appear as a paintbrush). Your formatting is applied to the row or column. To apply the same formatting to multiple rows or columns, double-click the Format Painter. Now you can continue to apply the formatting to as many rows or columns as you'd like. When finished, click the Format Painter button again to turn it off.

Microsoft Excel - My Workbook

	A	B	C	D	E
1	Corporate Sales, 1st Quarter				
2					
3			January	February	March
4	1	DVD	3200	2800	[illegible]5
5	2	Book	925	1100	1450
6	3	CD	1900	1150	975
7	4	Monitor	4100	3825	2700
8	5	Printer	1200	2425	1450
9	6	Scanner	2300	3125	2725
10	7	Media	475	325	600
11	8	Networking	1175	950	800
12	9	Storage	1350	1150	1000
13	10	Game	1200	1200	1175
14	11	Speaker	325	200	325
15	12	Camera	4225	4500	3875
16	13	Camcorder	3225	3800	2875
17	14	Apparel	125	175	175
18	15	Cable	300	475	750
19	16	Stereo	825	700	650
20	17	TV	2750	2900	3125

Use the mouse to apply the copied format to another object

Easy Access

WORKING WITH ACCESS

I used to think that "database" was the worst sound I'd ever heard until I started my car with a cat on the manifold. That's the worse sound I've ever heard! After that

Easy Access

working with access

happened, I thought I'd give databases another shot. And once I figured 'em out, I fell in love with 'em (not literally, that would be weird). I began making databases for just about anything and everything. The first one I created was for tracking the members of my "the-terrors-of-starting-your-car" therapy group (it took me a while). After that, it was off to the races. And to think, I owe my love of databases all to a cat. It's funny how things happen. It's not funny about the cat, that's sad.

YOUR VERY OWN TOOLTIPS

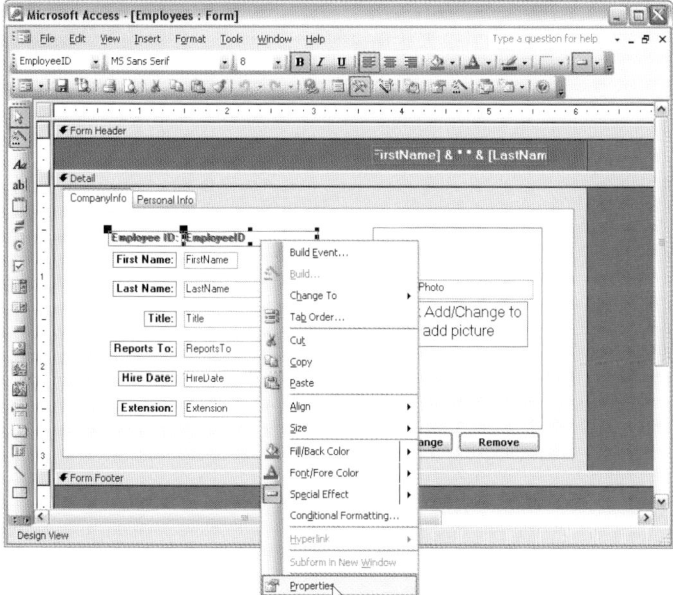

Aren't ToolTips sweet? They're very helpful and just plain fun. Really, I love 'em. So, you can only imagine how excited I was when I discovered how to make my own when I'm using a form in Access (File>New>Blank Database>Forms). Let me share how to do this: Open any form in Design View (View>Design View), then right-click the control that you want to add a ToolTip to. (In case you didn't know—a ToolTip [sometimes called a ScreenTip] is a tiny window that pops up when you position your mouse pointer over a control. It explains the control's function or offers help. You can turn these on and off by choosing Tools>Customize and selecting Show ScreenTips on Toolbars.) Anyway, once you've right-clicked the control, then click Properties in the shortcut menu. See if the control you've selected has the option to create a ToolTip by clicking the Other tab in the control's dialog and type your ToolTip in the ControlTip Text field, then close the dialog. Now, switch your form's view by choosing Form View from the View menu, then place your pointer over the control and there it is...your very own ToolTip.

IT'S YOUR DEFAULT

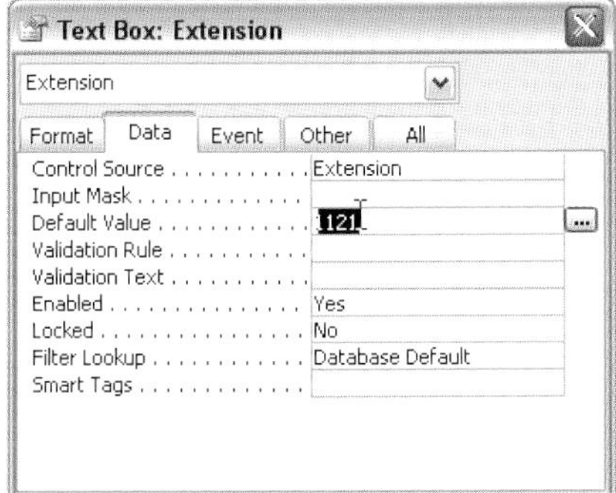

If a field generally will have the same data for each record, you can save time for users by changing the field's default value to display the data automatically for each new record created. Here's how: Open your form in Design View (View>Design View), right-click the control that you want to assign a default value to, and then click Properties in the shortcut menu. Next, click the Data tab on the control's dialog and type the recurring data in the Default Value field. Close the control's dialog when finished. Now, switch your form to Form View (View>Form View) and create a new record. You can now see your default value in that control's field. This will be the default value for each record until the user changes it.

I'M IMPORTANT!

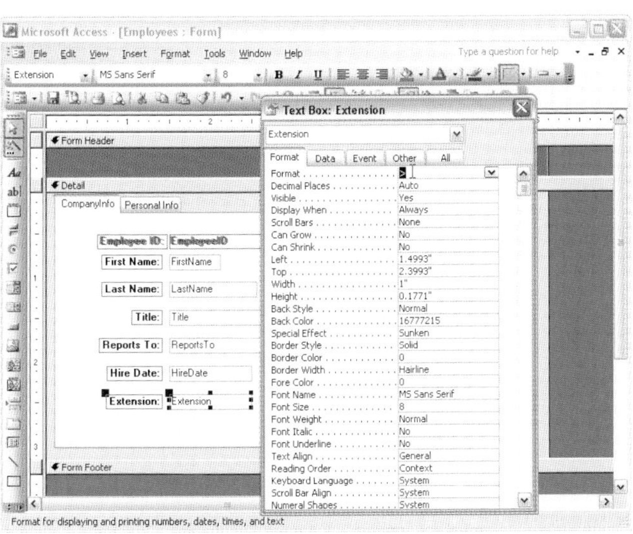

Here's a great way to bring attention to a field containing important data: Automatically show all text for a control's field in uppercase letters. To do this, make sure you're in Design or Form View by choosing either view from the View menu, then right-click the field where you want to apply this formatting and click Properties in the shortcut menu. Next, click the Format tab on the control's dialog and type ">" (press Shift-period) in the Format field, then close the dialog. Now all text for that control will be displayed in uppercase letters. You can't miss it. To display all text in lowercase letters, type "<" (Shift-comma) into the Format field.

SAY NO TO SNAP TO GRID

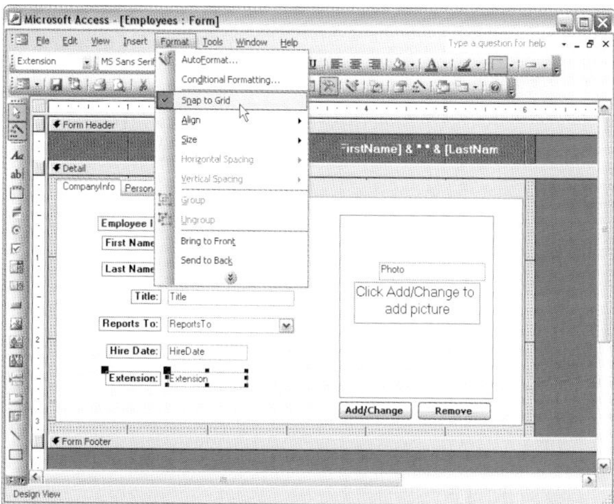

Grids are good; Snap to Grid is not. So, don't use it. You can turn off Snap to Grid by clicking Format>Snap to Grid in the menu bar. If you insist on using Snap to Grid, however, there will be times when you'll want to move your controls freely to place them in the correct positions. You can do this without turning off Snap to Grid: While in Design View (View>Design), just press-and-hold the Control key on your keyboard as you reposition the control. This will allow you to resize or place the control anywhere on your forms or reports without the controls snapping to your grid. If you decide that you want to snap a control to your grid after all, simply release the Control key before you release your mouse button.

INSTANT FIT

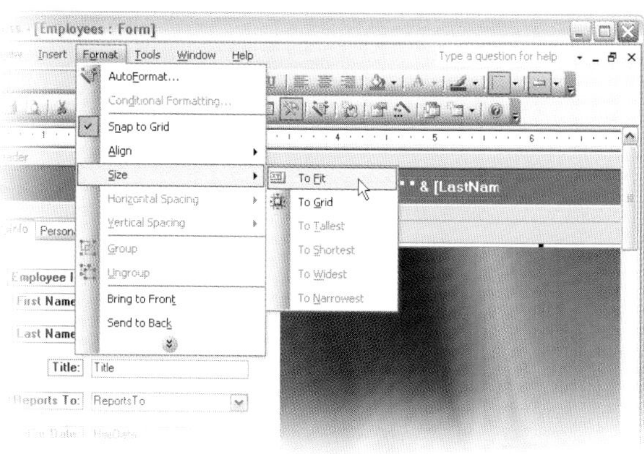

Instead of trying to resize your image box manually to fit your picture, use the To Fit command to adjust your image box to the exact dimension of your image. To resize an image box so that it fits your image, select the image box, then click Format>Size>To Fit in the menu bar. Your image box will expand or shrink to fit your image perfectly. This tip also works for fitting controls (e.g., text boxes, etc.) to text.

CAN YOU PICTURE IT?

Pictures just make things better, and this is very true for databases because databases are boring. They just are, and you should do anything that you can do to spice 'em up. Actually, images are fairly essential for any database. They can be your logo to help identify your company, photos of employees, or pictures that relay a message about the form being used. Fortunately, Access makes it easy to add these gems to your forms or reports. First, view your form or report in Design View by clicking View>Design View in the menu bar. Next, right-click any toolbar or menu and select Toolbox in the shortcut menu. Then, click the Image button on the Toolbox toolbar that appears and click-and-drag an image box to where you want the image to appear on your form or report, or simply click your mouse where you want the image to appear on the form. Now, using the Insert Picture dialog, browse your hard drive to locate the image, and then click OK when finished. Your image will appear in the image box. To add a caption, click the Label button on the Toolbox toolbar, click-and-drag to create a label box, then type your caption, and press Enter on your keyboard. Lastly, move the caption to arrange it within your image.

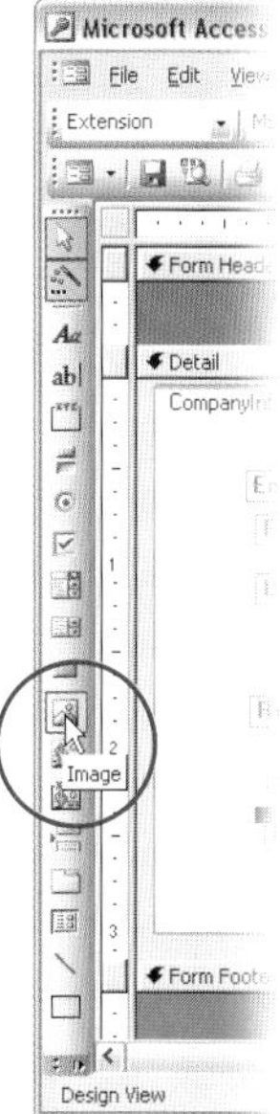

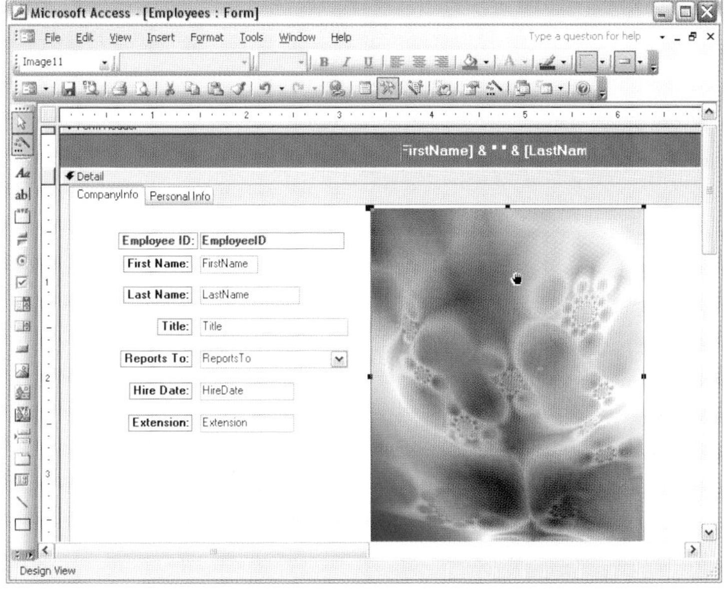

THE OBJECT OF SHORTCUTS

Typically, I work with the same object in a database or at the very least, I always use the same object when first opening a database. Well, you can speed up this process by actually creating a desktop shortcut to your favorite database object—a form, a report, etc. Here's how: Open the object you want to create a shortcut to (I used a form here) and in the object's Database window, right-click the object's icon, then click Create Shortcut in the shortcut menu. Next, click Browse to navigate to your desktop, and then click OK in the Create Shortcut dialog. Now you can close out of Access, go to your desktop, and there's your object's new shortcut. Double-click the shortcut to launch Access and go directly to your object, bypassing the default database window.

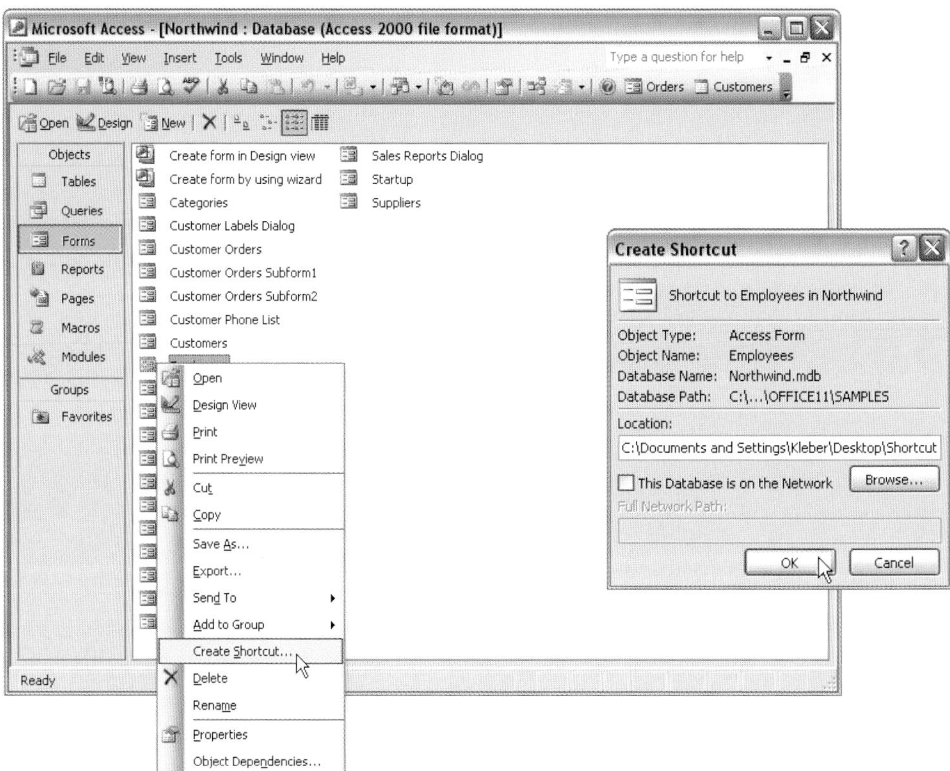

 ACCESS SPECIFICATIONS

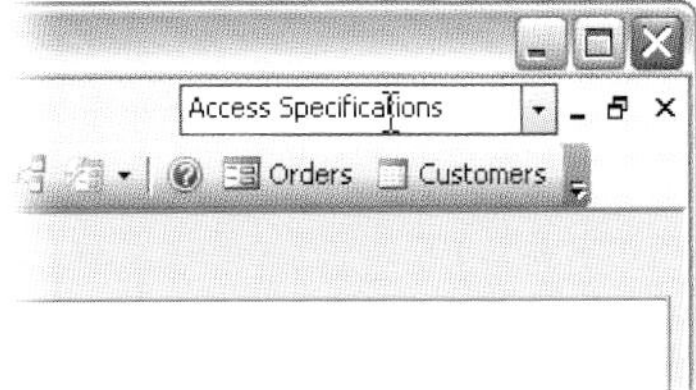

Have you ever wondered what Access is capable of, such as the maximum possible size of any database or the maximum possible number of records in a table? If so, then you can find out. In the "Type a question for help" field (in the top-right corner of the menu bar), type "Access Specifications" and then press Enter on your keyboard. This opens the Help pane. Click the Access Specifications link at the top of the task pane, which will display Access's capabilities for databases and projects.

 ALL I SEE ARE ASTERISKS

If you need to protect sensitive or confidential information when entering data into a field, you should set the control's Input Mask property to Password. To do this, open your form in Design View (View>Design View), then right-click the control's field that you want to protect, and click Properties in the shortcut menu. Next, click the Data tab in the control's dialog and click the Input Mask field to select it. Type "Password" in the Input Mask field (as in the first example) or click the Build button to the right of the field (it looks like an ellipsis) and choose Password from the Input Mask Wizard dialog (as in the second example), then click Finish. Now when you switch to Form View from the View menu, all data in that field will appear as asterisks (*).

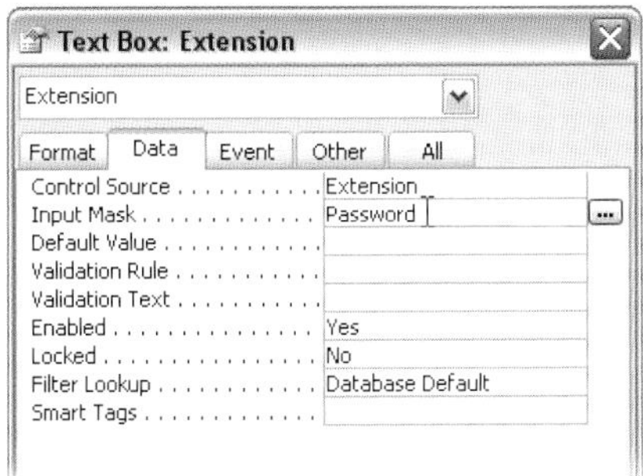

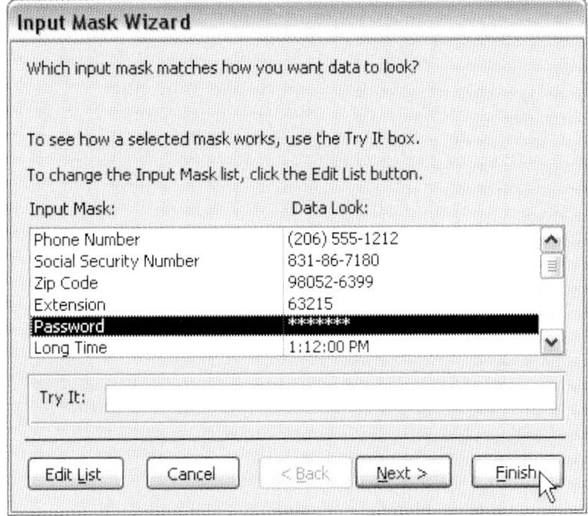

DON'T IMPORT—LINK

You don't always have to import your text files for use in your database; you can link to them instead. Here's how: From the menu bar, click File>Get External Data>Link Tables. Next, use the Link dialog to browse your hard drive to locate the text file you want to import (be sure to choose Text Files in the Files of Type drop-down menu in the Link dialog), and then click Link. Follow the Link Text Wizard to choose your import options, and then click Finish. Your file will appear in your object's Database window.

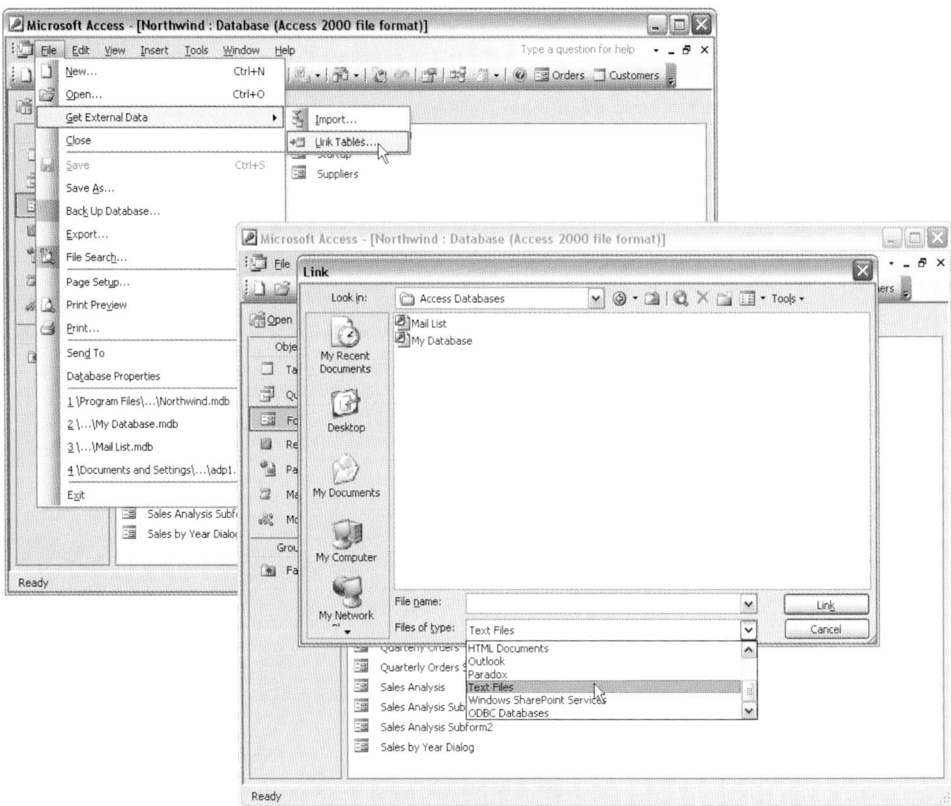

TAKE IT TO THE WEB

One of the coolest features of Access 2003 is its ability to convert forms and reports into webpages. I do it all the time for no reason at all and you can too. First select the form or report that you want to convert into a webpage by choosing Select Record or Select All from the Edit menu, and then click File>Save As in the menu bar. (*Note:* If you're using a report, make sure you're in Design View.) Type a name for your page in the Save Report/Form To field and choose Data Access Page from the As drop-down menu, and then click OK. This opens the New Data Access Page dialog. Next, choose a location on your hard drive to save your page and click OK. You've just created a webpage from your form/report. Double-click the page's icon saved on your hard drive to open it in your Web browser.

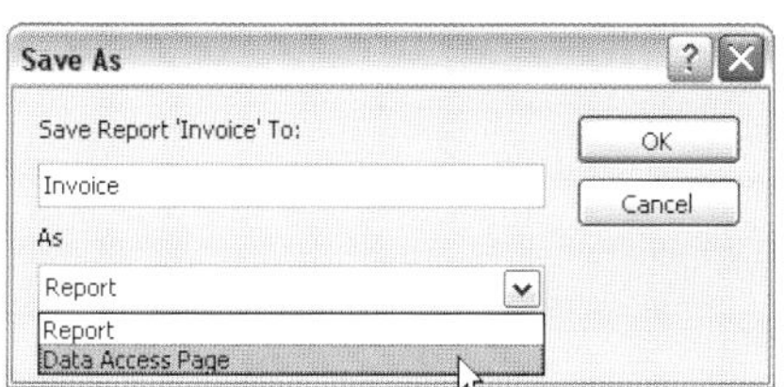

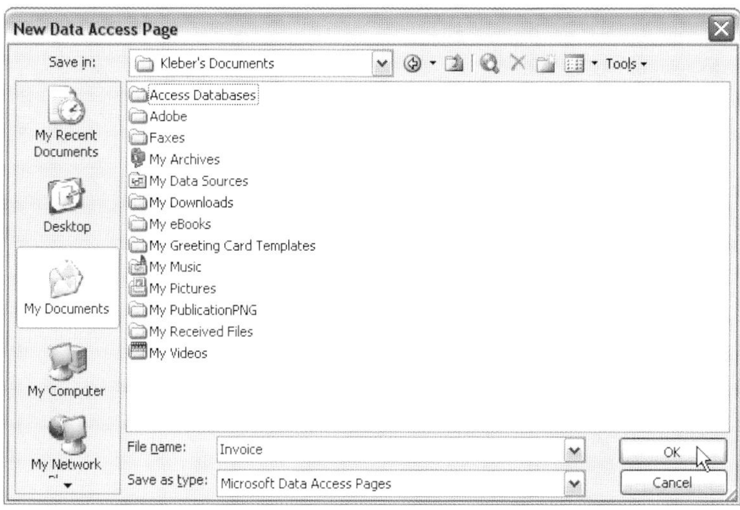

MENU BAR OBJECTS

I'm working in the same database 90% of the time, and I'm constantly switching back and forth between several database objects, which slows things down. To speed things back up, you can place objects on any toolbar or even in the program's menu bar: Simply drag-and-drop any database object from the Database window onto the program's menu bar (or toolbar of your choice). Now your favorite objects are always just a click away.

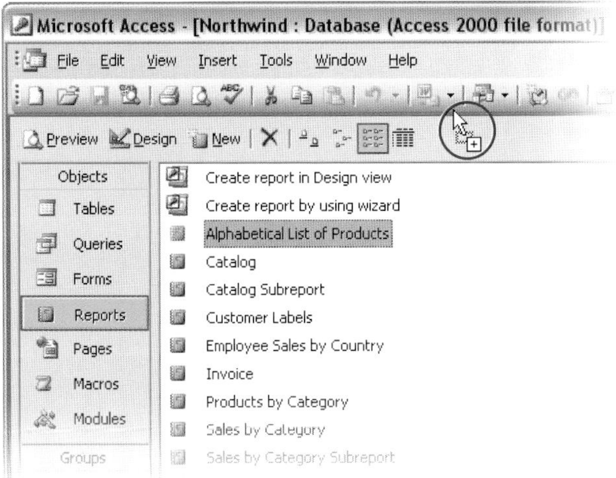

DON'T DOUBLE-CLICK

Anytime you can do anything faster, you should. So, why double-click to open an object when you can single-click instead? Click Tools>Options in the menu bar, and then in the View tab on the Options dialog, check Single-click Open, then click OK. I have no idea why this isn't the default option. It just makes sense to change it.

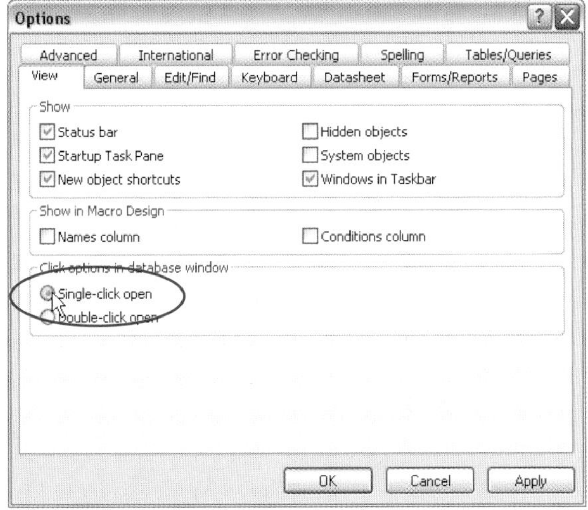

ZOOM ZOOM

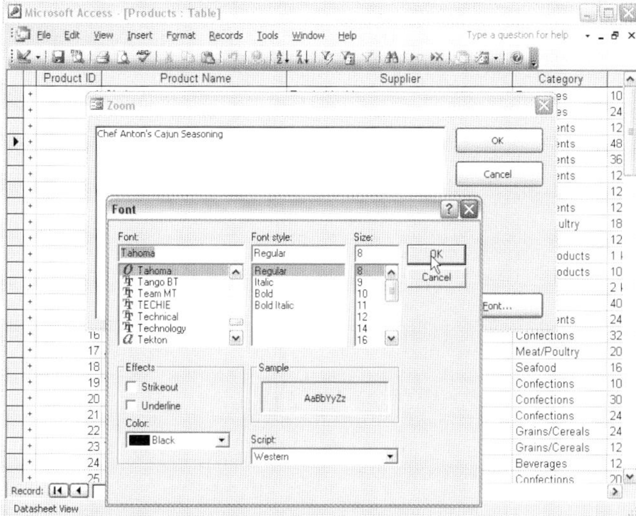

Let's face it—the old eyes just aren't what they used to be, and at higher monitor resolutions, your database's text can look something like alien hieroglyphics, making it almost impossible to edit. Fortunately, you can give your eyes a break. Click anywhere in the field that you want to edit and press Shift-F2 on your keyboard. Now, make any changes you'd like to the field's text. To change the font size or style, click the Font button. Click OK when finished.

INSTANTLY LAUNCH A FORM

To instantly launch a form from the Database window, click Tools>Startup in the menu bar, then click the Display Form/Page drop-down menu on the Startup dialog and select the form you want to automatically open when you open your database, then click OK. Now close your database and reopen it. The form you specified in Startup automatically opens.

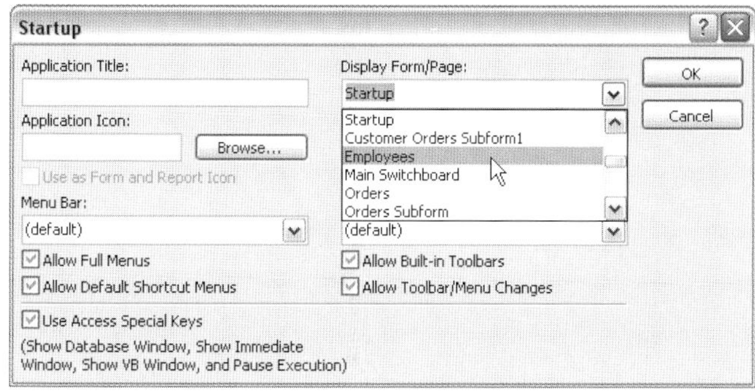

 INSTANTLY LAUNCH A RECORD

If you want to open a specific record automatically when opening a form, try this: First open the form in Design View (View>Design View), then click View>Properties in the menu bar. In the Event tab on the Form dialog, click the On Open field, and then click the Build button to the right (it looks like an ellipsis). Choose Code Builder in the Choose Builder dialog and click OK. This opens the Visual Basic window. Now, on a new line directly beneath Private Sub Form Open(Cancel As Integer), type: DoCmd. GoToRecord acForm, "your form name", acGoTo, #, (replacing # with the number of the record that you want to open first). Close the Visual Basic window, then save the changes (File>Save) and close the form. Now, open your form, and the designated record will appear first.

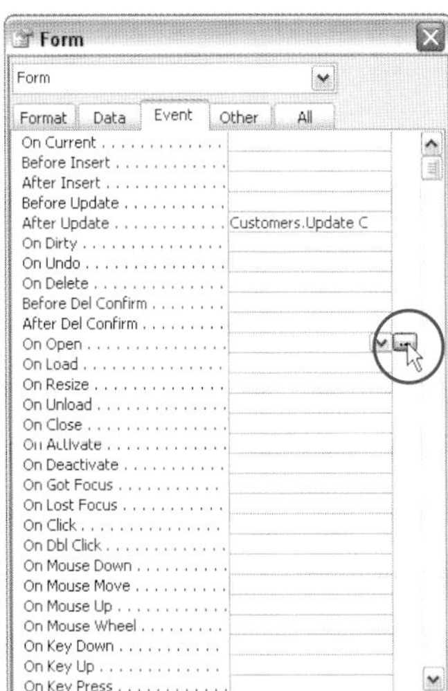

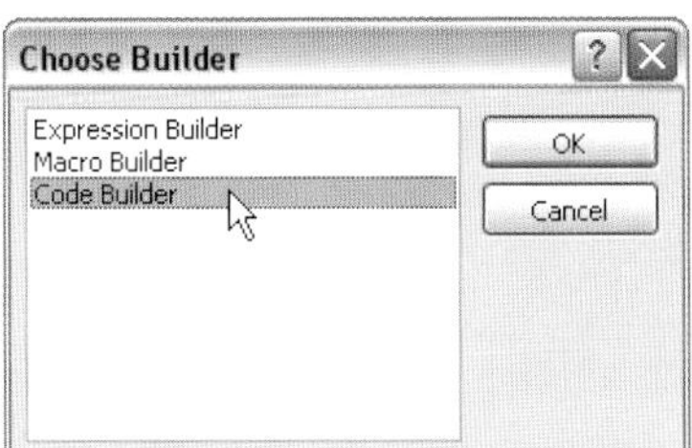

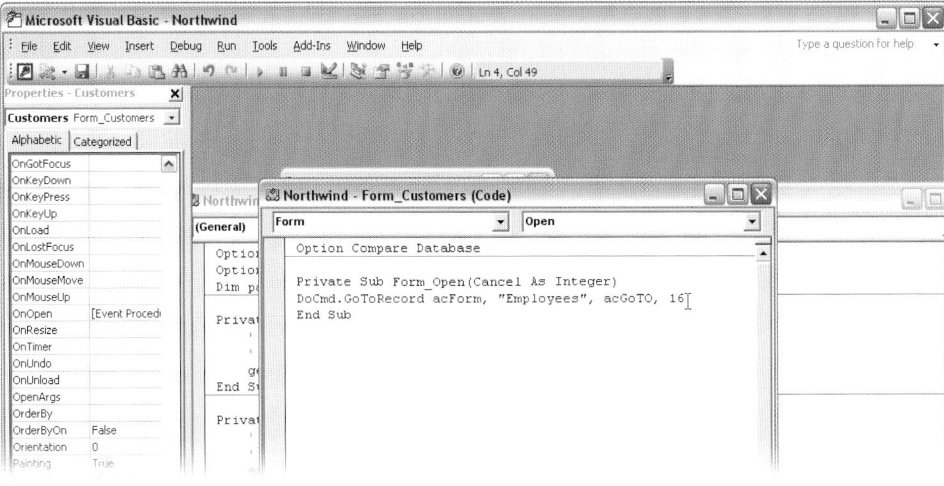

GET YOUR TABS IN ORDER

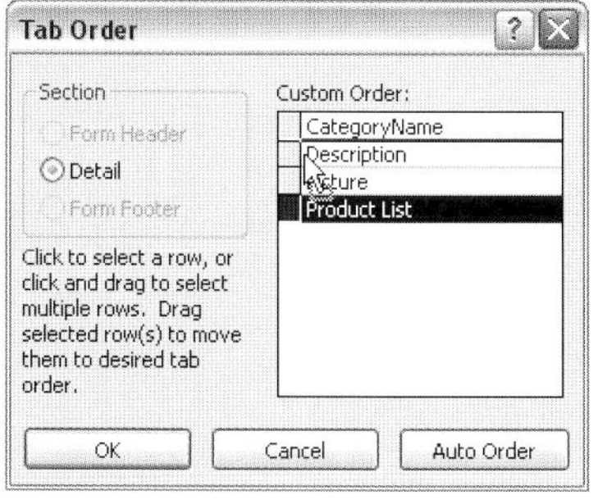

The tab order of any form is very important because pressing the Tab key on your keyboard jumps you to the next field to be completed. The sequence in which the Tab key selects a field can be important when navigating a form. To make your forms user-friendly, you should design your tab order to follow a logical progression, such as address, city, state, zip, and so on, and put product codes and other information at the bottom. This doesn't happen automatically, you have to assign your database's tab order; otherwise, Access will assign the tab order as your fields are created. To change your tab order, first switch your form to Design View (View>Design View), then click View>Tab Order in the menu bar. Now, put your controls into any order by dragging-and-dropping the selector boxes to the left of the controls in the Custom Order list. When finished, click OK. Now click Form View in the View menu, and press the Tab key. Your fields will highlight according to your new tab order.

HIDIN' OUT

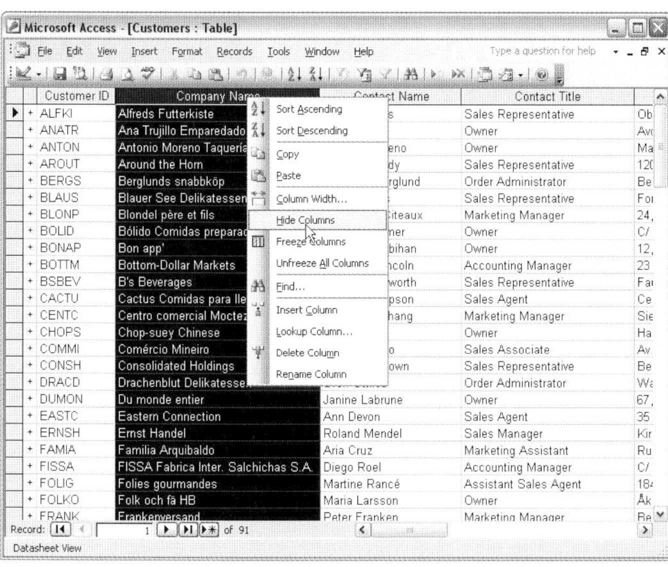

To quickly hide table columns, right-click the column header you want to hide and click Hide Columns in the shortcut menu. To view the column again, click Format>Unhide Columns in the menu bar, turn on the hidden column's checkbox in the Unhide Columns dialog, and click Close.

A BETTER VIEW

Tables can get ridiculously long, and this can make entering new data in tables tedious. Well, there's a way to make working in a table while in Datasheet View much easier—hide existing records before entering new ones. To do this, first open the table that you want to work with, then click Records>Data Entry in the submenu. Access hides all of the records, leaving only a new blank record. Now, go crazy. Each new record is added to your table. When you're done, click Records>Remove Filter/Sort.

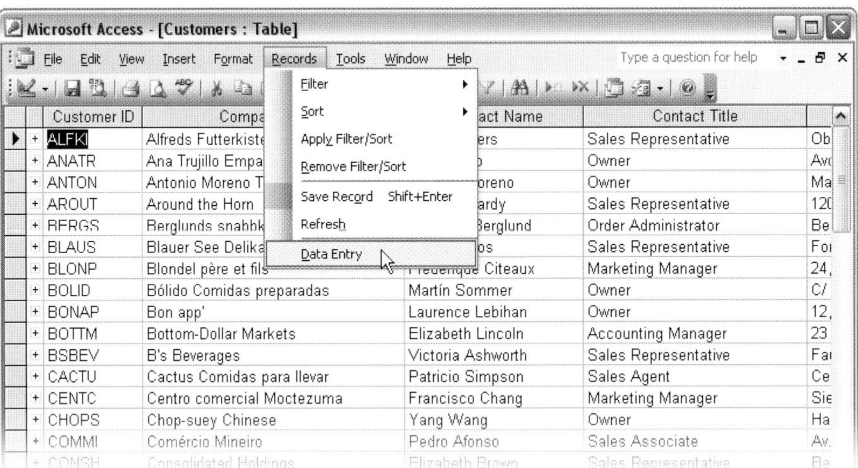

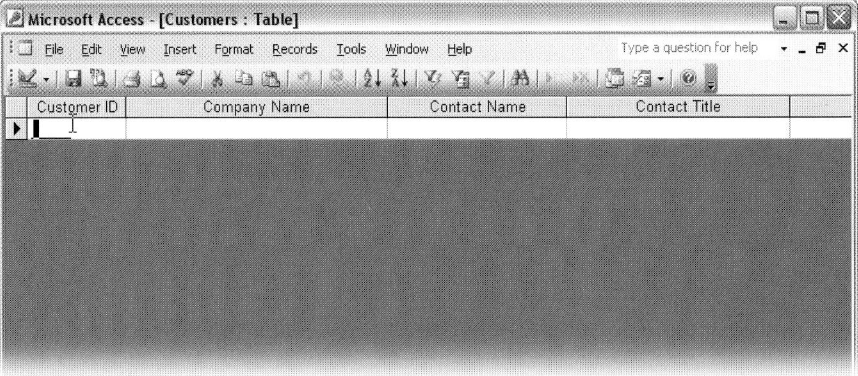

HOW'S YOUR RELATIONSHIP?

Trying to decipher the relationship between tables is impossible so don't ever try it (kidding). Actually, it's almost impossible to build an effective database without understanding the relationships between tables. Fortunately, Access offers a way to help with this: You can print a table relationships map. In Access's Database window, click Tables in the Objects list in the left column of the window. Now click Tools>Relationships in the menu bar. This will open the Relationships dialog and the Show Table dialog (if the Show Table dialog doesn't appear, right-click in any blank space in the Relationships dialog and choose Show Table in the shortcut menu). In the Show Table dialog, select the tables that you want in the Tables tab and click the Add button. When you're finished, click Close. Next, click File>Print Relationships in the menu bar, which opens the database's relationships layout in Print Preview. Click the Print button on the Print Preview toolbar, then click Close. Next, close the relationships Report window that appears and you'll be prompted to save the report. Click Yes to save or No to close without saving.

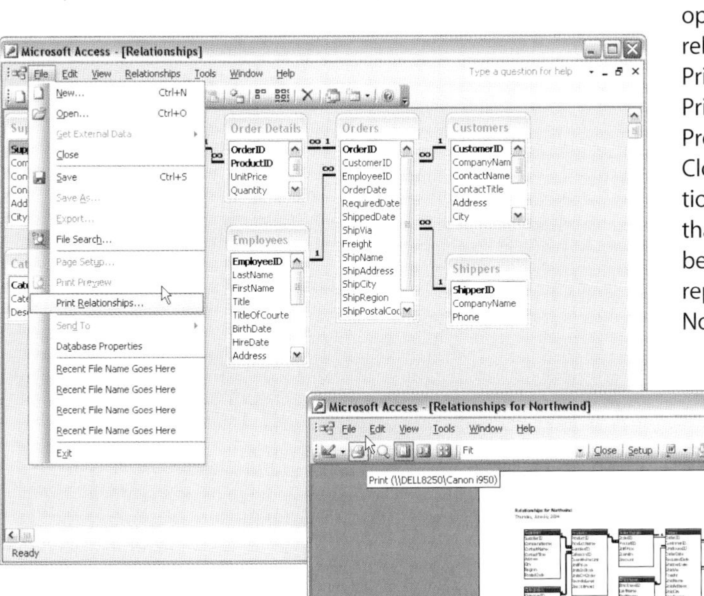

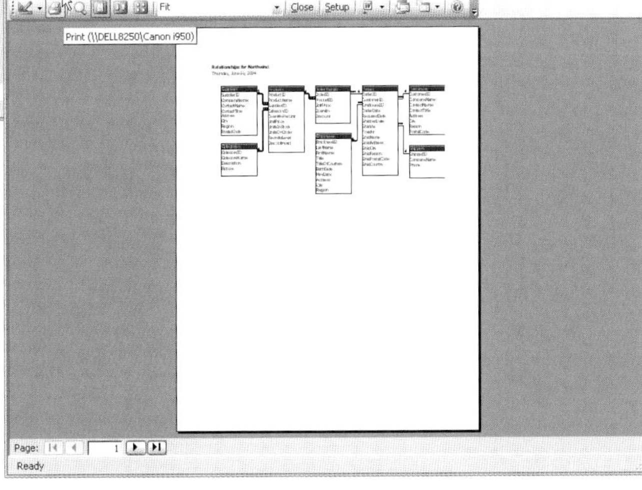

LINE 'EM UP

To align multiple controls on a form, first switch to Design View by clicking View>Design View in the menu bar, then select the controls and the control fields by pressing the Shift key as you click on each control that you want to align. Next, click Format>Align and select an alignment direction in the submenu (e.g., Left, Right, etc.). All of your controls will instantly align.

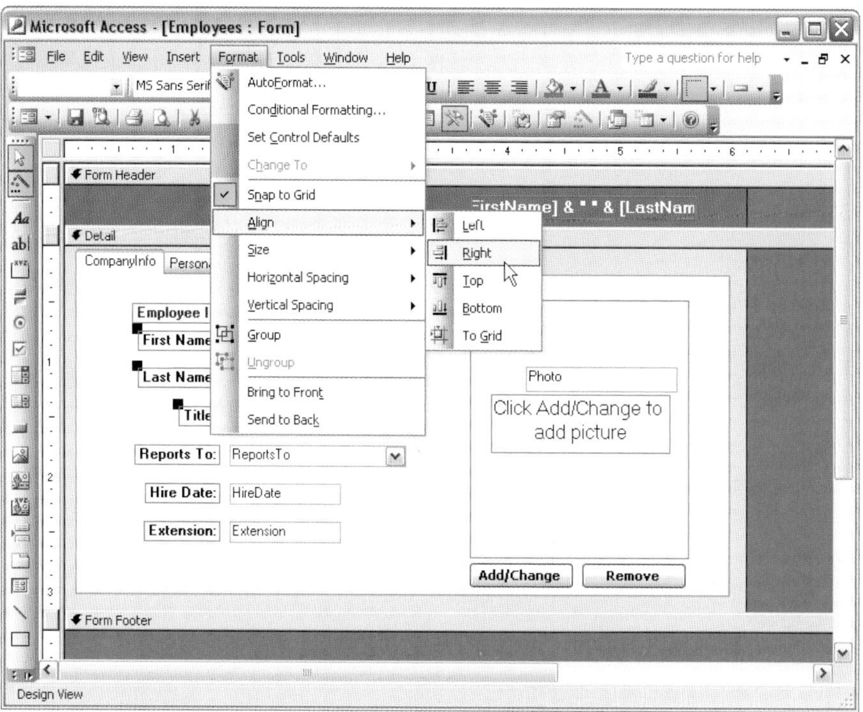

QUICK CALENDAR

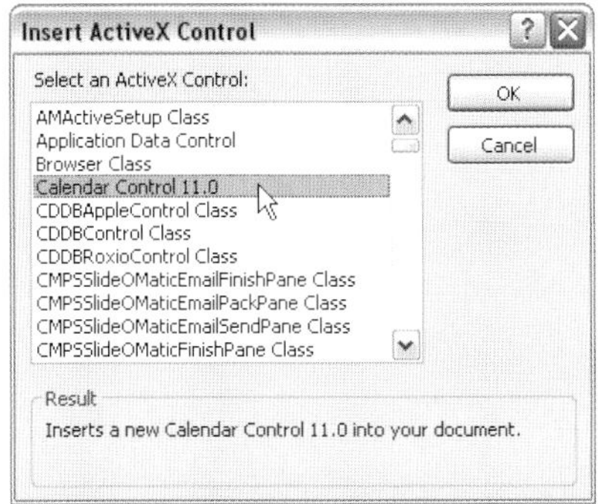

Adding a calendar to a form is easy. First, open your form in Design View (View>Design View). Then, click Insert>ActiveX Control in the menu bar, select Calendar Control 11.0 in the Insert ActiveX Control dialog, and click OK. Now, click-and-drag the calendar to any location on your form.

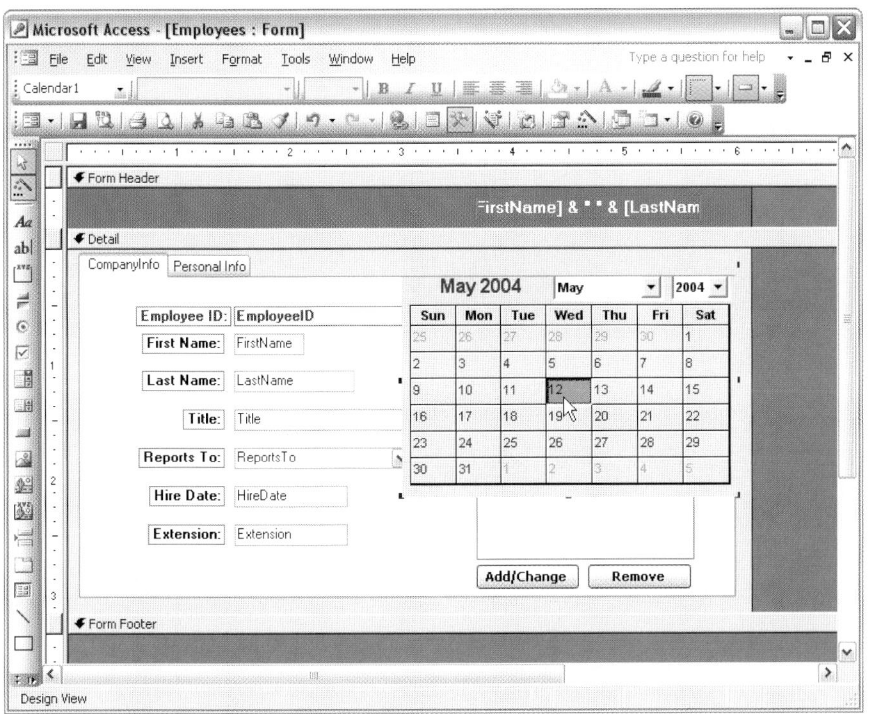

A BETTER PREVIEW

Layout Preview is better than Print Preview, but don't take my word for it: Open a report that contains a query or two, then click View>Print Preview. Are you still waiting for it to open? Still waiting? Reports with queries can sometimes take a while to generate a print preview; however, you don't experience such processing downtime when using Layout Preview. To view your report in Layout Preview, start off in Design View (View>Design View), then click View>Layout Preview in the menu bar and there it is. This is the same view as Print Preview, only faster in some cases. The only drawback to Layout Preview is that you can't edit your document as you can in Print Preview, but if you're like most users on the planet, you don't edit your reports in Print Preview anyway.

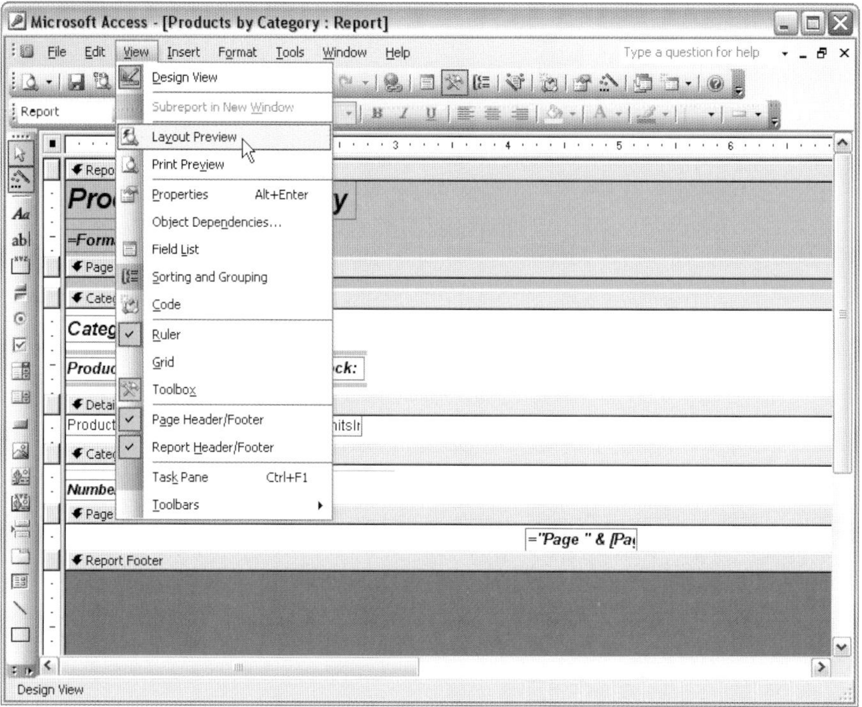

SHIFT SIZE

Adjusting the size of your controls is fairly straightforward: You grab a resize handle and drag it to resize; however, it's pretty tricky to be accurate when using the resize handles. Try this instead: While in Design View (View>Design View), click to select your control, press the Shift key on your keyboard, then use the arrow keys to increase or decrease the size of your control. Each press of an arrow key changes the control's size by 1/24th of an inch in any direction.

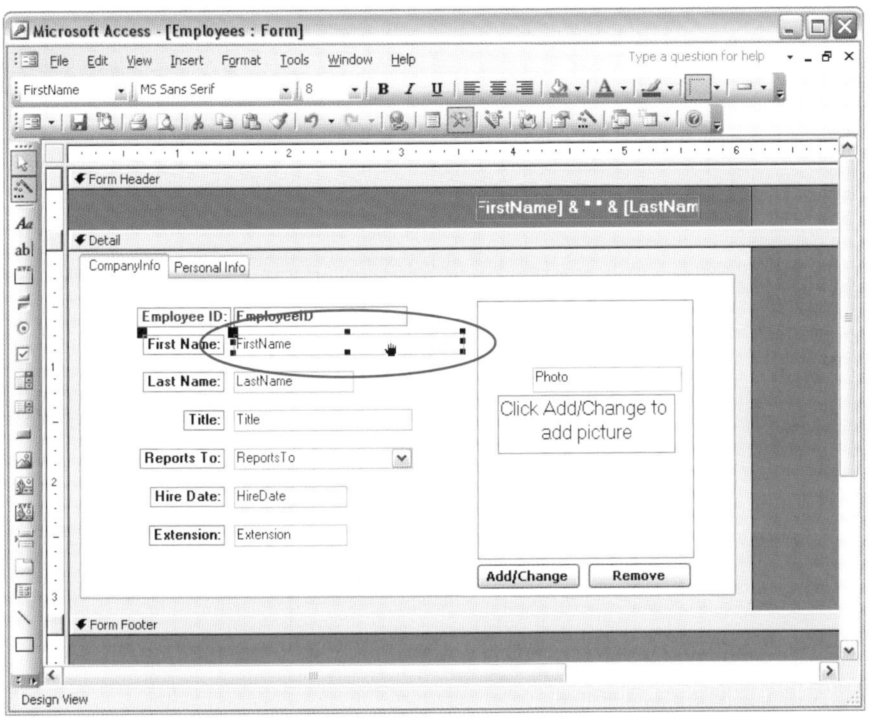

TITLE PAGES MADE EASY

Did you know that you could design and print a title page for your reports directly within Access? Bet you didn't. If you've ever gone through the hassle of creating one, then you'll love this tip. To create a title page from your existing report, first open your report in Design View (View>Design View), then lay out your title page in the report's header, adding any images and text. Next, right-click any blank space in the header and click Properties in the shortcut menu. Now, click the Format tab in the Section dialog and click the Force New Page field to select it, then choose After Section from the field's drop-down menu and close the dialog. Your report's header will now print on a separate sheet of paper.

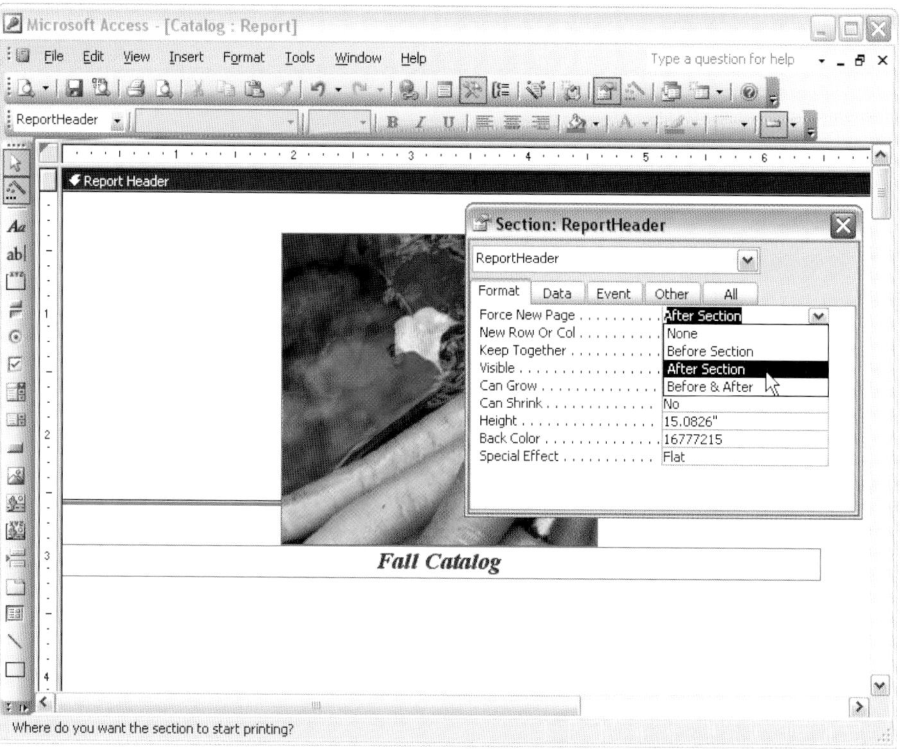

CAN'T CLOSE

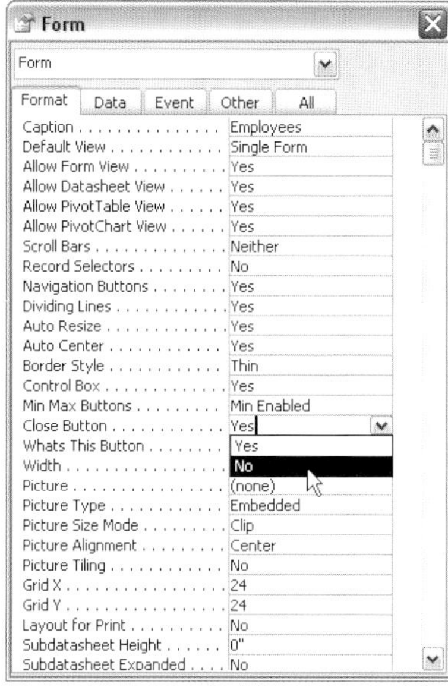

Want to make it harder for users to close forms? Of course you do, messing with people is half the fun of databases. Well, you can disable the form window's Close button so that users can't easily close your form. To do this, open your form in Design View by choosing Design View in the View menu. Then click View>Properties in the menu bar and click the Format tab in the Form dialog. Next, click the Close Button field to select it and choose No from the field's drop-down menu, and then close the dialog. Now users won't be able to use the Close button in the form's window. To return the Close button's function to its default state, repeat this tip but choose Yes in the field's drop-down menu. It's fun to mess with people.

CAN'T ADD

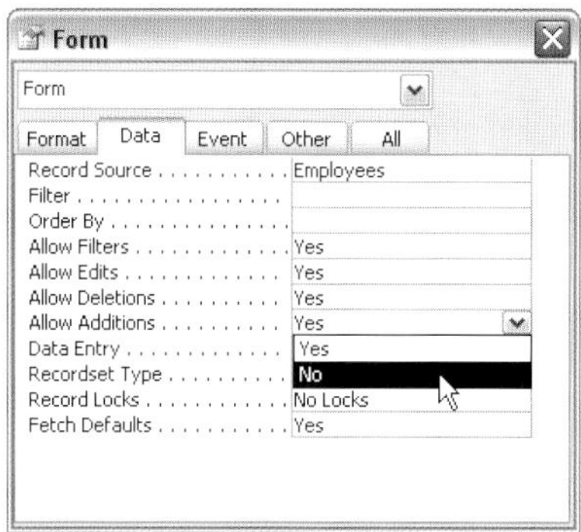

If you want to allow users to access data but don't want them to add new data, then do this: Open your form in Design View (View>Design View), select View>Properties in the menu bar, and click the Data tab in the Form dialog. Next, click the Allow Additions field and choose No from the field's drop-down menu, and then close the dialog. Now when you access the form in Form View (View>Form View), the New Record button will appear dimmed, indicating that this option is disabled.

SET THE TIMER

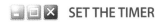

If you really want to see a look of confusion on people's faces, then automatically close your forms on 'em. If you time it just right, you can make 'em cry. Just kidding—we don't want to make anyone cry. There's actually a practical use for automatically closing a form. This is perfect for giving someone a limited amount of time to complete a form, perhaps in the form of a test or quiz. To do this, first open the form in Design View (View>Design View), click View>Properties in the menu bar, and then click the Event tab in the Form dialog. Next, click the Timer Interval field and type the number of seconds to leave the form visible once opened (1000 = 1 second). Next, click the On Timer field and click its Build button (it looks like an ellipsis) to the right. Choose Code Builder in the Choose Builder dialog and click OK. This opens the Visual Basic window. Now on a new line directly beneath Private Sub Form_Timer (), type: DoCmd.Close, "" (with a space between the comma and double quotation marks). Close the Visual Basic window, save the changes, and close the form. Now, open your form to test your timer. To change your timer setting back to its default, repeat this tip but enter a zero in the Timer Interval field, and delete any command in the On Timer field.

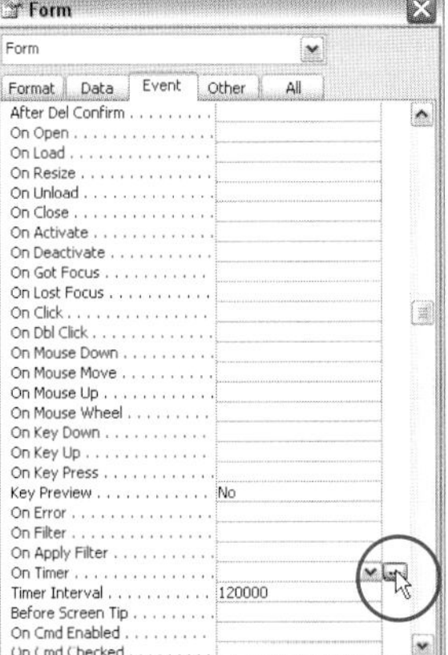

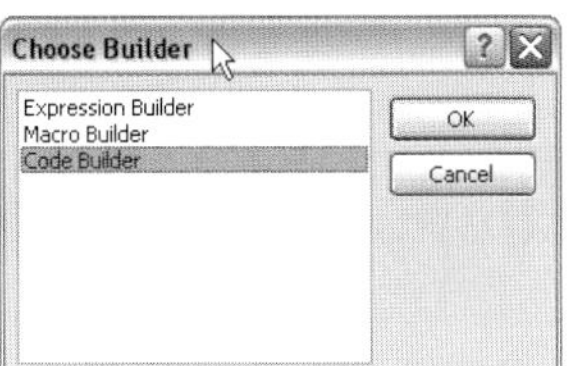

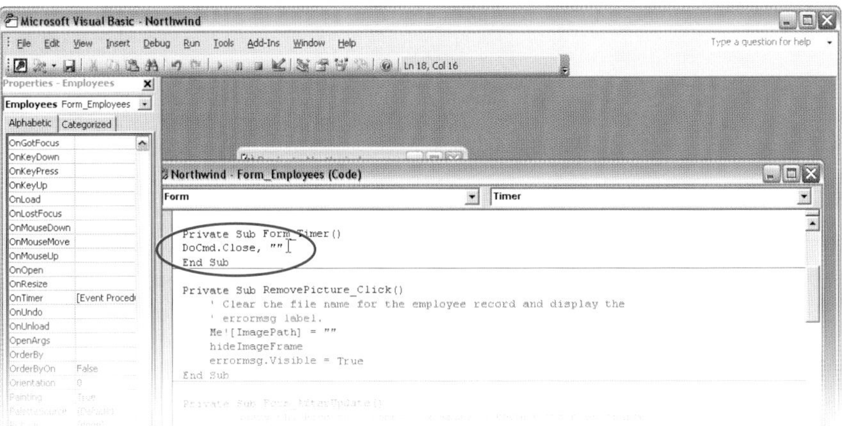

WHAT'S THIS?

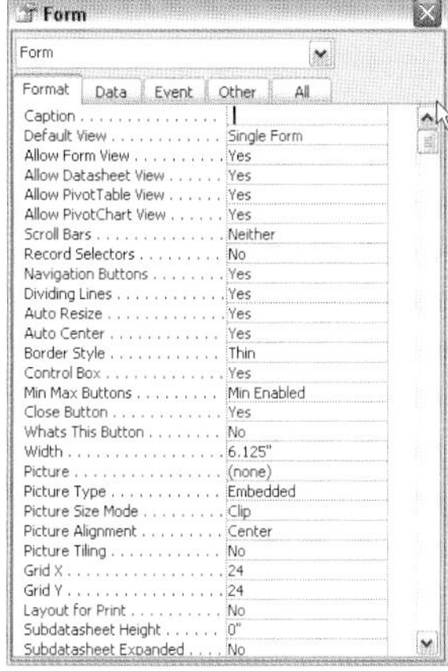

I'm not sure how many of you will actually use this tip, but I'm sure it's going to be exactly what someone was hoping to find. If you're secretive or just want to baffle people using your forms, don't give them titles. I know you're thinking, "You can't do that!" But you can. By default, your form has to have a title and it does, but you can change it. Here's how: Open your form in Design View (View>Design View), click View>Properties in the menu bar, and then click the Format tab in the Form dialog. Next, delete the form title from the Caption field, then type a single space into the Caption field, and close the dialog. Choose View>Form View in the menu bar, and your title's gone. Baffling isn't it? To see the title again, repeat this tip but enter your title in the Caption field instead of deleting it.

GETTIN' AROUND

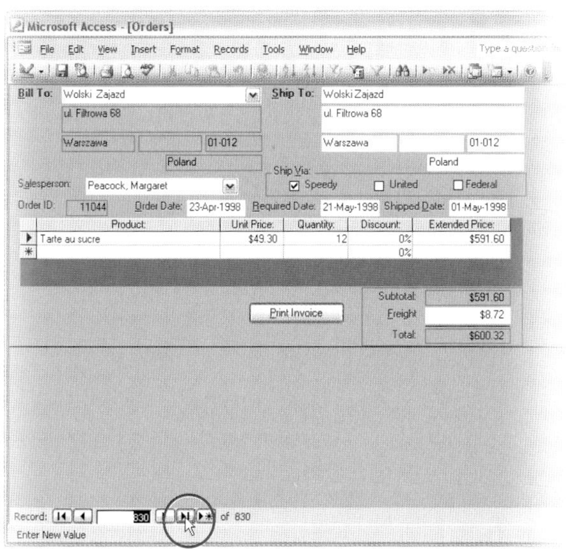

To quickly navigate your records in Access, try these handy keyboard shortcuts. To jump from field to field, press the Left and Right Arrow keys on your keyboard (instead of scrolling through records by clicking the Next Record or Previous Record buttons, as shown here). To advance to the next record in a database, press the Page Down key or press the Page Up key to advance to the top of your data list. You can get to the last record in a database by pressing Control-End, or press Control-Home to go to the first record in your database.

 SUPER-FAST APPEND

To append data records from the Database window, click Tables in the Objects list on the left-hand side of the window, then right-click the table that contains the records that you want to append to another table and click Copy in the shortcut menu. Next, right-click any blank space in the Database window and click Paste in the shortcut menu. This opens the Paste Table As dialog. Now, in the Table Name field, type the name of the target table to which you want to append the copied records, then select Append Data to Existing Table, and click OK. Your records are instantly added to the table you specified. *Note:* Your target table must have the same fields (headers) as the table you've copied.

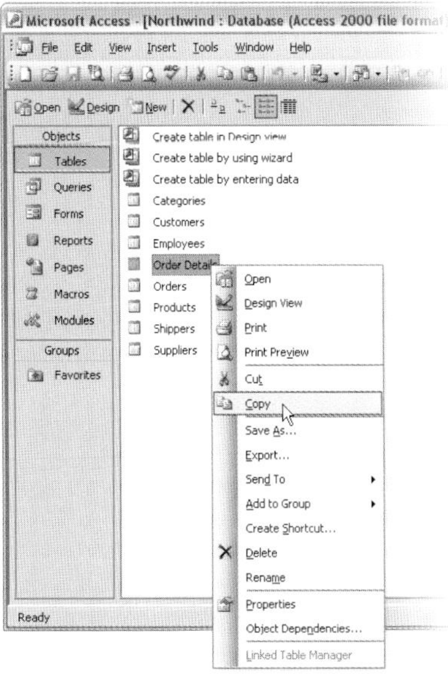

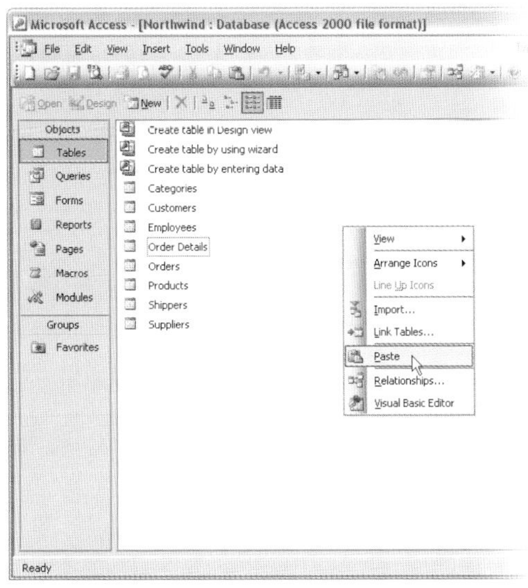

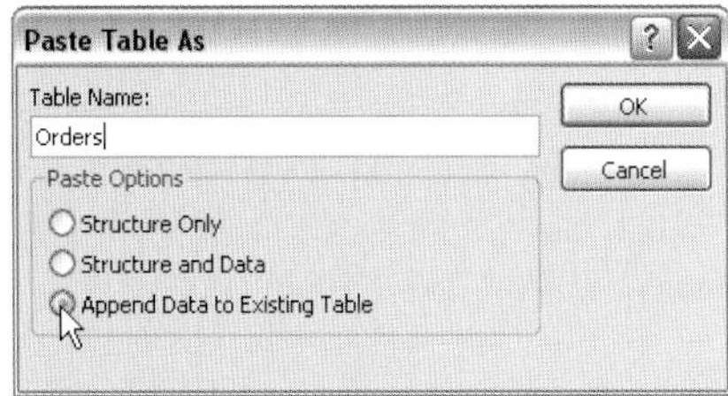

REPORT SNAPSHOT

There's a much better way to distribute reports than printing them—unless of course you're a tree killer, then go ahead (just kidding). Actually, the environment has nothing to do with this; it just makes good sense to share your reports in a digital format that allows the recipients greater control over storing, retrieving, and yes, even printing the report once they receive it. To do this, send a snapshot of your report. To create a snapshot of your report, select the report by clicking Reports in the Objects list on the left side of the Database window and clicking once on the report's icon to select it. Then click File>Export in the menu bar. Select Snapshot Format from the Save as Type drop-down menu in the Export Report As dialog. Select a location to save your snapshot, name it in the File Name field, and then click Export. Now, locate your saved snapshot report on your hard drive and double-click to open it. Cool, huh? Now, save it to disk or attach it to emails for distribution.

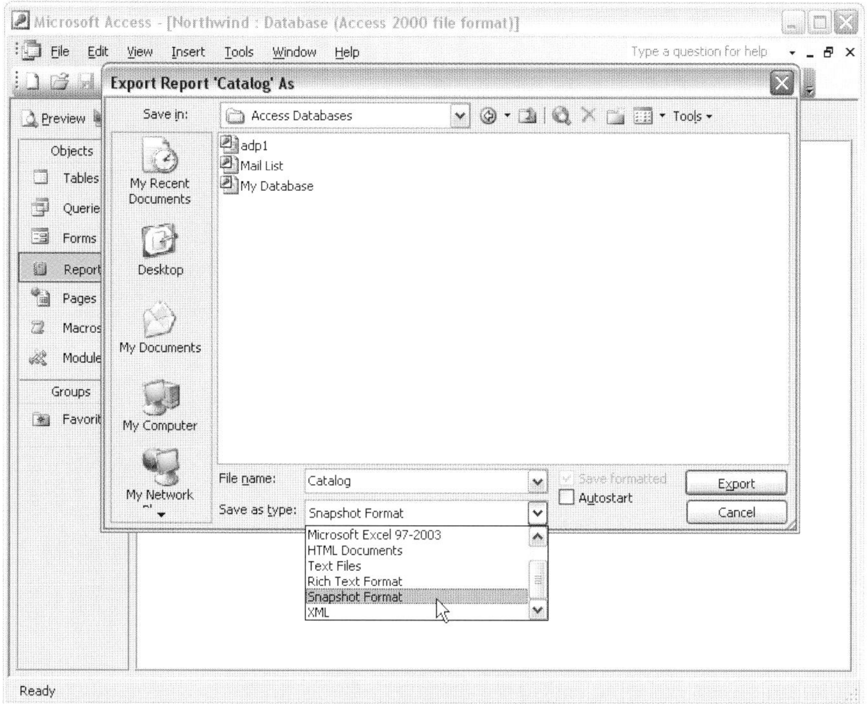

ANALYZE THIS!

Access databases are great, but you'll probably find that Access can't always give you the kind of data-crunching power that you want. I mean, it's not Excel. Well, maybe not, but it doesn't have to be. We can export our reports to Excel and data-crunch away anytime we want. Try this: In the Reports pane (which you open by clicking Reports in the Objects list of the Database window), select a report that you want to export to Excel, then, in the menu bar, click Tools>Office Links>Analyze It with Microsoft Office Excel. This launches Excel and opens your report. To save the report in Excel, click File>Save As on Excel's menu bar.

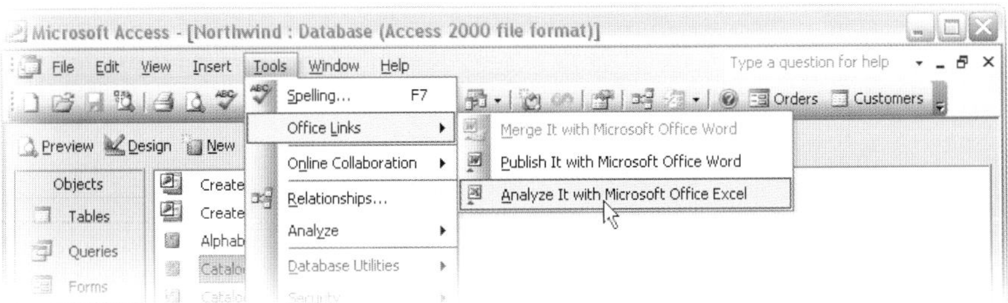

QUICK DATES

Here's a handy shortcut for entering dates into forms. You don't have to go to the trouble of typing the entire date into a field (for example, 21-July-2004). Simply type 7/21 instead. Access interprets this as a date and appends the current year to the end of your date (depending on the date settings for that field). Once you exit the field, 7/21 will automatically change to 21-July-2004.

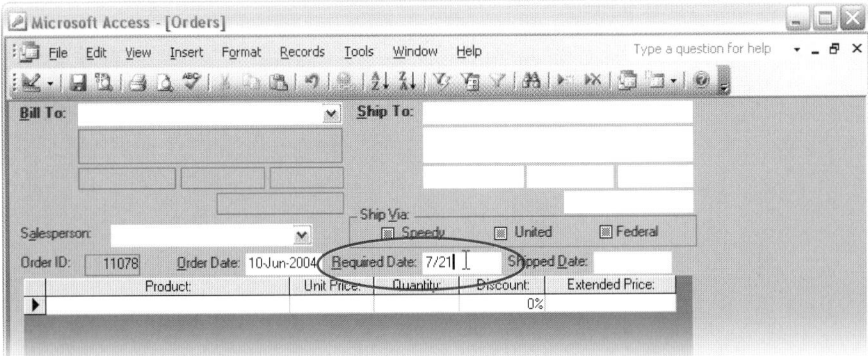

ONE-CLICK EXCEL

I always use Excel and Access together (especially when working with forms). They just go together…kind of like cookies and milk or pencil and paper. And, to make it easier to get to Excel, I place a command button directly on my form that launches Excel with a single click of my mouse. You can too. Open any form in Design View (View>Design View), right-click any menu or toolbar and select Toolbox, then click the Command Button tool on the Toolbox toolbar (it looks like a solid gray bar). Then, click on the form where you want to place the Command Button. This opens the Command Button Wizard. Click Application from the Categories window, then choose Run MS Excel from the Actions window, and click Finish. Return to Form View (View>Form View), and click the Excel Command Button to launch Excel anytime you'd like.

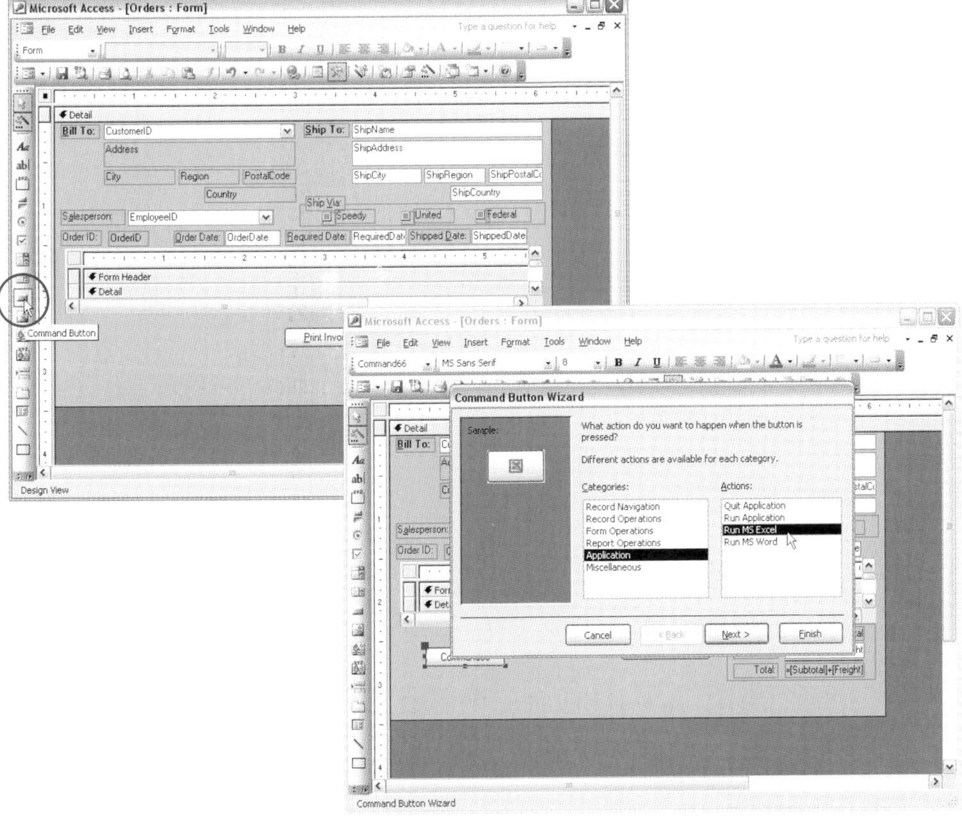

Get Published

WORKING WITH PUBLISHER

I know what you use Microsoft Publisher for: You use it for exactly the same thing that everybody else uses Microsoft Publisher for…creating greeting cards. Hands-down, it's

Get Published

working with publisher

the best program available for creating greeting cards, but that really is the tip of the iceberg, so to speak. Publisher is also perfect for creating newsletters, advertisements, flyers, brochures, and more. Now, while "professional" layout designers may smirk when you tell them that you created your brochure in Microsoft Publisher, there's always one thing that you'll have on Adobe InDesign and QuarkXPress users. You didn't drop 700 bucks for your software. That'll stick it to 'em. Honestly, there are few things that you can't do in Publisher, so before you take a withdrawal from your children's college fund for "professional" software, give Publisher a try. You'll be surprised at what you can do.

EDIT IN WORD

If you're going to edit text in Publisher (or any Office application), it's best to do it in Word. Word simply provides the best tools and capabilities for the task. And you can easily edit your Publisher text using Word. To do this, first select your text, then right-click it with your mouse, and click Change Text>Edit Story in Microsoft Word in the shortcut menu. This opens the selected text in Word. Now, make any changes, and when finished, click File>Close & Return to <*your document's title*> in Word's menu bar. Your edited text now appears in your publication.

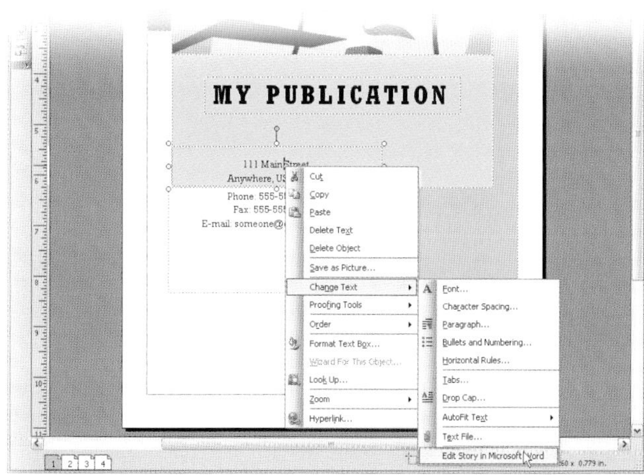

DELETE THE WHOLE THING

When you select a text box in Publisher and press Backspace on your keyboard, sometimes only the character to the right of the insertion point is deleted, not the entire text box, which probably isn't what you intended. You probably wanted to delete the entire text box. You still can—just press Control-Shift-X on your keyboard and the text box is gone.

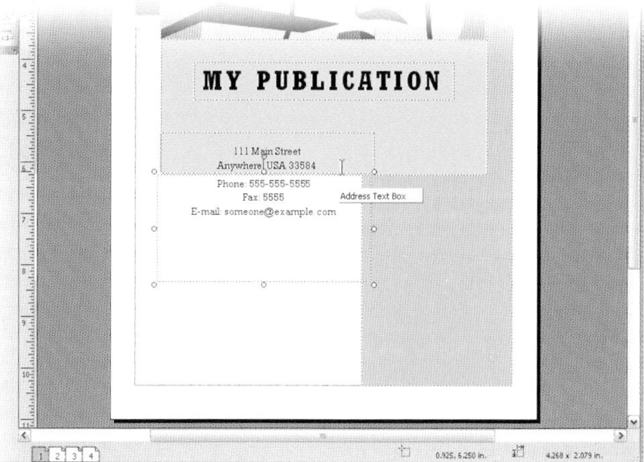

NAVIGATE WEB PUBLICATIONS

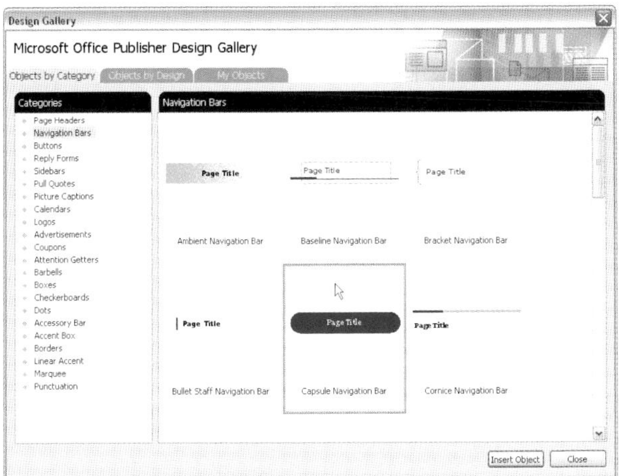

You can add navigation buttons to any Web publication by clicking Insert>Design Gallery Object in the menu bar. In the Objects by Category tab in the Design Gallery dialog, click Navigation Bars (this option only appears for publications saved as Web publications) in the Categories window, then select a button in the Navigation Bars window, and click Insert Object. This will open the Create New Navigation Bar dialog, where you can choose on which pages to insert the bar and choose to update navigation bar links automatically. Click OK when finished. Now click-and-drag your new navigation bar to position it in your document.

CUSTOMIZE COLOR SCHEMES

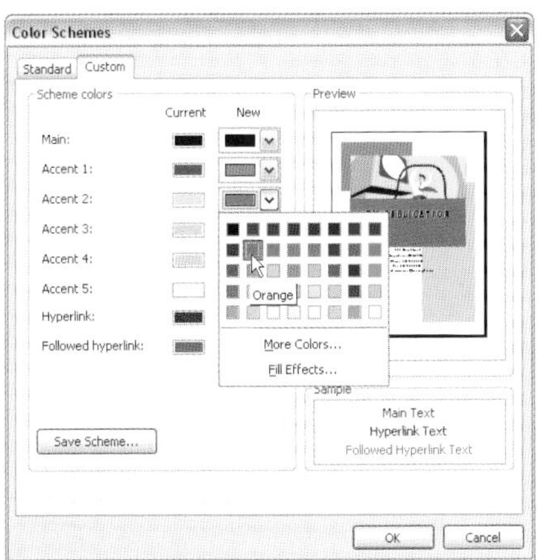

Keep this in mind when choosing any of Publisher's default publication designs: Don't worry about their colors. That's right, don't think twice about 'em. The colors don't matter because you can quickly change the entire color scheme. Here's how: Open any publication design from the New Publication task pane (File>New), then click Format>Color Schemes in the menu bar. Click the "Custom color scheme" link at the bottom of the Color Schemes task pane, then click the Custom tab on the Color Schemes dialog. All colors represented in the design are shown in the Current color column. To change any Current color, click the New color drop-down menu to the right and select a new color. You'll see your changes in the Preview window. When finished, click OK to apply your new color scheme.

GET PERSONAL

A real time saver in Publisher is its ability to automatically insert your personal information into publications. First, set up your info by clicking Edit>Personal Information in the menu bar, then update your information in the Personal Information dialog, and click Update when finished. To create a publication that includes your personal information, create a new document (File>New), then open the Quick Publication Options task pane by clicking the down-facing arrow to the left of the Close button on the New Publication task pane. Select the Personal Information With Picture icon in the Layout category (it's the last icon in the last row). You can also insert single fields of personal information by clicking Insert>Personal Information in the menu bar and selecting any of the available personal info tags.

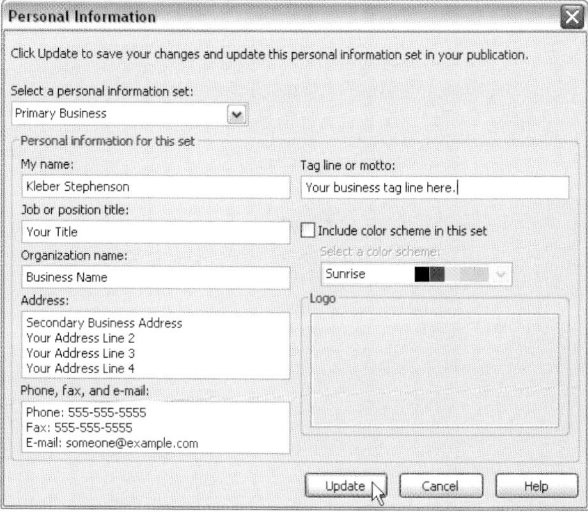

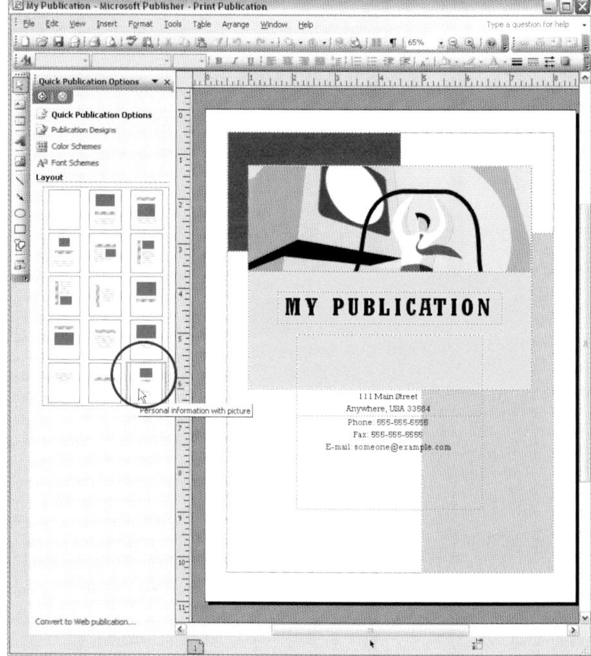

CONTROL GROUPS

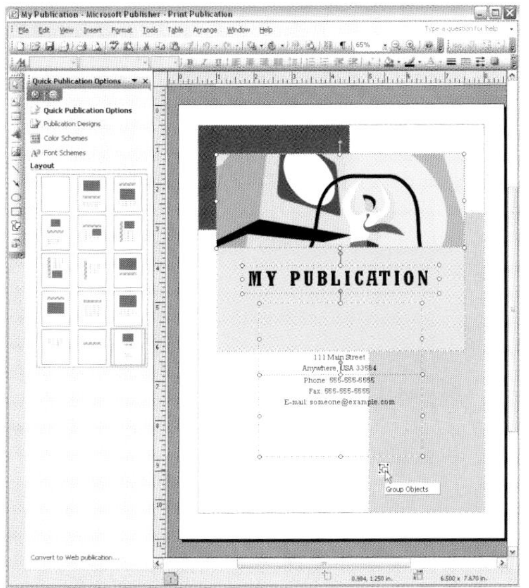

To group objects so they move together when laying out your publication, press-and-hold the Control key on your keyboard and click each object with your mouse—this selects each object. Anytime you select more than one object, the Group Objects icon will appear. Click this icon to group your selected objects and now you can move the group to any location on your layout. To ungroup your objects, simply click the Ungroup Objects Icon while your group is selected.

THAT SHOULD BE A PICTURE

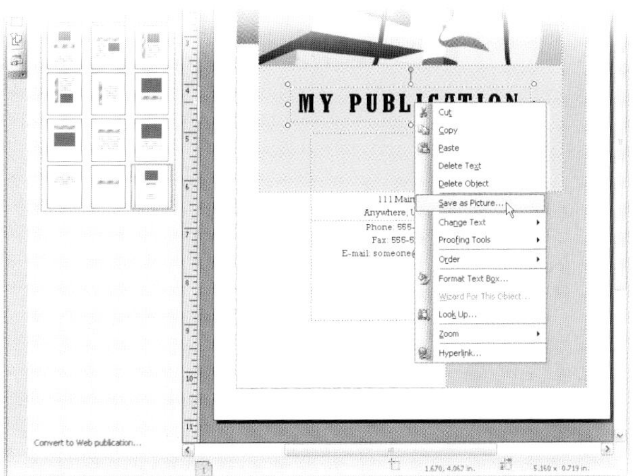

You can save just about any object—even text—as a picture in Publisher. To save objects as pictures, right-click an object and click Save as Picture in the shortcut menu. Choose a location on your hard drive to save your picture, choose the picture's format in the Save as Type field in the Save As dialog, and then click Save.

THE KEY TO THE WEB

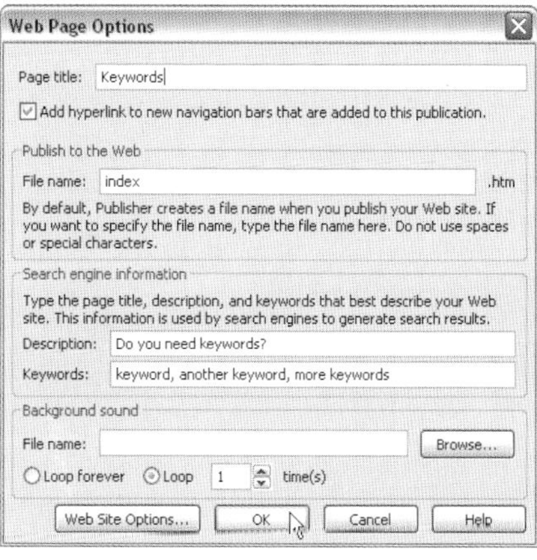

What's the point of posting your Web publication to the Web if no one can find it—probably no point at all. So, you're going to want to include keywords, or metatags, in your publication's HTML. Search sites such as Google and Yahoo index websites by the site's keywords. If your site doesn't have keywords, it won't be indexed by many search engines...so, make certain that you add keywords. Here's how: Open the title page of your Web publication, then click the Web Page Options button in the Web Tools toolbar (if you don't see the Web Tools toolbar, right-click the Standard toolbar in your Web document and click Web Tools). Next, complete the Web Page Options dialog, providing a Page Title and File Name. Now, under the Search Engine Information category, provide a description of your website, then in the Keywords field, enter keywords that will help to identify your website when someone searches for your products or services. Click OK when finished.

HEADIN' TO THE PRINTERS

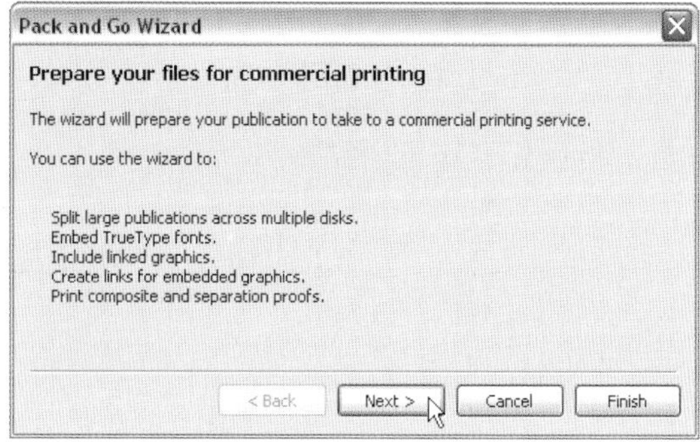

If you've created a business publication, such as a brochure or other informational literature, then you should consider having it professionally printed to get the best possible quality. Most Publisher users wouldn't know where to begin to do this but fortunately, Publisher makes getting your publication ready for a printer extremely easy. When you're ready to have your publication printed, click File>Pack and Go>To a Commercial Printing Service, then follow the Pack and Go Wizard to prepare your print job. When you're finished, simply take your publication's Pack and Go folder and its contents to your printer.

PUBLISHER-FRIENDLY PRINTERS

Okay, you're all excited about taking your files to the local printer, but when you get there and tell him that you have Microsoft Publisher files, he looks at you as if you were the "dumbest of a dumb, dumber, and dumbest trio." Believe it or not, not every printer appreciates the growing number of designers using Publisher to create publications. Well, you don't have to take it—you can take your business somewhere else. To find a local printer who will be happy to take your Publisher files, press F1 on your keyboard to open the Publisher Help task pane, then click Connect to Microsoft Office Online (that is, as long as you're connected to the Internet). This will launch your Web browser and take you to the Microsoft Office website. Click the Publisher link under the Microsoft Office category to the left and on the resulting webpage, click the "Find a local printer" link under the Browse Publisher category.

I'VE BEEN FRAMED

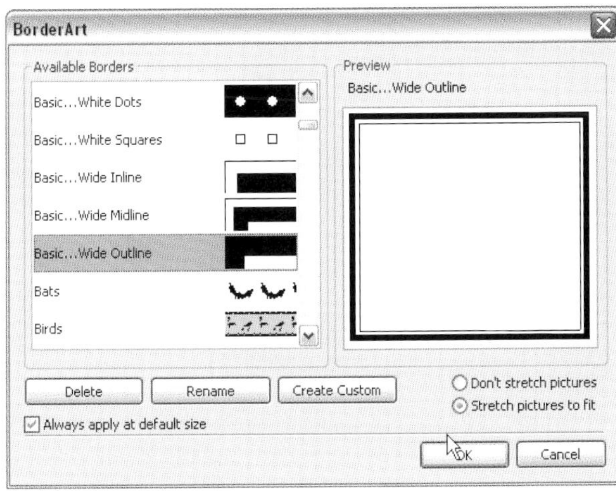

Know what makes pictures better? Frames! You can add frames or borders to your pictures by first selecting the picture that you want to apply a frame to, then clicking the Line/Border Style button in the Formatting toolbar, and clicking More Lines. Next, in the Colors and Lines tab in the Format Picture dialog, click BorderArt, select a border from the Available Borders category in the BorderArt dialog, and then click OK. In the Format Picture dialog, click OK again to apply the border to your picture.

FLOWING TEXT

You probably think that text boxes are boring, don't you? Well, you're wrong. You can create some very cool effects using text boxes, such as flowing text from one text box to another. Here's how: Create at least two text boxes (Insert>Text Box), then select the first text box. Next, click the Create Text Box Link button on the Connect Text Boxes toolbar (if you don't see the Connect Text Boxes toolbar, right-click the Standard toolbar and click Connect Text Boxes). Now click the second text box that you want the text to flow into (your mouse pointer will turn into a tiny pitcher). Repeat the steps as many times as necessary to link as many text boxes as you want. Now when you type your text, it will flow from text box to text box. You can even move the text boxes to any location on your page or resize your text boxes and the text will continue to flow into them.

TRANSPARENT SHAPES

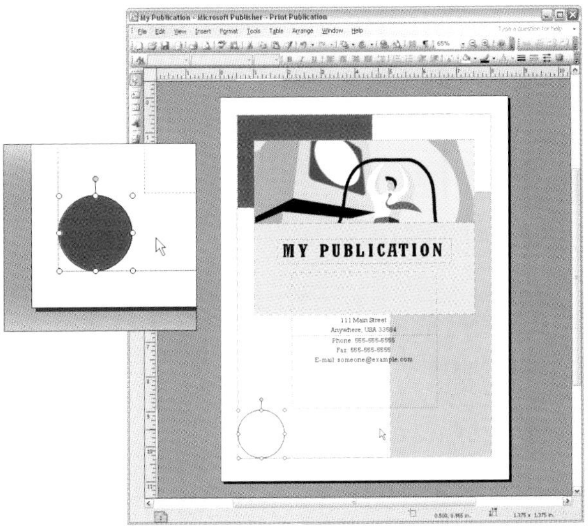

To make a shape transparent, try this: Click any shape (I used a red circle with a black border by clicking the Oval tool in the Drawing toolbar), then press Control-T on your keyboard. This will make the shape transparent (remove its fill color), but leave the shape's line color untouched.

PAINT YOUR FORMATTING

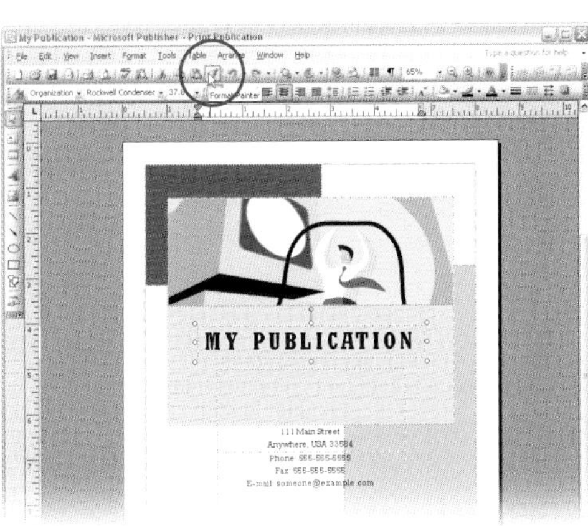

I like to play around with my text formatting in Publisher; for example, I'll apply different text formatting attributes to different boxes of text on a page just to get a feel for what looks best. When I find the text formatting that I want to use, I use Format Painter to apply it to all the text. Try this: Highlight the text with the formatting that you want to copy, then double-click the Format Painter button in the Standard toolbar to copy the text's formatting (your mouse pointer will change to a paintbrush). Next, simply click inside any additional text blocks where you want to apply the formatting. When finished, click the Format Painter button once more to turn it off. You can also use the Format Painter button to apply similar formatting to shapes.

DON'T STRESS OVER FONTS

If you're like me, you have about 30,000 fonts on your computer, and finding just a few that look good together can be a real chore. Well, don't stress—Publisher can help. To find just the right fonts for your presentation, click Format>Font Schemes in the menu bar, then select any font scheme in the Font Schemes task pane to instantly apply it to your publication.

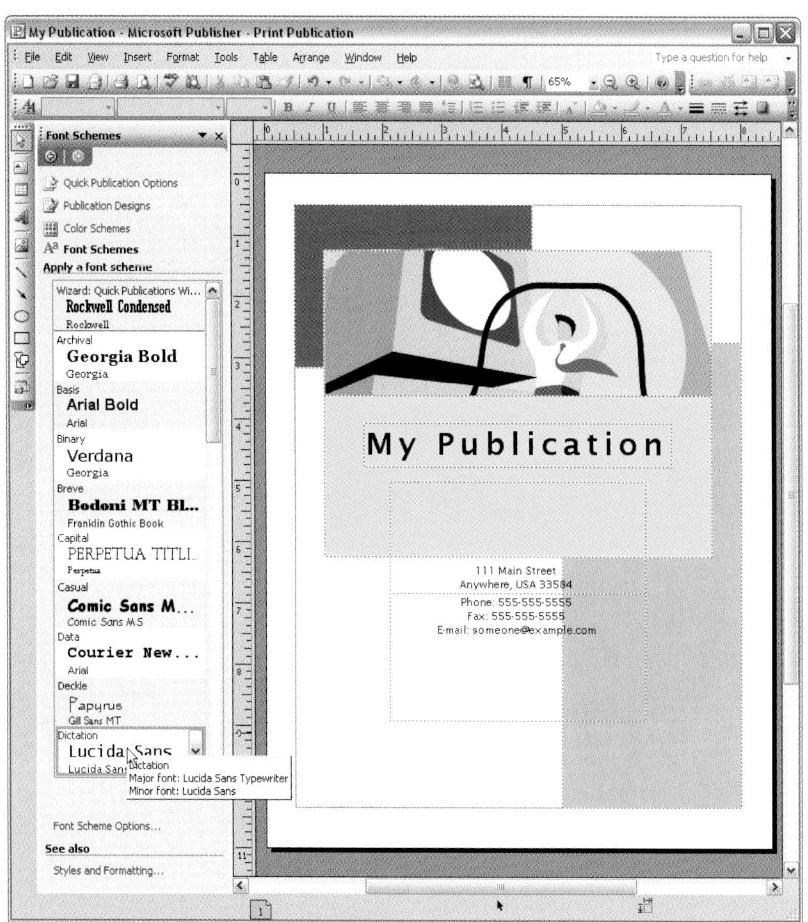

 WHAT ARE YOUR MEASUREMENTS?

Do you need to know the exact measurements of your objects? If you do, you're in luck—it's easy. Select any object, then look at the bottom-right corner of Publisher's program window. There it is—the exact measurement of your object.

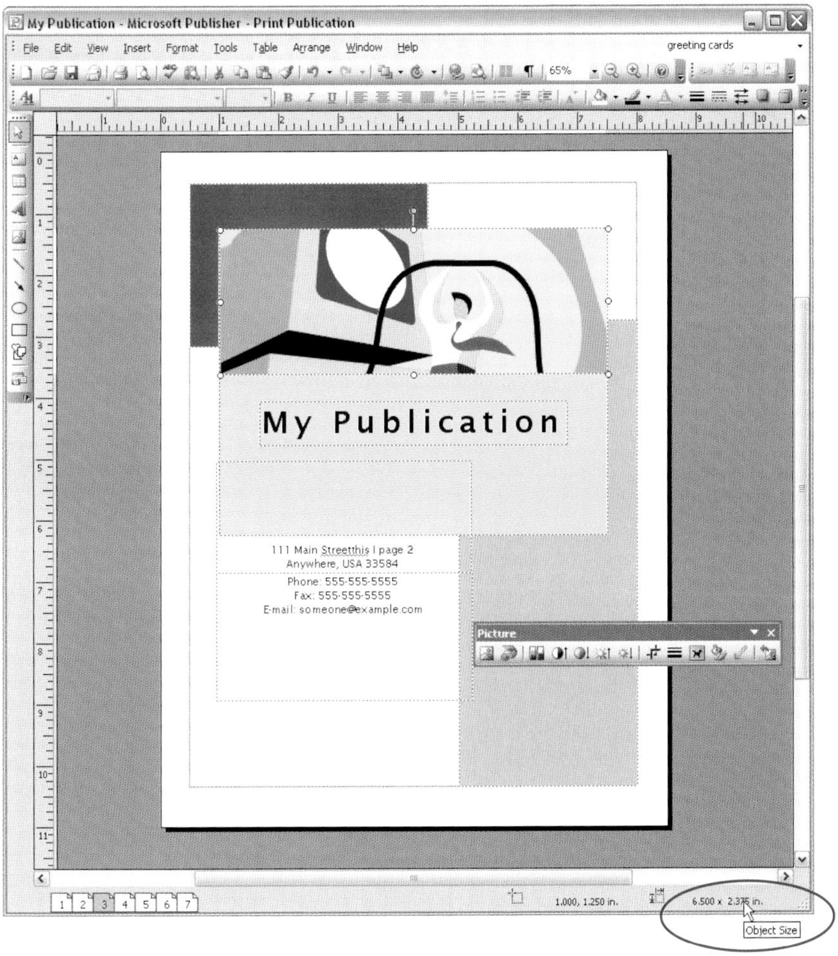

DRAG, DROP, MOVE

To move or rearrange your publication's pages, simply grab a page number's icon on the Page Sorter, located at the bottom-left corner of Publisher's view window, and drag-and-drop it into any order you'd like. *Note:* If you have two-page spreads, dragging-and-dropping will move both pages.

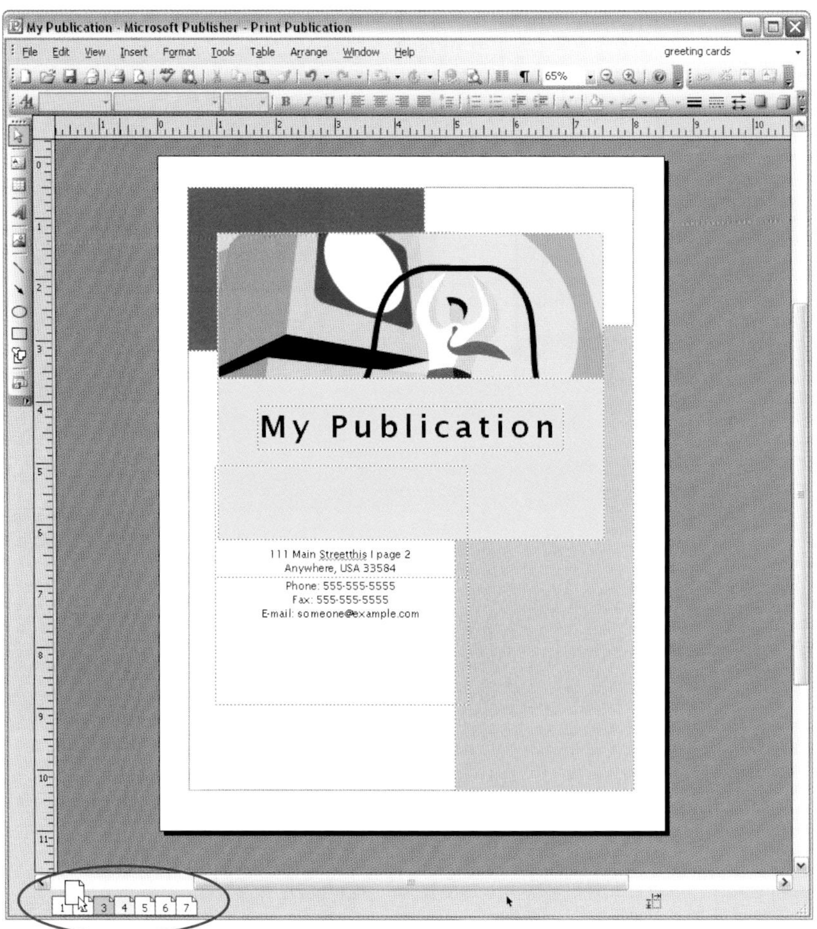

DRAG-AND-DROP DUPLICATES

In the previous tip, I showed you how to use the Page Sorter to move pages quickly, but you can also use it to create duplicates of pages. To do this, drag-and-drop any page that you want to duplicate while pressing-and-holding the Control key on your keyboard. This instantly creates a duplicate of the page and places it into your publication. *Note:* If you have two-page spreads, dragging-and-dropping will duplicate both pages.

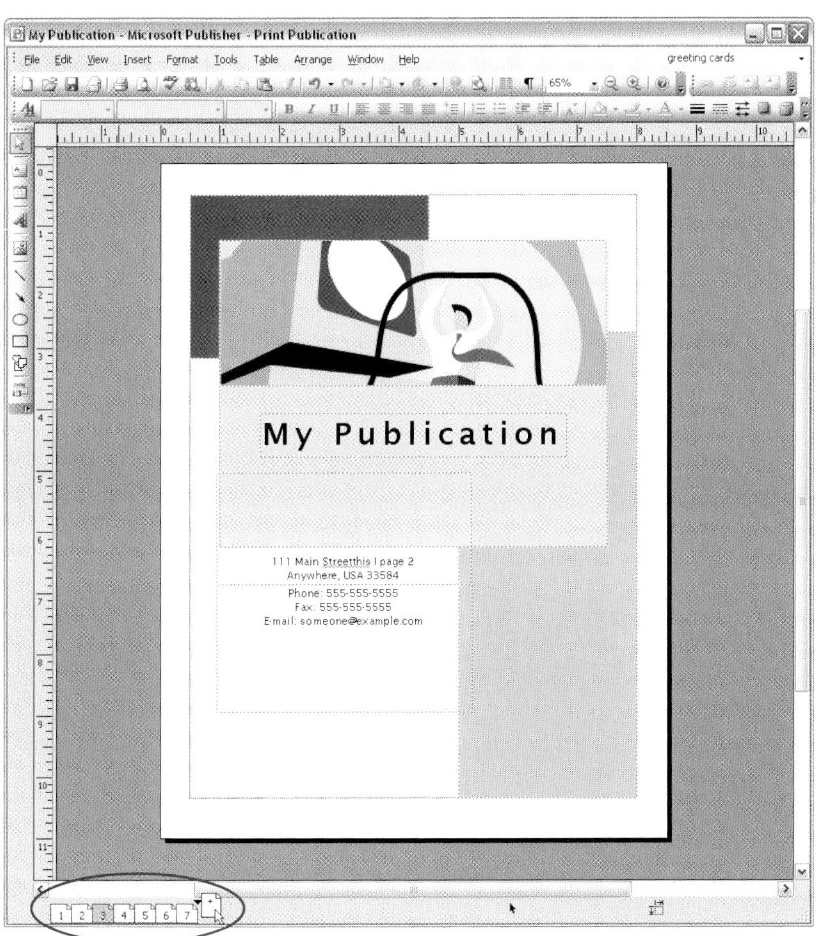

FAUX FRAME

When creating the layout for a publication, it can be useful to create empty picture frames to help with your design. For instance, you may not know exactly which picture you want to use yet, but you do know how large it will be and where it's going to be placed. When this happens, use an empty picture frame to lay out the page's elements until you find the right picture. To do this, click the Picture Frame button in the Objects toolbar (if you don't see the Objects toolbar, right-click any toolbar and click Objects) and click Empty Picture Frame. Then, drag out a frame with your mouse pointer onto the current presentation page. Now, resize and move it to where you want. Notice that the frame works exactly as a picture would: You can wrap text around it, rotate it, or anything that you could do with a picture. When you're ready to replace the frame with your picture, right-click the frame and on the shortcut menu, click Change Picture> From File (or select Clip Art to use Office's images), and browse for your image. Then click Insert, which inserts your picture into your frame. *Note:* You may have to resize your image frame once it's placed.

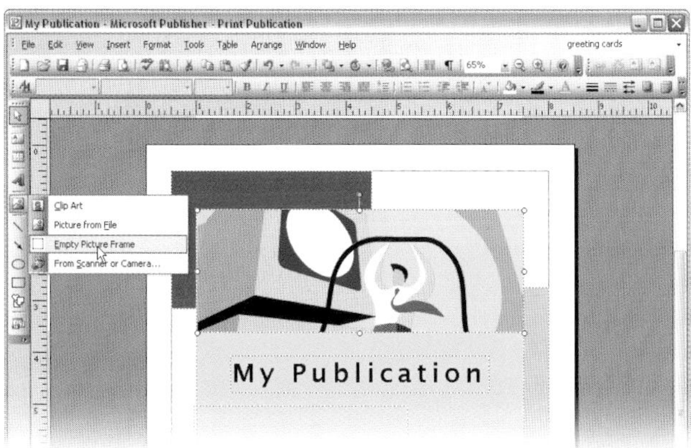

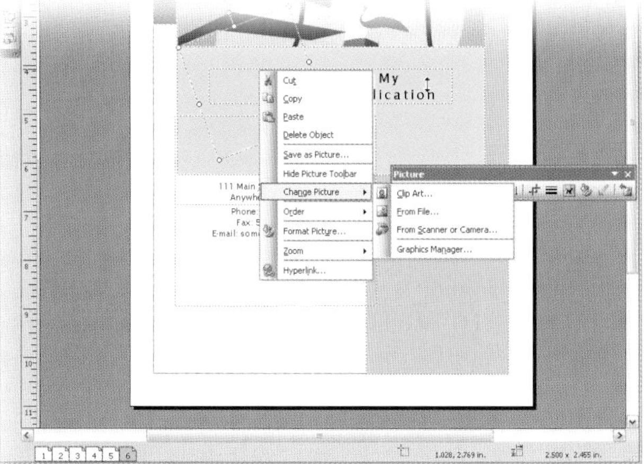

LINE UP

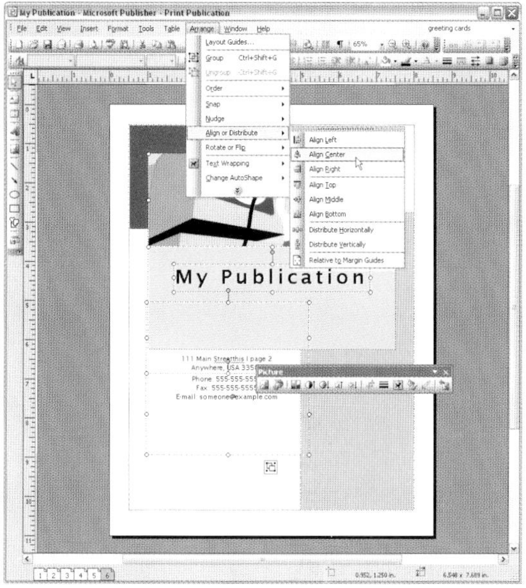

To line up your objects on a page, press-and-hold the Control key on your keyboard and click to select each object that you want to line up. Next, click Arrange>Align or Distribute and choose an alignment for your objects.

EXACT ROTATION

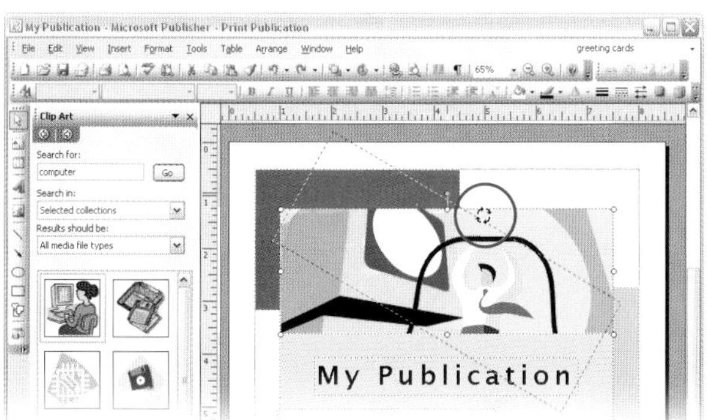

Rotating an object is easy: Just select the object, then pull the rotate picture handle at the top of the picture's frame to the left or right to rotate the object freely. But what if you want to be a little more exact with your rotation? If you need a little more precision when rotating your objects, hold the Shift key on your keyboard as you rotate an object. This rotates the object in 15° increments.

FIND THE RIGHT WORDS

If you're struggling to find the perfect quote or sentiment for your greeting cards, don't! Publisher offers an enormous collection of verses for just about any occasion. Open the New Publication task pane (File>New), click the Publications for Print folder, click Greeting Cards, select a category, then click on the card you want to create. To view the selection of verses for your new card, click the "Select a suggested verse" link at the bottom of the Greeting Card Options task pane, which opens the Suggested Verse dialog. Now, choose an occasion from the Category drop-down menu and click a verse in the Available Messages window to preview them.

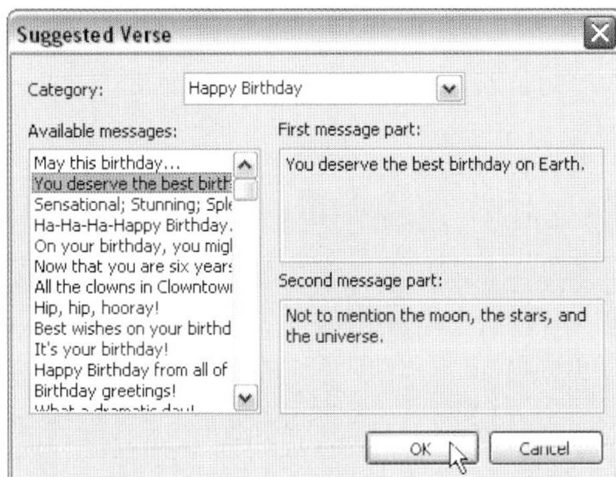

RULERS ANYWHERE

Sometimes guides just won't do it—you need rulers (View>Rulers), but you need them in the middle of your page. What now? Move the rulers! Press-and-hold the Shift key on your keyboard and then grab the rulers and drag-and-drop them wherever needed. To put them back, press-and-hold the Shift key and drag them back to the window's edge.

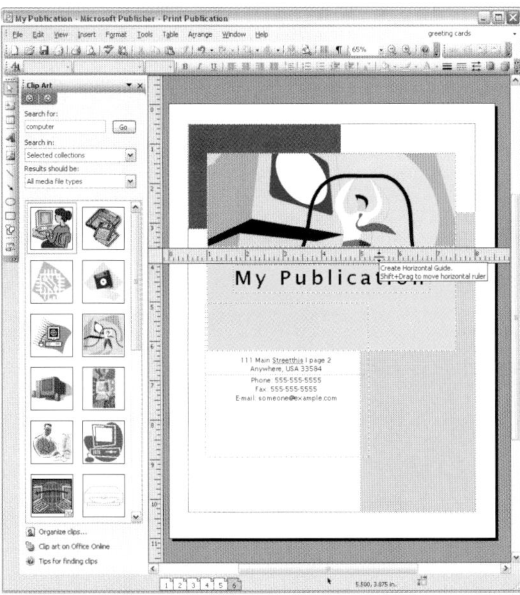

WRAP TEXT

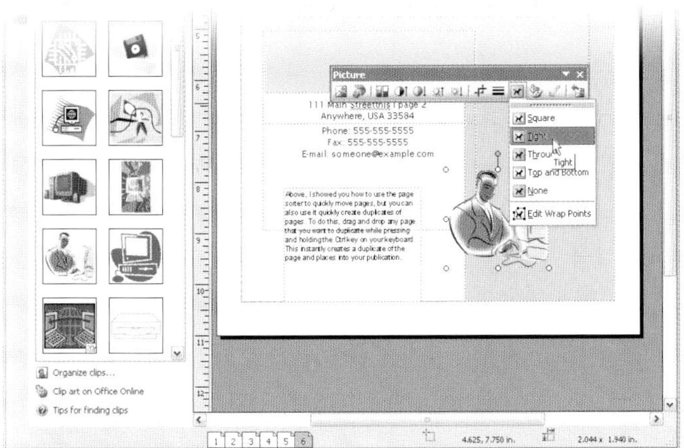

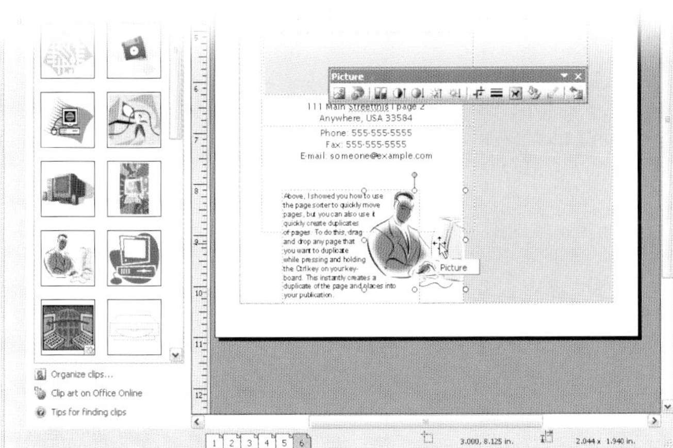

Publisher wraps text like a pro—it makes Word envious. To wrap text around pictures or objects, select the picture (this opens the Picture toolbar) that you want to wrap text around, and click the Text Wrapping button on the Picture toolbar. Choose the type of text wrap to apply. Now, move your picture over a text box (depending on how the objects are ordered—the picture is positioned in front of the text box by right-clicking the image and choosing Order>Bring to Front), and the text wraps automatically around the picture.

RECOLOR PICTURES

If you need to quickly recolor a picture to match your publication's color scheme, try this: Right-click the picture then click Format Picture in the shortcut menu. Next, click the Picture tab on the Format Picture dialog and click Recolor. Now, click the Color drop-down menu and select a color that more closely matches your color scheme. After you choose a replacement color, you can then choose to "Recolor the whole picture" or "Leave black parts black." When finished, click OK and your picture's new colors are applied.

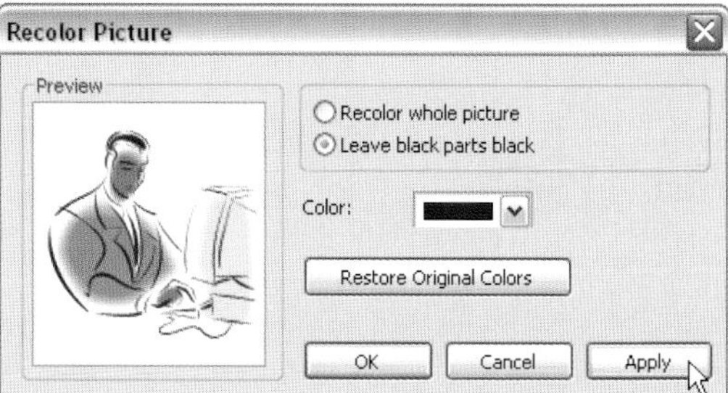

COLOPHON

The book was produced by the author and the design team using Dell and Macintosh computers, including a Dell Precision M60 2-GB 1.7-GHz Pentium M Processor, a Dell PWS650 1-GB 3.06-GHz, a Power Mac G5 Dual 2-GHz, a Power Mac G5 1.8-GHz, a Power Mac G4 1.25-GHz, a Power Mac G4 733-MHz, and a Power Mac G4 Dual 500-MHz. We used Sony Artisan, LaCie Electron Blue 22, and Apple Studio Display monitors.

Page layout was done using Adobe InDesign CS. The headers for each technique are set in Adobe MyriadMM_565 SB 600 NO at 11points on 12.5 leading, with the horizontal scaling set to 100%. Body copy is set using Adobe Myriad MM_400 RG 600 NO at 9.5 points on 11.5 leading, with the horizontal scaling set to 100%.

Screen captures were made with SnagIt and were placed and sized within Adobe InDesign CS. The book was output at 150 line screen, and all in-house printing was done using a Xerox Phaser 7700 DX.

Index

E

O

P

R

S

T

U

V

W

Z